HARRIET MARTINEAU

(1802–1876) was born in N
children in a strongly Unitar
of a successful cloth manufac
unhappy one: she felt hers
Suffering continually from ill-
well-educated, at a local Unit
school in Bristol – though her .... was interrupted
by advancing deafness, requiring her to use an ear trumpet
in later life.

Harriet Martineau's first article, 'Female Writers of
Practical Divinity' was published when she was nineteen
in a Unitarian magazine, *Monthly Repository*, to which she
became a regular contributor. Her twenties were beset by
misfortune: the death of her eldest brother was followed,
in 1826, by that of her father. Then her fiancé died, and
in 1829 the family business finally collapsed, leaving the
Martineaus penniless. This was the turning point in
Harriet's life.

Unable, because of her deafness, to become a governess
like her sisters, she contributed to the family income
through her writing: no longer made to put it aside in
favour of more 'womanly' pursuits, she became the bread-
winner of the family. With the enormous success of her
twenty-four part series, *Illustrations of Political Economy*,
she became a literary celebrity and moved to London. At
the age of thirty-five, she was offered the editorship of a
new economics periodical, but her adored brother James
disapproved, and so she refused it. Instead she turned to
fiction and wrote *Deerbrook* (also published by Virago).
She then collapsed into bed where she was to remain for
the next five years.

In 1855, thinking that she was about to die. she wrote
her autobiography at break-neck speed – and lived for
another twenty years. In those years, the happiest of her
life, she wrote widely and prolifically on the enfranchise-
ment of women, the abolition of slavery, education, travel
and hypnotism. Harriet Martineau died at the age of
seventy-four and was buried, by her own wishes, without
religious rites.

HARRIET MARTINEAU'S AUTOBIOGRAPHY

VOL. II.

Harriet Martineau
1850

HARRIET MARTINEAU'S
AUTOBIOGRAPHY

VOL. II.

With a New Introduction by Gaby Weiner

'Etiam capillus unus habet umbram suam'—PROVERB

And this dear freedom hath begotten me this peace,
that I mourn not that end which must be,
nor spend one wish to have one minute added
to the uncertain date of my years'—BACON

Virago

Published by VIRAGO PRESS Limited 1983
41 William IV Street, London WC2N 4DB

First published in Great Britain in three volumes,
the first two containing the complete text of the
Autobiography, and the third including memorials
by Maria Weston Chapman, by Smith, Elder, & Co., 1877

Virago edition offset from Smith,
Elder, & Co., third edition 1877

Introduction copyright © Gaby Weiner 1983

British Library Cataloguing in Publication Data

Martineau, Harriet
  Autobiography of Harriet Martineau.
  Vol. 2.
  1. Martineau, Harriet 1802–1876—Biography
  2. Authors, English—19th century—Biography
  I. Title
  828'.809   PR4984.M5Z/

ISBN 0-86068-430-X

The cover shows a detail from a water-colour
of Harriet Martineau's Ambleside drawing-
room painted in 1844. Reproduced by kind
permission of Robert David.
Portrait of Harriet Martineau reproduced by
kind permission of the National Portrait
Gallery, London.

Printed in Finland by Werner Söderström Oy,
a member of Finnprint

CONTENTS

OF

THE SECOND VOLUME.

————•◦•————

PERIOD IV.

PAGE

ILLUSTRATIONS TO VOL. II.

INTRODUCTION

This second volume of Harriet Martineau's *Autobiography* covers the period from her voyage to America in 1834, aged thirty-two and already famous, to her second long illness in 1855.

She wrote both volumes of the *Autobiography* at considerable speed, in three months, because she thought she was dying. In fact, she lived for a further twenty-one years, working much of the time as a journalist and writing as many as six leaders a week for the *Daily News*.

By the time she reached the stage of her life covered by this volume, Harriet Martineau had lived through the collapse of the family business and the deaths of her father, her much loved older brother Richard and her fiancé, John Hugh Worthington; despite these misfortunes, she had achieved national fame as the author of a bestselling series on political economy.

She had been born in 1802, the sixth of eight children of a Norwich Unitarian family. At the time of her birth, Harriet's father was a reasonably prosperous cloth manufacturer. Later, her ambitions for a literary career were given an urgent boost when the family business faltered in 1825 and finally failed four years later, obliging Harriet to become financially self-supporting. But she was unable to become a governess, the accepted occupation of the nineteenth-century impoverished 'genteel' female, due to the onset of chronic deafness, although she retained sufficient hearing throughout her life to communicate with the aid of an ear trumpet.

She had an extremely unhappy childhood, not only because of increasing ill-health but also because she felt unloved and unwanted at home, particularly by her mother. She was fortunate, however, in the exceptionally broad education that she received (unusually so for a young girl in the first two decades of the nineteenth century) and was able to immerse herself in the study of the Classics, literature and modern languages as a means of escape from family pressures.

Encouraged to write by her younger brother James, to whom she developed a close emotional attachment in adolescence, she published her first article on 'Female Writers of Practical Divinity' in the Unitarian periodical, the *Monthly Repository* in 1822, at the age of twenty. Ten years later, having published numerous articles and reviews, usually without payment, and having won the three major prizes in a Unitarian essay competition, Harriet Martineau hit upon the idea which was so successfully to transform her literary career in terms of both personal satisfaction and financial reward.

She decided to use a fictional form to describe, for lay people, the principles of the science of political economy – of considerable popular interest in the 1830s. Her scheme was to produce monthly stories, which, though fictional in theme and content, explained clearly the economic principles pioneered by Adam Smith and the supporters of Free Trade.

Initially she had difficulty in finding a publisher, but so successful was the series that she became an instant celebrity whose advice was sought by government ministers over the great Reform Bill of 1832 and whose presence was requested at important social gatherings. She also earned £2000 from her two years' work.

> I remember walking up and down the grassplat feeling my cares were over. And so they were. From that hour, I have never had any anxiety about employment than what I choose, not any real care about money....
> I think I may date my release from pecuniary care

from that 10th February 1832 [the publishing date of the first issue].[1]

A move from Norwich to London to complete the series led to her 'lionization' by London society and Harriet took every opportunity to meet those members of the literati, who until then had been for her only names in books and newspapers. She befriended and achieved equal intellectual standing with the most eminent people of the day, and the London social network itself was later to prove beneficial in the important literary and political contacts it provided when Harriet moved her home and place of work to Ambleside in the Lake District.

Among those she knew well were Samuel Rogers, the poet; Sidney Smith, the politician and friend of Florence Nightingale; Bulwer Lytton, the novelist; Elizabeth Barrett and Robert Browning; William Macready, the actor; Charles Eastlake, the painter; and Mary Somerville, the mathematician and scientist. She met the poets Southey and Coleridge, Charles and Erasmus Darwin, John Stuart Mill and Harriet Taylor and many other glittering figures of the time.

Notwithstanding her enjoyment of fame and success, Harriet Martineau had a deep commitment to erasing political and social inequalities and was a life-long campaigner on the 'Woman Question'. Since her twenties, she had been concerned about the social, political and educational differences between women and men, and in an article entitled 'Female Education'[2] in 1823, complained that whilst when girls and boys received the same education their progress was equal, irreparable injustice occurred when boys were then encouraged to continue their education, whereas girls' studies were curtailed by social duties and domestic commitments.

She returned to this theme time and time again in her books and newspaper articles, and in the *Autobiography*. Though criticizing women for their frivolous behaviour, she nevertheless believed that female educational and occupational opportunities should be extended.

> Let them [women] be educated, – let their powers be cultivated to the extent for which the means are already provided, and all that is wanted or ought to be desired will follow of course. Whatever a woman proves herself able to do, society will be thankful to see her do, – just as if she were a man.[3]

Later in life, her commitment to the 'Woman Question' was exhibited by her actively supporting the first women's colleges, by giving her backing to the female suffrage movement and in her opposition to the notorious Contagious Diseases Acts.

Harriet Martineau described her childhood and fame in London as her life's 'winter and stormy spring'.[4] The second volume of the *Autobiography* describes the summer of Harriet Martineau's life, when she felt happiest and most fulfilled. It is a confident portrayal of the middle years of a Victorian woman of letters, and as such offers much of enormous interest and value to the reader.

Gaby Weiner, London 1982

NOTES

1. Harriet Martineau, *Autobiography*, Smith, Elder, & Co., London, 1877, Vol. 1, p. 178.
2. Harriet Martineau, 'Female Education' in *Monthly Repository*, 1823.
3. Martineau, *Autobiography*, op. cit., Vol. 1, p. 401.
4. ibid., Vol. 2, p. 205.

FOURTH PERIOD.

SECTION III.

A LITTLE while before my departure for the United States, I met Mr. James Mill one evening, and had a good deal of conversation with him. By the way, he made the frankest possible acknowledgment of his mistake in saying what had so critically and mischievously alarmed Mr. Fox;—that political economy could not be conveyed in fiction, and that the public would not receive it in any but the didactic form. Having settled this business, he asked me how long I meant to be abroad; and then, whether I expected to understand the Americans in that time;—that is, two years. He was glad to find I had no such idea, and told me that five-and-twenty years before, he had believed that he understood the Scotch; and that in another five-and-twenty, he should no doubt understand the English; but that now he was quite certain that he understood neither the one nor the other. As this looked rather as if he supposed I went out on a book-making expedition, I told him that it was not so. I would not say that I certainly should not write a book on my return: but I had actually refused to listen to the úrgent recommendation of a gentleman who professed to have influence with the booksellers, to allow him to obtain for me advances of money for my travelling expenses from a publishing house which would be glad to advance £500 or so, on my engaging to let them publish the book on my return. I have since had strong reason to rejoice that I did not permit such intervention. My reply was that I would not bind myself by any pledge of the sort; and that my travelling money was in fact ready. The friend who gave me credits to the American banks offered to obtain from Lord Brougham the £100 he owed me, as part payment: but that also I declined,—kindly as it was meant; because I did not think it quite a proper way to obtain payment. I preferred going out free from all misgiving and anxiety about pecuniary matters; so I paid in my £400, and carried credits to that amount, without being under obligation to any body.—Mr. Bentley the publisher met me one day at dinner at Miss Berry's, and he sounded me about a book on America. I rather think, from his subsequent conduct, that that was his real object in getting an introduction to me, though he put forward another: —his desire to issue my Series in a new form. I told him as I told others, that I knew nothing of any American book, and that I was going to the United States with other objects,—the first of which was to obtain rest and recreation. I went and returned entirely free from any kind of claim on me, on any

hand, for a book. I can truly say that I travelled
without any such idea in my mind. I am sure that
no traveller seeing things through author spectacles,
can see them as they are; and it was not till I looked
over my journal on my return that I decided to write
'Society in America.' (I never can bear to think of
the title. My own title was 'Theory and Practice of
Society in America;' but the publishers would not
sanction it. They had better have done so).

My first desire was for rest. My next was to break
through any selfish 'particularity' that might be
growing on me with years, and any love of ease and
indulgence that might have arisen out of success,
flattery, or the devoted kindness of my friends. I
believed that it would be good for me to 'rough it'
for a while, before I grew too old and fixed in my
habits for such an experiment. I must in truth add
that two or three of my most faithful friends, intimate
with my circumstances, counselled my leaving home
for a considerable time, for the welfare of all who lived
in that home. My position had become a difficult
one there, even while my work afforded an incontest-
able reason for my being sought and made much of.
If my social position remained the same after the
work was done, my mother's happiness would not,
they thought, be promoted by my presence. This was
too obviously true already : and I took the advice of
my friends to go without any misgiving, and to stay
away as long as I found it desirable. I made provision for my mother's income not being lessened by
my absence : but she declined, for generous reasons,
all aid of that sort. She never touched the money I
left for the purpose, but received in my place a lady

who made an agreeable third in the little household.
I have already said that Lord Henley's suggestions
first turned my project in the direction of the United
States; and the reasons he urged were of course
prominent in my mind during my travels.

I was singularly fortunate in my companion. I
had been rather at a loss at first what to do about
this. There are great difficulties in joining a party
for so very long a journey, extending over so long a
time. To be with new friends is a fearful risk under
such an ordeal : and the ordeal is too severe, in my
opinion, to render it safe to subject an old friendship
to it. There was a plan for a time that the same
friends with whom I was to have gone to Italy (if the
continent had been my playground) should go with
me to America: but there were aged parents and
other reasons against their going so far; and my
friends and I went on our several ways.— It would
never do, as I was aware, to take a servant, to suffer
from the proud Yankees on the one hand and the de-
based slaves on the other: nor would a servant have
met my needs in other ways. Happily for me a lady
of very superior qualifications, who was eager to
travel, but not rich enough to indulge her desire,
offered to go with me, as companion and helper, if I
would bear her expenses. She paid her own voyages,
and I the rest: and most capitally she fulfilled her
share of the compact. Not only well educated but
remarkably clever, and, above all, supremely rational,
and with a faultless temper, she was an extraordinary
boon as a companion. She was as conscientious as
able and amiable. She toiled incessantly, to spare my
time, strength, and faculties. She managed the busi-

ness of travel, and was for ever on the watch to
supply my want of ears,—and, I may add, my de-
fects of memory. Among the multitudes of strangers
whom I saw, and the concourse of visitors who presented themselves every where, I should have made
hourly mistakes but for her. She seemed to make
none,—so observant, vigilant and retentive were her
faculties. We fulfilled the term of our compact without
a shadow of failure, but rather with large supereroga-
tion of good works on her part; and she returned under
the care of the excellent captain,—a friend of some
of my family,—who brought me home four months
later. I remained that much longer, for the purpose
of accompanying a party of friends to the Northern
Lakes, and some new territory which it was important
that I should visit. I could not afford this additional
trip to more than myself; and there was not room for
more than one: so my comrade preceded me homewards, sorry not to have taken that northern trip, but
well satisfied with the enterprise she had achieved.
She has been married for many years; and it is
pleasant still to talk over our American adventures in
her house or in mine. Her husband and children
must be almost as glad as she and I that she had the
spirit to go.

After leaving home, I paid visits to my family and
friends, (followed from place to place by my last proofs)
and was joined by Miss J. at Liverpool, a day or two
before we sailed. The first steam voyage to the United
States took place in 1838: and I set forth in 1834:
so there was no thought of a quicker passage than a
month. I did not wish for a shorter one; and when
it stretched out to forty-two days, I was not at all

discontented.   I have enjoyed few things more in life
than the certainty of being out of the way o the post,
of news, and of passing strangers for a whole month :
and this seems to show how over-wrought I must
have been at the close of my long work.   My felicity
would have been complete if I could have looked forward to a month of absolute idleness : but my constitutional weakness,—my difficulty in saying ' No,'
was in my way, and a good deal spoiled my holiday.
A friend, whom indeed I was bound to oblige, requested me to write for him a long chapter for a book
he contemplated, to be called ' How to Observe.'
The subject he gave me was Morals and Manners.
Before my return, his proposed volume was given up ;
and Mr. Knight was arranging about a series of
volumes, under that title.   The Chapter I wrote on
board ship served as the basis of my own volume for
that series ; and thus, the reluctant toil was not thrown
away.   But thoroughly reluctant it was.   The task
weighed upon me more than the writing of a quarto
volume would have done at another time : and circumstances of time and place were indeed most unfavourable to work of the kind.   My long confinement
within stringent bounds of punctuality had produced
bad effects,—narrowing my mind, and making my
conscience tender about work.   So, when that chapter
was done at last, I wrote no more till I was settled at
home again, in the autumn of 1836,—with two
small exceptions.   It was necessary to accede to a
request to bring out myself, while in America, two
volumes of ' Miscellanies,' under penalty of seeing it
done by some unauthorised person, with alterations,
and probably the introduction of pieces which would

be as new to me as to any body. In order to secure
the copyright to the American proprietors, I wrote an
essay for their edition: (on ' Moral Independence.')
Being asked to furnish a story for some Sunday school
festival, I wrote the little tale ' The Children who
lived by the Jordan.' These two trifles were all I
wrote for press, as far as I remember, for above two
years. I need not say that I had a large correspondence to sustain,—a correspondence perpetually increasing as my travel and my intercourses extended:
and I kept a very ample journal.

On the morning of the 4th of August, we were
summoned on board our ship,—the United States.
As I stood on the wharf in my sea-dress, watching
the warping out of the vessel, I saw an old acquaintance observing the same process. Sir James
Parke was one of the Judges then at Liverpool on
circuit; and he and some ladies were amusing themselves with seeing the American packet clear out. He
would hardly believe me when I told him I was going
to step on board presently; and for how long. He
was the last of my London acquaintances whom I saw
before that long absence.

I have said quite enough about that voyage, and
very nearly enough about my American travel, in the
two books I published after my return. One subject
remains nearly untouched in those books; and on that
alone I propose now to speak at any length. I refer
to my own personal connexion with the great controversy on negro slavery which was then just beginning to stir the American community. While
speaking largely of the controversy in my book, I
said as little as possible of my own relation to it,

because some undeserved suspicion of resentment on my own account might attach to my historical narrative ; and because it was truly my object to present an impartial view, and by no means to create an interest in my personal adventures. In this place I feel it right to tell my story. Supported as it is by documents in the hands of my Executor, and by the testimony of Americans who know me best, it will stand as a record of what really took place, in answer to some false reports and absurd misrepresentations. For one instance of what Americans,—even American gentlemen,— will persuade themselves to do in the case of the Slavery question, which seems to pervert all its advocates ;—I heard some time since that two American gentlemen, who were college youths when I saw them, claim the credit of having beguiled me into publishing some nonsensical stories with which they mystified me when I was the guest of their parents. I not only clearly remember that I had no conversation with those boys (who were shy of my trumpet) but I possess the best possible evidence that it is their present statement which is the mystifying one. By some lucky inspiration of prudence, I kept a lock-up copy of my American books, in which the name of every authority for every statement is noted in the margin. I have referred to this copy since I heard of the claim of these two gentlemen ; and I have called my biographer to witness that the names of the gentlemen in question do not once occur.—So many false things having been said about my American experiences, in regard to the anti-slavery agitation, during my life, it is probable that there may be more when I am no longer here to contradict them : and therefore it is that

I now give a plain account of what really took place. I do not altogether trust my memory for an experience which is however deeply impressed upon it. My journal, and my entire American correspondence on that subject are my warrant : and I have before me also the narrative as written down many years ago, from the same materials, and when my remembrance of the events of 1835 and 1836 was so fresh as to obviate any objection that can be made to my statement on the score of lapse of time.

It will be remembered that I wrote, near the beginning of my Series, a number called 'Demerara,' which was as open a committal of myself, on every ground, to hostility to slavery as was possible. I therein declared myself satisfied that slavery was indefensible, economically, socially, and morally. Every body who knew any thing about me at all, at home or in America, knew that from the spring of 1832 I was completely committed against slavery. The American passengers on board our ship were certainly aware of it before they saw me ; and so was a Prussian fellow-passenger, Dr. Julius, who had been introduced to me in London as a philanthropist going to America with a direct commission from the late King of Prussia to inquire into the state of prison discipline there. Every one on board regarded Dr. Julius as so commissioned ; but he told Miss J. and me, one day, when in a communicative mood, that he had sought the sanction of the King to his object, and believed he had obtained it : but that when he was admitted to an audience, to take leave, he found that the King had forgotten all about it (if he had really known) and that nothing could make him understand that this was a leave-taking visit, or why Dr. Julius presented himself, though the King approved of inquiries into prison-discipline. Whether there was a prevalent doubt about the reality of his commission, or whether his habit of petty concealment induced suspicion, I do not know; but the impression on board ship, and in American society afterwards, certainly was that there was something mysterious and doubtful about him. I was disposed to conclude, on the whole, that there was nothing worse in the case than that he was a Jew, and was anxious to conceal the fact. The clearest thing in the matter was that, with all his big talk, he was in a continual state of panic. He was afraid of the elements and of man : convulsed with terror during a storm ; and in great horror on the subject of Slavery, though the American ' reign of terror' was only then beginning, and it had not, I believe, been heard of in Europe. Mr. George Thompson had half-engaged a cabin in our ship for himself and his family, but was by some accident prevented sailing so soon. It was very well : for, while we were crossing the sea, the first serious pro-slavery riots were taking place in New York ;—those riots by which the Messrs. Tappan were driven from the city, their houses destroyed, and their furniture burnt in the streets.

The last news I heard of Dr. Julius was some time after my return to England; and I acknowledge that I was considerably disturbed by it. After I had left Washington, he petitioned for certain State Papers, and government information, either in my name expressly, or on the ground of our being fellow-travellers. I need not say that this was without any authority whatever from me, or that I took pains to disavow in the right quarter all connexion with Dr. Julius's inquiries. I was distinctly informed that the papers and information would not have been granted, but on the supposition that they were asked for by me, for my own use.

When we took in a pilot at Sandy Hook, we all observed how hastily he tossed down his bundle of newspapers for the amusement of the passengers, and then beckoned the captain to the stern; and we were not so absorbed in the newspapers as not to perceive that the conversation in the stern was earnest and long. Though there was a good deal about me and my reception in those newspapers, it never occurred to me that I was the subject of the conversation between the captain and pilot. When the pilot went to the wheel, the captain requested a private interview with an American lady who had talked with me a good deal during the voyage. Long after, I heard that he wanted to know from her what my opinions were upon Slavery; and, if anti-slavery, whether I had ever professed them publicly. It is odd that she did not tell him, (what she certainly knew) that I was completely committed to anti-slavery opinions by my writings. By her own account, her reply to the captain was that I was opposed to Slavery; but that I had been more than once heard to say on board, when questioned about my opinion of American institutions, that I went to learn, and not to teach. The captain seemed satisfied to let Slavery pass muster among 'American institutions;' and he declared that he should now know what to say. He avowed that if he had been less well satisfied, he should not have ventured to put me ashore: and he made it his particular request that

I should hear nothing of what had passed. The pilot had warned him that if Mr. Thompson was on board, he had better hide him in his cabin; for, if his presence was known in New York, he would be a dead man before night.

Knowing nothing of all this, being carefully kept ignorant while in New York, (as many resident ladies were) of the fact of the riots, and travelling for weeks among persons who either took no interest in the subject or anxiously ignored it, Miss J. and I long remained in a state of profound unconsciousness of the condition of society around us. It was not merely as travellers that we were thus kept in the dark. On the last occasion of my being at New York, I was assured by the ladies of Mrs. Jeffrey's family that I was entirely misinformed about there having been any disturbances there at all in the autumn of 1834. I told them the particulars,—some notorious, and others of unquestionable truth; but they believed me so little that they asked husband and brother about it, in the middle of dinner, in the presence of the servants. The gentlemen could not, of course, deny the facts; but they did their best to make light of them, on the one hand; and, on the other, accounted for their silence to the wondering ladies by declaring that they were ashamed of the whole business, and did not wish to alarm or annoy the ladies unnecessarily. Such was the bondage in which the inhabitants of the boasted republic were living so long ago as 1834. Such bondage was, to English women, an inconceivable and incredible thing, till the fact was forced on our observation by further and more various travel.

We went among the Sedgwicks, on our ascent of

the Hudson: we went to Niagara, and by Western
Pennsylvania to Philadelphia, where we staid six
weeks, proceeding to Baltimore (a Slave State) in
December. There was all this while scarcely any
thing to remind us of the subject of Slavery but the
virulent abuse of the Abolitionists in the newspapers.
I afterwards learned that the whole country was divided into three parties; the Pro-slavery multitude,
the Colonisationists (represented in Europe by the be-
fore-mentioned Elliot Cresson), and the Abolitionists.
The Colonisationists were simply a selection from the
Pro-slavery multitude, who did the Slave States the
service of ridding them of clever and dangerous slaves,
and throwing a tub to the whale of adverse opinion,
and easing lazy or weak consciences, by professing to
deal, in a safe and beneficial manner, with the otherwise hopeless difficulty. Care was taken, so early as
my visit to Philadelphia, and yet more at Baltimore
and Washington, that I should hear much in favour of
the Colonisation scheme, and nothing but horrors of
the Abolitionists. I acknowledge here, once for all,
that it is very probable that expressions unfavourable
to the Abolitionists may be fairly remembered and
quoted against me throughout the Southern and
Western States. I never wavered, of course, in my
detestation of Slavery; and I never intended to take
any part against the Abolitionists; but it is scarcely
possible to hear from day to day, for ten months, that
persons whom one has never seen are fanatical, bloodthirsty and so forth, without catching up some prejudice against them. We were constantly and gravely
informed, as a matter of fact, that Garrison and his
followers used incitements to the slaves to murder

their masters, and sent agents and publications into the South to effect insurrections. Till we had the means of ascertaining that these charges were totally and absolutely false,—Garrison and most of his followers being non-resistants, and thoroughly consistent opponents of physical force,—it was really impossible to remain wholly unimpressed by them. I steadily declared my intention to hear, when opportunity offered, what the Abolitionists, as well as others, had to say for themselves : but it certainly never entered my imagination that I could possibly find them the blameless apostles of a holy cause which I afterwards saw that they were.

The first perplexing incident happened at Philadelphia, ten or twelve weeks after our landing. A lady of that city whose manners were eminently disagreeable to us, beset us very vigorously,—obtruding her society upon us, and loading me with religious books for children,—some of her own writing, and some by others. When we made our farewell calls, we were not sorry to be told that this lady could see no visitors, as she had a cold. We were speeding away from the door, when a servant ran after us, with an unwelcome summons to the lady's chamber. She made me sit beside her on her sofa, while Miss J. sat opposite,—out of my hearing. The lady having somehow introduced the subject of the blacks, a conversation ensued between her and Miss J. of which I did not hear a syllable. I saw my companion look embarrassed, and could not conceive why, till the lady turned full upon me with, ' Can it be as your friend assures me ? She says that if any young person known to you was attached to a negro, you would not interfere to prevent their marrying.' I replied that I had no notion of interfering between people who were attached; that I had never contemplated the case she proposed; but that I did not believe I should ever interfere with lovers proposing to marry. The lady exclaimed against my thus edging off from the question,—which I had not the least intention of doing: and she drove her inquiries home. Mystery is worse than any other mischief in such matters; and I therefore replied that, if the union was suitable in other respects, I should think it no business of mine to interfere on account of complexion. The lady cried out in horror, 'Then you are an Amalgamationist!' 'What is that?' I asked: and then remonstrated against foreign travellers being classified according to the party terms of the country. I was not then aware of the extent to which all but virtuous relations are found possible between the whites and blacks, nor how unions to which the religious and civil sanctions of marriage are alone wanting, take place wherever there are masters and slaves, throughout the country. When I did become aware of this, I always knew how to stop the hypocritical talk against 'amalgamation.' I never failed to silence the cant by pointing to the rapidly increasing mulatto element of the population, and asking whether it was the priest's service which made the difference between holy marriage and abhorred 'amalgamation.' But I was not yet possessed of this defence when assailed by the Philadelphia saint.—When we rose to go, the woman insisted on kissing me, and poured out lamentations about my departure. The moment we were in the street, I said to my friend, ' You *must* be careful, and not get me or yourself into any more such scrapes till we know what people mean on this subject of the blacks.' Miss J. justified herself completely. She had been so questioned that she could not avoid saying as much as she did, unless by the more dangerous method of refusing to reply. This was the beginning of many troubles: but the troubles would have occurred from some other beginning, if we had escaped this.

The day before we left Philadelphia, Dr. Julius called at the house where we were staying. He had just arrived from New York. He burst into the room with an air of joy which did not look very genuine; and I presently saw that he was absent and uneasy. After staying an unconscionable time, while I was fidgetty about my preparations, he explained a long series of unintelligible nods and winks by asking to speak with me alone for a few minutes. My host, (a clergyman, and in character, though not in circumstances, the original of Hope in 'Deerbrook') left the room, taking his little boy with him: and then Dr. Julius, turning as white as the marble chimney-piece, said he came to warn me to proceed no further south than Philadelphia. He had not been two hours in the city before he heard that I had avowed myself an amalgamationist, and that my proceeding southwards would bring upon me certain insult and danger. It appeared to me that there was every reason why this conversation should *not* be private; and I summoned my host. While I repeated to him what Dr. Julius had been saying, he too turned as pale as ashes; and between his ghastly countenance, and the gesticulations of Dr. Julius, the scene was a strange one. Dr. Julius declared the whole city was ringing with the news.—After a moment's consideration, I declared that I should not alter my

plans in any respect. I was a well-known anti-slavery
writer before I thought of going to America; and my
desire to see the operation of the system of Slavery
could hardly be wrongly interpreted by any one who
took an interest in my proceedings. I was disposed
to trust to the openness of my plans, and the simplicity
of my purpose, and to the common sense of those
among whom I was going. Dr. Julius shrugged his
shoulders; and my host suggested a method by which
the difficulty might be probably obviated. The Editors
of the two leading Philadelphia newspapers were well
acquainted with me, and would undoubtedly, according to custom, give their report of me on my departure. They could with perfect truth, and would on
the slightest hint, declare that my opinions on slavery
were candidly held, and that they afforded no obstacle
to the most friendly intercourse with me. I positively
forbade any such movement on the part of my personal
friends, feeling that I should never succeed in seeing
the Americans as they were, if my road was paved for
me from one society to another. Knowing Dr. Julius's
tendency to panic, I felt little apprehension from any
thing he could say; and I particularly requested my
host and hostess not to alarm Miss J. with any account of what had passed. I took on myself the duty
which belonged to me, of enlightening her sufficiently
to put her own case into her own hands.

At Baltimore, further obscure intimations of danger
were conveyed to me: and at Washington, so many,
that I felt the time was come for laying the case before my companion. Reflecting that she and I had
discussed the whole matter of my anti-slavery opinions
before we left home; and that she was very prudent

and extremely clever, and fully able to take care of herself, all I thought it necessary to do was this.

In our own room at Washington, I spread out our large map, showed the great extent of Southern States through which we should have to pass, probably for the most part without an escort; and always, where we were known at all, with my anti-slavery reputation uppermost in every body's mind.—' Now, Louisa,' said I, ' does it not look awful? If you have the slightest fear, say so now, and we will change our route.'—' Not the slightest,' said she. ' If you are not afraid, I am not.' This was all she ever heard from me of danger.

The intimations I refer to came to me in all manner of ways. I was specially informed of imprisonments for opinions the same as are found in ' Demerara;' which indeed might well be under the laws of South Carolina, as I found them in full operation. Hints were offered of strangers with my views not being allowed to come away alive. But the most ordinary cunning or sensitiveness of the slave-holders would account for attempts like these to frighten a woman from going where she might see slavery for herself. I was more impressed by less direct warning; by words dropped, and countenances of anxiety and pity.— Before I left Washington, I wrote to my Philadelphia host and hostess, who were not only my most intimate American friends, but witnesses of the first attempt to alarm me. I told them of the subsequent incidents of the same kind, and that I had communicated them to no other person whatever, supposing that they might be only empty threats. As they might however be real, I wrote to assure these friends, and other

friends and my family through them, that I went into
the danger warily : and I requested that my letter
might be kept in evidence of this, in case of my never
returning.

As for the terms on which I went, I took timely
care that there should be no mistake about that. I
carried letters to some of the leading statesmen at
Washington; and the first to acknowledge them were
the senators from the Southern States. On the very
first day, several of these gentlemen came straight
from the senate, with their wives, not only to offer me
their services at Washington, but to engage us to
visit them at their homes, in our progress through
the South. Before I pledged myself to make any
visit whatever, I took care to make it understood that
I was not to be considered as silenced on the subject
of slavery by the hospitality of slave-owners. I made
an express reservation of my freedom in this matter,
declaring that I should not, of course, publish names
or facts which could draw attention upon individuals
in private life ; but that it must not be forgotten
that I had written upon Slavery, and that I should
write on it again, if I saw reason. They all made in
substance the same reply ; that my having published
'Demerara' was the main reason why they wished
me to visit them. They desired me to see their
'peculiar institution' for myself: they would show
me the best and the worst instances of its working ;
and their hope was — so they declared, — that 1
should publish exactly what I saw. The whole conduct and conversation of my southern entertainers
showed an expectation of seeing in print all that was
then passing. I often told them that they were much

more sure than I was that I should write a book. I
am not aware that there was ever any misunderstanding between them and me on this head; and if any
charge of my having accepted hospitalities from slave-
holders, and then denounced their mode of life has ever
been brought, or should ever be brought against me,
I repel it as wholly groundless. A fair lady of blue-
stocking Boston said of me after my book appeared,
'She has ate of our bread and drunk of our cup; and
she calls dear, delightful, intellectual Boston pedantic!' on which a countryman of the complainant
remarked, 'If she thinks Boston pedantic, did you
mean to bribe her, by a cup of tea, not to say so?'
The southerners might be more easily excused for this
sort of unreasonableness and cant: but I never heard
that they were guilty of it. Angry as they were
with my account of slavery, I am not aware that they
imputed ingratitude and bad manners to me in consequence.

It was not in the south that I saw or heard any
thing to remind me of personal danger: nor yet in
the west, though the worst inflictions of Lynch law
were beginning there about that time. My friend
and I were in fact handed on by the families of
senators, to the care and kindness of a long succession of them, from the day we reached Washington,
till we emerged from the Slave States at Cincinnati.
Governor Hayne and his friends, and Mr. Calhoun's
family secured every attention to us at Charleston;
and Colonel Preston was our host at Columbia. Judge
Porter, of the federal senate, and Chief Justice of the
Supreme Court of Louisiana, was the familiar friend
who took us in charge at New Orleans: and Mr. Clay

conducted us on board the steamer there,—his son-in-law being our escort up the Mississippi, and our host afterwards in Kentucky, where Mr Clay, whose estate adjoined, spent part of every day with us. No one of these, nor any other of our intimate acquaintance can ever, I am sure, have complained of my act of publishing on the institution which they exhibited to me, however they may dislike my opinions on it.

Our host at Charleston was a clergyman from the north, with a northern wife, who had rushed into that admiration of Slavery which the native ladies do not entertain. I never met with a lady of southern origin who did not speak of Slavery as a sin and a curse,—the burden which oppressed their lives; whereas Mrs. Gilman observed to me, in the slave-market at Charleston, in full view of a woman who, with her infant, was on the stand,—that her doctrine was that the one race must be subordinate to the other, and that if the blacks should ever have the upper hand, she should not object to standing on that table with her children, and being sold to the highest bidder. This lady's publications bear the same testimony. Her brother-in-law is Mr. Ellis Gray Loring of Boston, well known as an avowed Abolitionist, and a most generous contributor to the cause. The Gilmans adored this brother-in-law,—speaking of his abolitionism as his only fault. I was gratified by receiving, in their house, a message from him, to say that his wife and he would call on me as soon as I went into their neighbourhood, and that they begged I would reserve some time for a visit to them. I was aware that this excellent pair, and also Dr. and Mrs. Follen, were, though abolitionists, not 'bloodthirsty' nor 'fanatical.' One of my chief objects in meeting their advances was to learn what the abolitionists really thought, felt and intended. I had attended Colonisation meetings, whenever invited, and heard all that the advocates of slavery had to say; and I made no secret of my intention to give the same ample hearing to the Abolitionists, if they should desire to instruct me in their views and objects.

My first intercourse with any abolitionist took place when I was staying in Kentucky, on my way northwards, and when Mr. Clay was daily endeavouring, at his daughter's house or his own, to impress me in favour of slavery. A long and large letter from Boston arrived one day. The hand was strong and flowing; the wording wonderfully terse, the style wonderfully eloquent; but the whole appearing to me rather intrusive, and not a little fanatical. It was from her who has been my dear, honoured and beloved friend from that year to the present day. When I saw the signature ' Maria Weston Chapman,' I inquired who she was, and learned that she was one of the ' fanatics.' The occasion of her writing was that some saying of mine had reached her which showed, she thought, that I was blinded and beguiled by the slave-holders; and she bespoke for the abolitionists, in the name of their cause, a candid hearing. She then proceeded to remonstrance. I cannot bear to think of my answer. I have no clear remembrance of it; but I am sure it was repulsive, cold and hard. I knew nothing of what was before her eyes,—the beginning of the reign of terror in New England on the slave question; and I knew myself to be too thoroughly opposed to slavery to need caution from an

abolitionist. I was not aware of the danger of the
Colonisation snare. I was, in short, though an
English abolitionist, quite unaware of the conditions
of abolitionism in America. Mrs. Chapman received
my reply, and then myself, with a spirit of generosity,
disinterestedness and thorough nobleness which laid a
broad foundation for friendship between us, whenever
I should become worthy of it : but not one woman
in a thousand (and that one in a thousand only for
the sake of the cause) would have ever addressed me
again after receiving my letter, if my general impression of it is at all correct.

In August 1835, Miss J. and I were the guests of
a clergyman at Medford, near Boston : and there I saw
Dr. and Mrs. Follen, and Mr. and Mrs. Ellis Gray
Loring, and enjoyed sufficient intercourse with them
to find that some abolitionists at least were worthy of
all love and honour. We travelled in other parts of
Massachusetts before paying our Boston visits ; and it
was in passing through Boston, on my way from
Salem to Providence, that I saw, but without being
aware of it, the first outbreak of Lynch law that I
ever witnessed. In that August 1835, there had been
a public meeting in Boston (soon and long repented
of) to denounce, rebuke and silence the abolitionists ;
a proceeding which imposed on the abolitionists the
onus of maintaining the liberty of speech and action
in Massachusetts. How they did it, few or none can
have forgotten ; how, on the 21st of the following
October, the women held their proper meeting, well
knowing that it might cost them their lives ; how Mr.
Garrison was mobbed and dragged through the streets
towards the tar-kettle which he knew to be heating

near at hand, but was saved by the interference and
clever management of a stout truckman, who got him
into the gaol : and how Mrs. Chapman, the leader of
the band of confessors, remained in possession of the
moral victory of the day. Miss J. and I asked the meaning of the crowded state of the streets in the midst of
Boston that day; and our fellow-travellers in the coach
condescended to explain it by the pressure near the
post-office on foreign post day! At Providence, we
heard what had really happened. President Wayland
agreed with me at the time about the iniquitous and
fatal character of the outrage; but called on me, after
a trip to Boston, to relieve my anxiety by the assurance that it was all right,—the mob having been
entirely composed of gentlemen! Professor Henry
Ware, who did and said better things afterwards, told
me that the plain truth was, the citizens did not
choose to let such a man as Garrison live among them,
—admitting that Garrison's opinions on slavery were
the only charge against him. Lawyers on that occasion defended a breach of the laws; ladies were sure
that the gentlemen of Boston would do nothing im-
proper : merchants thought the abolitionists were
served quite right,—they were so troublesome to
established routine; the clergy thought the subject so
' low' that people of taste should not be compelled
to hear any thing about it; and even Judge Story,
when I asked him whether there was not a public
prosecutor who might prosecute for the assault on
Garrison, if the abolitionists did not, replied that he
had given his advice (which had been formally asked)
against any notice whatever being taken of the outrage,—the feeling being so strong against the dis-

cussion of slavery, and the rioters being so respectable in the city.   These things I myself heard and saw, or I would not ask any body to believe what I could hardly credit myself.   The rural settlements were sounder in principle and conduct; and so were the working men of Boston, and many young men not yet trammelled and corrupted by the interests of trade and the slavery of public opinion : but the public opinion of Boston was what I have represented in the autumn of 1835, when I was unexpectedly and very reluctantly, but necessarily, implicated in the struggle.

It was in the interval between that dispersed meeting of the abolitionists and their next righteous attempt to assemble, that Miss J. and I returned to the neighbourhood,—paying our first visit at Professor Henry Ware's at Cambridge.   Dr. and Mrs. Follen called on us there one morning ; and Dr. Follen said, with a mild and serious countenance, ' I wish to know whether we understood you rightly,— that you would attend an abolition meeting, if opportunity offered.'   I repeated what I had said before ; —that having attended Colonisation meetings, and all others where I thought I could gain light on the subject of slavery, I was not only willing but anxious to hear what the Abolitionists had to say, on their public as well as their private occasions.   Dr. Follen said that the opportunity might presently occur, as there was to be a meeting on the next Wednesday, (November 18th) adding that some were of opinion that personal danger was incurred by attending abolition meetings at present.   This was, of course, nothing to me in a case where a principle, political or moral, was involved ; and I said so.   Dr. Follen inquired whether, if I should receive an invitation to attend a meeting in a day or two, I would go. I replied that it must depend on the character of the meeting. If it was one at which ladies would merely settle their accounts and arrange their local affairs, I would rather defer it till a safer time : but if it was one where I could gain the knowledge I wanted, I would go, under any circumstances. Dr. Follen said the meeting would be of the latter kind : and that, as it was impossible to hold it at the Anti-slavery Office without creating a mob, the meeting was to be held at the house of Mr. Francis Jackson. This house was only just finished, and built according to the taste of this most faithful citizen, for himself and his daughters : but he said he would willingly sacrifice it, rather than the ladies of Boston should not have a place to meet in.

The Follens had not been gone many minutes before the invitation arrived. It was signed by the President and the Secretary of the Ladies' Society; and it included in its terms any friend whom I might like to take with me. The note was enclosed in one from Mr. Loring, proposing to call for Miss J. and me on the Wednesday, that we might dine early at his house and go to the meeting with his family party. His house was near Mr. Jackson's, and it was not considered safe to go otherwise than on foot. I had before satisfied myself as to the duty of not involving any of my hosts in any of my proceedings on the abolition question. But it was now necessary to give Miss J. time to consider the part she should take. Three ladies, all inadequate to the subject, were dining at Dr. Ware's that day ; and it was impossible at the moment to have any private conversation with my companion. I therefore handed her the letters across the table, with a sign of silence; and she had five hours for reflection before the guests departed. 'Have you read those letters?' I then inquired of her.— 'Yes.'—'Do you mean to go?'—'Certainly, if you do.'—'Shall I say so for you?'—'If you please.'—I therefore accepted both invitations for both of us, and returned to the drawing-room, where I soon found an opportunity of saying to my host and hostess, 'I do not ask or wish an opinion from you: but I tell you a fact. Miss J. and I are going to dine at Mr. Loring's on Wednesday, to attend an abolition meeting.' Dr. Ware turned round as he stood in the window, and said, 'You will be mobbed. You will certainly be mobbed.'—'Perhaps so,' I replied. I then explained that Mr. Loring was coming for us; so that none of our Cambridge friends would be seen in the streets, or involved in our proceeding. I was sorry to hear, the next morning, that my host had desired Mr. Loring not to trouble himself to fetch us, as Mrs. Ware had some shopping to do in Boston, and Dr. Ware would drive us there in his 'carry-all.'—From time to time during the intervening day, our host observed, 'You will certainly be mobbed:' and when I once more and finally explained that this would make no difference, he jokingly declared that he said it so often, partly to be proved right, if any accident should happen, and partly for a jest, if all went well.

At Mr. Loring's house we found Mrs. Chapman and one of her sisters, and the Rev. Samuel I. May. During dinner, the conversation was chiefly on the Southern slave-holders, whose part was taken by Miss J. and myself, so far as to plead the involuntariness of

their position, and the extreme perplexity of their case,
—over and above the evil conditions of prejudice and
ignorance in which they were brought up. Our line
of argument was evidently worth little in the estimate
of all present, who appeared to us, in our then half-in-
formed state, hard and narrow. But we were now in
the way to learn better. Mr. Loring was too ill to
eat or speak : and it was plain that he ought to have
been in bed : but he would not leave his wife's side on
that day.—Immediately after dinner it was time to
be gone. When I was putting on my shawl upstairs,
Mrs. Chapman came to me, bonnet in hand, to say,
'You know we are threatened with a mob again to-
day : but I do not myself much apprehend it. It
must not surprise us; but my hopes are stronger than
my fears.' I hear now, as I write, the clear silvery
tones of her who was to be the friend of the rest of my
life. I still see the exquisite beauty which took me
by surprise that day;—the slender, graceful form,—
the golden hair which might have covered her to her
feet;—the brillant complexion, noble profile, and
deep blue eyes;— the aspect, meant by nature to be
soft and winning only, but that day, (as ever since) so
vivified by courage, and so strengthened by upright
conviction, as to appear the very embodiment of heroism. 'My hopes,' said she, as she threw up her
golden hair under her bonnet, ' are stronger than my
fears.'

Mr. Loring and I walked first. Just before turning into the street where Mr. Jackson lived, he
stopped, and looking me full in the face, said, 'Once
more,—have you physical courage ? for you may need
it now.' On turning the corner we were pleased to

find only about a dozen boys yelling in front of Mr. Jackson's house, as often as the coloured women went up the steps. No one was detained there an instant. The door opened and shut as rapidly as possible. As it was a ladies' meeting, there were no gentlemen in the house but the owner, and the two who accompanied us. When all were admitted, the front door was bolted, and persons were stationed at the rear of the house, to keep a way clear for escape over the fence, if necessary. About a hundred and thirty ladies were assembled; all being members except Mrs. George Thompson, Miss J. and myself. The folding-doors between the two drawing-rooms were thrown back; and the ladies were seated on benches closely ranged in both rooms. The President's table was placed by the folding-door; and near her were seated the officers of the society. The three gentlemen overheard the proceedings from the hall. I may refer to my ' Retrospect of Western Travel,' (volume iii., page 153) for some account of the proceedings; and to an article of mine in the ' Westminster Review,' of December, 1838, entitled ' The Martyr Age of the United States,' for evidence of the perils dared by the women who summoned and held this meeting. To me the commotion was a small matter,—provided we got away safely. I was going home in less than a year; and should leave peril and slander behind me. But these women were to pass their lives in the city whose wrath they were defying; and their persecutors were fellow-citizens, fellow-worshippers, and familiar acquaintances. I trust that any who may have the least doubt of the seriousness of the occasion will look back to that year of terror, 1835, in that sketch in the

' Westminster Review' or other records.   The truth
is, it was one of the crises which occur in the life of a
youthful nation, and which try the quality of the
people, bringing out the ten righteous from among
the multitude who are doing evil.

In the midst of the proceedings which I have elsewhere detailed, a note was handed to me, written in
pencil on the back of the hymn which the party were
singing.   It was from Mr. Loring ; and these were
his words.   ' Knowing your opinions, I just ask you
whether you would object to give a word of sympathy
to those who are suffering here for what you have advocated elsewhere.   It would afford great comfort.'
The moment of reading this note was one of the most
painful of my life.   I felt that I could never be happy
again if I refused what was asked of me : but, to com-
ply was probably to shut against me every door in the
United States but those of the Abolitionists.   I should
no more see persons and things as they ordinarily
were : I should have no more comfort or pleasure in
my travels ; and my very life would be, like other
people's, endangered by an avowal of the kind desired.
George Thompson was then on the sea, having nar-
rowly escaped with his life ; and the fury against
' foreign incendiaries' ran high.   Houses had been
sacked ; children had been carried through the snow
from their beds at midnight : travellers had been
lynched in the market-places, as well as in the woods ;
and there was no safety for any one, native or foreign,
who did what I was now compelled to do.—Having
made up my mind, I was considering how this word
of sympathy should be given when Mrs. Loring came
up with an easy and smiling countenance and said—

'You have had my husband's note.   He hopes you
will do as he says; but you must please yourself, of
course.'   I said ' No : it is a case in which there is
no choice.'   ' O! pray do not do it unless you like it.
You must do as you think right.'   ' Yes,' said I :
' I must.'

At first, (out of pure shyness) I requested the President to say a few words for me : but, presently re-
membering the importance of the occasion, and the
difficulty of setting right any mistake that the President might fall into, I agreed to that lady's request
that I would speak for myself.   Having risen therefore, with the note in my hand, and being introduced
to the meeting, I said, as was precisely recorded at the
time, what follows.

' I have been requested by a friend present to say
something—if only a word—to express my sympathy
in the objects of this meeting.   I had supposed that
my presence here would be understood as showing my
sympathy with you.   But as I am requested to speak,
I will say what I have said through the whole South,
in every family where I have been ; that I consider
Slavery as inconsistent with the law of God, and as
incompatible with the course of his Providence.   I
should certainly say no less at the North than at the
South concerning this utter abomination—and I now
declare that in your *principles* I fully agree.'

I emphasized the word 'principles,' (involuntarily,)
because my mind was as yet full of what I had heard
at the South of the objectionable methods of the
Abolitionists.   I have already explained that I ascertained all reports of the kind to be entirely false.—
As I concluded, Mrs. Chapman bowed down her glow-

ing face on her folded arms, and there was a murmur
of satisfaction through the room, while outside, the
growing crowd (which did not however become large)
was hooting and yelling, and throwing mud and dust
against the windows.

Dr. Ware did the brave act of driving up to Mr.
Jackson's door, to take us home.   On our road home,
he questioned me about the meeting.   ' What have
you been doing?' he asked.   ' Why,' said I, ' I have
been speaking.'—' No! you have not!' he exclaimed
in alarm.   I told him that I was as sorry for it as he
could be; but that it was wholly unavoidable.   He
communicated the fact, first to his wife and then to
his brother-in-law, at home, in a way which showed
how serious an affair they considered it.   They could
only hope that no harm would come of it.   As I heard
nothing about it for nearly three weeks, I began to
hope so too.—During those three weeks, however,
the facts got into print.   Dr. Follen went to the Anti-
slavery office one day, and found the Secretary and
Mr. May revising the report of the meeting,—Mr.
May taking extreme care that my precise words should
be given.   Nothing could be more accurate than the
report, as far as I was concerned.

About three weeks after the meeting, I was staying
at the Rev. Dr. Walker's, at Charlestown,—a suburb
of Boston, the weather being extremely bad with
snow-storms, so that visiting was almost out of the
question,—considering that a windy and immensely
long bridge stretches between Charlestown and Boston.
The weather prevented my being surprised that so few
people came ; but my host and hostess were in daily
expectation of some remark about their seclusion from

society.   It was not till many months afterwards that
I was told that there were two reasons why I was not
visited there as elsewhere.   One reason was that I had
avowed, in reply to urgent questions, that I was disappointed in an oration of Mr. Everett's : and the
other was that I had publicly condemned the institution of Slavery.   I hope the Boston people have outgrown the childishness of sulking at opinions, not in
either case volunteered, but obtained by pressure.   At
the time, I could not have conceived of such pettish-
ness; and it was now nearly twenty years ago ; so we
may hope that the weakness is more or less outgrown,
—so little as the indulgence of it can matter to passing strangers, and so injurious as such tendencies are
to permanent residents.   At length, some light was
thrown on the state of my affairs, which I found every
body knew more of than Miss J. and myself.

Miss Peabody of Boston was staying at Dr. Walker's
at the same time with ourselves.   The day before she returned home, she happened to be in the Doctor's library
when his newspaper came in.   It was the leading paper
in Boston, conducted by Mr. Hale, the brother-in-law
of Mr. Everett.   Mr. Hale knew me,—having travelled
a whole day in company with me, during which the
party conversed abundantly.   His paper contained, on
this day, an article on my attending an abolition meeting, very bad in itself, but made infinitely worse by
giving, with its sanction, large extracts from a New
York paper of bad repute (The Courier and Enquirer)
—those extracts being, to speak plainly, filthy.   Dr.
Walker and Miss Peabody burned the paper, hoping
that I might not hear of it.   In the course of the
morning, however, Miss Tuckerman called, in com-

pany with two other ladies, and was evidently full of something that she was eager to say. With a solemn countenance of condolence she presently told me that she had never seen Dr. Channing so full of concern as on that day, on the appearance of a most painful article in the 'Daily Advertiser;' and she proceeded to magnify the misfortune in a way which astonished me. I begged her to tell Dr. Channing, not to be troubled about it, as I was, in the first place, prepared for the consequences of what I might say or do; and, in the next, I acknowledge no foreign jurisdiction in the case. The next time I saw Dr. Channing, he quietly observed that it was all a mistake about his having been troubled on my account. His anxiety was for Mr. Hale, not for me. He did not offer an opinion then or ever afterwards, as to whether I was right or wrong in regard to that act: and I never inquired. I found from others, some time afterwards, that he had written a strong remonstrance to Mr. Hale, declaring that he would not throw up the newspaper, as many other citizens did that day; because, having the independence of the newspaper press at heart, he thought it unjustifiable to desert an Editor for one slip, however great. Many others thought differently; and Mr. Hale lost so many subscribers before night as to be in a thorough ill-humour about the whole business. His excuse to the public for having delayed the 'exposure' of me so long was, like that of the New York editor, that he had not credited the fact of my attending an abolition meeting till he saw it confirmed in the Liberator, though daily assured of it by many anonymous letters.—In the course of that strange day, many other papers came out, full of fury against me, till Miss Peabody was almost frantic with grief. She had to return to Boston in the evening. Two hours after her return, late in the snowy night, a special messenger brought a letter from Miss Peabody, requiring an immediate answer. The letter told me that the Abolitionists were far from grateful for what I had done, while all the rest of society were alienated; and the justification of this assertion was that an abolition lady had made a saucy speech about it at the supper table of the boarding-house. (I was glad to find afterwards that this was a mistake,—the lady being no Abolitionist, and her meaning being also misapprehended by Miss Peabody.) The main business of the letter was to tell me that there was one newspaper not yet committed against me,—the 'Atlas'; and the Editor had just promised Miss Peabody to wait the return of her messenger for any explanation that I or my friends might send. My reply was, of course, that I had no explanation to give,—the report in the Liberator, on which all this censure was grounded, being perfectly accurate. I requested Miss Peabody to repeat to me no more conversations which were not intended for me to hear, and to burn no more newspapers, which I had a right to see. Next morning, the 'Atlas' came out against me, as strong as all the rest. I was truly concerned for Dr. and Mrs. Walker, who could obtain no guests to meet me but their own relatives, and those, I believe, only by special entreaty.

The day after the declaration of hostilities, while two ladies, yet ignorant of the hubbub, were calling on me, a coach drove up, and Mr. Loring entered, looking like a corpse from the grave. He had been confined to his bed ever since the day of the meeting, had risen from it that morning, to be wrapped in blankets, and put into the coach, and came over the long bridge, and through wind and snow to relieve his mind. He intimated that he must see me alone. I asked him if he could wait till the ladies were gone. 'I can wait all day,' he replied. When I could go to him, I took Miss J. with me as a witness, as I did on all occasions of importance, lest my deafness should cause mistake, or the imputation of it. With strong emotion, Mr. Loring said, 'I find I have injured you; and I have come to know if I can make reparation.' My good friend thought he could never be happy again! I bade him be comforted, telling him that the responsibility of the act of avowal was mine at bottom. The suggestion was his; the decision was mine. 'Thank God!' he exclaimed: 'then my mind is relieved. But the question is, what can I do?' 'Nothing,' I told him:—'that is, supposing the account is accurately given in the papers which have copied from the "Liberator."' I asked him whether he had the Advertiser with him. Yes, he had; but he never *could* show it me. I desired to see it, as I could not form a judgment without. He threw it into my lap, and walked to the window, and up and down the room, paler, if possible, than before. The facts were correctly stated, and I had therefore only to send my friend home, desiring him to get well and trust me to bear the consequences of saying abroad what I had long ago printed at home. He left me much relieved, as he said; but he was long in getting over it. When Miss J. and I were staying at his house some weeks afterwards, we observed with pain the cloud that came over the faces of himself and his wife at every slight and insult, public and private, offered to me. I took occasion one day, when they and I were alone, to rebuke this, reminding them that when they devoted themselves to the cause, it was with a determination to bear, for themselves and each other, all its consequences; and that they ought to exert the same faith on behalf of their friends. To this they agreed, and never looked grave on the matter again.

As I anticipated, I saw nothing of Boston society, for some time, but what I had seen before; and at no time was I admitted as I should since have been, if I had accepted the invitations sent me in recent years, to go and see what reparation awaited me. I am told that many people who were panic-stricken during that reign of terror are heartily ashamed now of their treatment of me. I should be glad if they were yet more ashamed of the flatteries and worship with which the Americans received and entertained me, till I went to that meeting. The 'enthusiasm' of which they boasted, and which, I hereby declare, and my companion can testify, was always distasteful to me, collapsed instantly when I differed publicly from them on a sore point: and their homage was proved to be, like all such idolatries, a worship of the ideal, and no more related to myself, in fact, than to the heroine of a dream. There was something diverting, but more vexatious, in the freaks and whims of imaginative people, during the season of my being (in American phrase) 'Lafayetted' in the United States; that is, during the first half of my stay; and the converse experience of the last few months was not devoid of amusement, though it was largely mingled with disgust. The 'lion-hunters' who embarrassed me with invitations which I had no inclination to accept, now backed out of their liability with a laughable activity. Mrs. Douglass Cruger, of New York, who amused and bored Sir Walter Scott so wonderfully, and of whom most English celebrities have curious anecdotes to tell, was one of the most difficult to deal with, from her pertinacity in insisting that I should be her guest when I made my stay at New York: but, before I went there, I had made my abolition avowal; and never was there such a list of reasons why a hostess could not invite guests, as Mrs. Cruger poured out to me when we met in a crowd at a ball; nor any thing so sudden as her change of tone, with some hesitation lingering in it, when she saw that I was well received after all. A somewhat similar instance was that of General and Mrs. Sullivan, of Boston, with whom Miss J. and I had travelled for many days together, and who had been urgent in their entreaties that we would spend a long time with them in Boston. On the appearance of the Advertiser article, they ceased their attentions, taking no further notice of me than once inviting me to a family party. Moreover, Dr. Channing inquired of some friends of mine whether I had been informed of the manner in which the Sullivans were speaking of me throughout Boston; for that I ought to be put on my guard against looking for, or accepting, attentions from persons who so treated my name. Again, I called one day on Mr. and Mrs. C. G. L., with whom we had had friendship on the Mississippi, and who had been then, and were always afterwards, kind to us in every possible way.

I found Mr. L. ill, and almost unable to speak from a swelled face. Mrs. L. explained for him that he was wretched on my account, and had had two sleepless nights. Three gentlemen had called on him, entreating him to use his influence in persuading me not to expose myself to the censure and ridicule of the whole country. In answer to all that I said, Mrs. L. pleaded the wretchedness of her family in hearing 'such things' said of me : and she continued piteously beseeching me not to do ' such things.' She said all Boston was in an uproar about it. Alas ! no power availed to put ' all Boston in an uproar ' about the intolerable lot of millions of slaves, or about the national disgrace of their fate. My friends could lie awake at night from concern about what their neighbours were saying of a passing stranger, to whom Boston opinion would be nothing a year hence ; and they could not spare a moment, or an emotion, for the negro mother weeping for her children, nor for the crushed manhood of hundreds of thousands of their countrymen whose welfare was their natural charge. In vain I told my friends how ashamed I was of my troubles being cared for, and how much better their grief and agitation might be bestowed on real sufferers whom they *could* aid, than on me who complained of nothing, and needed nothing. But really the subservience to opinion in Boston at that time seemed a sort of mania ; and the sufferers under it were insane enough to expect that their slavery was to be shared by a foreigner accustomed to a totally different state of society.

For a considerable time, my intercourse was confined to the Abolitionists and their friends, and my

own former friends; but before the end of my stay,
it seemed to be discovered that I was not the monster
that had been described; and sundry balls and parties
were given for my entertainment. In other States,
however, the prejudice remained as long as I was in
the country, and some time after, giving place at
length to an earnest desire (to judge by the warmth
of invitations from various quarters) that I would return, and see their country in what my correspondents
call its normal state. I am pleased to find, however,
within the last few days, that in the South I am still
reviled, as I was twenty years ago, and held up, in the
good company of Mrs. Chapman and Mrs. Stowe, to
the abhorrence of the South. If I am proud of my
company, in one sense, I am ashamed of it in another.
Mrs. Chapman and Mrs. Stowe have really sacrificed
and suffered, and thrown their whole future into the
cause; whereas mine is so cheap a charity that I blush
to have it associated with theirs. By their side, I am
but as one who gives a half-penny to a beggar, in
comparison with those who have sold all their goods
to feed the poor.

From Boston I went to New York; and, though
several months had passed, the impression against me
was so strong that my host, on whose arm I entered
a ball-room, was 'cut' by fourteen of his acquaintance on that account. When he told me this, as a
sign of the time, he related that, seeing a group of
gentlemen gathered round a pompous young man who
was talking vehemently, he put his head in to see
what it was all about, when he heard the following;
—'My verdict is that Harriet Martineau is either an
impertinent meddler in our affairs, or a woman of

genius without common sense.' My host replied,
with equal solemnity, ' If, sir, such be your sentence,
Miss Martineau must bear it as she may !' thus ex-
ploding the serious business with a general laugh.
These instances are mere samples of social rudenesses
too numerous to be related.

To return to the 'Daily Advertiser';—in about ten
days, an article appeared which the Editor declared to
be his *amende*, and which the public seemed to consider
such. The Editor professed to choose, from among an
amazing number, a letter which was afterwards avowed
to be by Mr. Minot, a respected Boston merchant, and
a connexion of the Sedgwicks. The insertion of this
letter was considered by all who understood the principle involved in the case an aggravation of the original
offence against that principle. It observed that
American travellers were allowed in England, by courtesy, the liberty of expressing their opinions on all
subjects ; and it was to be hoped that Boston would
not refuse a similar courtesy to a distinguished lady
who was allowed in private relations to be, &c., &c.,
and to whom a debt of gratitude was owing for her
writings. I have strong reason to believe that the
discussions arising out of this treatment of me,—the
attacks and the yet worse *amende*,—roused the minds
of many young citizens to a consideration of the whole
subject of freedom of opinion, and made many converts
to that, and also to Abolitionism. One clear consequence of my conversation and experience together
was that the next prosecution for Blasphemy in Massachusetts was the last. An old man, above seventy,
was imprisoned in a grated dungeon for having printed
that he believed the God of the Universalists to be ' a

chimera of the imagination.' Some who had listened to my assertions of the rights of thought and speech drew up a Memorial [1] to the Governor of the State for a pardon for old Abner Kneeland,— stating their ground with great breadth and clearness, while disclaiming any kind of sympathy with the views and spirit of the victim. The prime mover being a well-known religious man, and Dr. Channing being willing to put his name at the head of the list of requisitionists, the principle of their remonstrance stood out brightly and unmistakeably. The religious corporations opposed the petitioners with all their efforts; and the newspapers threw dirt at them with extraordinary vigour; so that the Governor did not grant their request: but when old Abner Kneeland came out of his prison every body knew that that ancient phase of society had passed away, and that there would never again be a prosecution for Blasphemy in Massachusetts. The civil rights of Atheists have not since been meddled with, though those of the coloured race and their champions are still precarious or worse.

The general indignation which I encountered at every step was, however disagreeable, far less painful to me than some experience among my personal friends. A letter from my Philadelphia host (the same who turned pale at Dr. Julius's news) grieved me much. He told me that his first intimation of what I had done was from the abuse in the newspapers; that his great hope was that I had not acted without purpose; but that still, under any circumstances, he could not but greatly lament the act, as he

[1] Appendix A.

feared it would totally ruin the effect upon the American public of any book I might write.   In my reply, I reminded him of his own exhortation to me to forget all about writing a book, in order that my own impressions and ideas of what I witnessed might be true and free.   He abandoned his objection to my attending the meeting, but still wished that I had not further committed myself.   When I visited Philadelphia some months afterwards, I found the aspect of society much changed towards me : and my hostess and her coterie of friends surrendered none of their objections to what I had done.   How changed is the whole scene now!   That host of mine has become one of the most marked men in the cause.   The scales fell from his eyes long years ago, and he perceived that there can be small virtue in preaching and teaching which covers up the master sin and sorrow of the time.   He has seen from his pulpit a large proportion of his hearers rise and go away on his first mention of the subject on which they most needed to hear him.   He has undergone social reproach and family solicitude for doing what I did—under the same objection, but at infinitely greater risk, and under temptations to silence which scarcely another in his profession has had grace to resist.   In those days, however, I had to feel that I must stand alone ; and, far worse, my friend's disapprobation (he being the most unworldly and upright of men) could not but cause some perplexity in my mind, even in so simple an action as this, in the midst of a clamour which left me scarcely any quietness for reflexion.   I found it best to accept this new trouble as retribution, if I had indeed been wrong, and to defer too close a questioning of past acts to a calmer time. If any are surprised that I could be shaken even thus far, I can only say that they cannot conceive of the hubbub of censure in which I was living,—enough to confound the soberest senses.

On one occasion my indignation was fairly roused. Among the passengers in my voyage out was the Rev. Charles Brooks, who showed me great kindness, during our whole acquaintance, and whose first wife was a special friend of mine. I was their guest at the time of the anniversary festival of Forefathers' Day, at Plymouth, and I accompanied them to the celebration. The first incident of the day was a rather curious one. The orator of the occasion was Senator Sprague, whom I had known well at Washington. He took particular pains to have me seated where I could hear him well ; and then he fixed his eye on me, as if addressing to me particularly the absurd abuse of England which occupied much of his address, and some remarks which were unmistakeably intended for my correction. On our returning to our quarters while the gentlemen went to dinner, an aged lady who could not brave the cold out of doors, asked me how I liked Mr. Sprague's address; on which her daughter burst out with an exclamation which I have never forgotten. The blood rose to her temples, and she threw her bonnet on the table as she cried 'O mother! I am sick of this boasting and exaltation of ourselves over others. When I think of what we might be and what we are, I want to say only " God be merciful to us sinners ! " ' While we were dressing for the ball, the gentlemen were dining. When Mr. Brooks came for us, he bent over my chair to inform me that my health had been pro-

posed by the President to the Sons of the Pilgrims,
and drunk with honour ; and that it had fallen to him
to return thanks for me, as my nearest friend present.
I was struck by his perplexed and abashed countenance ; but I might have gone to the ball believing his
tale without deduction but for an accident which gave
me some notion of what had really taken place.   Mr.
Brooks, who always went out of the room, or at least
covered his face with a screen, when the subject of
anti-slavery was mentioned, would willingly have kept
from me if it had been possible, all knowledge of the
toast : but it was not possible ; and he told me himself
in order that I might know only what was convenient
to him, at the risk of my making myself ridiculous at
the ball.   Happily, there was some one who served me
better.—The method in which the President had introduced my health was this.   After designating ' the
Illustrious Stranger' who was to be toasted, he said
that he was confident no son of the Pilgrims would refuse to drink, considering that the lady in question
was their guest, and how they and their children were
indebted to her for her writings.   Considering these
things, could they not forgive her, if, holding absurd
and mischievous opinions, she had set them in operation in a sphere where she had no concern ?   Could
they not forgive one such act in a guest to whom they
were under such large obligations ?—What Mr.
Brooks took upon him to say for me, I was never able,
with all my pains, to ascertain ; for the newspapers
gave merely an intimation that he acknowledged the
toast.   From his unwillingness that I should hear exactly what passed, I have always trembled to think what
surrender of principle he may have made in my name.

From Boston, the abuse of me ran through almost
every paper in the Union. Newspapers came to me
from the South, daring me to enter the Slave States
again, and offering mock invitations to me to come
and see how they would treat foreign incendiaries.
They would hang me : they would cut my tongue out,
and cast it on a dunghill ; and so forth.   The calum-
nies were so outrageous, and the appeal to the fears of
the slave-holders so vehement that I could feel no surprise if certain interested persons were moved to plot
against my life. My name was joined with George
Thompson's, (who had already escaped with difficulty):
I was represented as a hired agent, and appeals were
made to popular passions to stop my operations.   I believe that almost all the extreme violences perpetrated
against Abolitionists have been by the hands of slave-
traders, and not by the ordinary kind of American citizens.   The slave-traders on the great rivers are (or were
then) generally foreigners,—outcasts from European
countries,—England and Ireland among the number.
These desperate men, driving a profitable trade, which
they believe to be endangered by the Abolitionists,
were not likely to scruple any means of silencing their
enemies.   Such, and such only, have I ever believed to
have designed any violence against me.   Such as these
were the instigators of the outrages of the time,—the
floggings in the market-places, as in Amos Dresser's
case,—the tarrings and featherings of travellers who
were under suspicion of anti-slavery opinion, and the
murder of Lovejoy on his own threshold, in Illinois, on
account of his gallant and heroic defence of the liberty
of the press on the subject of Slavery.
    These fellows haunted the Ohio at the time when I

was about to descend the river with a party of friends, on a visit to the West, which was to occupy the last three months of my stay in America. The party consisted of Dr. and Mrs. Follen and their child, and Mr. and Mrs. Loring. We intended first to visit Mr. Birney at Cincinnati, and afterwards to meet a brother of Dr. Follen's, who had a farm in Missouri. We knew that we could not enter Missouri with safety; but Mr. Follen was to cross the river, and join us in Illinois. Every thing was arranged for this in the winter, and we were rejoicing in the prospect, when the consequences of my abolition avowal interfered to spoil the plan. Miss J. and I were staying at Dr. Channing's towards spring, when, on our return about eleven o'clock one night from a visit, we were rather surprised to find Mr. Loring sitting in Dr. Channing's study. We were surprised, not only on account of the lateness of the hour, but because Mr. Loring was not then a visiting acquaintance of Dr. Channing's. Both of us were struck with the air of gloom in everybody's face and manner. We attempted conversation; but in vain: nobody supported it. Presently, Dr. Channing crossed the room to say to me 'I have requested Mr. Loring to remain, in order to tell you himself the news he has brought. I desire that you should hear it from his own lips.' It appeared that Mr. Loring had been waiting some hours. He told us that an eminent merchant of the city, with whom he was previously unacquainted, had that day called on him to say that he felt it his duty to give some intelligence to my friends of a matter which nearly concerned my safety. He took no interest whatever in the abolition question, on the one side or the other ; but he could not allow the personal safety of a stranger to be imperilled without giving warning. He had been in the West on business, and had there learned that I was expected down the Ohio in the spring : that certain parties had sworn vengeance against me ; and that they had set a watch upon the steamboats, where I should be recognised by my trumpet.   At Cincinnati, the intention was to prosecute me, if possible ; and, at any rate, to prevent my going further.   Much worse things were contemplated at the slave-holding city of Louisville.   My going upon the Ohio at all would not be permitted, the gentleman was sure, by any who cared for my security ; and he explained that he was reporting what he positively knew, from the testimony of his own ears, as well as by trustworthy information ; and that the people to be feared were not the regular inhabitants of the towns, but the hangers-on at the wharves ; and especially the slave-traders.   This gentleman's first business on his return was to ascertain who were my most intimate friends, and to appeal to them to prevent my going near the Ohio.—All this seemed so incredible to me that I made light of it at first : but the party looked more and more grave, and Mr. Loring said : ' Well, then, I must tell you what they mean to do.   They mean to lynch you.'   And he proceeded to detail the plan.   The intention was to hang me on the wharf before the respectable inhabitants could rescue me.

Not wishing to detain Mr. Loring, as it was just midnight, I gave at once, as my decision, what seemed plain to my own mind.   I told him that I had less means of judging what was likely to happen than

natives of the country; and I would leave it to my
own party to determine what should be done. I supposed that none of them would think of relinquishing
such a scheme for mere threats; and if they were not
afraid, neither was I. The decision must rest with
them.—The gloom of the ' good-night' which the
Channings gave me oppressed me even more than
what I had just heard. While pondering the affair in
the middle of the night, I recurred to what my brother
James had suggested in a recent letter. He had ab-
stained from giving any opinion of what I had done,
as none from such a distance could be of any value:
but he had proposed that I should transmit my papers
piecemeal to England; for the obvious reason that destroying my papers would be the aim of the enemy,
in order to prevent my publication of my journals at
home. I had no immediate means of transmitting my
papers: but I had obtained permission from a clergyman who was not an Abolitionist to deposit my papers
in his unsuspected keeping. I had resolved now that
this should be my first work in the morning.

After breakfast, while I was sealing up my parcel
Dr. Channing stood beside me, more moved than I had
ever seen him. He went to his bookshelves, and came
back again, and went again, as if to look at his books,
but in truth to wipe away the tears that rolled down
under his spectacles. What he said I remember, and
the tone of his voice, as if it was five minutes ago. 'I
am ashamed,' he said, ' that after what you have done
for the people of this country, there should be any part
of it in which you cannot set your foot. We are accustomed to say that we are under obligations to you;
and yet you are not safe among us. I hope that as

soon as you return home, you will expose these facts
with all the boldness of which you are capable.' I
replied that I should not publish, in my accounts of
America, any personal narrative of injury: for, besides
the suspicion and odium that attach to a narrative of
personal sufferings from insult, it was to me a much
more striking fact that native citizens, like himself
and Mr. Garrison and others, to whom the Constitution expressly guarantees the liberty of traversing all
the States as freely as any one of them, should be excluded by intimidation from half the States of the
Union.   Dr. Channing said, ' As to this journey, you
must indeed give it up. I think, if you consider that
no immediate call of duty takes you to the Ohio, and
that your destruction might involve that of the whole
party, you will feel it to be your duty to change your
plan.'   My party unhesitatingly decided this for me.
Mrs. Loring declared that she would not go; and the
gentlemen were of opinion that the risk was too serious.   I had myself no idea how I should suffer or act
in circumstances so new.   We therefore gave up the
idea of visiting Messrs. Birney and Follen, and determined on another route.

During that spring, as during many preceding
months, there were lynchings of Abolitionists in various parts of the country, and threatenings of more.
Wherever we went, it was necessary to make up our
minds distinctly, and with the full knowledge of each
other, what we should say and do in regard to the
subject which was filling all men's minds.   We resolved, of course, to stand by our anti-slavery principles, and advocate them, wherever fair occasion
offered: and we never did omit an opportunity of

saying what we knew and thought. On every steamboat, and in every stage (when we entered public
conveyances) the subject arose naturally; for no subject was so universally discussed throughout the country, though it was interdicted within the walls of the
Capitol at Washington. Mr. Loring joined in the
conversation when the legal aspects of the matter were
discussed; and Dr. Follen when the religious and
moral and political bearings of Slavery were the subject. Mrs. Follen and Mrs. Loring were full of facts
and reasons about the working of Abolitionism in its
head quarters. As for me, my topic was Texas, in regard to which I was qualified to speak by some recent
inquiries and experience at New Orleans. This was
three years before the annexation of Texas, and while
the adventurers under Colonel Austin were straining
every nerve to get Texas annexed. They thought that
if, among other devices, they could obtain any sort of
sanction from the British government, or could induce
English settlers, in any considerable number, to go to
Texas, their chances of every sort would be improved.
My visit to New Orleans was seized on, among other
incidents, for the prosecution of this chance. After
duly preparing me by sending me 'information' in
the shape of bragging accounts of the country, they
sent a deputation to me at New Orleans, consisting of
the notorious Mrs. Holley (who did more than perhaps any other individual for the annexation of Texas)
and two or three companions. Concealing from me the
fact that Colonel Austin was at that very time in jail
at Mexico, my visitors offered me in the name of the
Texan authorities, an estate of several thousand acres
in a choice part of the country, and every aid and

kindness that could be rendered, if I would bind myself to live for five years in Texas, helping to frame
their Constitution, and using my influence to bring
over English settlers. The conversation was to me
a most ludicrous one, from the boasts made by my
guests of their happy state of society, though my
questions compelled them to admit that they were
living without a Constitution, or any safeguard of
law; and in fact subject to the dictatorship of Colonel
Austin, a mere adventurer, and then actually in the
hands of the Mexicans, who were far too merciful in
releasing him after a few months imprisonment. One
plea was urged on me which it was hoped I should find
irresistible. There was to be no slave-trade or slavery
in Texas. I knew there was none before the Americans
intruded themselves; but I could not, and did not, believe in this piece of ostentatious virtue in a set of
southern speculators who staked their all on the preservation of Slavery in the United States. I was not
surprised to find that, in the absence of an avowed slave-
trade, there were negroes conveyed from Louisiana,
and landed at night on a spit of sand on the frontier,
whence in the morning they immigrated into Texas,
where they were not to be slaves:—O dear, no!—
not slaves, but apprentices for ninety-nine years! I
gave my visitors a bit of my mind, in return for their
obliging offer. An English visitor, a scholar and
a minister of religion, was deluded by similar offers
and suggestions; and deeply concerned he was that I
would not go into the enterprise. He wrote repeatedly
to offer his assistance for any number of years, and implored me to consider well before I rejected so unequalled an opportunity of usefulness. He offered to

come and see me wherever I might stop on the Mississippi; and he fully believed he should induce me to
turn back. Poor gentleman! his was a mournful
story. His wife died of consumption on the bank of
the Mississippi, just as I reached New Orleans; and
he and his children were in their first desolation when
he made up his mind to embrace the Texan enterprise.
Soon after I answered his final appeal to me to go, I
heard of his death by fever. The disease of the country
laid him low at the outset of his first season. His
children were most benignantly cared for by the
American citizens. One died; but the two little
daughters were adopted,- one by a planter's lady in
the West, and the other by an English lady in the
North.—My attention being thus turned towards
Texas, I was qualified to bring the subject under Dr.
Channing's notice as the interest of it deepened; and
to converse upon it in our northern journey when we
were perpetually encountering citizens who had been
listening to the boasts of Austin's emissaries, at New
York or elsewhere.— Dr. Channing's ' Letter ' on the
Annexation of Texas is perhaps the most honoured
in England of all his writings. The credit of origin-
ating it belongs in the first place, and chiefly, to Mr.
David Child, who furnished an admirable history of
the province, and of its sufferings from the Americans,
in the Anti-slavery Quarterly Review. From that article I avowedly derived the facts which I gave as the
basis of my own account of the Texas business, in my
' Society in America.' I besought Dr. Channing's
especial attention to that chapter; and the whole subject so moved him that he sat down and wrote that
noble ' Letter,' by the moral effect of which the

annexation of Texas was unquestionably deferred for two years. It is not often that the writings of divines have even that much effect in bridling the lust of ambition and cupidity.

Our route had for its chief objects (after Niagara) the Northern Lakes. The further we went, the more we heard of lynchings which had lately taken place, or were designed for the next Abolitionists who should come that way. At Detroit, Mr. Loring entered the reading-room of the hotel, immediately on our arrival; and while he read the newspaper, he heard one citizen telling another how during the temporary absence of the latter, there had been a lynching of a fellow who pretended to be a preacher, but was suspected to be an Abolitionist. The speaker added that a party of Abolitionists was expected; and that everything was in readiness to give them a similar reception. He finished off with saying that lynching did not look well in newspapers, or sound well at a distance; but that it was the only way. Our Abolitionism could be no secret, ready as we always were to say what we knew and thought: and that very evening, I had the pleasure of so far converting the Governor of the State (Michigan) as to possess him with a true idea of Garrison, and to obtain his promise,—which was indeed freely offered, as we took leave,—to protect, to the utmost of his power, every Abolitionist within the boundary of the State.

The woods of Michigan were very beautiful; but danger was about us there, as everywhere during those three months of travel. It was out of such glades as those of Michigan that mobs had elsewhere issued to stop the coach, and demand the victim, and inflict the

punishment earned by compassion for the negro, and
assertion of true republican liberty. I believe there was
scarcely a morning during those three months when it
was not my first thought on waking whether I should
be alive at night. I am not aware that the pleasure of
that glorious journey was materially impaired by this ;
yet I learned by that experience to sympathise with
the real griefs of martyrdom, and to feel something
different from contemptuous compassion for those who
quail under the terror of it.—At Pittsburg, sitting by
our open window one hot night, we heard an uproar at
a distance, the cause of which my companions truly
divined to be a pro-slavery riot. ' What can it be?'
I exclaimed, as it drew nearer. ' Only a little execra-
tion coming this way,' replied Dr. Follen, smiling,
referring to our reputation as execrated persons. We
were not the objects that night, however: but the
houses of several free negro families were destroyed.
What we met with was, usually, prodigious amazement, a little scorn, and a great many warnings.

After so many weeks, during which the idea of
danger had become the rule, and safety the exception,
we were struck with a kind of astonishment when we
entered the great cities,—Philadelphia and New York,
—where the comfortable citizens assumed an air of
scepticism about the critical state of the country which
was truly marvellous in republicans. I have mentioned before how the ladies of one of the first families
in New York were kept in ignorance of riots so serious that one might almost as soon expect the ladies of
Birmingham and Bristol to have been unaware of the
High-church and Reform riots of 1791 and 1831.
We now found that selfish, or aristocratic, or timid

citizens had kept themselves as ignorant of the dangers of their neighbours as the same kind of men of every country are in times of great moral revolution. Quiet and complacent were the smiles with which some who ought to have known better declared their disbelief even that threats had been offered to a guest and a woman; and various were the excuses and special reasons given for the many instances of violence to their own citizens which could not be denied. Some were sorry that I believed such threats to myself, and such inflictions upon others as were as certainly and notoriously true as the days of the month on which they happened. Some would not listen to the facts at the time: others, who could not doubt them at the time, have tried to get rid of the belief since, but are incessantly thrown back upon the old evidence by the new troubles which arise from day to day out of the cursed and doomed institution of Slavery. I happened to witness the opening of the martyr age of its reformers; and I am thankful that I did witness it. There were times when I was sorry that I was not the victim of the struggle, instead of Lovejoy, or some other murdered citizen. I was sorry, because my being a British subject would have caused wider and deeper consequences to arise from such a murder than followed the slaughter of native Abolitionists,—despised and disowned by their government for their very Abolitionism. The murder of an English traveller would have settled the business of American Slavery (in its federal sense) more speedily than perhaps any other incident. It is no wonder that some Americans, who shut their eyes to the whole subject, should disbelieve in any body being in any danger, and that others should try to make me forget my share of it. The latest and most general method of propitiating me has been by inviting me to go again, and see what Abolitionists my acquaintances have become,—every where north of Mason and Dixon's line.

When I returned home, the daily feeling of security, and of sympathy in my anti-slavery views gave me a pleasure as intense as if I had returned from a long exile, instead of a tour of recreation. I was not left without paltry disturbances, however. In the preface to 'Society in America,' I invited correction as to any errors in (not opinion, but) matters of fact. After this, I could not, of course, decline receiving letters from America. Several arrived, charged double, treble, even quadruple postage. These consisted mainly of envelopes, made heavy by all manner of devices, with a slip of newspaper in the middle, containing prose paragraphs, or copies of verses, full of insults, and particularly of taunts about my deafness. All but one of these bore the post-mark of Boston. I was ashamed to mention this back to America; and I hope that most of this expensive and paltry insult was the work of one hand.

My story seems a long one: but I do not think it could have been honestly omitted in a history of my life: and it seems to be worth telling for another reason,—that it may afford material for an instructive comparison between the state of the cause, (and of American society as determined by it,) in 1835 and 1855. When I was at Washington, the leading statesmen were, or declared themselves to be, confident that the abolition of Slavery would never be even named in Congress; to which I replied that when

they could hedge in the wind and build out the stars
from their continent, they might succeed in their proposed exclusion : and now, at the end of twenty years,
what has come of the attempt ?   It was prosecuted
with all diligence. A rigid censorship in the Southern
States expunged from English and other classics every
reference to Slavery, and every perilous aspiration
after freedom.   Abolitionists were kept out by the
most vigilant cruelty, which inflicted torture on mere
suspicion.   Free negroes were lodged in prison, even
when they were British sailors ; as indeed they are
still liable to be.   The right of petition to Congress
was temporarily abolished.   Every liberty, personal
and social, was sacrificed in the attempt to enforce
silence on that one sore subject.   And now the whole
world rings with it.   Congress can, in fact, talk about
nothing else : for, whatever subject a debate may
ostensibly be upon, it always merges in a wrangle on
Slavery.   The entire policy of the Republic has been
shaped by it ; and the national mind also, in as far as
the public mind depends on the national policy in a
democratic republic.   The moral deterioration has been
more rapid than the most cautious of the early Presidents could have apprehended, or than the despots of
the world could have hoped.   Because it was necessary
to obtain new territory for the support of the destructive institution, a process of aggression and annexation
was entered upon ; and that policy has dragged back
the mind and morals of the people into that retrograde
state in which territorial aggrandisement is the national aim.   This, again, implicates foreign nations in
the interest of the question.   It was not enough that
every political movement in the United States was

modified by this great controversy ;—that it ruined, and still ruins, every statesman who takes the immoral side ;—that it destroyed the career and broke the hearts of the most eminent of them,—of Calhoun, of Clay, and of Webster ;—that it shattered the reputation of more, and is now rendering absolutely certain the dissolution of the Union, in one way or another, and with more or less chance of its virtuous reconstitution :—it was not enough that all this has happened at home, amidst the most desperate efforts to cover up the difficulty under an enforced silence :—it has enlisted almost every people and ruler in the world on the one side or the other. The Czars are making friendships with the slave power, as the most hopeful ally on earth of Russian tyranny. Spain is immediately interested, because Cuba is the next morsel for which the ogre lusts. The friendship of Western Europe, otherwise so certain to be cordial and durable, is rendered in the last degree precarious by the lawless and barbaric proceedings of the pro-slavery Americans. The depressed nationalities of Europe, who might otherwise look up to America for protection and aid, can now only blush at the disgrace reflected by America on republicanism all over the world, and sigh at the hopelessness of any real assistance from a nation which cannot aid freedom abroad because it has to take care of its own slavery, and beware of its victims at home. That which was the protest of almost a solitary voice when I went to America has now expanded into a world-wide controversy.—It was in 1831 that Garrison, the apostle of the deepest and broadest cause of our century, said those immortal words. ' I am aware that many

object to the severity of my language; but is there
not cause for severity? I *will* be as harsh as truth,
and as uncompromising as justice. I am in earnest—
I will not equivocate—I will not excuse—I will not
retreat a single inch—AND I WILL BE HEARD.' This
humble printer, so speaking after the first taste of
persecution, a quarter of a century ago, has made himself 'heard' round the globe and from pole to pole.
There is no saying what fates and policies of nations
were involved in those first utterances of his.   The
negroes first heard him by some untraceable means;
and the immediate consequence was the cessation of
insurrection.   There were frequent risings of the
slaves before; and there have been none since.   But
the lot of the negro race is by no means the only or
the chief fate involved in the controversy.   Every
political and social right of the white citizens has been
imperilled in the attempt to enforce silence on the
subject of slavery.   Garrison will be recognised hereafter, not only as at present,—as the Moses of the
enslaved race, leading them out of their captivity,—but
as more truly the founder of the republic than
Washington himself.   Under the first Presidents,
democratic republicanism made a false start.   It has
bolted from the course, and the Abolitionists are
bringing it back to the starting-post.   If it is found
capable of winning the race against old despotisms
and temporary accommodations of constitutional monarchy, the glory of the consummation will be awarded
more plentifully to the regenerators of the republic
than to its originators, great as they were; for they
left in it a fatal compromise.—But I must not
enlarge further on this subject, on which I have

written abundantly elsewhere. I could say much; and it requires self-denial to abstain from a statement of what Garrison's friends, Mr. and Mrs. Henry Grafton Chapman, and their relatives on both sides of the house, contributed to the cause by deeds and sufferings. But my peculiar connexion with Mrs. Chapman in this memoir renders it impossible to speak as I would. Happily, the claims of that privileged family are and will be understood without any appeal from me to the veneration and gratitude of society.

The accident of my arriving in America in the dawning hour of the great conflict accounts for the strange story I have had to tell about myself. Any person from England, so arriving, pledged as I was to anti-slavery views, and conspicuous enough to draw attention to those views, was sure to meet with just such treatment;—a blinding incense first; and then, if the incense failed to blind, a trial of the method of intimidation. Other English persons were indeed so prepared for and received. Some did not understand their position, and went unconsciously into the snare. Some took fright. Some thought prudence necessary, for the sake of some other cause which they had more at heart. Some were even converted by the romancing of the slave-owners. Some did their duty. It is not, and it never will be, forgotten how Lord Carlisle did his, when, as Lord Morpeth, he traversed the whole country, never failing in the kindliness and candour which adorn his temper, while never blinking the subject of slavery, or disguising his anti-slavery convictions. The reign of terror (for travellers at least) was over before he went;

and he would have been safe under any circumstances :
but he was subject to insults and slander, and was
abundantly visited with a laborious contempt : and in
bringing this upon himself and bearing it good-
humouredly, he threw his mite into the treasury which
is to redeem the slaves.   He seems to have been
pitied and excused in somewhat the same style as
myself by persons who assumed to be our protectors.
When I had conversed on board a steamboat with a
young lady of colour, well educated and well mannered,
and whom I had been acquainted with at Philadelphia,
I was of course, the object of much wrath and denun-
ciation on deck ; and my spontaneous protectors
thought themselves generous in pleading that I ought
to be excused for such conduct, on the ground of the
' narrowness of my foreign education ! ' Such were
the vindications with which Lord Carlisle also was
insulted when he was vindicated at all.

It was impossible, during such a crisis, to avoid
judging conspicuous persons more or less by their
conduct in regard to the great conflict of their time.
Ordinary persons might be living as common-place
people do in such times,—in utter unconsciousness
of their position. As in the days of Noah, such
people buy and sell and build and plant, and are
troubled by no forecast of what is to happen.   But in
a republic, it cannot be so with the conspicuous citizens.
The Emersons, for instance, (for the adored Charles
Emerson was living then :)—they were not men to
join an association for any object ; and, least of all, for
any moral one : nor were they likely to quit their
abstract meditations for a concrete employment on
behalf of the negroes.   Yet they did that which made

me feel that I knew them, through the very cause in which they did not implicate themselves. At the time of the hubbub against me in Boston, Charles Emerson stood alone in a large company in defence of the right of free thought and speech, and declared that he had rather see Boston in ashes than that I, or anybody, should be debarred in any way from perfectly free speech. His brother Waldo invited me to be his guest, in the midst of my unpopularity, and, during my visit, told me his course about this matter of slavery. He did not see that there was any particular thing for him to do in it then : but when, in coaches or steamboats or any where else, he saw people of colour ill-used, or heard bad doctrine or sentiment propounded, he did what he could and said what he thought. Since that date, he has spoken more abundantly and boldly the more critical the times became ; and he is now, and has long been, completely identified with the Abolitionists in conviction and sentiment, though it is out of his way to join himself to their organisation.—The other eminent scholars and thinkers of the country revealed themselves no less clearly,—the literary men of Boston and Cambridge sneering at the controversy as ‘ low ’ and disagreeable, and troubling to their repose, and Edward Everett, the man of letters *par excellence*, burning incense to the south, and insulting the Abolitionists while they were few and weak, endeavouring to propitiate them as they grew strong, and finally breaking down in irretrievable disgrace under a pressure to which he had exposed himself by ambition, but which he had neither courage nor conscience to abide. I early saw in him the completest illustration I met with of the influences of

republican life upon a man of powers without principle, and of knowledge without wisdom. He was
still worshipped through vanity, when I knew him,
though his true deserts were well enough understood
in private : he had plenty of opportunity to retrieve
his political character afterwards: he obtained in
England, when ambassador, abundance of the admiration which he sacrificed so much to win; and
then at last, when the hour arrived which must test
his quality, he sank, and must abide for the rest of
his life in a slough of contempt from which there is
no rescue. This is precisely what was anticipated
twenty years ago by (not his enemies, for I believe he
then had none, but) friends who mourned over his
quitting a life of scholarship, for which he was eminently qualified, for one of political aspiration. They
knew that he had not self-reliance or courage enough for
effective ambition, nor virtue enough for a career of
independence.   It is all over now; and the vainest of
men, who lives by the breath of praise, is placed for the
sad remnant of his days between the scorn of the
many and the pity of the few. Vindicators he has
none, and I believe no followers.—The Sedgwicks
were beginning to be interested in the great controversy ; but they were not only constitutionally
timid,—with that American timidity which we
English can scarcely conceive of,—but they worshipped the parchment idol,—the Act of Union ;
and they did not yet perceive, as some of them have
done since, that a human decree which contravenes
the laws of Nature must give way when the two are
brought into conflict. I remember Miss Sedgwick
starting back in the path, one day when she and I

were walking beside the sweet Housatonic, and snatching her arm from mine when I said, in answer to her inquiry, what I thought the issue of the controversy must be. 'The dissolution of the Union!' she cried. 'The Union is sacred, and must be preserved at all cost.' My answer was that the will of God was sacred too, I supposed; and if the will of God which, as she believed, condemned Slavery should come into collision with the federal constitution which sanctioned it, the only question was which should give way,—the Divine will or a human compact. It did not appear to me then, any more than now, that the dissolution of the Union need be of a hostile character. That the elimination of the two pro-slavery clauses from the constitution must take place sooner or later was always clear to me; but I do not see why the scheme should not be immediately and peaceably reconstituted, if the Americans will but foresee the necessity in time. The horror expressed by the Sedgwicks at what seemed so inevitable a consequence of the original compromise surprised me a good deal: and I dare say it seems strange to themselves by this time: for Miss Sedgwick and others of her family have on occasion spoken out bravely on behalf of the liberties of the republic, when they were most compromised. I had a great admiration of much in Miss Sedgwick's character, though we were too opposite in our natures, in many of our views, and in some of our principles, to be very congenial companions. Her domestic attachments and offices were charming to witness; and no one could be further from all conceit and vanity on account of her high reputation in her own country. Her authorship did not constitute her life; and she led a complete life, according to her measure, apart from it : and this is a spectacle which I always enjoy, and especially in the case of a woman. The insuperable difficulty between us,—that which closed our correspondence, though not our good will, was her habit of flattery ;—a national weakness, to which I could have wished that she had been superior. But her nature was a timid and sensitive one ; and she was thus predisposed to the national failing ;—that is, to one side of it ; for she could never fall into the cognate error,—of railing and abuse when the flattery no longer answers. She praised or was silent. The mischief was that she praised people to their faces to a degree which I have never considered it necessary to permit. I told her that I dreaded receiving her letters because, instead of what I wished to hear, I found praise of myself. She informed me that, on trial, she found it a *gêne* to suppress what she wanted to say ; and thus it was natural for us to cease from corresponding. I thought she wanted courage, and shrank from using her great influence on behalf of her own convictions; and she thought me rash and rough. She thought ' safety ' a legitimate object of pursuit in a gossiping state of society; and I did not care for it,—foreigner as I was, and witnessing, as I did, as critical a struggle as has ever agitated society. I said what I thought and what I knew of the Websters and the Everetts, and other northern men who are now universally recognised as the disgrace rather than the honour of the region they represented. Their conduct, even then, authorised my judgment of them : but she, a northern woman, shared the northern caution, if not the sectional vanity, which admired

and upheld, as long as possible, the men of genius and
accomplishment who sustained the intellectual reputation of New England.   Through all our differences of
view and temperament, I respected and admired Miss
Sedgwick, and I was sorry to be absent from England
in 1839 when she was in London, and when I should
have enjoyed being of any possible use to her and her
connexions, who showed me much hospitality and
kindness in their own country.   What I think of Miss
Sedgwick's writings I told in a review of her works
in the Westminster Review of October, 1837.   Her
novels, and her travels, published some years later,
had better be passed over with the least possible
notice ; but I think her smaller tales wonderfully
beautiful ;—those which, as ' Home ' and ' Live and
Let Live,' present pictures of the household life of
New England which she knows so well, and loves so
heartily.

Of Webster, as of Clay, Calhoun, President Jackson
and others, I gave my impressions in my books on
America, nearly twenty years ago.   I will not repeat
any thing I then and there said : but will merely
point out how their fate corresponded with their ordeal.   ' My dear woman,' said Mr. Webster to me at
his own table, laying his finger on my arm to em-
phasize his words,—' don't you go and believe me
to be ambitious.   No man can despise that sort of
thing more than I do.   I would not sacrifice an hour
of my ease for all the honours and powers in the
world.'   Mr. Clay made no protestations of the sort
to me ; nor Mr. Calhoun, whom, with all his absurdi-
ties, I respected by far the most of the three, in the
long run.   All were hugely ambitious : but Calhoun

was honest in the main point. He lived and died for the cause of Slavery; and, however far such a career is from the sympathies of English people, the openness and directness of his conduct were at least respectable. He was infatuated by his sectional attachments: but he was outspoken and consistent. Mr. Clay never satisfied me of his sincerity on the great question of his time; but there was much, outside of that trying matter, that was interesting and even honourable;—a genuine warmth, a capacity for enthusiasm, and vast political ability. Our intercourse amounted to friendship at last; but his unworthy conduct during the closing years of his life overthrew my esteem, and destroyed my regard for him. While professing a desire to provide for the future abolition of Slavery, he prevented in some parts its immediate abolition, and he extended in others the area of its prevalence. He was as well aware as any body of the true character of the Colonisation scheme of which he accepted the Presidency; and he continued to laud it to foreigners as an agency of emancipation, when he knew that it was established and upheld by slaveholders like himself, for the protection and security of the institution of Slavery. His personal ambition was as keen as Webster's; and the failure of both in their aspirations for the Presidentship destroyed them both. In regard to genius, both were of so high an order, and their qualifications were so little alike, that there is no need to set the one above the other. Webster's training was the higher; his position as a Massachusetts man the more advantageous, morally and politically; his folly and treachery in striving to win the supreme honours of the state by winning the South, through the sacrifice of the rights and liberties of the North, were, of necessity, more extreme and more conspicuous than any double dealing of Mr. Clay's ; his retribution was the more striking ; and the disgrace which he drew down on his last days was the more damning of the two.   But both these men, who might have rivalled the glory of Washington himself, by carrying the state through a stress as real and fearful as that of eighty years ago, will be remembered as warnings and not as examples.   As far as appears, they were the last of the really great men who led the statesmanship of the republic ; and to their failure, moral and political, may perhaps be mainly charged the fatal mischief which now hangs as a doom over the state, that the best men decline entering political life, and that there is every inducement for the least capable and the least worthy to be placed in the highest seats.   The ablest men of their generation did not attempt to reverse, or even to retard the retrogression of their country ; but, on the contrary, for their own ends they precipitated it.   I feared this when I observed their proceedings on the spot ; and they afterwards proved the fact to all the world ; and sad has the spectacle been.   There is not even the consolation that, being dishonest, they failed ; for their failure was on account of their eminence and not their dishonesty.   They were put aside to make way for knaves of an obscure cast, who might more readily beguile or evade the indignation of the world, which would not waste on a Fillmore or a Pierce the reprobation which would have attended on a Webster or a Clay who had done their deeds and committed their *laches*.   Already, so long ago as twenty years, there was a striking contrast between the speech and manner of venerable elders, like Madison and Chief Justice Marshall, and those of the aspiring statesmen, Webster, Clay, and, in a smaller way, Everett and other second-rate politicians. The integrity, simplicity and heart-breathing earnestness of the aged statesmen were singularly contrasted with the affectations, professions, cautious procedures, and premeditated speech of the leaders of the time. How rapid and how great the deterioration has been since, every new page of American history bears witness. Still, there is no reason for despair. A safe issue is always possible, and most probable, where there is any principled and active body of true patriots, like the Abolitionists of the United States. Their light shines the brighter for the gathering darkness about them ; and they belong to a people who, however scared at new dangers for a time, cannot for ever love darkness rather than light. The choice is being offered to them more and more plainly ; and my knowledge of them, personal and by study, gives me every hope that their choice will be the right one, if only they are compelled to make it before the lust of territorial aggrandisement has become overwhelming by indulgence.

In Margaret Fuller's Memoirs there is a letter which she declared she sent to me, after copying it into her common-place book. It is a condemnatory criticism of my ' Society in America ; ' and her condemnation is grounded on its being what she called ' an abolition book.' I remember having a letter from her ; and one which I considered unworthy of her and of the occasion, from her regarding the anti-slavery subject as simply a low and disagreeable one, which should be left to unrefined persons to manage

while others were occupied with higher things : but I
do not think that the letter I received was the one
which stands in her common-place book. I wish that
she had mentioned it to me when my guest some
years afterwards, or that my reply had appeared with
her criticism. However, her letter, taken as it stands,
shows exactly the difference between us. She who
witnessed and aided the struggles of the oppressed in
Italy must have become before her death better aware
than when she wrote that letter that the struggle for
the personal liberty of millions in her native republic
ought to have had more of her sympathy, and none of
the discouragement which she haughtily and com-
placently cast upon the cause. The difference between
us was that while she was living and moving in an
ideal world, talking in private and discoursing in
public about the most fanciful and shallow conceits
which the transcendentalists of Boston took for philosophy, she looked down upon persons who acted
instead of talking finely, and devoted their fortunes,
their peace, their repose, and their very lives to the
preservation of the principles of the republic. While
Margaret Fuller and her adult pupils sat ' gorgeously
dressed,' talking about Mars and Venus, Plato and
Göthe, and fancying themselves the elect of the earth
in intellect and refinement, the liberties of the republic were running out as fast as they could go, at a
breach which another sort of elect persons were devot-
ing themselves to repair : and my complaint against
the ' gorgeous ' pedants was that they regarded their
preservers as hewers of wood and drawers of water,
and their work as a less vital one than .the pedantic
orations which were spoiling a set of well-meaning

women in a pitiable way. All that is settled now. It
was over years before Margaret died. I mention it
now to show, by an example already made public by
Margaret herself, what the difference was between me
and her, and those who followed her lead. This
difference grew up mainly after my return from
America. We were there intimate friends; and I
am disposed to consider that period the best of her
life, except the short one which intervened between
her finding her real self and her death. She told me
what danger she had been in from the training her
father had given her, and the encouragement to
pedantry and rudeness which she derived from the
circumstances of her youth. She told me that she
was at nineteen the most intolerable girl that ever
took a seat in a drawing-room. Her admirable candour, the philosophical way in which she took herself
in hand, her genuine heart, her practical insight, and,
no doubt, the natural influence of her attachment to
myself, endeared her to me, while her powers, and her
confidence in the use of them, led me to expect great
things from her. We both hoped that she might go
to Europe when I returned, with some friends of hers
who would have been happy to take her: but her
father's death, and the family circumstances rendered
her going out of the question. I introduced her to
the special care of R. Waldo Emerson and his wife:
and I remember what Emerson said in wise and gentle
rebuke of my lamentations for Margaret that she
could not go to Europe, as she was chafing to do, for
purposes of self-improvement. 'Does Margaret Fuller,
—supposing her to be what you say,—believe her
progress to be dependent on whether she is here or

there?' I accepted the lesson, and hoped the best.
How it might have been with her if she had come to
Europe in 1836, I have often speculated. As it was,
her life in Boston was little short of destructive. I
need but refer to the memoir of her. In the most
pedantic age of society in her own country, and in its
most pedantic city, she who was just beginning to rise
out of pedantic habits of thought and speech relapsed
most grievously. She was not only completely spoiled
in conversation and manners : she made false estimates
of the objects and interests of human life. She was
not content with pursuing, and inducing others to
pursue, a metaphysical idealism destructive of all
genuine feeling and sound activity : she mocked at
objects and efforts of a higher order than her own,
and despised those who, like myself, could not adopt
her scale of valuation. All this might have been
spared, a world of mischief saved, and a world of good
effected, if she had found her heart a dozen years
sooner, and in America instead of Italy. It is the
most grievous loss I have almost ever known in private
history,—the deferring of Margaret Fuller's married
life so long. The noble last period of her life is,
happily, on record as well as the earlier. My friendship with her was in the interval between her first
and second stages of pedantry and forwardness : and
I saw her again under all the disadvantages of the
confirmed bad manners and self-delusions which she
brought from home. The ensuing period redeemed
all ; and I regard her American life as a reflexion,
more useful than agreeable, of the prevalent social
spirit of her time and place ; and the Italian life as
the true revelation of the tender and high-souled

woman, who had till then been as curiously concealed from herself as from others.

If eccentricities like Margaret Fuller's, essentially sound as she was in heart and mind, could arise in American society, and not impair her influence or be a spectacle to the community, it will be inferred that eccentricity is probably rife in the United States. I certainly thought it was, in spite (or perhaps in consequence) of the excessive caution which is prevalent there in regard to the opinion of neighbours and society. It takes weeks or months for an English person to admit the conception of American caution, as a habit, and yet more as a spring of action : and the freedom which we English enjoy in our personal lives and intercourses must find an equivalent in Americans somehow or other. Their eccentricities are, accordingly, monstrous and frequent and various to a degree incredible to sober English people like myself and my companion. The worst of it is, there seem to be always mad people, more or fewer, who are in waiting to pounce upon foreigners of any sort of distinction, as soon as they land, while others go mad, or show their madness, from point to point along the route. Something of the same sort happens elsewhere. A Queen, or a Prime Minister's secretary may be shot at in London, as we know ; and probably there is no person eminent in literature or otherwise who has not been the object of some infirm brain or another. But in America the evil is sadly common. The first instance I encountered there was of a gentleman from the West who foretold my arrival in his country, and the time of it, before I had any notion of going, and who announced a new revelation which I was to aid

in promulgating ; and this incident startled and dismayed me considerably. I am not going into the
history of the freaks of insanity in that case or any
other. Suffice it that, in any true history of a life,
this liability must be set down as one condition of
literary or other reputation. The case of the poor
' High Priest ' at Philadelphia was not the only one
with which I was troubled in America ; and I have
met with others at home, both in London and since I
lived at Ambleside.

I encountered one specimen of American oddity
before I left home which should certainly have lessened
my surprise at any that I met afterwards. While I
was preparing for my travels, an acquaintance one
day brought a buxom gentleman, whom he introduced
to me under the name of Willis. There was something rather engaging in the round face, brisk air and
enjouement of the young man ; but his conscious
dandyism and unparalleled self-complacency spoiled
the satisfaction, though they increased the inclination
to laugh. Mr. N. P. Willis's plea for coming to see
me was his gratification that I was going to America :
and his real reason was presently apparent ;—a desire
to increase his consequence in London society by
giving apparent proof that he was on intimate terms
with every eminent person in America. He placed
himself in an attitude of infinite ease, and whipped his
little bright boot with a little bright cane while he
ran over the names of all his distinguished countrymen and country-women, and declared he should send
me letters to them all. This offer of intervention
went so very far that I said (what I have ever since
said in the case of introductions offered by strangers),

while thanking him for his intended good offices, that I was sufficiently uncertain in my plans to beg for excuse beforehand, in case I should find myself unable to use the letters. It appeared afterwards that to supply them and not to have them used suited Mr. Willis's convenience exactly. It made him appear to have the friendships he boasted of without putting the boast to the proof. It was immediately before a late dinner that the gentlemen called; and I found on the breakfast-table, next morning, a great parcel of Mr. Willis's letters, enclosed in a prodigious one to myself in which he offered advice. Among other things, he desired me not to use his letter to Dr. Channing if I had others from persons more intimate with him; and he proceeded to warn me against two friends of Dr. and Mrs. Channing's, whose names I had never heard, and whom Mr. Willis represented as bad and dangerous people. This gratuitous defamation of strangers whom I was likely to meet confirmed the suspicions my mother and I had confided to each other about the quality of Mr. Willis's introductions. It seemed ungrateful to be so suspicious: but we could not see any good reason for such prodigious efforts on my behalf, nor for his naming any countrywomen of his to me in a way so spontaneously slanderous. So I resolved to use that packet of letters very cautiously; and to begin with one which should be well accompanied.—In New York harbour newspapers were brought on board, in one of which was an extract from an article transmitted by Mr. Willis to the 'New York Mirror,' containing a most audacious account of me as an intimate friend of the writer. The friendship was not stated as a matter of fact, but so conveyed that it cost me much trouble to make it understood and believed, even by Mr. Willis's own family, that I had never seen him but once ; and then without having previously heard so much as his name. On my return, the acquaintance who brought him was anxious to ask pardon if he had done mischief, —events having by that time made Mr. Willis's ways pretty well known. His partner in the property and editorship of the ' New York Mirror ' called on me at West Point, and offered and rendered such extraordinary courtesy that I was at first almost as much perplexed as he and his wife were when they learned that I had never seen Mr. Willis but once. They pondered, they consulted, they cross-questioned me ; they inquired whether *I* had any notion what Mr. Willis could have meant by writing of me as in a state of close intimacy with him. In like manner, when, some time after, I was in a carriage with some members of a pic-nic party to Monument Mountain, a little girl seated at my feet clasped my knees fondly, looked up in my face, and said ' O ! Miss Martineau ; you are *such* a friend of my uncle Nathaniel's !' Her father was present ; and I tried to get off without explanation. But it was impossible,—they all knew how very intimate I was with ' Nathaniel :' and there was a renewal of the amazement at my having seen him only once. I tried three of his letters; and the reception was in each case much the same,—a throwing down of the letter with an air not to be mistaken. In each case the reply was the same, when I subsequently found myself at liberty to ask what this might mean. ' Mr. Willis is not entitled to write to me : he is no acquaintance of mine.' As for the two ladies of whom I was especially to beware, I became exceedingly well acquainted with them, to my own advantage and pleasure ; and, as a natural consequence, I discovered Mr. Willis's reasons for desiring to keep us apart. I hardly need add that I burned the rest of his letters. He had better have spared himself the trouble of so much manœuvring, by which he lost a good deal, and could hardly have gained anything. I have simply stated the facts because, in the first place, I do not wish to be considered one of Mr. Willis's friends ; and, in the next, it may be useful, and conducive to justice, to show, by a practical instance, what Mr. Willis's pretensions to intimacy are worth. His countrymen and countrywomen accept, in simplicity, his accounts of our aristocracy as from the pen of one of their own coterie; and they may as well have the opportunity of judging for themselves whether their notorious ' Penciller' is qualified to write of Scotch Dukes and English Marquises, and European celebrities of all kinds in the way he has done.

For some weeks, my American intercourses were chiefly with literary people, and with leading members of the Unitarian body,—far more considerable in America than among us. All manner of persons called on us ; and every conceivable attention and honour was shown us, for the first year. Of this nothing appears in my journal, except in the facts of what we saw and did. Such idolatry as is signified by the American phrase,—that a person is Lafayetted, —is not conceivable in England : and its manifestations did not appear to me fit matter for a personal journal. Not a word is to be found in that journal

therefore of either the flatteries of the first year or
the insults of the second. A more difficult matter
was how to receive them. I was charged with hard-
ness and want of sympathy in casting back praise
into people's faces: but what can one do but change
the subject as fast as possible? To dwell on the
subject of one's own merits is out of the question;
but to disclaim praise is to dwell upon it. If one is
silent one is supposed to 'swallow everything.' I
see nothing for it but to talk of something else on
the first practicable opening. While under the novelty
of this infliction of flatterers, it was natural to turn to
those most homelike of our acquaintance,—the chief
members of the Unitarian body, clergymen and others.
Among them we found a welcome refuge, many a
time, from the hubbub which confounded our senses:
and exemplary was the kindness which some few of
the body showed me even throughout the year of my
unpopularity. But before that my destiny had led
me much among the families of statesmen, and the
interests of political society: and finally, as I have
shown, the Abolitionists were my nearest friends, as
they have ever since remained.

It was while my companion and I were going from
house to house in the Unitarian connexion, between Philadelphia and our visits to our Congressional friends, that
an incident occurred which is worth relating as curious
in itself, and illustrative of more things than one. Our
host in Philadelphia (an Unitarian clergyman, as I
have said) had a little boy of six who was a favourite
of mine,—as of a good many other people. Mr.
Alcott, the extraordinary self-styled philosopher,
whose name is not unknown in England, was at Phil-

adelphia at that time, trying his hand on that strange
management of children of which I have given my
opinion elsewhere.* Little Willie went to Mr. Alcott
sometimes; and very curious were the ideas and accounts of lessons which he brought home. Very early
in my visit, Willie's father asked me whether I could
throw any light on the authorship of a parable which
was supposed to be English, and which the children
had learned from Mr. Alcott's lips. This parable,
called 'The Wandering Child,' was creating such a
sensation that it was copied and sent in all directions.
It seemed to me, when Willie recited it, that I had
somewhere seen it; but the impression was so faint as
to be entirely uncertain, even to that extent. From
Philadelphia, we went to the house of another clergyman at Baltimore; and there one of the first questions
asked by my host was the origin of that parable. He
had used the extraordinary license of taking the
parable for the text of a recent sermon, instead of a
passage of scripture; and his friends wanted to know
where it came from. He was sadly disappointed that
we could not tell him. More enquiries were made even
at Washington, where we had no particular connexion
with Unitarians. At Charleston we found in our
host an Unitarian clergyman who knew more of the
'Monthly Repository' than any English readers I
was acquainted with. He possessed it; and he had a
fancy to look there for the parable,—some notion of
having seen it there remaining on his mind. I went
with him to his study; and there we presently found
the parable,—in a not very old volume of the Monthly

* Society in America, vol. iii., page 175.

Repository, and, to my unspeakable amazement, with my own signature, V., at the end of it. By degrees my associations brightened and began to cohere; and at last I perfectly remembered when and where the conception occurred to me, and my writing the parable in my own room at Norwich, and carrying it down to my mother whom I saw in the garden, and her resting on her little spade as she listened.

The readers of Dr. Priestley's Life will not pronounce on me, (as I was at first disposed to pronounce on myself) that I was losing my wits. Dr. Priestley tells how he once found in a friend's library a pamphlet on some controverted topic which he brought to his friend with praise, as the best thing he had seen on the subject. He wanted to know,—the title-page being torn off,—who wrote it. His friend stared as my Charleston host did; and Dr. Priestley began to fear that he was losing his faculties: but he remembered (and this was my plea after him) that what we give out from our own minds, in speech or in writing, is not a subject of memory, like what we take in from other minds: and that there are few who can pretend to remember what they have said in letters, after a few years. There was the fact, in short, that we had completely forgotten compositions of our own; and that we were not losing our faculties.

Here is the parable which went through such curious adventures:—

THE WANDERING CHILD.

'In a solitary place among the groves, a child wandered whithersoever he would. He believed himself alone, and wist not that one watched him from the thicket, and that the eye of his parent was on him continually; neither did he mark whose hand had opened a way for him thus far. All things that he saw were new to him; therefore he feared nothing. He cast himself down in the long grass, and as he lay he sang till his voice of joy rang through the woods. When he nestled among the flowers, a serpent arose from the midst of them; and when the child saw how its burnished coat glittered in the sun like a rainbow, he stretched forth his hand to take it to his bosom. Then the voice of his parent cried from the thicket "Beware!" And the child sprang up, and gazed above and around, to know whence the voice came; but when he saw it not, he presently remembered it no more.

He watched how a butterfly burst from its shell, and flitted faster than he could pursue, and soon rose far above his reach.

When he gazed and could trace its flight no more, his father put forth his hand, and pointed where the butterfly ascended, even into the clouds.

But the child saw not the sign.

A fountain gushed forth amidst the shadows of the trees, and its waters flowed into a deep and quiet pool.

The child kneeled on the brink, and looking in, he saw his own bright face, and it smiled upon him.

As he stooped yet nearer to meet it, the voice once more said "Beware!"

The child started back; but he saw that a gust had ruffled the waters, and he said within himself, "It was but the voice of the breeze."

And when the broken sunbeams glanced on the moving waves, he laughed, and dipped his foot that the waters might again be ruffled : and the coolness was pleasant to him. The voice was now louder, but he regarded it not, as the winds bore it away.

At length he saw somewhat glittering in the depths of the pool; and he plunged in to reach it.

As he sank, he cried aloud for help.

Ere the waters had closed over him, his father's hand was stretched out to save him.

And while he yet shivered with chillness and fear, his parent said unto him, " Mine eye was upon thee, and thou didst not heed ; neither hast thou beheld my sign, nor hearkened to my voice. If thou hadst thought on me, I had not been hidden."

Then the child cast himself on his father's bosom and said,—" Be nigh unto me still ; and mine eyes shall wait on thee, and my ears shall be open unto thy voice for evermore." '

I need say no more of my American travels. Besides that I have given out my freshest impressions in the two works on America which were published in the year after my return, it is as impossible to me here as in other parts of this Memoir to give any special account of my nearest and dearest friends. To those who have seen by the volumes I refer to how I lived and travelled with Dr. and Mrs. Follen no avowal or description of our intercourse can be necessary ; and the relation in which Mrs. Chapman stands to me now, in the most deliberate and gravest hour of my life, renders it impossible to lay open our relation further to the world. I will simply state one fact which may show, without protestation, what my near and dear American friends were to me. They and I did not

half believe, when I came away, that we had parted :
and it was some years before I felt at all sure that I
should not live and die in America, when my domestic
duties should, in the course of nature, have closed.   It
was my Tynemouth illness, in fact, which decided the
conflict.   Something of a conflict it was.   If I had
gone to America, it would have been for the sole object of working in the cause which I believed then,
and which I believe now, to be the greatest pending
in the world.   While my mother lived, my duty was
clear—to remain with her if she and the family desired it.   I did not think it the best arrangement;
especially when I witnessed the painful effect on her
of the resumption of my London life and acquaintances : but she and the others wished things to go on
as they were; and I never thought of objecting.   I
did my utmost to make the two old ladies under my
charge happy.   It did not last very long,—only two
years and a half, when I broke down under the anxiety
of my position.   During that time, the vision of a
scheme of life, in which the anti-slavery cause (for the
sake of the liberties of every kind involved in it) should
be my vocation, was often before me,—not as a matter
of imagination, but for decision by the judgment,
when the time should arrive.   The immediate objections of the judgment were two :—that, in the first
place, it seldom or never answers to wander abroad for
duty ; every body doing best what lies nearest at hand :
and, in the second place, that my relation to Mrs.
Chapman required my utmost moral care.   The discovery of her moral power and insight was to me so
extraordinary that, while I longed to work with and
under her, I felt that it must be morally perilous to

lean on any one mind as I could not but lean on hers.
Thus far, whenever we had differed, (and that had not
seldom happened) I had found her right : and so deeply
and broadly right as to make me long to commit myself to her guidance.   Such a committal can never be
otherwise than wrong; and this it was which, more
than any thing, made me doubt whether I ought to
contemplate the scheme.   As usual in such cases,
events decided the matter.   My mother was removed
from under my care by my own illness ; and, when I
had recovered, and she died at an advanced age, I had
a clear course of duty to pursue at home, in which perhaps there may be as decided an implication of human
liberties of thought, action and speech as in the anti-
slavery cause itself.

To a certain extent, my travels in America answered
my purposes of self-discipline in undertaking them.
Fearing that I was growing too much accustomed to
luxury, and to an exclusive regularity in the modes of
living, I desired to 'rough it' for a considerable
time.   The same purpose would have been answered
as well, perhaps, and certainly more according to my
inclination, if I could have been quiet, instead of
travelling, after my great task was done ;—if I could
have had repose of body and peace of mind, in freedom
from all care.   This was impossible ; and the next
best thing was such a voyage and journey as I took.
America was the right country too, (apart from the
peculiar agitation it happened to be in when I
arrived); the national boast being a perfectly true
one,—that a woman may travel alone from Maine to
Georgia without dread of any kind of injury.   For
two ladies who feared nothing, there was certainly

nothing to fear. We had to ' rough it ' sometimes, as every body must in so new and thinly peopled a country ; but we always felt ourselves safe from ill usage of any kind. One night, at New Orleans, we certainly did feel as much alarmed as could well be ; but that was nobody's fault. From my childhood up, I believe I have never felt so desolating a sense of fear as for a few moments on that occasion,—which was simply this.

A cousin of mine whom I saw at Mobile had a house at New Orleans, inhabited by himself or his partner, as they happened to be there or at Mobile. My cousin kindly offered us the use of this house during our stay, saying that we might thus obtain some hours of coolness and quiet in the morning which would be unattainable in a boarding-house, or in the capacity of guests. The ' people,' that is, the slaves, received orders to make us comfortable, and the partner saw that all orders were obeyed. We arrived at about ten in the forenoon,—exceedingly tired,— not only by long travel in the southern forests, but especially by the voyage of the preceding night, -in hot, thundery weather, a rough sea, and in a steam- boat which so swarmed with cockroaches that we could not bring ourselves to lie down.—It was a day of considerable excitement. We found a great heap of letters from home ; we saw many friends in the course of the day ; and at night I wrote letters so late that my companion, for once, went to bed before me. We had four rooms forming a square, or nearly : —two sitting-rooms, front and back ; and two bed- rooms opening out of them, and also reaching, like them, from the landing at the top of the stairs to the street front. On account of the heat, we decided to put all our luggage (which was of considerable bulk) into one room, and sleep in the other. The beds were very large, and as hard as the floor,—as they should be in such a climate. Mosquito nets hung from the top; and the room was plentifully provided with sponging baths and water.—Miss J. was in bed before I finished my writing : and I therefore did not call her when I found that the French window opening on the balcony could not be shut, as the spring was broken. Any one could reach the balcony from the street easily enough ; and here was an entrance which could not be barred ! I set the heaviest chair against it, with the heaviest things piled on it that I could lay my hands on. I need not explain that New Orleans is, of all cities in the civilised world, the most renowned for night robbery and murder. The reputation is deserved ; or was at that time : and we had been in the way of hearing some very painful and alarming stories from some of our friends who spoke from their own experience. Miss J. was awake when I was about to step into bed, and thoughtlessly put out the candle. I observed on my folly in doing this, and on our having forgotten to inquire where the slave-quarter was. Here we were, alone in the middle of New Orleans, with no light, no bell, no servants within reach if we had had one, and no idea where the slaves were to be found ! We could only hope that nothing would happen : but I took my trumpet with me within the mosquito curtain, and laid it within reach of Miss J.'s hand, in case of her having to tell me any news. I was asleep in a trice. Not so Miss J.

She gently awoke me after what seemed to her a very long time; and, putting the cup of my tube close to her mouth, whispered slowly, so that I could hear her, 'There is somebody or something walking about the room.' I whispered that we could do nothing: and that, in our helpless state, the safest way was to go to sleep. 'But I can't,' replied she. I cannot describe how sorry I was for her, sitting up listening to fearful sounds that I could not hear. I earnestly desired to help her: but there was nothing that I could do. To sit up, unable to hear anything, and thus losing nerve every minute, was the worst thing of all for us both. I told her to rouse me again if she had the slightest wish: but that I really advised her going to sleep, as I meant to do. She again said she could not. I did; and it must be remembered how remarkably tired I was. After another space, Miss J. woke me again, and in the same cautious manner said, 'It is a man without shoes; and he is just at your side of the bed. We each said the same thing as before; and again I went to sleep. Once more she woke me; and this time she spoke with a little less caution. She said he had been walking about all that time,—for hours. He had pushed against the furniture, and especially the washstand, and seemed to be washing his hands: and now he had gone out at the door nearest the stairs. What did I think of her fastening that door? I feared she would let the mosquitoes in if she got up; and there were two other doors to the room; so I did not think we should gain much. She was better satisfied to try; and she drove a heavy trunk against the door, returned without letting in any mosquitoes, and at last obtained some

sleep.   In the morning we started up to see what we
had lost.   My watch was safe on the table.   My rings
were not there ; but we soon spied them rolled off to
the corners of the room.   The water from the baths
was spilled ; and our clothes were on the floor ; but we
missed nothing.

We agreed to say and do nothing ungracious to the
servants, and to make no complaint ; but to keep on
the watch for an explanation of the mystery ; and, if
evening came without any light being thrown on the
matter, to consult our friends the Porters about spending another night in that room.—At breakfast, the
slave women, who had been to market, and got us
some young green peas and other good things, hung
over our chairs, and were ready to gossip, as usual.   I
could make nothing of their jabber ; and Miss J. not
much : but she persevered on this occasion ; and, before
breakfast was over, she gave me a nod which showed
me that our case was explained.   She had been playing with a little black dog the while : and she told me
at length that this little black dog belonged to the
personage at the back of my chair ; but that the big
dog, chained up in the yard, belonged to my cousin ;
and that the big dog was the one which was unchained
the last thing at night, and allowed the range of the
premises, to deal with the rats, which abounded in that
house as in every other in New Orleans.   The city being
built in a swamp, innumerable rats are a necessary consequence.   The intruder was regarded very differently
the next night ; and we had no more alarms.   I own
that the moments when my companion told me that
a man without shoes was walking about the room, and
when, again, she heard him close by my bedside, were

those of very painful fear.   I have felt nothing like it, on any other occasion, since I grew up.

Safe as we were from ill usage, our friends in America rather wondered at our fearlessness about the perils of the mere travel.   We were supposed, before we were known, to be finé ladies ; and fine ladies are full of terrors in America, as elsewhere.   When it was seen that we could help ourselves and had no groundless fears, some of our friends reminded us that their forests and great rivers were not like our own mailroads ; and that untoward accidents and detentions might take place, when we should be glad of such aid as could be had from its being known who we were. Chief Justice Marshall, the survivor of the great men of the best days of the republic, and the most venerated man in the country, put into my hands ' a general letter,' as he called it, commending us to the good offices of all citizens, in case of need.   The letter lies before me ; and I will give it as a curiosity. No occasion of peril called it forth for use ; but it was a show, in many a wild place,—gratifying the eyes of revering fellow-citizens of the majestic old Judge. Here it is.

' I have had the honour of being introduced to, and of form-ing some acquaintance with, Miss Martineau and Miss J——, two English ladies of distinction who are making the tour of the United States.   As casualties to which all travellers, es-pecially those of the female sex, are liable may expose these ladies to some difficulties in situations remote from those popu-lous towns in which they may find persons to whom they will be known, it gives me pleasure to state that these ladies have the fairest claims to the aid, protection and services which their possible situation may require : that they are of high worth and character, and that I shall, individually, feel myself under obligations to any gentleman who, in the event described, shall be in any manner useful to them.   J. MARSHALL.'

A parting act of gallantry has puzzled me many a time; and the more I have thought of it, the less have I known what to make of it. For many months it had been settled, as I have mentioned, that I was to return in Captain Bursley's ship,—he being a friend, in virtue of mutual friendships on both sides the water. Some days before I sailed, my last American host undertook the business of paying my passage, and changing my American money for English. We were not aware of any extraordinary precipitation in settling this business. When I was out at sea, however, a fellow passenger, one of our party of six, put into my hands a packet of money. It was the amount of my fare; and my fellow-passenger either could not or would not tell me who sent it. She said she was as helpless in the matter as I was. All that she could tell me was that somebody had gone, in supposed good time, to pay my passage, was disconcerted to find I had paid it, and could think of no other way than returning the money through a fellow-passenger.—I know no more of the motive than of the person or persons. Whether it was shame at the treatment I had received on the anti-slavery question, or a primitive method of hospitality, or any thing else, I have never been able to satisfy myself, or to get any light from any body. I could do nothing, and say nothing. The only certain thing about the case is that the act was meant in kindness: and I need not say that I was grateful accordingly.

The New York host whom I have referred to was an intimate friend of our captain: and he knew enough of one or two of the passengers to be pretty well aware that there would be moral tempests on

board, however fair the weather might be overhead.
He and his wife kindly forbore to give me any hint of
coming discomfort which could not be avoided; but
they begged me to keep a very full journal of the
voyage, and send it to them, for their private reading.
I did so: and they next requested that I would agree
to a proposal to print it,—the names being altered;
and the most disgraceful of the incidents (e.g., a plot
for the seduction of an orphan girl) being omitted.
The narrative accordingly appeared in the 'Penny
Magazine' of October and November, 1837, under
the title of 'A Month at Sea.' As it may amuse
somebody to see, in such detail, what such a voyage
was like, the narrative will be found in the Appendix.*
It is enough to say here that I had the advantage of
the companionship of Professor and Mrs. Farrer, of
Harvard University; of Lieutenant Wilkes, who was
on his way to England to prepare for the American
Exploring Expedition, of which he was Commander;
and of two or three younger members of the party,
who were good-humoured and agreeable comrades, in
the midst of a set of passengers who were as far as
possible from being either.

We arrived at Liverpool on the 26th of August,
1836; and there I found several members of my family
awaiting me.

* Appendix B.

SECTION IV.

My mother and I spent two months among my brothers and sisters before returning home to settle for the winter. I was aware that I must presently make up my mind about a book or no book on America: but I had no idea how soon my decision would be called for. As I have mentioned, I declined the offer made before I left home to obtain an advance of £500 from a publisher, who would be glad thus to secure the book. Mr. Murray also sent me a message through a mutual friend, intimating his wish to publish my travels on my return. In America such applications were frequent: and on all occasions my reply was the same; that I did not know, nor should till I got home, whether I should write on the subject at all. One personal application made to me in New York at once amused and shocked me. I had not then, and I have not to this day, got over the wonder and disgust caused by the tone in which so serious and unworldly a vocation as that of authorship is spoken of; and, of all the broad instances of such coarseness that I have met with, this New York application affords the very grossest. Mr. Harper, the head of the redoubtable piratical publishing house in New

York, said to me in his own shop, ' Come, now ; tell me what you will take for your book.'—' What book ? '—' O ! you know you will write a book about this country. Let me advise you.'—' But I don't know that I shall write one.'—' O ! but I can tell you how easily you may do it. So far as you have gone, you must have picked up a few incidents. Well ! then you might Trollopize a bit, and so make a readable book. I would give you something handsome for it. Come ! what will you take ? '

Even people who know nothing of books in a mercantile view seem to have as little conception of the true aim and temper of authorship as the book-merchants themselves, who talk of a book as an ' article,'—as the mercer talks of a shawl or a dress. A good, unselfish, affectionate woman, whom I really love, showed me one day how she loves me still as in the old times when I was not yet an author, by evidencing her total lack of sympathy in my thoughts and feelings about my work. I am to her the Harriet of our youth,—the authorship being nothing more between us than something which has made her happy for me, because it has made me happy. I like this,—the being loved as the old Harriet : but, still, I was startled one day by her congratulating me on my success in obtaining fame. I had worked hard for it, and she was so glad I had got it ! I do not like disclaiming, or in any way dwelling on this sort of subject ; but it was impossible to let this pass. I told her I had never worked for fame. ' Well then,—for money.' She was so glad I was so successful, and could get such sums for my books. This, again, could not be let pass. I assured her I had never written, or omitted to write,

any thing whatever from pecuniary considerations.
'Well, then,' said she, 'for usefulness. I am determined to be right. You write to do good to your
fellow-creatures. You must allow that I am right
now.' I was silent; and when she found that I could
allow no such thing, she was puzzled. Her alternatives were exhausted. I told her that I wrote because
I could not help it. There was something that I
wanted to say, and I said it: that was all. The fame
and the money and the usefulness might or might not
follow. It was not by my endeavour if they did.

On landing at Liverpool, I found various letters
from publishers awaiting me. One was from Mr.
Bentley, reminding me of his having met me at Miss
Berry's, and expressing his hope of having my manuscript immediately in his hands. My reply was that
I had no manuscript. Another letter was from Messrs.
Saunders and Otley to my mother, saying that they
desired the pleasure of publishing my travels. I was
disposed to treat with them, because the negotiation
for the 'Two Old Men's Tales' had been an agreeable one. I therefore explained to these gentlemen
the precise state of the case, and at length agreed to
an interview when I should return to town. My
mother and I reached home before London began to
fill; and I took some pains to remain unseen for two
or three weeks, while arranging my books, and my
dress and my other affairs. One November morning,
however, my return was announced in the 'Morning
Chronicle;' and such a day as that I never passed,
and hoped at the time never to pass again.

First, Mr. Bentley bustled down, and obtained entrance to my study before any body else. Mr. Colburn

came next, and had to wait. He bided his time in
the drawing-room. In a few minutes arrived Mr.
Saunders, and was shown into my mother's parlour.
These gentlemen were all notoriously on the worst
terms with each other; and the fear was that they
should meet and quarrel an the stairs. Some friends
who happened to call at the time were beyond measure
amused.

Mr. Bentley began business. Looking hard into
the fire, he 'made no doubt' I remembered the promise I had made him at Miss Berry's house. I had
no recollection of having promised any thing to Mr.
Bentley. He told me it was impossible I should forget having assured him that if any body published for
me, except Fox, it should be himself. I laughed at the
idea of such an engagement. Mr. Bentley declared it
might be his silliness; but he should go to his grave
persuaded that I had made him such a promise. It
might be his silliness, he repeated. I replied that indeed it was; as I had a perfect recollection that no
book of mine was in question at all, but the Series,
which he had talked of putting among his Standard
Novels. He now offered the most extravagant terms
for a book on America, and threw in, as a bribe, an
offer of a thousand pounds for the first novel I should
write. Though my refusals were as positive as I could
make them, I had great difficulty in getting rid of
him: and 1 doubt whether I was so rude to Mr.
Harper himself as to the London speculator.—Mr.
Colburn, meantime, sent in his letter of introduction,
which was from the poet Campbell, with a message
that he would shortly return. So Mr. Saunders entered next. I liked him, as before; and our conversa-

tion about the book became quite confidential. I
explained to him fully my doubt as to the reception of
the work, on the ground of its broad republican character. I told him plainly that I believed it would
ruin me, because it would be the principle of the book
to regard every thing American from the American
point of view : and this method, though the only fair
one, was so unlike the usual practice, and must lead to
a judgment so unlike what English people were prepared for, that I should not be surprised by a total
condemnation of my book and myself. I told him
that, after this warning, he could retreat or negotiate,
as he pleased : but that, being thus warned, he and not
I must propose terms : and moreover, it must be understood that, our negotiation once concluded, I could
listen to no remonstrance or objection, in regard to
the contents of my book. Mr. Saunders replied that
he had no difficulty in agreeing to these conditions,
and that we might now proceed to business. When
he had ascertained that the work would consist of
three volumes, and what their probable size would be,
the amusing part of the affair began. ' Well, Ma'am,'
said he, ' What do you propose that we should give
you for the copyright of the first edition ? ' ' Why,
you know,' said I, ' I have written to you, from the
beginning, that I would propose no terms. I am quite
resolved against it.'—' Well, Ma'am; supposing the
edition to consist of three thousand copies, will you
just give me an idea what you would expect for it ? '
—' No, Mr. Saunders: that is your business. I wait
to hear your terms.'

So I sat strenuously looking into the fire,—Mr.
Saunders no less strenuously looking at me, till it was

all I could do to keep my countenance. He waited
for me to speak ; but I would not ; and I wondered
where the matter would end, when he at last opened
his lips. ' What would you think, Ma'am, of £900 for
the first edition ? '—' Including the twenty-five copies
I stipulated for ? '—' Including twenty-five copies of
the work, and all proceeds of the sale in America,
over and above expenses.' I thought these liberal
terms ; and I said so ; but I suggested that each party
should take a day or two for consideration, to leave no
room for repentance hereafter. I inquired whether
Messrs. Saunders and Otley had any objection to my
naming their house as the one I was negotiating with,
as I disliked the appearance of entertaining the prof-
fers of various houses, which yet I could not get rid
of without a distinct answer to give. Apparently
amused at the question, Mr. Saunders replied that it
would be gratifying to them to be so named.

On the stairs, Mr. Saunders met Mr. Colburn, who
chose to be confident that Campbell's introduction
would secure to him all he wished. The interview was
remarkably disagreeable, from his refusing to be refused, and pretending to believe that what I wanted
was more and more money. At last, on my giving
him a broad hint to go away, he said that, having no
intention of giving up his object, he should spend the
day at a coffee-house in the neighbourhood, whence he
should shortly send in terms for my consideration.
He now only implored a promise that I would not
finally pass my word that day. The moment he was
gone, I slipped out into the Park to refresh my mind
and body ; for I was heated and wearied with the con-
ferences of the morning. On my return, I found that

Mr. Colburn had called again : and while we were at dinner, he sent in a letter, containing his fresh terms. They were so absurdly high that if I had had any confidence in the soundness of the negotiation before, it would now be overthrown.   Mr. Colburn offered £2,000 for the present work, on the supposition of the sale of I forget what number, and £1,000 for the first novel I should write.   The worst of it was, he left word that he should call again at ten o'clock in the evening.   When we were at tea, Mr. Bentley sent in a set of amended proposals ; and at ten, Mr. Colburn arrived.   He set forth his whole array of ' advantages,' and declared himself positive that no house in London could have offered higher terms than his.   I reminded him that I had been telling him all day that my objections did not relate to the amount of money ; and that I was going to accept much less : that it was impossible that my work should yield what he had offered, and leave anything over for himself ; and that I therefore felt that these proposals were intended to bind me to his house,—an obligation which I did not choose to incur.   He pathetically complained of having raised up rivals to himself in the assistants whom he had trained, and concluded with an affected air of resignation which was highly amusing.   Hanging his head on one side, and sighing, he enunciated the sentiment : ' When, in pursuing any praiseworthy object, we have done all we can, and find it in vain, we can but be resigned.'   With great satisfaction I saw him lighted down stairs, and heard the house-door locked, at near midnight, on the last of the booksellers for that day. From that time forward, Mr. Colburn was seen, on the appearance of any of my works, to declare himself

' singularly unfortunate' in having been always too late. He professed to have the best reason to know that if he had been a day or so earlier in his application, he would have been my publisher. This was in each case a delusion. I never, for a moment, encouraged any such expectation: and when, in course of time, Mr. Colburn's piracies of Sparks's Washington and other works were brought before the law courts, I was glad to have avoided all connection with the house. —The only reasons for dwelling on the matter at all are that, in the first place, it is desirable to put on record exactly what did happen on an occasion which was a good deal talked about; and next, because it may be well to show how the degradation of literature comes about, in times when speculating publishers try to make grasping authors, and to convert the serious function of authorship into a gambling match. The way in which authors allowed themselves to be put up to auction, and publishers squabbled at the sale was a real and perpetual grief to me to witness. It reminded me but too often of the stand and the gesticulating man with the hammer, and the crowding competitors whom I had seen jostling each other in the slave-markets of the United States. I went to bed that night with a disgusted and offended feeling of having been offered bribes, all day long, with a confidence which was not a little insulting.

My transactions with Messrs. Saunders and Otley were always very satisfactory. I did not receive a penny from the sale of my American books in the United States, though my American friends exerted themselves to protect the work from being pirated: but the disappointment was the fault of my publishers'

agent ; and they were as sorry for it as I was. Soon
after the appearance of 'Society in America,' Mr.
Saunders called on me to propose a second work, which
should have more the character of travel, and be of a
lighter quality to both writer and reader. I had plenty
of material ; and, though I should have liked some
rest, this was no sufficient reason for refusing. The
publishers offered me £600 for this, in addition to the
attendant advantages allowed with the former work.
—Even through these liberal and honourable publishers, however, I became acquainted with one of the
tricks of the trade which surprised me a good deal.
After telling me the day of publication, and announc-
ing that my twenty-five copies would be ready, Mr.
Saunders inquired when I should like to come to their
back parlour, ' and write the notes.'—' What notes ? '
—' The notes for the Reviews, you know, Ma'am.'
He was surprised at being obliged to explain that
authors write notes to friends and acquaintances connected with periodicals, ' to request favourable notices
of the work.' I did not know how to credit this ; and
Mr. Saunders was amazed that I had never heard of
it. ' I assure you, Ma'am, —— —— does it ; and
all our authors do it.' On my emphatically declining,
he replied ' As you please, Ma'am : but it is the
universal practice, I believe.' I have always been related to the Reviews exactly like the ordinary public.
I have never inquired who had reviewed me, or known
who was going to do so, except by public rumour. I
do not very highly respect reviews, nor like to write
them ; for the simple reason that in ninety-nine cases
out of a hundred, the author understands his subject
better than the reviewer. It can hardly be otherwise

while the author treats one subject, to his study of which his book itself is a strong testimony; whereas the reviewer is expected to pass from topic to topic, to any extent, pronouncing, out of his brief survey. on the results of deep and protracted study. Of all the many reviews of my books on America and Egypt, there was not, as far as I know, one which did not betray ignorance of the respective countries. And, on the other hand, there is no book, except the very few which have appeared on my own particular subjects, that I could venture to pronounce on; as, in every other case, I feel myself compelled to approach a book as a learner, and not as a judge. This is the same thing as saying that reviewing. in the wholesale way in which it is done in our time, is a radically vicious practice; and such is indeed my opinion. I am glad to see scientific men, and men of erudition, and true connoisseurs in art, examining what has been done in their respective departments: and everybody is glad of good essays, whether they appear in books called Reviews or elsewhere. But of the reviews of our day, properly so called, the vast majority must be worthless, because the reviewer knows less than the author of the matter in hand.

In choosing the ground of my work, 'Society in America,'— (which should have been called, but for the objection of my publishers, 'Theory and Practice of Society in America,') I desired fairness in the first place: and I believed it was most fair to take my stand on the American point of view,—judging American society, in its spirit and methods, by the American tests,—the Declaration of Independence, and the constitutions based upon its principles. It

had become a practice so completely established to
treat of America in a mode of comparison with
Europe, that I had little hope of being at first understood by more than a few. The Americans themselves
had been so accustomed to be held up in contrast
with Europeans by travellers that they could not
get rid of the prepossession, even while reading my
book. What praise there was excited vanity, as if such
a thing had never been heard of before : and any
censure was supposed to be sufficiently answered by
evidence that the same evils existed in England. I
anticipated this ; and that consternation would be
excited by some of my republican and other principles.
Some of this consternation, and much of the censure
followed, with a good deal that I had not conceived
of. All this was of little consequence, in comparison
with the comfort of having done some good, however
little, in both countries. The fundamental fault of
the book did not become apparent to me for some
time after ;—its metaphysical framework, and the
abstract treatment of what must necessarily be a
concrete subject. The fault is not exclusively mine.
It rests with the American theory which I had taken
for my standpoint : but it was the weakness of an
immature mind to choose that method of treatment ;
just as it was the act of immature politicians to make
after the same method the first American constitution,
—the one which would not work, and which gave
place to the present arrangement. Again, I was
infected to a certain degree with the American
method of dissertation or preaching ; and I was also
full of Carlylism, like the friends I had left in the
Western world. So that my book, while most care-

fully true in its facts, had a strong leaning towards the American fashion of theorising; and it was far more useful on the other side of the Atlantic than on this. The order of people here who answer to the existing state of the Americans took the book to heart very earnestly, if I may judge by the letters from strangers which flowed in upon me, even for years after its publication. The applications made to me for guidance and counsel,—applications which even put into my hand the disposal of a whole life, in various instances,--arose, not from agreement in political opinion, nor from discontent with things at home; but from my hearty conviction that social affairs are the personal duty of every individual, and from my freedom in saying what I thought. The stories that I could tell, from letters which exist among my papers, or from those which I thought it right to burn at once, would move the coldest, and rouse the laziest. Those which touched me most related to the oppressions which women in England suffer from the law and custom of the country. Some offered evidence of intolerable oppression, if I could point out how it might be used. Others offered money, effort, courage in enduring obloquy, every thing, if I could show them how to obtain, and lead them in obtaining, arrangements by which they could be free in spirit, and in outward liberty to make what they could of life. I feel strongly tempted to give here two or three narratives: but it would not be right. The applicants and their friends may be living; and I might be betraying confidence, though nearly twenty years have elapsed. Suffice it that though I now disapprove the American form and style of the book, not the less standing by my choice of the American point of view, I have never regretted its boldness of speech. I felt a relief in having opened my mind which I would at no time have exchanged for any gain of reputation or fortune. The time had come when, having experienced what might be called the extremes of obscurity and difficulty first, and influence and success afterwards, I could pronounce that there was nothing for which it was worth sacrificing freedom of thought and speech. I enjoyed in addition the consolidation of invaluable friendships in America, and the acquisition of new ones at home. Altogether, I am well pleased that I wrote the book, though I now see how much better it might have been done if I had not been at the metaphysical period of my life when I had to treat of the most metaphysical constitution and people in the world.

Some of the wisest of my friends at home,—and especially, I remember Sydney Smith and Carlyle,— gently offered their criticism on my more abstract American book in the pleasant form of praise of the more concrete one. The 'Retrospect of Western Travel' was very successful,—as indeed the other was, though not, I believe, to the extent of the publishers' expectations. Sydney Smith showed but too surely, not long after, in his dealings with American Repudiation, that he did not trouble himself with any study of the Constitution of the United States; for he crowded almost as many mistakes as possible into his procedure,— supposing Congress to be answerable for the doings of Pennsylvania, and Pennsylvania to have repudiated her debts; which she never did. Readers who thus read for amusement,

and skip the politics, liked my second book best : and
so did those who, like Carlyle, wisely desire us to see
what we can, and tell what we see, without spinning
out of ourselves systems and final causes, and all
manner of notions which, as self-derived, are no part
of our business or proper material in giving an
account of an existing nation.   Carlyle wrote me
that he had rather read of Webster's cavernous eyes
and arm under his coat-tail, than all the political
speculation that a cut and dried system could suggest.
I find before me a memorandum that Lord Holland
sent me by General Fox a motto for the chapter on
Washington.   How it came about, I do not exactly
remember ; but I am sure my readers, as well as I,
were obliged to Lord Holland for as exquisite an
appropriation of an exquisite eulogy as was ever proposed.   The lines are the Duke of Buckingham's on
Lord Fairfax.

> ' He might have been a king
> But that he understood
> How much it was a meaner thing
> To be unjustly great than honourably good.'

It was in September of that year (1837) that I began to keep a Diary.   My reason was that I saw so
many wise people, and heard so much valuable conversation, that my memory would not serve me to retain
what I was sorry to lose.   I continued the practice for
about five years, when I found it becoming, not only
burdensome, but, (as I was ill and living in solitude,)
pernicious.   I find, by the first portion of my Diary,
that I finished the ' Retrospect of Western Travel '
on the first of December, 1837, having written a good

many other things during the autumn, of which I now
remember nothing. It was in August of that year
that the Editor of the Westminster Review (then the
property of Mr. J. S. Mill) called on me, and asked
me to write a review of Miss Sedgwick's works. I
did so for the October number, and I believe I supplied
about half-a-dozen articles in the course of the next
two years,—the best known of which is ' The Martyr
Age of the United States,'—a sketch of the history
of Abolitionism in the United States, up to that time.
I find mention in my Diary of articles for the ' Penny
Magazine,' before and after the one already referred
to,—the ' Month at Sea :' and I remember that I
earned Mr. Knight's ' Gallery of Portraits,' and some
other valuable books in that pleasant way. The most
puzzling thing to me is to find repeated references to a
set of Essays called 'The Christian Seer,' with some
speculation on their quality, while I can recal nothing
whatever about them,—their object, their subject,
their mode of publication, or any thing else. I can
only hope that others have forgotten them as completely as I have; for they could not have been worth
much, if I have never heard or thought of them since.
They seem to have cost me some pains and care; and
they were probably not the better for that.—The
entry in my Diary on the completion of the 'Retrospect' brings back some very deep feelings. ' I care
little about this book of mine. I have not done it
carelessly. I believe it is true: but it will find no place
in my mind and life; and I am glad it is done. Shall
I despise myself hereafter for my expectations from
my novel ? '

Great were my expectations from my novel, for this

reason chiefly;—that for many years now my writing had been almost entirely about fact:—facts of society and of individuals: and the constraint of the effort to be always correct, and to bear without solicitude the questioning of my correctness, had become burdensome. I felt myself in danger of losing nerve, and dreading criticism on the one hand, and of growing rigid and narrow about accuracy on the other. I longed inexpressibly for the liberty of fiction, while occasionally doubting whether I had the power to use that freedom as I could have done ten years before. The intimate friend, on whose literary counsel, as I have said, I reposed so thankfully, and at whose country-house I found such sweet refreshment every autumn, was the confidante of my aspirations about a novel; and many a talk she and I had that autumn about the novel I was to write in the course of the next year. She never flattered me; and her own relish of fiction made her all the more careful not to mislead me as to my chances of success in a new walk of literature. But her deliberate expectation was that I should succeed; and her expectation was grounded, like my own, on the fact that my heart and mind were deeply stirred on one or two moral subjects on which I wanted the relief of speech, or which could be as well expressed in fiction as in any other way,—and perhaps with more freedom and earnestness than under any other form. After finishing my American subjects, I was to take a holiday,—to spend whole days without putting pen to paper; and then I was to do my best with my novel.

Such was the scheme: and so it went on up to the finishing of the year's engagements, and the first day

of holiday, when I found reason to suspect that I had
been under too long a strain of work and of anxiety.
During that summer, I failed somewhat in strength,
and, to my own surprise, in spirits. I told no person
of this, except the friend and hostess just referred to.
Within two years we found that I had already begun
to sink under domestic anxieties, and the toil which
was my only practicable refuge from them. The illness which prostrated me in 1839 was making itself
felt,—though not recognised,—in 1837. I was
dimly aware of overstrained strength, on the first
experiment of holiday, when something happened
which threw me into great perturbation. Nothing
disturbs me so much as to have to make a choice
between nearly equal alternatives; and it was a very
serious choice that I had to make now.—A member
of an eminent publishing firm called on me on the
eleventh of December, to propose that his house should
set up a periodical which was certainly much wanted,
—an Economical Magazine,—of which I was to have
the sole charge. The salary offered was one which
would have made me entirely easy about income: the
subject was one which I need not fear to undertake:
the work was wanted: and considerations like these
were not strongly balanced by the facts that I felt tired
and longed for rest, or by the prospect of the confinement which the editorship would impose. The vacilla-
tion of my mind was for some days very painful. I
find, two days later, this entry. 'In the morning, I
am *pro*, and at night, and in the night, *con* the scheme.
I wonder how it will end. I see such an opening in
it for things that I want to say! and I seem to be the
person to undertake such a thing. I can toil—I am

persevering, and in the habit of keeping my troubles to myself. If suffering be the worst on the *con* side, let it come. It will be a fine discipline of taste, temper, thought and spirits. But I don't expect —— and —— will accede to my last stipulations. If not, there's an end. If they do, I think I shall make the plunge.' Two days later :—' After tea, sat down before the fire with pencil and paper, to make out a list of subjects, contributors and books, for my periodical. Presently came a letter from —— and ——, which I knew must nearly decide my fate in regard to the project. I distinctly felt that it could not hurt me, either way, as the *pros* and *cons* seem so nearly balanced that I should be rather thankful to have the matter decided for me. —— and —— grant all that I have asked; and it looks much as if we were to proceed. So I went on with my pondering till past ten, by which time I had got a sheetful of subjects.' I certainly dreaded the enterprise more than I desired it. ' It is an awful choice before me! Such facilities for usefulness and activity of knowledge; such certain toil and bondage; such risk of failure and descent from my position! The realities of life press upon me now. If I do this, I must brace myself up to do and suffer like a man. No more waywardness, precipitation, and reliance on allowance from others! Undertaking a man's duty, I must brave a man's fate. I must be prudent, independent, serene, good-humoured; earnest with cheerfulness. The possibility is open before me of showing what a periodical with a perfect temper may be:—also, of setting women forward at once into the rank of men of business. But the hazards are great, I wonder how it will end.' I had consulted two or three intimate friends, when I wrote these entries; and had written to my brother James for his opinion. The friends at hand were all in favour of my undertaking the enterprise. If the one remaining opinion had been in agreement with theirs, I should have followed the unanimous advice: but on the nineteenth, I find, 'James is altogether against the periodical plan.' I wrote my final refusal on that day; and again I was at liberty to ponder my novel.

My doctrine about plots in fiction has been given at sufficient length. It follows of course that I looked into real life for mine. I attached myself strongly to one which it cost me much to surrender. It is a story from real life which Miss Sedgwick has offered in her piece called 'Old Maids,' in her volume of 'Tales and Sketches,' not likely to be known in England: —a story of two sisters, ten years apart in age, the younger of whom loves and finally marries the betrothed of the elder. Miss Sedgwick told me the real story, with some circumstances of the deepest interest which she, for good reasons, suppressed, but which I might have used. If I had wrought out this story, I should of course have acknowledged its source. But I deferred it,—and it is well I did. Mrs. S. Carter Hall relates it as the story of two Irish sisters, and impresses the anecdote by a striking wood-cut, in her 'Ireland:' and Mrs. Browning has it again, in her beautiful 'Bertha in the Lane.'

I was completely carried away by the article on St. Domingo in the Quarterly Review, (vol. xxi.) which I lighted upon, one day at this time, while looking for the noted article on the Grecian Philosophy in the same volume. I pursued the study of Toussaint

L'Ouverture's character in the Biographie Universelle; and, though it is badly done, and made a mere patchwork of irreconcilable views of him, the real man shone out into my mind, through all mists and shadows. I went to my confidante, with a sheetful of notes, and a heartful of longings to draw that glorious character,—with its singular mixture of negro temperament, heathen morality, and as much of Christianity as agreed with the two. But my friend could not see the subject as I did. She honestly stood by her objections, and I felt that I could not proceed against the counsel of my only adviser. I gave it up: but a few years after, when ill at Tynemouth, I reverted to my scheme and fulfilled it: and my kind adviser, while never liking the subject in an artistic sense, graciously told me that the book had kept her up, over her dressing-room fire, till three in the morning. —There was a police report, during that winter, —very brief,—only one short paragraph,—which moved me profoundly, and which I was sure I could work out into a novel of the deepest interest. My fear was that that one paragraph would affect other readers as it did me, and be remembered, so that the catastrophe of my tale would be known from the beginning: so we deferred that plot, meaning that I should really work upon it one day. The reason why I never did is that, as I have grown older, I have seen more and more the importance of dwelling on things honest, lovely, hopeful and bright, rather than on the dark and fouler passions and most mournful weaknesses of human nature. Therefore it was that I reverted to Toussaint, rather than to the moral victim who was the hero of the police-court story.

What then was to be done? We came back, after
every divergence, to the single fact (as I then believed
it) that a friend of our family, whom I had not seen
very often, but whom I had revered from my youth
up, had been cruelly driven, by a match-making lady,
to propose to the sister of the woman he loved,— on
private information that the elder had lost her heart
to him, and that he had shown her attention enough
to warrant it.   The marriage was not a very happy
one, good as were the persons concerned, in their
various ways. I altered the circumstances as much as
I could, and drew the character, not of our English
but of an American friend, whose domestic position
is altogether different: and lo! it came to my knowledge, years afterwards, that the story of our friend's
mischance was not at all true. I was rejoiced to hear
it.   Not only was I relieved from the fear of hurting
a good man's feelings, if he should ever read 'Deerbrook:' but 'Deerbrook' was a fiction, after all, in
its groundwork.

The process was an anxious one. I could not at all
tell whether I was equal to my enterprise. I found in
it a relief to many pent-up sufferings, feelings, and
convictions : and I can truly say that it was uttered
from the heart. But my friend seemed nearly as
doubtful of success as I was. She feared to mislead
me ; and she honestly and kindly said less than she felt
in its favour.   From the time when one day I saw a
bright little tear fall on her embroidery, I was nearly
at ease ; but that was in the last volume. I have often
doubted whether I could have worked through that
fearful period of domestic trouble, with heart and hope
enough to finish a book of a new kind, but for a sin-

gular source of refreshment,—a picture. Mr. Vincent Thompson and his lady took me to the private view of the pictures at the British Institution; and I persisted in admiring a landscape in North Wales by Baker, to which I returned again and again, to feast on the gush of sunlight between two mountains, and the settling of the shadows upon the woods at their base. Mr. Thompson at length returned too, and finally told me that it *was* a good picture. Several weeks afterwards, I heard an unusual lumbering mode of coming up-stairs; and Mr. Thompson was shown in, bearing the picture, and saying that as I should certainly be getting pictures together some time or other, Mrs. Thompson had sent me this to begin with. I sat opposite that landscape while writing ' Deerbrook;' and many a dark passage did its sunshine light me through. Now that I live among mountains, that landscape is as beautiful as ever in my eyes: but nowhere could it be such a benefaction as in my little study in Fludyer Street, where dingy red walls rose up almost within reach, and idle clerks of the Foreign Office lolled out of dusty windows, to stare down upon their opposite neighbours.

I was not uneasy about getting my novel published. On May-day, 1838, six weeks before I put pen to paper, I received a note from a friend who announced what appeared to me a remarkable fact;—that Mr. Murray, though he had never listened to an application to publish a novel since Scott's, was willing to enter into a negotiation for mine. I was not aware then how strong was the hold on the public mind which ' the silver-fork school' had gained; and I discovered it by Mr. Murray's refusal at last to publish

'Deerbrook.' He was more than civil;—he was kind, and, I believe, sincere in his regrets. The execution was not the ground of refusal. It was, as I had afterwards reason to know, the scene being laid in middle life. I do not know whether it is true that Mr. Lockhart advised Mr. Murray to decline it ; but Mr. Lockhart's clique gave out on the eve of publication that the hero was an apothecary. People liked high life in novels, and low life, and ancient life ; and life of any rank presented by Dickens, in his peculiar artistic light, which is very unlike the broad daylight of actual existence, English or other : but it was not supposed that they would bear a presentment of the familiar life of every day. It was a mistake to suppose so ; and Mr. Murray finally regretted his decision. Mr. Moxon, to whom, by Mr. Rogers's advice, I offered it, had reason to rejoice in it. 'Deerbrook' had a larger circulation than novels usually obtain ; two large editions having been long exhausted, and the work being still in constant demand.—I was rather amused at the turn that criticism took among people of the same class as my personages,—the class which I chose because it was my own, and the one that I understood best. It was droll to hear the daughters of dissenting ministers and manufacturers expressing disgust that the heroine came from Birmingham, and that the hero was a surgeon. Youths and maidens in those days looked for lords and ladies in every page of a new novel.—My own judgment of 'Deerbrook' was for some years more favourable than it is now. The work was faithful in principle and sentiment to the then state of my mind ; and that satisfied me for a time. I should now require more of myself,

if I were to attempt a novel,—(which I should not
do, if I were sure of living another quarter of a century.)   I should require more simplicity, and a far
more objective character,—not of delineation but of
scheme.   The laborious portions of meditation, ob-
truded at intervals, are wholly objectionable in my
eyes.   Neither morally nor artistically can they be
justified.   I know the book to have been true to the
state of thought and feeling I was then in, which I
now regard as imperfect and very far from lofty:—I
believe it to have been useful, not only in overcoming a
prejudice against the use of middle-class life in fiction,
but in a more special application to the discipline of
temper; and therefore I am glad I wrote it: but I
do not think it would be fair to judge me from it,
any later than the time in which it was written.

When Mr. Murray perceived that the book had a
decided though gradual success, he sent a mutual
friend to me with a remarkable message, absolutely
secret at the time, but no longer needing to be so.
He said that he could help me to a boundless fortune,
and a mighty future fame, if I would adopt his
advice.   He advised me to write a novel in profound
secrecy, and under appearances which would prevent
suspicion of the authorship from being directed
towards me.   He desired to publish this novel in
monthly numbers; and was willing to pledge his
reputation for experience on our obtaining a circulation as large as had ever been known.   It would give
him high satisfaction, he declared, to see my writings
on thousands of tables from which my name would
exclude every thing I published under it: and he
should enjoy being the means of my obtaining such

fortune, and such an ultimate fame as I might confidently reckon on, if I would accept his offer. I
refused it at once. I could not undertake to introduce
a protracted mystery into my life which would
destroy its openness and freedom. This was one
reason: but there was a far more serious one ;—more
important because it was not personal. I could not
conscientiously adopt any method so unprincipled in
an artistic sense as piecemeal publication. Whatevei
other merits it may have, a work of fiction cannot
possibly be good in an artistic sense which can be cut
up into portions of an arbitrary length. The success
of the portions requires that each should have some
sort of effective close; and to provide a certain number
of these at regular intervals, is like breaking up the
broad lights and shadows of a great picture, and
spoiling it as a composition. I might never do any
thing to advance or sustain literary art ; but I would
do nothing to corrupt it, by adopting a false principle
of composition. The more license was afforded by
the popular taste of the time, the more careful should
authors be to adhere to sound principle in their art.
Mr. Murray and our friend evidently thought me very
foolish ; but I am as sure now as I was then that, my
aim not being money or fame, I was right.

While pondering my novel, I wrote (as I see by
my diary) various small pieces, stories, and didactic
articles, for special purposes,—religious or benevolent,
American and English : and in April and May I
cleared my mind and hands of a long-standing engagement. The chapter which I mentioned having
written at sea, on ' How to observe Morals and
Manners,' was, by the desire of the proposer and of

Mr. Knight, to be expanded into a volume; and this piece of tough work, which required a good deal of reading and thinking, I accomplished this spring. The earlier numbers of the ' Guide to Service,' beginning with ' The Maid of All Work,' were written in the same spring. In the first days of June, I wrote an article on ' Domestic Service in England' for the Westminster Review: and then, after a few days with my friends the Fs. on one of our Box Hill expeditions, I was ready and eager to sit down to the first chapter of my first novel on my birthday,— June 12th, 1838. By the end of August I had finished the first volume, and written ' The Lady's Maid,' for the ' Service ' series. As I then travelled, it was November before I could return to ' Deerbrook.' I finished it on the 1st of the next February; and it was published before Easter.

The political interests of this period were strong. The old King was manifestly infirm and feeble when I last saw him, in the spring of 1837. I was taking a drive with Lady S——, when her carriage drew up to the roadside and stopped, because the King and Queen were coming. He touched his hat as he leaned back, looking small and aged. I could not but feel something more than the ordinary interest in the young girl who was so near the throne. At a concert at the Hanover Square Rooms, some time before (I forget what year it was) the Duchess of Kent sent Sir John Conroy to me with a message of acknowledgment of the usefulness of my books to the Princess: and I afterwards heard more particulars of the eagerness with which the little lady read the stories on the first day of the month. A friend of mine who was

at Kensington palace one evening when my Political
Economy series was coming to an end, told me how
the Princess came, running and skipping, to show her
mother the advertisement of the ' Illustrations of
Taxation,' and to get leave to order them.   Her
' favourite ' of my stories is ' Ella of Garveloch.'—It
was at breakfast that we heard of the King's death.
In the course of the morning, while I was out, a
friend came to invite my old ladies to go with him to
a place near, where they could at their ease see the
Queen presented to the people.   They went into the
park, and stood in front of the window at St. James's
Palace, where, (among other places) the sovereigns are
proclaimed and presented. Scarcely half-a-dozen people
were there; for very few were aware of the custom.
There stood the young creature, in the simplest mourning, with her sleek bands of brown hair as plain as her
dress.   The tears ran fast down her cheeks, as Lord
Melbourne stood by her side, and she was presented to
my mother and aunt and the other half-dozen as their
sovereign.—I have never gone out of my way to see
great people ; but the Queen went abroad abundantly,
and I saw her very often.   I saw her go to dissolve
Parliament ; and on the 9th of November, to the
Guildhall banquet ; and several times from Mr.
Macready's box at the theatre.   It so happened that
I never saw her when she was not laughing and talking, and moving about.   At a tragedy, and going to
a banquet and to dissolve her predecessor's parliament,
it was just the same.   It was not pleasant to see her,
when Macready's ' Lear' was fixing all other hearts
and eyes, chattering to the Lord Chamberlain, and
laughing, with her shoulder turned to the stage.   I

was indignant, like a good many other people : but, in the fourth act, I saw her attention fixed ; and then she laughed no more. She was interested like the rest of the audience ; and, in one way, more than others. Probably she was the only person present to whóm the play was entirely new.   I heard from one who knew her and the incidents of that evening too well to be mistaken, that the story was absolutely new to her, inasmuch as she was not previously aware that King Lear had any daughters. In remarkable contrast with her was one of the gentlemen in attendance upon her, —the Lord Albemarle of that day.   He forgot every thing but the play,—by degrees leaned forward between the Queen and the stage, and wept till his limp handkerchief would hold no more tears.

Those were the days when there was least pleasure to the loyal in seeing their Queen. At her accession, I was agreeably surprised at her appearance. The upper part of her face was really pretty, and there was an ingenuous and serene air which seemed full of promise.   At the end of a year, the change was melancholy. The expression of her face was wholly altered. It had become bold and discontented. That was, it is now supposed, the least happy part of her life.   Released from the salutary restraints of youth, flattered and pampered by the elated Whigs who kept her to themselves, misled by Lord Melbourne, and not yet having found her home, she was not like the same girl that she was before, nor the same woman that she has been since.   Her mother had gone off the scene, and her husband had not come on ; and in the lonely and homeless interval there was much cause for sorrow to herself and others.   The Whigs about her made a

great boast of the obligations she was under to Lord
Melbourne : but the rest of the world perceives that
all her serious mistakes were made while she was in
Lord Melbourne's hands, and that all went well
after she was once fairly under the guidance of Sir
Robert Peel, and happy in a virtuous home of her
own.

I was at her Coronation : and great is the wonder
with which I have looked back to the enterprise ever
since.   I had not the slightest desire to go, but every
inclination to stay at home: but it was the only coronation likely to happen in my lifetime, and it was a clear
duty to witness it.   I was quite aware that it was an
occasion (I believe the only one) on which a lady could
be alone in public, without impropriety or inconvenience : and I knew of several daughters of peeresses
who were going singly to different parts of the Abbey,
their tickets being for different places in the building.
Tickets were offered me for the two brothers who were
then in London ; but they were for the nave ; and I
had the luck of one for the transept-gallery.   The
streets had hedges of police from our little street to the
gates of the Abbey ; and none were allowed to pass
but the bearers of tickets ; so nothing could be safer.
I was aware of all this, and had breakfasted, and was
at our hall-door in time, when one of my brothers, who
would not believe it, would not let me go for another
half-hour, while he breakfasted.   As I anticipated, the
police turned him back, and I missed the front row
where I might have heard and seen every thing.   Ten
minutes sooner, I might have succeeded in witnessing
what would never happen again in my time.   It was
a bitter disappointment ; but I bent all my strength to

see what I could from the back row. Hearing was out of the question, except the loudest of the music. —The maids called me at half-past two that June morning,—mistaking the clock. I slept no more, and rose at half-past three. As I began to dress, the twenty-one guns were fired which must have awakened all the sleepers in London. When the maid came to dress me, she said numbers of ladies were already hurrying to the Abbey. I saw the grey old Abbey from my window as I dressed, and thought what would have gone forward within it before the sun set upon it. My mother had laid out her pearl ornaments for me. The feeling was very strange of dressing in crape, blonde and pearls at four in the morning. Owing to the delay I have referred to, the Poets' Corner entrance was half full when I took my place there. I was glad to see the Somervilles just before me, though we presently parted at the foot of the staircase. On reaching the gallery, I found that a back seat was so far better than a middle one that I should have a pillar to lean against, and a nice corner for my shawl and bag of sandwiches. Two lady-like girls, prettily dressed, sat beside me, and were glad of the use of my copy of the service and programme. The sight of the rapid filling of the Abbey was enough to go for. The stone architecture contrasted finely with the gay colours of the multitude. From my high seat I commanded the whole north transept, the area with the throne, and many portions of galleries, and the balconies which were called the vaultings. Except a mere sprinkling of oddities, every body was in full dress. In the whole assemblage, I counted six bonnets. The scarlet of the military officers mixed in well; and the

groups of the clergy were dignified; but to an unac-
customed eye the prevalence of court-dresses had a
curious effect. I was perpetually taking whole groups
of gentlemen for quakers till I recollected myself.
The Earl Marshal's assistants, called Gold Sticks,
looked well from above, lightly flitting about in white
breeches, silk stockings, blue laced frocks, and white
sashes. The throne, an armchair with a round back,
covered, as was its footstool, with cloth of gold, stood
on an elevation of four steps, in the centre of the area.
The first peeress took her seat in the north transept
opposite at a quarter before seven : and three of the
bishops came next. From that time, the peers and
their ladies arrived faster and faster. Each peeress
was conducted by two Gold Sticks, one of whom
handed her to her seat, and the other bore and
arranged her train on her lap, and saw that her coronet,
footstool and book were comfortably placed. I never
saw anywhere so remarkable a contrast between youth
and age as in those noble ladies. None of the decent
differences of dress which, according to middle-class
custom, pertain to contrasting periods of life seem to
be admissible on these grand court occasions. Old
hags, with their dyed or false hair drawn to the top of
the head, to allow the putting on of the coronet, had
their necks and arms bare and glittering with
diamonds : and those necks and arms were so brown
and wrinkled as to make one sick ; or dusted over with
white powder which was worse than what it disguised.
I saw something of this from my seat in the transept
gallery, but much more when the ceremonial was over,
and the peeresses were passing to their carriages, or
waiting for them. The younger were as lovely as the

aged were haggard. One beautiful creature, with a transcendent complexion and form, and coils upon coils of light hair, was terribly embarrassed about her coronet. She had apparently forgotten that her hair must be disposed with a view to it : and the large braids at the back would in no way permit the coronet to keep on. She and her neighbour tugged vehemently at her braids : and at last the thing was done after a manner, but so as to spoil the wonderful effect of the simultaneous self-coroneting of all the peeresses.— About nine, the first gleams of the sun slanted into the Abbey, and presently travelled down to the peeresses. I had never before seen the full effect of diamonds. As the light travelled, each peeress shone like a rainbow. The brightness, vastness, and dreamy magnificence of the scene produced a strange effect of exhaustion and sleepiness. About nine o'clock, I felt this so disagreeably that I determined to withdraw my senses from the scene, in order to reserve my strength (which was not great at that time) for the ceremonial to come. I had carried a book ; and I read and ate a sandwich, leaning against my friendly pillar, till I felt refreshed.

The guns told when the Queen had set forth : and there was renewed animation. The Gold Sticks flitted about ; there was tuning in the orchestra ; and the foreign ambassadors and their suites arrived in quick succession. Prince Esterhazy, crossing a bar of sunshine, was the most prodigious rainbow of all. He was covered with diamonds and pearls ; and as he dangled his hat, it cast a dancing radiance all round. While he was thus glittering and gleaming, people were saying, I know not how truly, that he had to redeem those jewels from pawn, as usual, for the occasion.—At half-past eleven, the guns told that the Queen had arrived: but, as there was much to be done in the robing-room, there was a long pause before she appeared.   A burst from the orchestra marked her appearance at the doors, and the anthem 'I was glad' rang through the Abbey.   Every body rose: and the holders of the first and second rows of our gallery stood up so high that I saw nothing of the entrance, nor of the Recognition, except the Archbishop of Canterbury reading at one of the angles of the platform.   The 'God save the Queen' of the organ swelled gloriously forth after the recognition. The services which followed were seen by a very small proportion of those present.   The acclamation when the crown was put on her head was very animating: and in the midst of it, in an instant of time, the peeresses were all coroneted:—all but the fair creature already described.   In order to see the enthroning, I stood on the rail behind our seats, holding by another rail.   I was in nobody's way; and I could not resist the temptation, though every moment expecting that the rail would break.   Her small dark crown looked pretty, and her mantle of cloth of gold very regal.   She herself looked so small as to appear puny.   The homage was as pretty a sight as any;—trains of peers touching her crown, and then kissing her hand.   It was in the midst of that process that poor Lord Rolle's disaster sent a shock through the whole assemblage.   It turned me very sick.   The large, infirm old man was held up by two peers, and had nearly reached the royal footstool when he slipped through the hands of his supporters, and

rolled over and over down the steps, lying at the
bottom coiled up in his robes. He was instantly
lifted up ; and he tried again and again, amidst
shouts of admiration of his valour. The Queen at
length spoke to Lord Melbourne, who stood at her
shoulder, and he bowed approval ; on which she
rose, leaned forward, and held out her hand to
the old man, dispensing with his touching the crown.
He was not hurt, and his self-quizzing on his misad-
venture was as brave as his behaviour at the time. A
foreigner in London gravely reported to his own
countrymen, what he entirely believed on the word of
a wag, that the Lords Rolle held their title on the
condition of performing the feat at every coronation.

The departure of a large proportion of the assemblage when the Communion-service began afforded me
a good opportunity for joining some friends who, like
myself, preferred staying to see more of the Queen in
the Abbey, to running away for the procession. I then
obtained a good study of the peers, and of the Queen
and her train-bearers when she returned to the throne.
The enormous purple and crimson trains, borne by her
ladies, dressed all alike, made the Queen look smaller
than ever. I watched her out at the doors, and then
became aware how fearfully fatigued I was. I never
remember any thing like it. While waiting in the
passages and between the barriers, several ladies sat or
lay down on the ground. I did not like to sink down
in dust half a foot deep, to the spoiling of my dress
and the loss of my self-respect ; but it was really a terrible waiting till my brothers appeared at the end of
the barrier. The crowd had rendered our return im-

possible till then; and even then, we had to make a circuit. I satisfied my thirst, and went to sleep; and woke up to tea, and to keep house with my mother, while every body else went out to see the illuminations. I did not; but was glad to go to bed at midnight, and sleep eight hours at a stretch, for once.

It was a wonderful day; and one which I am glad to have witnessed; but it had not the effect on me which I was surprised to observe in others. It strengthened, instead of relaxing my sense of the unreal character of monarchy in England. The contrast between the traditional ascription of power to the sovereign and the actual fact was too strong to be overpowered by pageantry, music, and the blasphemous religious services of the day. After all was said and sung, the sovereign remained a nominal ruler, who could not govern by her own mind and will; who had influence, but no political power; a throne and crown, but with the knowledge of every body that the virtue had gone out of them. The festival was a highly barbaric one, to my eyes. The theological part especially was worthy only of the old Pharaonic times in Egypt, and those of the Kings in Palestine. Really, it was only by old musical and devotional association that the services could go down with people of any reverence at all. There was such a mixing up of the Queen and the God, such homage to both, and adulation so like in kind and degree that, when one came to think of it, it made one's blood run cold to consider that this was commended to all that assemblage as religion. God was represented as merely the King of kings and Lord of lords;—the lowest of the low views in which the Unknown is regarded or described. There is, I

believe, no public religious service which is not offensive to thoughtful and reverent persons, from its ascription of human faculties, affections, qualities and
actions to the assumed First Cause of the universe : but
the Jewish or heathen ascription to him of military and
aristocratic rank, and regal prerogative, side by side
with the same ascription to the Queen, was the most
coarse and irreverent celebration that I was ever a witness to. The performance of the Messiah, so beautiful
and touching as a work of art, or as the sincere homage of superstition, is saddening and full of shame
when regarded as worship. The promises—all broken;
the exultation—all falsified by the event ; the prophe-
cies—all discredited by the experience of eighteen
centuries, and the boasts of prevalence, rung out gloriously when Christianity is dying out among the fore-
most peoples of the earth ;—all these, so beautiful as
art or history, are very painful when regarded as religion.   As an apotheosis of Osiris, under his ancient
name, or his more modern image of Christ, the Messiah
of Handel is the finest treat in the whole range of art :
but it is too low for religion.   Yet more striking was
the Coronation service to me, in the same light. Splendid and moving as addressed to a Jehovah, on the
coronation of a Solomon, it was offensive as offered to
the God of the nineteenth century in the Western
world.—I have refreshed my memory about the incidents of that twenty-eighth of June, 1838, from my
Diary. The part which least needs refreshing is this
last. I remember remarking to my mother on the impiety of the service, when a copy of it was kindly sent
to me the evening before; and I told her when the celebration was over, that this part of it had turned out

even worse than I expected ; and that I could not
imagine how so many people could hear it as a matter
of course.

One of the strongest interests of the year 1838 was
Lord Durham's going out as Governor-General of the
North American colonies.   I have given my account
of that matter in my History of the Peace, and I will
not enlarge on it now.   I was concerned when I heard
of his acceptance of the post, because the difficulties
appeared all but insuperable at best ; and I knew
too much of Lord Brougham's jealousy and Lord
Melbourne's laxity to hope that he would be duly
supported from home, or even left unmolested.   He
said himself that he felt ' inexpressible reluctance ' to
undertake the charge : but his confiding temper misled him into trusting his political comrades,—Lord
Melbourne and his Ministry—for ' cordial and ener-
getic support,'—and his political opponents,—Lord
Brougham and those who pulled his wires,— for
' generous forbearance.'   In talking over the matter
one day with our mutual friend, Lady Charlotte
Lindsay, I did not conceal my regret and apprehension.   She called one day, soon after, to tell me
honestly that she had told Lord Durham, the night
before, that I was not sanguine about his success.   He
questioned her anxiously as to my exact meaning ; and
she referred him to me.   I had no wish to disturb him,
now that it was too late, with my bad opinion of those
in whose hands he was placing his fate : and I did not
do so.   I answered all his questions about Canada and
the United States as well as I could.   Charles and
Arthur Buller obtained introductions and information
from me ; and Charles spent many hours by my fire-

side, diligently discussing business, and giving me the
strongest impression of his heart being deep in his
work.   His poor mother, who worshipped him, came
one day, just before they sailed, nervous and flushed,
and half laughing, telling me what a fright she had
had:—that she had been assured that the Hastings
man-of-war, in which her sons were to attend Lord
Durham, would certainly sink from the weight of the
Governor-General's plate. This was a specimen of the
vulgar jokes of the Brougham clique : and it produced
an effect on others than poor Mrs. Buller.   Lord
Chandos founded a motion on it,—objecting to the
expense to the country !—the Governor-General going
out unsalaried, to save a group of colonies to the
empire in an hour of extreme danger !

The intolerable treatment he met with shocked me
as much as if I had anticipated any thing better : and
his own magnanimous conduct on his return moved me
as deeply as if I had not known him to be capable of it.
He was calm, cheerful, winning in his manners as ever,
and quite willing to trust his friends for their friendship
while himself desiring no demonstration of it which
should overthrow the tottering Government, and em-
barrass the Queen for his sake.   Lady Durham necessarily resigned her office about the Queen's person :
but no word or sign of reproach ever reached her royal
mistress for her fatal fickleness in first writing an autograph letter of the warmest thankfulness for his ordinances, and then disallowing those same ordinances,
and permitting every kind of insult to be offered to the
devoted statesman who had sacrificed his comfort and
ease in her service, and was about to yield his life
under the torture which she allowed to be inflicted on

him. To the last moment, her old friends, who might
have expected something very different from her sense
of early obligation, maintained that she meant well,
but was misguided. When I last saw Lord Durham
it was in his own house in Cleveland Row, when a note
was brought in from the Colonial Office, the contents
of which he communicated to me :—that he could not
have any copies of his own Report without paying four
shillings and threepence apiece for them. He had gone
unsalaried, had spent 10,000*l*. out of his private property, and had produced a Report of unequalled value,
at an unparalleled sacrifice ; and he was now insulted
in this petty way. He smilingly promised me a four-
and-threepenny Report notwithstanding.—His successor, Lord Sydenham (who had not yet got his
patent) was diligently studying Canadian affairs every
day, with Lord Durham and the Bullers, in order to
carry out their scheme. We had a world of talk about
the Western Continent that night : but I never much
liked Poulett Thomson. He had great qualities,—a
very remarkable industry, and personal fortitude, long
and thoroughly tested : but he was luxurious, affectedly
indolent in manner, and with a curious stamp of mean-
ness on both person and manners. I never saw him
again, either. He was on the eve of departure for his
government, whence he never returned. If I remember right, that was the day of Lord Normanby's ap-
pointment to the Colonial Office. He complained, half
in earnest, of the hardship of never getting a foreign
tour, like other people,—passing as he had done from
Jamaica to Ireland, and now having all the colonies ou
his hands. I entirely agreed with him as to the weight
of the charge : whereupon he asked me what I should

have done first, if I had been in his place that day.
My answer was that I should have gone immediately
to the globe, to see where the forty-three colonies were
that I was to govern. He laughed; but I thought it
a serious matter enough that any minister should be
burdened with a work which it was so impossible that
he should do properly. Well!—that night I bade
Lord and Lady Durham farewell, little imagining that
I should never more see either of them. I knew he
was more delicate in health even than usual; and
that he was exerting himself much to keep up till the
Ministry or the session should close. ' Till Easter '
politicians said the Ministry might last; and this was
a pretty good hit, as the Bedchamber Question came
on just after Easter. Before that time I was abroad;
and I was brought home on a couch, and carried
through London at once to Newcastle-on-Tyne, where
I staid some months at my brother-in-law's. Repeated invitations to Lambton Castle came to me
there; but I was too ill to leave the house. In the
course of the next spring, Lord Durham was ordered
to the south of Europe; but he got no further than
Cowes, where he died in July,—the vitality of his
heart and animation of his mind flattering the hopes
of his family to the last. Lady Durham took her
young family to Italy, but died before they had reached
their destination. For his death I was prepared : but
the news of hers was a great shock. I was very ill
then; and when the orphaned girls came to see me at
Tynemouth, I behaved (it seemed to me) unpardon-
ably. I could not stop my tears, in the presence of
those who had so much more reason and so much more
right to be inconsolable. But I always have felt, and

I feel still, that that story is one of the most tragic I
have ever known. In my early youth I had been accustomed to hear my revered eldest brother say that
the best man in the House of Commons—the one who
would turn out a hero and a statesman in the worst
or the best of times,—was John George Lambton.
I had watched his career through the worst of times
till he came into power, and made the Reform Bill. I
then became acquainted with him, and found in him
a solid justification of the highest hopes ; and now he
was dead, in middle life, broken-hearted by injury,
treachery and insult ; and his devoted wife presently
followed him.

Their eldest daughter was profoundly impressed by
the serious responsibilities which rested on her as the
head of the family during her brother's boyhood ; and
she took me along with her in her efforts and her
cares. It was she and I who originated the ' Weekly
Volume,'—our scheme being taken up and carried
out by Mr. Charles Knight, in the way which is so
well known. The singular satisfaction has been hers
of seeing the redemption of Canada carried out by her
husband from her father's beginning. She has the
best possible consolation for such a fate as that of her
parents that their work has been gloriously achieved
by one whom she has made their son.

On looking at my Diary, I am not at all surprised
that it was considered desirable for me to take another
journey in the autumn of 1838. I was sorry to leave
' Deerbrook ' at the end of the first volume : but
there was every other reason why I should take the
refreshment of a journey after two years of close work,
and no other reason why I should not. Either the

growing domestic anxiety or the ever-increasing calls
of work and of society would have been enough for
the strongest and gayest-hearted : and I had both
kinds of burdens on me. I find in my Diary more and
more self-exhortations and self-censures about the sufferings of that year 1838. I had by that time resolved
on the wisdom which I try to this day to practise :—
longing for quiet, and yet finding it impossible in the
nature of things that my life should be anything but
a busy, public, and diversified one,—*to keep a quiet
mind.*   I did strive ; and to a considerable extent I
succeeded ; but my nerves were, and had long been,
overstrained ; and my wisest friends continued to advise me to leave home more frequently than my inclination would have disposed me to do.   My mother
was well pleased to let me go on this occasion, as my
rooms would be at her disposal for her hospitalities ;
and I therefore agreed to join a party of friends, to
attend the meeting of the British Association at Newcastle first, and then proceed to the Lake District,
which I had never seen, and into Scotland, visiting
both Western and Northern Highlands.   It is always
pleasant, I find, to have some object in view, even in
the direction of a journey of pleasure : and this was
supplied to me by Mr. Knight's request that I would
explore the topography of Shakspere's Scotch play
now ; and of the Italian plays when I went to the continent the next year.   'Do this for me,' said Mr.
Knight, 'and I will give you ten copies of my
Shakspere.'   Two copies of the Shakspere satisfied
me ; for indeed the work was purely pleasurable.   A
few months after that time, my companions were
walking Padua through and through with me, for the

shrewish Katherine's and delectable Portia's sake; and
looking for Juliet at Verona, and exploring the Jew
quarter at Venice, and fixing on the very house whence
Jessica eloped; and seeing at the arsenal what Othello
meant by his business at the Sagittary.   In like manner we now traced out the haunts of Macbeth, living
and dead.   When we were at Lord Murray's, at
Strachur, his brother gave us a letter of introduction
which opened to us all the known recesses of Glammis
Castle.   We sat down and lingered on the Witches'
Heath, between Nairn and Forres, and examined
Cawdor Castle.   Best of all, we went to Iona, and saw
Macbeth's grave in the line of those of the Scottish
kings.   I have seen many wonders and beauties in
many lands; but no one scene remains so deeply impressed on my very heart as that sacred Iona, as we saw
it, with its Cathedral standing up against a bar of yellow western sky, while the myrtle-green tumbling sea
seemed to show it to be unattainable.   We had reached
it however; and had examined its relics with speechless
interest.   I do not know whether any of the air of the
localities hangs about those notes of mine in Mr.
Knight's Shakspere; but to me, the gathering up of
knowledge and associations for them was almost as
pleasant work as any I ever had to do.

We were tempted to go to Newcastle by sea, by a
steamer having been engaged to convey a freight of
savans.   A curious company of passengers we were on
board the Ocean:—sound scientific men; a literary
humbug or two; a statistical pretender or two; and a
few gentlemen, clerical or other.   When we entered
Shields Harbour, the whole company were on deck, to
see Tynemouth Priory, and the other beauties of that

coast; and the Shields people gathered on the quays
to stare at the strange vessel. When they hailed, and
asked who we were, the great men on the deck
shouted in reply ' *savans*,' 'philosophers,' ' nonde-
scripts.'

That was the Meeting of the British Association at
which (Dr. Lardner being present) the report was in-
dustriously spread that the Great Western,—the first
steamer to America on her first voyage,—' had been
seen in the middle of the Atlantic, broken-backed, and
in great distress.' The words sank heavily upon my
heart; for I was acquainted with several persons on
board; and it shed more or less gloom over the whole
week. Many observed at the time that it was just the
thing likely to be said by Dr. Lardner and his friends,
considering his pledges of his scientific reputation on
the impossibility of crossing the Atlantic by steam;
and in this every body agreed: but the suspense was
painful; and it outlasted the week; as it was intended
to do. Dr. Lardner's final disgraces had not yet taken
place; but I saw how coldly he was noticed, when he
was not entirely ignored : and when I curtseyed to him
at the ball, I was warned by a friend not to notice
him if I could avoid it. I was glad then that I had
not entertained his proposal when, as editor of the
Encyclopedia which goes under his name, he wrote to
me, and called, and endeavoured to obtain my promise
to write a volume for him. A cousin of mine, who is
so little fond of the pen as to find letter-writing a
grievance, was highly amused at receiving (I think
while I was abroad) a flattering letter from Dr.
Lardner, requesting a volume from her for his series.
Not very long after that Newcastle meeting, he made

his notorious flight to America; and I have heard
nothing of him since.

What I saw of that meeting certainly convinced
me of the justice, in the main, of Carlyle's sarcasms
on that kind of celebration. I have no doubt of the
opportunity afforded for the promotion of science in
various ways: but the occasion is really so sadly
spoiled (or was in those days) by the obtrusions of
coxcombs, the conceit of third-rate men with their
specialities, the tiresome talk of one-idead men, who
scruple no means of swelling out what they call the
evidence of their doctrines, and the disagreeable footing of the ladies, that I internally vowed that I would
never again go in the way of one of those anniver-
saries. I heard two or three valuable addresses; but,
on the whole, the humbugs and small men carried all
before them: and, I am sorry to say, Sir John
Herschel himself so far succumbed to the spirit of the
occasion as to congratulate his scientific brethren on
the 'crowning honour' among many, of the presence
of the fair sex at their sections! That same fair sex,
meantime, was there to sketch the *savans*, under
cover of mantle, shawl or little parasol, or to pass the
time by watching and quizzing the members. Scarcely
any of the ladies sat still for half an hour. They
wandered in and out, with their half-hidden sketch-
books, seeking amusement as their grandmothers did
at auctions. I was in truth much ashamed of the
ladies; and I wished they had staid at home, preparing hospitalities for the tired *savans*, and showing
themselves only at the evening promenade in the
Green Market, and at the ball. The promenade was
really a pretty sight,—not only from the beauty of

the place and its decorations, but on account of the presence of the Quaker body, who, excluded from the other forms of social amusement, eagerly grasp at this one lawful exception. They made the very most of it; and I, for one, can testify to their capacity for staring at an anti-slavery confessor. My sister, who bore a family likeness to me, proposed to dress her hair like mine, borrow a trumpet from a deaf friend who was present, and walk up and down the opposite side, to draw off my 'tail,' which was declared to be 'three times as long a O'Connell's.'

It was the accident of Professor Daubeny putting some American newspapers into my hand one day that week which occasioned the appearance of one of my most heart-felt writings. The Editor of the Westminster Review was impressed by what I showed and told him of the life and murder of Lovejoy, the first American witness unto death in the cause of liberty of speech; and he requested from me a vivid historical sketch of the cause, from the beginning to Lovejoy's murder. This was the origin of 'The Martyr Age of the United States' which has been elsewhere sufficiently referred to. It appeared in the Christmas number of the Westminster Review.

With joy we left the crowded scene which was such a mixture of soundness and pretence, wisdom and vanity, and matter for pride and shame, and betook ourselves to the Lake District. I had never seen it before, and had no distinct anticipation of seeing it again. What should I have felt, if I had been told that, after one more painful stage of my life, I should make my home in that divine region till death! It was on the 2nd of September that we drove through

Ambleside, from Bowness to Grasmere, passing the
field in which I am now abiding,—on which I am at
this moment looking forth.   I wonder whether my
eye rested for a moment on the knoll whereon my
house now stands.   We returned through Ambleside
to go to Patterdale; and a pencil entry in my diary
calls up the remembrance of the soft sadness with
which we caught 'our last view of Windermere;'—
that Windermere which was to become to me the
most familiar of all waters.

While at Strachur, Lord Murray's seat in Argyle-
shire, we found ourselves treated with singular hospitality.   Lord Murray placed the little Loch Fyne
steamer at our disposal.   He and Lady Murray
insisted on receiving our entire party; and every
facility was afforded for all of us seeing every thing.
Every Highland production, in the form of fish, flesh
and fowl, was carefully collected: salmon and Loch
herrings, grouse pies, and red-deer soup, and so forth.
What I best remember, however, is a conversation
with Lord Murray by the loch side.   He invited me
there for a walk; and he had two things to say.   He
wanted me to write some papers on prison management,
for Chambers's Journal, or some other popular periodical, for the purpose of familiarising the Scotch with the
principle of punishment, and the attendant facts of
American imprisonment   He lost his Prisons Bill in the
preceding session, and wanted the support of Scotch
public opinion before the next.   This being settled, he
wrote to Messrs. Chambers at Edinburgh; and I there
saw one of the brothers for the first time.   The papers
were agreed upon, written and published.   Mr. Robert
Chambers I did not see till some few years later,

when he called on me at Tynemouth, during my
recovery by mesmerism, for the purpose of investigating the subject.   Our acquaintance, then begun, has
since ripened into friendship, both on his own account,
and for the sake of his brother-in-law and sister, Mr.
and Mrs. Wills, who, becoming known to me through
my being a contributor to 'Household Words,' have
largely increased the pleasures of my latest years by
their friendly offices of every kind, and their hearty
affection.   Edinburgh was quite a different place to
me when I went for my third Scotch journey, in 1852,
by Mr. Robert Chambers's charming home being open
to me; and London has a new familiar interest to me
now that I have another home there at Mr. Wills's.

   To return to that walk with the Lord Advocate. He
wished to know my opinion on a subject which was
then more talked of than almost any other;—our
probable relations with Russia.   I hardly know now
how the notion came to spread as it did that the Czar
had a mind to annex us: but it was talked over in all
drawing-rooms, and, as I now found, in the Cabinet.
I had nothing to say,—so astonished was I to hear
it thus gravely and expressly brought forward.   I
could only say that the idea of our ever submitting
to Russia seemed too monstrous to be entertained.
Lord Murray had no formed opinion to produce; but
he offered,—' as a speculation,—just as a ground
for speculation,'—the fact that for centuries no
quarter of a century had passed without the incorpora-
tion of some country with Russia; some country
which no doubt once regarded its absorption by Russia
as the same unimaginable thing that our own appeared
to us now.   He said that if we commit two stone

bottles to the stream, and one breaks the other, it is
nearly an even chance whether it will break or be
broken next time : but, when the same has broken a
score, the chances are almost anything to nothing that
it will break the twenty-first. Therefore he thought
we might as well not be so entirely complacent and
secure as we were, but think over such a liability
with some little sobriety and sense. So there was a
new and very horrible speculation for me to carry
away with me : and highly curious it is to recur to
now (August, 1855) when we find that Russia, after
nearly twenty years' more leisure for preparation,
cannot meet us at sea, or win a battle on land. At
least, after a year and a half of warfare she has as
yet done neither.

From Strachur, we pursued our way to the Western
Islands : and, after being weather-bound in Mull, we
accomplished the visit to Iona which I have referred
to. We saw Staffa, and had the captain's spontaneous
promise to take us round by Garveloch, that I might
see the homes of the personages about whom I had
written so familiarly : but the weather was too rough ;
and I did not see the Garveloch Isles till a glorious
sunny day in July, 1852.

It was October before we reached Edinburgh : and
there my kind companions and I parted. Miss Rogers
and a young friend were staying at Lord Jeffrey's,
where I met them ; and Miss Rogers urged me to
take a seat in her carriage as far as Newcastle, where
I was to stop for a week or two. We saw Abbotsford
and Dryburgh under great advantages of weather ;
but my surprise at the smallness and toy-character of
Abbotsford was extreme. It was impossible but that

both Scott and Lockhart must know what a good Scotch house is ; and their glorification of this place shakes one's faith in their other descriptions.

That journey of 1838 was beneficial to me to a certain extent ; and it would have been more so, but for its close. I was called home from Newcastle under circumstances which made my long solitary mail journey a very heavy one, full of apprehension and pain. I was, though without being fully conscious of it, becoming too ill to bear the shocks of that unhappy year as I had borne all manner of shocks, all my life. The internal disease which was soon to prostrate me entirely had made considerable progress, though I had no more than a vague notion that there was something wrong. The refreshment from the journey was not lasting ; but its pleasures were. One of the noticeable things about it was that it introduced me to Mrs. Crowe, whose acquaintance has since yielded me very great pleasure. And she, again, has been the main cause or occasion of my friendship with Dr. Samuel Brown and his wife, who have been intimates of my latest years,—too much so to permit more than such a notice as this. Another marked thing about that autumn trip was that it introduced me to that pleasant experience of middle age,—the consideration of the young. I had always been among the youngest at home in my childhood ; and of late years had ministered, in the capacity of youngster, to my old ladies. Now, for the first time, I experienced the luxury of being tended as an elderly person. Though some years younger than the two heads of our travelling party, I was of their generation ; and the four young people were most attentive in saving us elders fatigue, making

tea, giving us the sofas and warm corners, and so on.
From that time I have taken rank among the elders,
and enjoyed the comfort of it.

The readers of my ' Retrospect of Western Travel '
may remember the story [1] of the slave child Ailsie,
whose mistress died at New Orleans, leaving that
beautiful little creature to be a most embarrassing
charge to the widower. My description of this child,
and of the interest felt in her fate by me and mine,
reached the eye of the widower ; and he wrote to entreat me to take charge of the girl (by that time
twelve years old). He avowed his inability to protect
her, and offered to send over a yearly allowance for her
maintenance, if I would receive and adopt her. I declined the annual allowance because my friend's money
was derived from slave-labour, and I would not touch
it ; but otherwise, I accepted his proposal, and did not
see why he should not lodge in a bank, for her ultimate benefit, such money as he believed her to have
earned. I intended first to train her as my little maid,
and have her attend a school near, so that I might
ascertain what she was most fit for. All this winter,
we were in daily expectation of her arrival. Her little
bed awaited her in my room ; and we had arranged
about having her vaccinated at once, and clothed like
English children, instead of having her brilliant eyes
and beautiful mulatto face surmounted by the yellow
turban which became her so well. But Ailsie, for
whose reception all arrangements were complete when
I went to Scotland, did not appear all the winter ; and
I wrote again, very urgently, to her master. I had to

[1] Retrospect of Western Travel, vol. ii., page 146.

make arrangements again when I went to the continent in April ; but his final letter came at last. It was the letter of an almost broken-hearted man ; and it almost broke our hearts to read it. He, Irish by birth, had never been more or less reconciled to ' the peculiar institution.' Involved in it before he was of age, he had no power to extricate himself from it,—at least till he had paid off all the liabilities under which young planters enter life. His beloved young wife had received this child as a gift from her mother in Tennessee,—the child's life being in danger on her native plantation, through the fierce jealousies which attend upon a system of concubinage. It never occurred to the widower that he could not freely dispose of his wife's little slave : but his mother-in-law demanded the girl back again. In her ripening beauty she was too valuable to be given to me. For what purposes she was detained as of course, there is no need to describe. She was already lost and gone ; and I have never heard of her since. Her voice often comes back upon my memory, and her vivid affectionate countenance, as she pulled at her mistress's gown, and clasped her knees with the anxious question,—' Ain't you well ? ' This one illustration of the villany of the system roused more indignation and sympathy in many hearts than a whole row of books of argument or description of Slave institutions in the abstract. I could not have done for Ailsie what I purposed, as my affairs turned out ; but there were many of my friends who could, and who were anxious to assume the charge. But she was never to be heard of more.

The continental journey that I have referred to was undertaken chiefly for the sake of escorting an invalid cousin to Switzerland.　As soon as ' Deerbrook ' was published, and my ' Guides to Service ' finished, the weather was fine enough to permit our departure. Two mutual friends joined us ; and our party thus consisted of four ladies, a maid-servant and a courier. We crossed to Rotterdam on the 17th of April, went up the Rhine, and by the usual route to Lausanne, except that one of my companions slipped across the frontier with me, for the sake of seeing Toussaint L'Ouverture's prison and grave.　I was furnished with a copious and comprehensive passport for myself and maid, obtained by the Lord Advocate's kindness from the Secretary of State, as the Austrian interdict against my entrance into the empire might otherwise be still an impediment.　My friend offered to personate my maid just for the day which would take us from the frontier to the castle of Joux.　We excited great wonder at the *douane*, of course, with our destitution of baggage, and our avowed intention of leaving France in the afternoon ; but we accomplished our purpose, and it was virtually decided that ' The Hour and the Man ' should be written.

While I was walking up a hill in Germany, one of my companions had observed to another that I was, in her opinion, on the verge of some terrible illness. It was at Venice that the extent of my illness became unquestionable.　My cousin had been deposited at her place of abode ; and the rest of us had gone on to Venice, intending to take a look at her at Lausanne on our return.　My illness, however, broke up all our plans.　My kind nurses contrived a couch for me in the carriage ; and on that I was brought home by the straightest road,—by the Via Emilia, and the St.

Gothard down the Rhine, where we were joined by one of my brothers and a brother-in-law. We took passage to London, from Antwerp: and I was soon on my mother's couch in Fludyer Street. Not to remain, however. I was conveyed without delay to Newcastle-upon-Tyne, to be under the care of my brother-in-law; and from that neighbourhood I did not remove for nearly six years.

Here closed the anxious period during which my reputation, and my industry, and my social intercourses were at their height of prosperity; but which was so charged with troubles that when I lay down on my couch of pain in my Tynemouth lodging, for a confinement of nearly six years, I felt myself comparatively happy in my release from responsibility, anxiety, and suspense. The worst sufferings of my life were over now; and its best enjoyments and privileges were to come,—though I little knew it, and they were as yet a good way off.

FIFTH PERIOD.

SECTION I.

TO THE AGE OF FORTY-THREE.

THE little volume which I wrote during my illness,
—'Life in the Sick-room,'—tells nearly as much
as it can be interesting or profitable for any body to
hear about this period of my life. The shorter I can
make my narrative of it, the better on all accounts.
Five years seem a long time to look forward; and five
years of suffering, of mind or body, seem sadly like
an eternity in passing through them: but they collapse
almost into nothingness, as soon as they are left
behind, and another condition is fairly entered on.
From the monotony of sick-room life, little beyond
the general impression remains to be imparted, or
even re-called; and if it were otherwise, I should
probably say little of that dreary term, because it is
not good to dwell much on morbid conditions, for any
other purpose than scientific study, for the sake of
the prevention or cure of the suffering in other cases.
I am aware that the religious world, proud of its
Christian faith as the 'Worship of Sorrow,' thinks
it a duty and a privilege to dwell on the morbid con-

ditions of human life ; but my experience of wide
extremes of health and sickness, of happiness and
misery, leads me to a very different conclusion. For
pathological purposes, there must be a study of morbid
conditions ; but that the study should be general,—
that it should be enforced as a duty, and held up as
a pleasure—seems to me one of those mistakes in
morals which are aggravated and protracted by the
mischievous influence of superstition. Tracts and
religious books swarm among us, and are thrust into
the hands of every body by every body else, which
describe the sufferings of illness, and generate vanity
and egotism about bodily pain and early death,—
rendering these disgraces of our ignorance and barbarism attractive to the foolish and the vain, and actually
shaming the wholesome, natural desire for 'a sound
mind in a sound body.' The Christian superstition,
now at last giving way before science, of the contemptible nature of the body, and its antagonism to
the soul, has shockingly perverted our morals, as well
as injured the health of Christendom : and every book,
tract, and narrative which sets forth a sick-room as a
condition of honour, blessing and moral safety, helps
to sustain a delusion and corruption which have
already cost the world too dear. I know too much of
all this from my own experience to choose to do any
thing towards encouragement of the morbid appetite
for pathological contemplation,—physical or moral.
My youthful vanity took the direction which might be
expected in the case of a pious child. I was patient in
illness and pain because I was proud of the distinction,
and of being taken into such special pupilage by God ;
and I hoped for, and expected early death till it was

too late to die early. It is grievous to me now to think what an amount of time and thought I have wasted in thinking about dying,—really believing as I did for many years that life was a mere preparation for dying : and now, after a pretty long life, when I find myself really about to die, the event seems to me so simple, natural, and, as I may say, negative in comparison with life and its interests, that I cannot but marvel at the quantity of attention and solicitude I lavished upon it while it was yet so far off as to require no attention at all. To think no more of death than is necessary for the winding up of the business of life, and to dwell no more upon sickness than is necessary for its treatment, or to learn to prevent it, seems to me the simple wisdom of the case,—totally opposite as this is to the sentiment and method of the religious world.

On the other hand, I do not propose to nourish a foolish pride by disguising, through shame, the facts of sickness and suffering. Pain and untimely death are, no doubt, the tokens of our ignorance, and of our sins against the laws of nature. I conceive our business to be to accept these consequences of our ignorance and weakness, with as little personal shame on the one hand as vanity or pride on the other. As far as any sickness of mine can afford warning, I am willing to disclose it; and I have every desire to acknowledge my own fault or folly in regard to it, while wholly averse to treat it as a matter of sentiment,— even to the degree in which I did it, sincerely enough, in ' Life in the Sick-room,' a dozen years ago. I propose, therefore, to be now as brief as I can, and at the same time, as frank, in speaking of the years between

1839 and 1845.—I have mentioned before, in regard
to my deafness, that I have no doubt of its having
been seriously aggravated by nervous excitement, at
the age when I lived in reverie and vanities of the
imagination; and that it was suddenly and severely
increased by a sort of accident. That sort of accident
was the result of ignorance in a person whom I need
not point out: and thus it seems that my deafness is
largely ascribable to disobedience to the laws of nature.
And thus in regard to the disease which at this time
was laying me low for so many years. It was unquestionably the result of excessive anxiety of mind,
—of the extreme tension of nerves under which I had
been living for some years, while the three anxious
members of my family were, I may say, on my hands
—not in regard to money, but to care of a more important kind. My dear aunt, the sweetest of old ladies,
was now extremely old, and required shielding from
the anxiety caused by the other two. My mother was
old, and fast becoming blind; and the irritability
caused in her first by my position in society, and next
by the wearing trial of her own increasing infirmity,
told fearfully upon my already reduced health. My
mother's dignified patience in the direct endurance of
her blindness was a really beautiful spectacle: but the
natural irritability found vent in other directions; and
especially was it visited upon me. Heaven knows, I
never sought fame; and I would thankfully have given
it all away in exchange for domestic peace and ease:
but there it was! and I had to bear the consequences.
I was overworked, fearfully, in addition to the pain of
mind I had to bear. I was not allowed to have a
maid, at my own expense, or even to employ a work-

woman: and thus, many were the hours after midnight
when I ought to have been asleep, when I was sitting
up to mend my clothes. Far worse than this, my
mother would not be taken care of. She was daily
getting out into the crowded streets by herself, when
she could not see a yard before her. What the distress
from this was to me may be judged of by the fact that
for many months after my retreat to Tynemouth, I
rarely slept without starting from a dream that my
mother had fallen from a precipice, or over the bannis-
ters, or from a cathedral spire; and that it was my
fault. These cares, to say nothing of the toils, had
long been wearing me down, so that I became subject
to attacks of faintness, on occasion of any domestic
uneasiness; and two or three intimate friends, as well
as some members of the family, urged my leaving
home as frequently as possible, for my mother's sake
as well as my own, as my return was always a joyful
occasion to her. My habits and likings made this
moving about a very irksome thing to me; and especially when arrangements had to be made about my
work,—from which I had never any holiday. I loved,
as I still love, the most monotonous life possible: but
I took refuge in change, as the only relief fiom a pressure of trouble which was breaking me down,—I was
not aware how rapidly. An internal disease was gain-
ing ground for months or years before I was aware of
it. A tumour was forming of a kind which usually
originates in mental suffering; and when at last I
broke down completely, and settled myself in a lodging
at Tynemouth, I long felt that the lying down, in
solitude and silence, free from responsibility and domestic care, was a blessed change from the life I had

led since my return from America.   My dear old aunt soon died: my mother was established at Liverpool, in the neighbourhood of three of her children; and the other claimant of my anxious care emigrated. It is impossible to deny that the illness under which I lay suffering for five years was induced by flagrant violations of the laws of nature : and I then failed to appropriate the comforts with which Christians deprave their moral sense in such a case, as I also felt unable to blame myself individually for my incapacity. No doubt, if I had felt less respect and less affection for my mother, I might have taken the management of matters more into my own hands, and should have felt her discontent with me less than I did; and again, if I had already found the supports of philosophy on relinquishing the selfish complacencies of religion, I should have borne my troubles with strength and ease. But, as it was, I was neither proud or vain of my discipline on the one hand, nor ashamed of it on the other, while fully aware that it was the result of fault and imperfection, moral and intellectual.

On my return from Italy, ill, my sister and her husband hospitably urged my taking up my abode with them, at least till the nature and prospects of my case were ascertained.   After spending a month at a lodging in their neighbourhood, in Newcastle-upon-Tyne, I removed to their hospitable house, where I was taken all possible care of for six months.   They most generously desired me to remain : but there were various reasons which determined me to decline their kindness. It would have been clearly wrong to occupy their guest chamber permanently, and to impose restraints upon a healthy household : and, for my own part, I had an unspeakable longing for stillness and solitude. I therefore decided for myself that I would go to a lodging at Tynemouth, where my medical brother-in-law could reach me by railway in twenty minutes, while I was removed from the bustle and smoke of Newcastle by an interval of nine miles. With an affectionate reluctance and grudging, my family let me try this as an experiment,—all of them being fully convinced that I could not long bear the solitude and monotony, after the life of excitement and constant variety to which I had been accustomed for above seven years. I was right, however, and they were wrong. On the sofa where I stretched myself after my drive to Tynemouth, on the sixteenth of March, 1840, I lay for nearly five years, till obedience to a newly-discovered law of nature raised me up, and sent me forth into the world again, for another ten years of strenuous work, and almost undisturbed peace and enjoyment of mind and heart.

I had two rooms on the first floor in this house of my honest hostess, Mrs. Halliday, who little imagined that March day, that the luck was happening to her of a lodger who would stay, summer and winter, for nearly five years. I had no servant with me at first ; for I was not only suddenly cut off from my literary engagements, and almost from the power of work, but I had invested £1,000 of my earnings in a deferred annuity, two years before ;—a step which seemed prudent at the time, and which I still consider to have been so ; but which deprived me of immediate resources. It was not long before two generous ladies, (sisters) old friends of mine, sent me, to my amazement, a bank note for £100, saying that my illness had probably interfered with certain plans which they knew I entertained. The generosity was of a kind which it was impossible to refuse, because it extended through me to others. I took the money, and applied it as intended. I need hardly say that when my working days and my prosperity returned, I repaid the sum, which was, as I knew it would be, lodged in the hands of sufferers as needy as I was when it came to me.

I was waited upon in my lodging by a sickly-looking, untidy little orphan girl of fourteen,—untidy, because the state of her eyes was such that she could not sew, or have any fair chance for cleanliness. She was the niece and dependent of my hostess, by whom she was scolded without mercy, and, it seemed to me, incessantly. Her quiet and cheerful submission impressed me at once : and I heard such a report of her from the lady who had preceded me in the lodgings and who had known the child from early infancy, that I took an interest in her, and studied her character from the outset. Her character was easily known ; for a more simple, upright, truthful, ingenuous child could not be. She was, in fact, as intellectually incapable as morally indisposed to deception of any kind. This was ' the girl Jane ' who recovered her health by mesmerism in companionship with me, and whom I was required by the doctors, and by the Athenæum, to ' give up' as ' an impostor,' after five years' household intercourse with her, in addition to my indirect knowledge of her, through my neighbour, from the age of three. I may mention here that my unvarying good opinion of her was confirmed after the recovery of both by the experience of her household qualities for seven

TYNEMOUTH.

FROM THE SICKROOM WINDOW.

years, during which period she lived with me as my cook, till she emigrated to Australia, where she has lived in high credit from the beginning of 1853 till now. This Jane, destined to so curious an experience, and to so discreditable a persecution (which she bore in the finest spirit), was at the door of my Tynemouth lodging when I arrived : and many were the heart-aches I had for her, during the years that her muscles looked like dough, and her eyes like .... I will not say what. I suffered from the untidiness of my rooms, I own ; and I soon found that my Norfolk notions of cleanliness met with no response at Tyne-mouth. Before long, I was shifted from purgatory to paradise in this essential matter. An uncle and some cousins, who had always been kind to me, were shocked to find that I was waited upon by only the people of the house ; and they provided me with a maid, who happened to be the cleanliest of her sex. She remained with me during the whole of my illness : and never, in all that time, did I see a needless grain of dust on the furniture, nor a speck on the window panes that was not removed next morning.

For the view from my window, and the details of my mode of life as an invalid I must refer all who wish to know my Tynemouth self to ' Life in the Sick-room.' They will find there what the sea and shore were to me, and how kind friends came to see me, and my family were at my call ; and for what reasons, and how peremptorily, I chose to live alone. One half year was rendered miserably burdensome by the cheating intrusion of an unwelcome and uncon-genial person who came (as I believed because I was told) for a month, and stayed seven, in a lodging next

door.   More serious mischiefs than the immediate
annoyance were caused by this unwarrantable liberty
taken with my comfort and convenience; and the
suffering occasioned by them set me back in health
not a little : but with the exception of that period, I
obtained the quiet I so needed and desired.

During the first half of the time, I was able to
work,—though with no great willingness, and with
such extreme exhaustion that it became at length
necessary to give up every exertion of the kind.
' Deerbrook' had come out in the spring of 1839,
just before my illness declared itself.   That conception
being wrought out and done with, I reverted to the
one which I had held in abeyance, through the
objections made to it by my friend Mrs. ————,
whom alone I consulted in such matters, and on whose
knowledge of books and taste in literature I reposed
my judgment.   Now that she was far away, my
affections sprang back to the character and fortunes
of Toussaint L'Ouverture.   I speedily made up my
mind to present that genuine hero with his actual
sayings and doings (as far as they were extant) to
the world.   When I had been some time at Tynemouth, finding my strength and spirits declining, I
gave up the practice of keeping a diary, for two
reasons which I now think good and sufficient;—
first, that I found it becoming a burden; and next
that a diary, kept under such circumstances, must be
mainly a record of frames and feelings,—many of
them morbid, and few fit for any but pathological
uses : but I cannot be sorry that I continued my
journal for some months, as it preserves the traces of
my progress in a work which I regard with some

affection, though, to say the truth, without any admiration whatever. I find, in the sickly hand-writing of that spring of 1840, notices of how my subject opened before me, and of how, as I lay gazing upon the moon-lit sea, in the evenings of April and May, new traits in the man, new links between the personages, and a clearer perception of the guiding principle of the work disclosed themselves to me. I find, by this record, that I wrote the concluding portion of 'The Hour and the Man' first, for the same reason that I am now writing the fifth period of this Memoir before the fourth,—lest I should not live to do the whole. It was on Saturday, the 2nd of May, 1840, that I began the book, with Toussaint's arrival at the Jura. My notice is that I was sadly tired with the effort, but more struck than ever with the springing up of ideas by the way, in the act of writing, so much more than in that of reading,—though in reading, the profit is more from the ideas suggested than from those received. This work was a resource, and some anxiety to me, all summer: on the 17th of November, I corrected the last proof-sheet, and before the end of the month, the opinions of my friends were, for the most part, known to me. I find in my diary of this period, under the date of November 26th, an entry which it may be worth while to give here, both as an authentication of some things I have said elsewhere, and as saving explanations which might appear like afterthoughts, in regard to a point in my character which has been important to my happiness, if not to matters of higher consequence. 'A letter from Moxon about the publication of my book holds out a very poor prospect. Under 500 copies are subscribed for. He offers me twenty-five copies more, both of it and of " Deerbrook," if I like to have them,—showing that he does not expect to sell them. If the book succeeds after this, it will be by its own merits purely. This seems the only good derivable from the news. Yet, as I sat at work, my spirits rose, the more I thought it over. It always is the way with me, and has been since I grew up, that personal mortifications (except such as arise from my own faults, and sometimes even then) put me in a happy state of mind. This is the news of all others (about my own affairs) which I had rather not have had: yet I don't know when I have been more cheery than now, in consesequence of it. It is always so with hostile reviewers; —the more brutal, the more animating, in a very little while. In that case it is that one's feelings are engrossed in concern for the perpetrators, and in an anxious desire to do them good,—and looking forward to the day when their feelings will be healthier.' The lighting upon this entry reminds me of some marked days of my literary life, made happy by this tendency in me; and especially the two days which might seem to have been the most mortifying;—that of the publication of the brutal review of my Political Economy series in the Quarterly, and that on which I received the news from the publisher of the total failure (as far as money was concerned) of my ' Forest and Game Law tales,'—of which no more than 2,000 copies have been sold to this day. In the first case, there was every sort of personal insult which could make a woman recoil; and in the other there was that sense of wasted labour which to me, with my strong economic faculty, was always excessively disa-

greeable : yet did both carry with them so direct an
appeal to one's inner force, and especially to one's
disinterestedness, that the reaction was immediate, and
the rebound from mortification to joyful acquiescence
was one of the most delightful experiences I have ever
had. Those several occasions are white days in the
calendar of my life.—As for the success of 'The
Hour and the Man' and 'Deerbrook,' it is enough to
say that both passed through two editions, and have
been purchased of me for a third.[1]

Before my book was well out, I had planned the
light and easy work (for which alone I was now fit)
of a series of children's tales, for which a friend then
nursing me suggested the capital title of 'The Playfellow.' While in spirits about the reception of my
novel, I conceived the plot of the first of those tales,
—'Settlers at Home,' concerning which I find this
entry in my diary. 'How curious it would be to
refer back to the sources of as many ideas as possible,
in any thing one writes! Tait's Magazine of last year
had an article of De Quincy's which made me think
of snow-storms for a story:—then it occurred to me
that floods were less hackneyed, and would do as well
for purposes of adventure and peril. But De Quincy's
tale (a true one) is fairly the origin of mine.—Floods
suggested Lincolnshire for the scene, and Lauder's
book (Sir Thomas Dick Lauder's "Floods in Moray-
shire," read many years before) for the material. For
Lincolnshire I looked into the Penny Cyclopedia, and
there found references to other articles,—particularly
"Axholme." Hence,—finding *gypsum* in that region,

---

[1] I find that 'The Hour and the Man' is re-issued.

—came the precise scene and occupations. A paragraph in a Poor Law Report on a gipsy "born in a long meadow," suggested (together with fishers and fowlers in the marshes) the Roger of my tale.' I finished this first of my four volumes of 'The Playfellow' by the end of the year,—of my first year of solitary residence at Tynemouth. The close was, on the whole, satisfactory. I found the wintry aspects of the sea wonderfully impressive, and sometimes very beautiful. I had been visited by affectionate members of my own family, and by friends,—one of whom devoted herself to me with a singular power of sympathy, and consummate nursing ability. I had reason to hope that my book had done good to the Anti-slavery cause by bringing into full notice the intellectual and moral genius of as black a negro as was ever seen ; and I had begun a new kind of work,—not too heavy for my condition of health, and sure of a prosperous circulation in Mr. Knight's hands. All this was more or less spoiled in actual experience by the state of incessant uneasiness of body and unstringing of nerves in which I was ; but it was one year of the five over, and I can regard it now, as I did even then (blank as was the future before me,) with some complacency. The remnant of life was not wholly lost, in regard to usefulness : and, as to the enjoyment, that was of small consequence.

The second volume of 'The Playfellow' was wrought upon the suggestion of a friend, for whose ability in instigation I had the highest respect. By this time I hardly needed further evidence that one mind cannot (in literature) work well upon the materials suggested by another: but if I had needed such

evidence, I found it here. The story of 'the Prince'
was by far the least successful of the set, except among
poor people, who read it with wonderful eagerness.
Some of them called it 'the French revelation,' and
the copy in Lending Libraries was more thumbed than
the others; but among children and the general
reading public, there was less interest about it than any
of the rest. I suppose other authors who have found,
as I have, that plenty of friends have advice to give
them how to write their books, (no two friends agreeing
in their advice) have also found themselves called self-
willed and obstinate, as I have, for not writing their
books in some other way than their own. In this case,
I liked the suggestion, and felt obliged by it, and did
my best with it ; and yet the result was a failure, in
comparison with those which were purely self-derived.
Throughout my whole literary career, I have found
the same thing happen; and I can assure any young
author who may ever read this that he need feel no
remorse, no misgiving about conceit or obstinacy, if
he finds it impossible to work so well upon the
suggestions of another mind as upon those of his own.
He will be charged with obstinacy and conceit, as I
have been. He is sure of that, at all events; for
among a dozen advisers, he *can* obey only one ; and
the other eleven will be offended. He had better
make it known, as I had occasion to do, that advice
is of value in any work of art when it is asked, and
not otherwise ; and that in a view more serious than
the artistic,—when convictions have to be uttered,—
advice cannot, by the very nature of things, be taken,
because no conscience can prescribe or act for another
—This seems to be the place for relating what my

own practice has been in this important matter. In
regard to literature, and all other affairs, my method
has been to ask advice very rarely,—always to follow
it when asked,—and rarely to follow unasked advice.
In other words, I have consulted those only whom I
believed to be the very best judges of the case in
hand ; and, believing them the very best judges, I
have of course been thankful for their guidance :
whereas, the officious givers of unsought advice are
pretty sure not to be good judges of the case in
hand ; and their counsel is therefore worth nothing
The case of criticism as to what is already wrought is
different. I have accepted or neglected that, according as it seemed to me sound or unsound; and I
believe I have accepted it much oftener than not. I
have adopted subjects suggested by others invariably
with ill-success. I have always declined assistance as
to the mode of treating my own subjects from persons
who could not possibly be competent to advise, for
want of knowing my point of view, my principle, and
my materials. I was rather amused, a few weeks ago,
by the proffer of a piece of counsel, by an able man
who, on the mere hearing that I was too ill to defer any
longer the writing of this Memoir, wrote to me his advice how to do it,—to make it amusing, and ' not too
abstract,' &c., &c., while in total ignorance of the
purposes with which I was undertaking the labour,—
whether to make an ' amusing ' book, or for a more
serious object. It reminded me of an incident which
I may relate here, though it occurred three years
before the time under notice. It is so immediately
connected with the topic I am now treating, that
there could not be a better place for it.

When I was writing ' Society in America,' a lady of my acquaintance sat down in a determined manner, face to face with me, to ask me some questions. A more kind-hearted woman could not be ; but her one requirement was that all her friends,—or at least all her protégés,—should let her manage their affairs for them,—either with her own head and hands, or by sending round her intelligence or her notions, so as to get somebody else to do the managing before the curtain while she prompted from behind. This lady brought her sister up to me, one day, in her own house, and they asked me, point blank, whether I was going to say any thing about this, that, and the other, in my book on America. Among the rest, they asked whether I was going to say something about the position of women in the United States. I replied ' Of course. My subject is Society in America ; and women constitute one half of it.' They entreated me ' to omit that.' I told them that the thing was done ; and that, when the book appeared, they would see that it was necessary. Finding me impracticable (conceited and obstinate, of course) they next called on my mother, for the purpose of alarming her into using her influence with me. They reckoned without their host, however ; for my mother was thoroughly sound in doctrine, and just and generous in practice, on that great matter. She told them that she never interfered with my work,—both because she considered herself incompetent to judge till she knew the whole bearing of it, and because she feared it would be turned into patch-work if more minds than one were employed upon it without concert. Foiled in this direction, the anxious meddler betook

herself to a mutual friend,—a literary man,—the
Edinburgh reviewer of my Political Economy tales,—
and most unwarrantably engaged his interference. He
did not come to me, or write, but actually sent a
message through a third friend, (who was most reluctant to convey it) requesting me to say nothing
about the position of women in America, for fear of
the consequences from the unacceptableness of the
topic, &c., &c.   When matters had come to this pass,
it was clear that I must plainly assert the principle of
authorship and the rights of authors, or be subject to
the interference of meddlers, and in constant danger
of quarrels from that time forward.   I therefore
wrote to my reviewer the letter which I will here cite.
It was not sent at once, because our intermediary
feared it would hurt him so deeply as to break off our
intercourse : but he questioned her so closely as to
learn that there *was* a letter; and then he read it,
declared we could never quarrel, and sent the reply
which, in fairness to him, I append to my letter. The
reply shows that he no more discerned the principle of
the case after reading my letter than before; and in
fact, if he had been restricted in his habit of advising
every body on all occasions, he would have felt his
occupation gone : but his kindly and generous temper
abundantly compensated for that serious mistake in
judgment, and our good understanding remained un-
impaired to the day of his death.

'March 5th, 1837.
  My dear friend,

    'I have received through Mrs. W———a message
from you, advising me not to put into my book any opinions concerning what are vulgarly called the "Rights of Woman."
    ' My replying to you is rendered unnecessary by the fact that

what I have to say on that subject at present has been printed these two months : but I think it desirable to write, to settle at once and for ever this matter of interference with opinions, or the expression of them. You and I differ so hopelessly on the very principle of the matter, that I have no expectation of converting you : but my declaration of my own principle may at least guide you in future as to how to treat me on such matters.

'I say nothing to *you* of the clear impertinence (in some through whom I conclude you had your information) of questioning an author as to what is to be in his book, in order to remonstrate, and get others to remonstrate, against it. You will agree with me in this. It was in answer to questions only that I mentioned the subject at all to some friends of ours.

'Nor need I tell you how earnestly I have been besought by various persons to say nothing about Democracy, nothing about Slavery, Commerce, Religion, &c.; and again, to write about nothing else but each of these. In giving me advice how to write my book, you are only following a score of other friends, who have for the most part far less weight with me.

'But you ought to know better than they what it is to write a book. You surely must know that it is one of the most sacred acts of conscience to settle with one's own intellect what is really and solemnly believed, and is therefore to be simply and courageously spoken. You ought to be aware that no second mind can come into the council at all ;—can judge as to what are the actual decisions of the intellect, or felt obligations of the conscience.—If you regard a book in the other aspect, of a work of Art, are you not aware that only one mind can work out the conceptions of one mind ? If you would not have the sculptor instructed how to bring out his Apollo ; or Handel helped to make an oratorio,— on the same principle you should not interfere with the very humblest efforts of the humblest writer who really has anything to say. In the present case, the appearance of my book will show you the impossibility of anyone who does not know the scheme of it being able to offer acceptable advice. I analyse society in America,—of which women constitute the half. I test all by their own avowed democratic principles. The result, you see, is inevitable.

'Either you think the opinions objectionable, or you kindly fear the consequences to myself, or act from a more general regard to my influence. Probably you are under all three fears. If the opinions are objectionable, controvert them. The press is as open to you as to me. But do not seek to suppress the persuasions of a mind which, for aught you know, has been as patient, and careful, and industrious in ascertaining its convictions as your own.

'Perhaps you fear for my influence. I fully agree with an American friend of mine who says, in answer to the same plea addressed to him as an Abolitionist, "I do not know what influence is good for if it is not to be used." For my own part, I have never sought influence : and by God's blessing I never will seek it, nor study how to use it, as influence. This is a care which God has never appointed to creatures so incapable of foresight as we are. Happily, all we have to do is to be true in thought and speech. What comes of our truth is a care which we may cast, with our other cares, upon Him.

'This is answer enough to your kind concern for myself. I know well enough what are likely to be the consequences of a perfectly free expression of opinion on any moral subject whatever. I will not say how I can bear them : but I must try. You and I differ as to what I can do; and what, if I am to render any service to society, is the kind of service which I am likely to render. You estimate what would be commonly called my talent far higher than I do. We will not dispute about what can be proved only by the event. But I will tell you what I *know*, —that any human being, however humble or liable to error, may render an essential service to society by making, through a whole lifetime, a steady, uncompromising, dispassionate declaration of his convictions as they are matured. This is the duty to which I some time ago addressed myself. What my talents, my influence, my prosperity may turn out to be, I care little. What my fidelity may be eventually proved to have been, I do care,—more than for life, and all that makes life so sweet as it is. My best friends will not seek to divert me from my aim.

'You may think I am making too serious a matter of this. I can only say that I think it a very serious one. The encroachment of mind upon mind should be checked in its smallest beginning, for the sake of the young and timid who shrink from asserting their own liberty.

'May I ask you not to destroy this letter : but to keep it as a check upon any future solicitudes which may arise out of your friendship for me ?   When shall we see you ?

'Believe me, &c., &c.,

'H. MARTINEAU.'

'My dear friend,

'Many thanks for the unreservedness of your letter, which I only got yesterday, when I called on Mrs. W————. It sets me quite at ease, in this instance, on the serious question of self-reproach at the reluctance and almost cowardice with which I usually set about to offer my advice to my friends. It would be personally an infinite relief to me if all those in whom I am interested would release me from what I feel to be one of the most painful obligations of friendship, by telling me, with equal frankness, that advice tendered under any of the points of view which you enumerate was an undue encroachment of mind on mind.

'Do not imagine that my personal interest in your happiness and usefulness will be one jot less sincere when the expression of it is limited within the conditions which you require.

'If I can call to-day, &c., &c.,

'W. EMPSON.'

I will add only one more incident in connexion with this subject. The friend who suggested the taking the life of Louis XVII. for my tale was one of my rebukers for not taking counsel;—that is, for not adopting all his suggestions when he would suggest a dozen volumes in the course of a single evening. I adopted more of his than of any body's, because I often admired them. (I wrote 'How to Observe' at his request, and a good many things besides.) He one day desired to be allowed to see and criticise the first chapter of my 'Retrospect of Western Travel.' I gave him the MS. at night; and in the morning he produced it, covered with pencil marks. I found on examination, and I convinced him, that he had altered about half the words;—on an average, every other word in the chapter: and I put it to him what would become of my book if I submitted the MS.

to other friendly critics, equally anxious to deal with it.   He could not answer the question, of course ; so he called me conceited and obstinate, and I rubbed out his pencil marks,—-without any detriment on either side to our friendship.   My chapter would have cut a curious figure, dressed in his legal phraseology ; as I should expect his legal opinions to do, if I were to express them in my own unprofessional style.   Painters complain of interference : musicians, I believe, do not. Amateurs let *them* alone.   It is to be hoped that, some time or other, literary works of art,—to say nothing of literary utterance being a work of conscience,— will be left to the artist to work out, according to his own conception and conviction.   At present, it seems as if few but authors had any comprehension whatever of the seriousness of writing a book.

There is something to be told about the origin of the third volume of ' The Playfellow.'   I had nearly fixed on a subject of a totally different kind when Mr. Laing's book on Norway fell in my way, and set my imagination floating on the fiords, and climbing the slopes of the Dovre Fjeld.   I procured Inglis's Travels and every thing that I could get hold of about the state of Norway while connected with Denmark; and hence arose ' Feats on the Fiord.'   Two or three years afterwards, a note from Mr. Laing to a relative of his in Scotland travelled round to me, in which he inquired whether his relative could tell him, or could learn, when and for how long I had resided in Norway, as he concluded I had, on the evidence of that story. I had the pleasure of transmitting to him the fact that I knew scarcely any thing about Norway, and had chosen another scene and subject, when his book caught

my fancy, and became the originator of my tale.   I
hope he enjoyed the incident as much as I did.

The fourth and last volume,—' The Crofton Boys,'
—was written under the belief that it was my last
word through the press.   There are some things in it
which I could not have written except under that persuasion.   By that time, I was very ill, and so sunk in
strength that it was obvious that I must lay aside the
pen.   I longed to do so ; and yet I certainly had
much enjoyment in the free outpouring of that book.
When it was sealed up and sent, I stretched myself on
my sofa, and said to myself, with entire sincerity, that
my career as an author was closed.   I find an entry in
my Diary of the extreme need in which I was,—not
of idleness, but of my mind being free of all *engagement* to work.   I was under the constant sense of
obligation to do what I am doing now,—to write my
life ; but otherwise I was at liberty and leisure.   The
strictest economy in my way of living was necessary
from the time of my ceasing to earn ; but my relations
now, as I explained before, enabled me to have a servant.   My lodgings were really the only considerable
expense I had besides ; for I had left off dining from
total failure of appetite, and my consumption of food
had become so small that the wonder was how life
could be supported upon it.

To finish the subject of my authorship during this
period, I will now tell how my anonymous volume,
'Life in the Sick-room,' came into existence, and how
I, who never had a secret before or since, (as far as
I can now remember) came to have one then.—In
the book itself it is seen what I have to say on the
subject of sympathy with the sick.   When I had been

living for above three years alone (for the most part)
and with merely the change from one room to another,
—from bed to sofa,—in constant uneasiness, and
under the depression caused both by the nature of my
disease and by heavy domestic cares, I had accu-
mulated a weight of ideas and experiences which I
longed to utter, and which indeed I needed to cast off.
I need not repeat (what is amply explained in the
book) that it was wholly my own doing that I lived
alone, and why such was my choice; and the letters
which I afterwards received from invalids satisfied me,
and all who saw those letters, that my method was
rational and prudent. It was not because I was destitute of kind nurses and visitors that I needed to pour
out what was in my mind, but because the most perfect
sympathy one can meet with in any trial common to
humanity is reached by an appeal to the whole mind
of society.   It was on the fifteenth of September
1843 that this mode of relief occurred to me, while I
lay on my sofa at work on my inexhaustible resource,
fancy-work. I kept no diary at that time; but I find
inserted under that date in a note-book, ' A new and
imperative idea occurred to me,—" Essays from a Sick-
room."' This conception was certainly the greatest
refreshment I had during all those heavy years.
During the next few days, while some of my family
were with me, I brooded over the idea; and on the
nineteenth, I wrote the first of the Essays. I never
wrote anything so fast as that book. It went off like
sleep. I was hardly conscious of the act, while writing
or afterwards,—so strong was the need to speak.   I
wrote the Essays as the subject pressed, and not in the
order in which they stand. As I could not speak of

them to any body I suspended the indulgence of writing them while receiving the visits which I usually had in October,—preparatory to the long winter solitude ; and it was therefore November when I finished my volume. I wrote the last Essay on the fourth. It was now necessary to tell one person ;— viz., a publisher. I wrote confidentially to Mr. Moxon who, curiously enough, wrote to me on the same day, (so that our letters crossed,) to ask whether I was not able, after so long an interval of rest, to promise him some work to publish. My letter had a favourable reception : he carefully considered my wishes, and kept my secret, and I corrected my last proof on the twenty-sixth of November. On the seventh of December, the first news of the volume being out arrived in the shape of other letters than Mr. Moxon's. I was instantly and universally detected, as I had indeed supposed must be the case. On that day my mother and eldest sister came over from Newcastle to see me. It was due to them not to let them hear such a fact in my history from the newspapers or from strangers; so, assuring them that it was the first time I had opened my lips on the subject, and that Mr. Moxon was the only person who had known it at all, I told them what I had done, and lent them my copy to take home. They were somewhat hurt, as were one or two more distant friends, who had no manner of right to be so. It proved to me how little reticence I can boast of, or have the credit for, that several friends confidently denied that the book was mine, on the ground that I had not told them a word about it,—a conviction in which I think them perfectly justified. There could not be a stronger proof of how I *felt* that book than my inability to speak of it except to my unknown comrades in suffering.   My mother and sister had a special trial, I knew, to bear in discovering how great my suffering really was: and I could not but see that it was too much for them, and that from that time forward they were never again to me what they had been.

What the 'success' of the book was, the fact of a speedy sale of the whole edition presently showed. What my own opinion of it is, at the distance of a dozen years, it may be worth while to record.   My note-book of that November says that I wrote the Essays from the heart, and that there never was a truer book as to conviction.   Such being the fact, I can only now say that I am ashamed, considering my years and experience of suffering, that my state of mind was so crude, if not morbid, as I now see it to have been.   I say this, not from any saucy elevation of health and prosperity, but in an hour of pain and feebleness, under a more serious and certainly fatal illness than that of 1843, and after ten intervening years of health and strength, ease and prosperity.   All the facts in the book, and some of the practical doctrine of the sick-room, I could still swear to: but the magnifying of my own experience, the desperate concern as to my own ease and happiness, the moaning undertone running through what many people have called the stoicism, and the total inability to distinguish between the metaphysically apparent and the positively true, make me, to say the truth, heartily despise a considerable part of the book.   Great allowance is to be made, no doubt, for the effect of a depressing malady, and of the anxieties which caused it, and for an exile of years from fresh air, exercise, and change of scene.   Let such allowance be made ; but the very demand shows that the book is morbid, —or that part of it which needs such allowance. Stoical!   Why, if I had been stoical I should not have written the book at all :—not *that* book ; but, if any, one wholly clear of the dismal self-consciousness which I then thought it my business to detail.   The fact is, as I now see, that I was lingering in the metaphysical stage of mind, because I was not perfectly emancipated from the *débris* of the theological.   The day of final release from both was drawing nigh, as I shall have occasion to show : but I had not yet ascertained my own position.   I had quitted the old untenable point of view, and had not yet found the one on which I was soon to take my stand.   And, while attesting the truth of the book on the whole, —its truth as a reflexion of my mind of that date, —I still can hardly reconcile with sincerity the religious remains that are found in it. To be sure, they are meagre and incoherent enough ; but, such as they are, they are compatible, I fear, with only a metaphysical and not a positive order of sincerity.   I had not yet learned, with decision and accuracy, what *conviction* is. I had yet no firm grasp of it ; and I gave forth the contemporary persuasions of the imagination, or narratives of old traditions, as if they had been durable convictions, ascertained by personal exertion of my faculties. I suffered the retribution of this unsound dealing,—the results of this crude state of mind,—in the latent fear and blazoned pain through which I passed during that period; and if any one now demurs to my present judgment, on the score of lapse

of time and change of circumstances, I would just
remind him that I am again ill, as hopelessly, and
more certainly fatally, than I was then. I cannot be
mistaken in what I am now feeling so sensibly from
day to day,—that my condition is bliss itself in
comparison with that of twelve years ago; and that
I am now above the reach (while my brain remains
unaffected by disease) of the solicitudes, regrets,
apprehensions, self-regards, and in-bred miseries of
various kinds, which breathe through these Sick-room
Essays, even where the language appears the least
selfish and cowardly. I should not now write a Sick-
room book at all, except for express pathological
purposes : but, if I did, I should have a very different
tale to tell. If not, the ten best years of my life,—
the ten which intervened between the two illnesses,—
would have been lost upon me.

Before I dismiss this book, I must mention that its
publisher did his duty amply by it and me. I told
him at first to say nothing to me about money, as I
could not bear to think of selling such an experience
while in the midst of it. Long after, when I was in
health and strength, he wrote that circumstances had
now completely changed, and that life was again open
before me; and he sent me a cheque for £75. On
occasion of another edition, he sent me £50 more.

The subject of money reminds me that by this time
a matter was finally settled which appears of less
consequence to me than many have supposed,—
probably because my mind was clear on the point
when the moment of action came. On my first going
to reside in London, at the end of 1832, a friend of
Lord Brougham's told me that there was an intention

on the part of government to give me a pension which should make me independent for life.   The story then told me I believed, of course, though it was not long bofore I found that it was almost entirely one of Lord Brougham's imaginations or fictions.   He said that Lord Grey, then Premier, wished to make me independent, that I might not be tempted, or compelled, to spend my powers (such as they were) on writing for periodicals : that he (Lord Brougham) had spoken to the King about it, and that the King had said divers gracious things on the occasion ; but that the two Ministers had judged it best for me to wait till my Political Economy Series was finished, lest the Radicals should charge me with having been bought by the Whigs.   Fully believing this story, I consulted, confidentially, three friends,—a Tory friend, my Whig Edinburgh reviewer, and my brother James.   The first two counselled my accepting the pension,—seeing no reason why I should not.   My brother advised my declining it.   If it had then been offered, I believe I should have accepted it, with some doubt and misgiving, and simply because I did not then feel able to assign sufficient reasons for doing an ungracious act. —The next I heard of the matter was a year afterwards, when I was two-thirds through my long work. Lord Durham then told me, after inquiring of Lord Grey, that the subject had never been mentioned to the King at all ; but that Lord Grey intended that it should be, and that I should have my pension.   Some months afterwards, when I was about to go to America, Lord Grey sent to Lord Durham for my address, for the avowed purpose of informing me of the intended gift.   I left England immediately after, and fully

understood that, on my return, I should be made easy
for life by a pension of £300 a year. Presently, the
Whigs went out, and Sir R. Peel was Premier for five
months, to be succeeded by the Whigs, who were in
power on my return. But, meantime, my mind had
become clear about refusing the pension. When at a
distance from the scene of my labours, and able to
think quietly, and to ascertain my own feelings at
leisure, the latent repugnance to that mode of provision came up again, and I was persuaded that I
should lose more independence in one way than I
should gain in another. I wrote to Lord Durham
from America, requesting him to beg of Lord Grey
that the idea might be laid aside, and that no application might be made to me which would compel me to
appear ungrateful and ungracious. Lord Grey saw
that letter of mine ; and I supposed and hoped that
the whole subject was at an end.

After my return, however, and repeatedly during
the next two years (1837 and 1838) some friends of
the government, who were kind friends of my own,
remonstrated with me about my refusal. I could
never make them understand the ground of my dislike of a pension. One could see in it nothing but
pride, and held up to me the name of Southey, and
others whom I cordially honoured, and told me that I
might well accept what they had not demurred to.
Another chid me for practically censuring all acceptors
of pensions ; whereas, it was so earnestly my desire to
avoid all appearance of such insolence and narrowness,
that I entreated that the express offer might not be
made. As for Lord Brougham, he said testily, before
many hearers, when my name was mentioned,--

' Harriet Martineau ! I hate her ! ' Being asked
why, he replied, ' I hate a woman who has opinions.
She has refused a pension,—making herself out to be
better than other people.' Having done all I could
to be quiet about the matter, and to avoid having to
appear to imply a censure of other people by an open
refusal, I took these misconstructions as patiently as I
could ; and I can sincerely declare that I never did,
in my inmost mind, judge any receiver of a pension
by my own action in a matter which was more one
of feeling than of judgment or principle. When my
part was taken beyond recal, a friend of mine showed
me cause for belief that it would have been convenient
for me to have accepted a pension at that time, on
account of an exposure of some jobbery, and a consequent stir about the bestowal of pensions. Certainly,
the few most popular pensioners' names were paraded
in parliament and the newspapers in a way which I
should not relish ; and though no suspicion of my
name being desired for justificatory reasons had any
thing to do with my refusal, I was more than ever
satisfied with what I had done when I saw the course
that matters were taking.

The subject was revived at the close of 1840,
through an old friend of mine ; and again in August
1841, just before Lord Melbourne went out of
office. Mr. Charles Buller wrote to me to say
that Lord Melbourne understood how my earnings
were invested (in a deferred annuity) and was
anxious to give me present ease in regard to money :
that he was sorry to have no more to offer at the
moment than £150 a year, (which however I was
given to understand might be increased when oppor-

tunity offered ; and that my answer must be immediate, as Lord Melbourne was going out so soon as to
require the necessary information by return of post.
I was very ill the evening that this letter arrived,—
too ill to write myself : but my brother Robert and
his wife happened to be with me ; and my brother
transmitted my reply.*   I did not feel a moment's
hesitâtion about it.   While fully sensible of Lord
Melbourne's kindness, I felt that I could not, with
satisfaction to myself, accept such a boon at his hands,
or as a matter of favouritism from any minister.   I
should have proudly and thankfully accepted ease and
independence in the form of a pension bestowed by
parliament, or by some better judge than Minister or
Sovereign can easily be : but, distinct and generous
as were the assurances given that the pension was
offered for past services, and ought not to interfere
with my political independence, I felt that practically
the sense of obligation would weigh heavily upon me,
and that I could never again feel perfectly free to
speak my mind on politics.   At that time, too, the
popular adversity was very great ; and I preferred
sharing the poverty of the multitude to being helped
out of the public purse.   From time to time since, I
have been made sensible of the prudence of my decision ; and especially in regard to that large undertaking of a subsequent period,—my 'History of the
Thirty Years' Peace.'   No person in receipt of a
pension from government, bestowed by Lord Mel-
burne, could have written that History ; and I have
had more satisfaction and pleasure from that work

* Appendix C.

than any amount of pension could have given me.
My family,—the whole clan,—behaved admirably
about the business, except the adviser in the former
case, who had changed his mind, and blamed me for
my decision. All the rest, whether agreeing with
me or not as to my reasons or feelings, said very
cordially, that, as such were my reasons and feelings,
I had done rightly; and very cheering to me, in those
sickly days of anxious conscience, was their generous
approval. Some of the newspapers insulted me: but
I did not care for that. All the mockery of strangers
all over the world could be nothing in comparison
with the gratification afforded by one incident, with
which the honoured name of Lady Byron is connected.
Lady Byron, with whom I had occasionally corresponded, wrote to a visitor of mine at that time that
henceforth no one could pity me for narrow circumstances which were my own free choice: but that she
thought it hard that I should not have the pleasure
of helping people poorer than myself. She had
actually placed in the bank, and at my disposal,
£100 for beneficent purposes: and, lest there should
be any possible injury to me from the circumstances
becoming known, she made the money payable to
another person. How rich and how happy I felt
with that £100! It lasted nearly the whole time of
my illness; and I trust it was not ill-spent.

During the whole time of my illness, comforts and
pleasures were lavishly supplied to me. Sydney Smith
said that every body who sent me game, fruit and
flowers was sure of Heaven, provided always that they
punctually paid the dues of the Church of England.
If so, many of my friends are safe. Among other

memorials of that time which are still preserved and
prized in my home are drawings sent me by the Miss
Nightingales, and an envelope-case, (in daily use) from
the hands of the immortal Florence.   I was one of
the sick to whom she first ministered; and it happened
through my friendship with some of her family.

Some time after the final settlement of this pension
business, some friends of mine set about the generous
task of raising a Testimonial Fund for my benefit.
It is necessary for me to offer the statement, as expressly and distinctly as possible, that I had nothing
whatever to do with this proceeding, and that I did
every thing in my power to avoid knowing any particulars while the scheme was in progress.   This
declaration, indispensable to my honour, is rendered
necessary by the behaviour of one person whose indiscretion and double-dealing involved me in trouble
about the testimonial business.   It is enough to say
here that so determined was I to hear nothing of the
particulars of the affair that, when I found it impossible to prevent that officious person telling me all she
knew, and representing me as compelling her to tell
it, in excuse for her own indiscretion, I engaged my
aunts, who were then lodging close by, to come in
whenever that visitor entered,—to stop her when she
spoke on the forbidden subject, and to bear witness
that it was my resolute purpose to hear nothing about
it.   One of my dear aunts was always instantly on
the spot, accordingly, to the discomfiture of the gossip,
who complained that she never saw me alone : and at
last, (but not till I was liable to serious injury in the
minds of many people) I succeeded in being so completely outside of the affair as to be ignorant of all

but the first steps taken. To this day I have never seen the list of subscribers, nor heard, probably, more than ten or twelve of them. The money raised was mainly invested, with the entire approbation of the managers of the business, in the Long Annuities,— the object being to obtain the largest income procurable from £1,400 for the period during which it was then supposed that I might live. I have since enjoyed ten years of health, (after many months more of that sickness) and it seemed probable that I should outlive that investment. Now again the scene is changed; and it appears that I shall leave the remnant of the kindly gift behind me. I do not know that I could better express the relief and satisfaction that I derived from that movement of my friends than by citing here the circular in which I made my acknowledgments.

'TO THE CONTRIBUTORS TO A TESTIMONIAL TO
H. MARTINEAU.

'My dear friends,

'To reach you individually from my retirement is not very easy; and to convey to you the feelings with which I accept your kindness is impossible: yet I cannot but attempt to present to each of you my acknowledgments, and the assurance of the comfort I feel, from day to day, in the honour and independence which you have conferred upon me. By your generous testimony to my past services you have set me free from all personal considerations, in case of my becoming capable of future exertion. The assurance which I possess of your esteem and sympathy will be a stimulus to labour, if I find I have still work to do: and if I remain in my present useless condition, it will be a solace to me under suffering, and a cordial under the depressions of illness and confinement.

'I am, with affectionate gratitude,

'Your Friend and Servant,

'Tynemouth,   'HARRIET MARTINEAU.'
October 22nd, 1843.'

SECTION II.

AFTER what I have said of my Sick-room Essays, which were written only the year before my recovery, it may seem strange to say that my mind made a progress worth noting during the five heavy years from 1839 to 1844 : but, small as my achievements now appear to me, there *was* achievement.   A large portion of the transition from religious inconsistency and irrationality to free-thinking strength and liberty was gone over during that period.   Not only had I abundant leisure for thought, and undiminished faculty of thought, but there was abundance of material for that kind of meditation which usually serves as an introduction to a higher.   I was not yet intellectually capable of a wide philosophical survey, nor morally bold enough for a deep investigation in regard to certain matters which I had always taken for granted : but the old and desultory questions—such as that of ' a divine government,' a ' future life,' and so on— were pressed upon me by the events and experiences of those years.   At the outset of the period, my revered and beloved friend, Dr. Follen, was lost by the burning of the Lexington steam-packet, under circumstances which caused anguish to all who heard

the story. Just about the same time, my old instructor,
who had for years of my youth been my idol, Dr.
Carpenter, perished in a singularly impressive manner,
—by being thrown overboard, no doubt by a lurch of
the steamer in which he was traversing the Medi-
terranean. The accident happened in the evening, so
that he was not missed till the morning. The hour
was shown by the stopping of his watch,—his body
being afterwards cast upon the Italian coast. A
strange and forlorn mode of death for a minister, the
idol of a host of disciples, and for a family-man whose
children would thankfully, any one of them, have
given their lives to prolong his !—During that period,
my grandmother, the head of one side of our house,
died ; and, on the other, the beloved old aunt who had
lived with us, and the old uncle whose effectual
sympathy in my great enterprise of the Political
Economy Series I described in its place ; and three
cousins of my own generation ; and a nephew
of the generation below. Several friends of my
father and mother, to whom I had looked up during
my childhood and youth, slipped away during the
period when I was lying waiting for death as my
release from dreary pain : and also a whole group of
my political friends, acquired since I entered the world
of literature. Lord and Lady Durham died, after
having sympathised with me in my illness ; and Lord
Sydenham, who had made me known to them in
my writings : and Lord Congleton : and Thomas
Drummond, who had been the medium of some of my
communications with Lord Grey's government : and
Lord Henley, who had suggested and determined my
going to America : and old Lord Leicester, who had

been, under the name of Mr. Coke, my early ideal of
the patriot gentleman of England; and others of less
note, or a remoter interest to myself.   Most various
and impressive had been the modes of their death.
Some few by mere old age and ordinary disease; but
others by heart-break, by over-anxious toil in the
public service, by suicide, and by insanity!   Then,
among my American friends, there were several whom
I had left not long before, in the full exercise of important functions, and in the bright enjoyment of
life;—Judge Porter of Louisiana, one of the leading
Senators of the United States, and perhaps the most
genial and merry of my American friends; Dr. Henry
Ware, the model of a good clergyman; and Dr.
Channing, who had just cheered me by his fervent
blessing on my portraiture of Toussaint L'Ouverture.
And then again, there were literary men who were
much connected with the last preceding phase of my
life;—Southey, after his dreary decline, and Campbell;
and Dr. Dalton, who remains a venerable picture in
my memory; and John Murray, who had refused
(with hesitation) to publish 'Deerbrook,' and had
found the refusal a mistake.   And there were others,
who were living influences to me, as they were to
multitudes more who had never seen them,—as
Grace Darling, of whom every storm of that same sea
reminded me.   The departure of these and many
more kept the subject of death vividly before me, and
compelled me to reduce my vague and fanciful speculations on 'the divine government' and human
destiny to a greater precision and accuracy.   The old
perplexity about the apparent cruelty and injustice of
the scheme of 'divine government' began at last to

suggest the right issue. I had long perceived the worse than uselessness of enforcing principles of justice and mercy by an appeal to the example of God. I had long seen that the orthodox fruitlessly attempt to get rid of the difficulty by presenting the two-fold aspect of God,—the Father being the model of justice, and the Son of love and mercy,—the inevitable result being that he who is especially called God is regarded as an unmitigated tyrant and spontaneous torturer, while the sweeter and nobler attributes are engrossed by the man Jesus,—whose fate only deepens the opprobrium of the Divine cruelty: while the heretics whose souls recoil from such a doctrine, and who strive to explain away the recorded dogmas of tyranny and torture, in fact give up the Christian revelation by rejecting its essential postulates. All this I had long seen: and I now began to obtain glimpses of the conclusion which at present seems to me so simple that it is a marvel why I waited for it so long;—that it is possible that we human beings, with our mere human faculty, may not understand the scheme, or nature, or fact of the universe! I began to see that we, with our mere human faculty, are not in the least likely to understand it, any more than the minnow in the creek, as Carlyle has it, can comprehend the perturbations caused in his world of existence by the tides. I saw that no revelation can by possibility set men right on these matters, for want of faculty in man to understand any thing beyond human ken; as all instruction whatever offered to the minnow must fail to make it comprehend the action of the moon on the oceans of the earth, or receive the barest conception of any such action.

Thus far I began to see now. It was not for long
after that I perceived further that the conception itself
of moral government, of moral qualities, of the necessity of a preponderance of happiness over misery,
must be essentially false beyond the sphere of human
action, because it relates merely to human faculties.
But this matter,—of a truer stand-point,—will be
better treated hereafter, in connexion with the period
in which I perceived it within my horizon. As to
death and the question of a future life,—I was some
time in learning to be faithful to my best light,—
faint as it yet was. I remember asserting to a friend
who was willing to leave that future life a matter of
doubt, that we were justified in expecting whatever
the human race had agreed in desiring. I had long
seen that the 'future life' of the New Testament
was the Millennium looked for by the apostles, according to Christ's bidding,—the glorious reign of 1,000
years in Judea, when the Messiah should be the
Prince, and his apostles his councillors and functionaries, and which was to begin with the then
existing generation. I had long given up, in moral
disgust, the conception of life after death as a matter
of compensation for the ills of humanity, or a police
and penal resource of 'the divine government.' I
had perceived that the doctrines of the immortality
of the soul and the resurrection of the body were
incompatible ; and that, while the latter was clearly
impossible, we were wholly without evidence of the
former. But I still resorted, in indolence and prejudice, to the plea of instinct,—the instinctive
and universal love of life, and inability to conceive of
its extinction. My Sick-room book shows that such

was my view when I wrote those essays : but I now feel pretty certain that I was not, even then, dealing truly with my own mind,—that I was unconsciously trying to gain strength of conviction by vigour of assertion. It seems to me now that I might then have seen how delusive, in regard to fact. are various genuine and universal instincts ; and, again, that this direction of the instinct in question is by no means so universal and so uniform as I declared it to be. I might then have seen, if I had been open-minded, that the instinct to fetishism, for instance, is more general,—is indeed absolutely universal, while it is false in regard to fact; and that it is, in natural course, overpowered and annihilated by higher instincts, leading to true knowledge.

In such progress as I did make, I derived great assistance from the visits of a remarkable variety of friends, and from the confidence reposed in me during tête-à-tête conversations, such as could hardly have occurred under any other circumstances. Some dear old friends came, one at a time, and established themselves at the inn or in lodgings near, for weeks together, and spent with me such hours of the day as I could render (by opiates) fit for converse with them. Others stopped at Tynemouth, in the midst of a journey, and gave me a day or two ; and with many I had a single interview which was afterwards remembered with pleasure. During many a summer evening, while I lay on my window-couch, and my guest of the day sat beside me, overlooking the purple sea, or watching for the moon to rise up from it, like a planet growing into a sun, things were said, high and deep, which are fixed into my memory now, like stars in a dark firmament. Now a philosopher, now a poet, now a moralist, opened to me speculation, vision, or conviction ; and numerous as all the speculations, visions and convictions together, were the doubts confided to my meditation and my discretion. I am not going to violate any confidence here, of course, which I have considered sacred in life. I refer to these conversations with the thoughtful and the wise merely to acknowledge my obligations to them, and to explain certain consequences to myself which may perhaps be best conveyed by an anecdote.—During the latter part of my Tynemouth sojourn, a friend, who could minister to me in all manner of ways except philosophy, was speaking of the indispensableness of religion, and of her mode of religion especially, to a good state of mind. Not at all agreeing with her, I told her I had had a good deal of opportunity of knowing states of mind since I lay down on that sofa ; and that what I had seen had much deepened the impression which I had begun to have long before,—that the best state of mind was to be found, however it might be accounted for, in those who were called philosophical atheists. Her exclamation of amazement showed me that I had said something very desperate : but the conversation had gone too far to stop abruptly. She asked me what on earth I could mean : and I was obliged to explain. I told her that I knew several of that class,—some avowed and some not ; and that I had for several years felt that they were among my most honoured acquaintances and friends ; and that now that I knew them more deeply and thoroughly, I must say that, for conscientiousness, sincerity, integrity, seriousness, effective intellect, and the true religious spirit, I knew nothing

like them. She burst out a laughing, and said she
could conceive how, amidst fortunate circumstances,
they might have been trained to morality ; but how
they could have the religious spirit, she could in no
way conceive. It seemed to her absolute nonsense.
I explained what I meant, being very careful, according
to my state of mind at that time, to assure her that I
was not of their way of thinking : nevertheless, it did
seem to me, I said, that the philosophical atheists were
the most humble-minded in the presence of the mys-
teries of the universe, the most equable in spirit and
temper amidst the affairs of life, the most devout in
their contemplation of the unknown, and the most
disinterested in their management of themselves, and
their expectations from the human lot ;—showing, in
short, the moral advantages of knowledge (however
limited) and of freedom (however isolated and mournful) over superstition as shared by the multitude. I
have reason to believe that, amazed as my visitor was,
she was not so struck as to derive benefit from the
statement of an unusual experience like mine, in my
sudden translation from the vividness of literary and
political life in London to the quietness of the sick-
room and its converse. She had not forgotten the
conversation many years afterwards : but it had not
borne fruit to her. On the contrary, she was so
shocked at my opinions, as avowed in the ' Letters on
Man's Nature and Development' as to be one of the
very few who retreated from intercourse with me on
account of them. There was a pretext or two for
ceasing to correspond ; but I believe there is no doubt
that my heresies were the cause. What I said to her
I siad to several other people ; and I doubt whether

any one of them was unprepared for what was pretty
certain to be the result when I had once attained to
the estimate of the free-thinkers of my acquaintance
which I have just recorded.

SECTION III.

ABOUT the middle of the period of this illness, Sir
E. L. Bulwer Lytton wrote to me an earnest suggestion that I should go to Paris to consult a somnambule
about the precise nature and treatment of my disease.
He said I should probably think him insane for
making such a proposition, but offered to supply me
with his reasons, if I would listen to him. My reply
was that I needed no convincing of the goodness of
his advice, if only the measure was practicable. I had
long been entirely convinced of the truth of the insight
of somnambules, and should have been thankful to be
able to make use of it : but there were two obstacles
which appeared insurmountable. I could not move,
in the first place. My medical adviser, my brother-
in-law, had much wished to take me to London, for
other opinions on my case; but my travelling was
altogether out of the question. Sir Charles Clarke
had come into Northumberland afterwards, and he
had visited me, and, after a careful inquiry into the
case, had decided that the disease was incurable.
After this, it was agreed on all hands that I could not
travel. In the next place, I had to explain that the
penalty on my consulting a somnambule, even if one

could be brought to me, was, not only the loss of my medical comforts at Tynemouth, but of family peace, —so strong was the prejudice of a part of my family against mesmerism. There the matter rested till May 1844, when, in the course of a fortnight, there were no less than three letters of advice to me to try mesmerism. My youngest sister wrote to me about a curious case which had accidentally come under the notice first, and then the management, of her husband, —a surgeon :—a case which showed that insensibility to pain under an operation could be produced, and that epilepsy of the severest kind had given way under mesmerism, when all other treatment had long been useless. Mr. and Mrs. Basil Montagu wrote to entreat me to try mesmerism, and related the story of their own conversion to it by seeing the case of Ann Vials treated by their ' dear young friend, Henry Atkinson,' —of whom I had never heard. The third was from a wholly different quarter, but contained the same counsel, on very similar grounds. Presently after, I was astonished at what my brother-in-law said in one of his visits. He told me that Mr. Spencer Hall, of whom I had never heard, was lecturing in Newcastle on mesmerism ; that he (my brother) had gone to the lecture out of curiosity, and had been put into the chair, on the clear understanding that he accepted the post only to see fair play, and not at all as counte-nancing mesmerism, of which he fairly owned that he knew nothing whatever : that he had been deeply impressed by what he saw, and was entirely perplexed, —the only clear conviction that he had brought away being of the honesty and fairness of the lecturer, who was the first to announce such failures as occurred ; and

that he (my brother) was anxious to see more of the
lecturer, and disposed to advise my trying the experiment of being mesmerised, as possibly affording me
some release from the opiates to which I was obliged
to have constant recourse. I was as much pleased as
surprised at all this, and I eagerly accepted the proposal that Mr. Spencer Hall should be brought to see
me, if he would come. Some of my family were
sadly annoyed by this proceeding; but as the move
was not mine, I felt no scruple about accepting its
benefits. For between five and six years, every thing
that medical skill and family care could do for me had
been tried, without any avail; and it was now long
since the best opinions had declared that the case was
hopeless,—that, though I might live on, even for
years, if my state of exhaustion should permit, the
disease was incurable. I had tried all the methods,
and taken all the medicines prescribed, ' without ' as
my brother-in-law declared in writing, ' any effect
whatever having been produced on the disease '; and,
now that a new experiment was proposed to me by
my medical attendant himself, I had nothing to do
but try it. This appears plain and rational enough to
me now, as it did then; and I am as much surprised
now as I was then that any evil influence should have
availed to persuade my mother and eldest sister that
my trial of mesmerism was a slight to the medical
adviser who proposed it, and my recovery by means
of it a fit occasion for a family quarrel. For my part
—if any friend of mine had been lying in a suffering
and hopeless state for nearly six years, and if she had
fancied she might get well by standing on her head
instead of her heels, or reciting charms or bestriding

a broomstick, I should have helped her to try: and thus was I aided by some of my family, and by a further sympathy in others: but two or three of them were induced by an evil influence to regard my experiment and recovery as an unpardonable offence ; and by them I never was pardoned. It is a common story. Many or most of those who have been restored by mesmerism have something of the same sort to tell ; and the commonness of this experience releases me from the necessity of going into detail upon the subject.

I may also omit the narrative of my recovery, because it is given in ' Letters on Mesmerism ' which I was presently compelled to publish. There is among my papers my diary of the case,—a record carefully kept from day to day of the symptoms, the treatment, and the results. The medical men, and the few private friends who have seen that journal (which I showed to my medical adviser) have agreed in saying that it is as *cool* as if written by a professional observer, while it is so conclusive as to the fact of my restoration by the means tried in 1844, that ' we must cease to say that any thing is the cause of any other thing, if the recovery was not wrought by mesmerism.' These are the words which are before me in the hand-writing of a wholly impartial reader of that journal.

I had every desire to bear patiently any troubles sure to arise in such a case from professional bigotry, and popular prejudice ; but I must think that I had more than my share of persecution for the offence of recovery from a hopeless illness by a new method.— Occasion of offence was certainly given by some advocates of mesmerism, strangers to me, by their putting letters into the newspapers, praising me for my experiment, and ridiculing the doctors for their repugnance to it; and one at least of these officious persons made several mistakes in his statement. I knew nothing of this for some time; and then only by the consequences. I must repeat here, what I have said elsewhere, that Mr. Spencer Hall had nothing to do with all this. Though he might naturally have been pleased with his own share in the business, and though many men would have considered themselves released from all obligation to silence by the publicity the matter soon obtained, he remained honourably silent, till he had my express permission to tell the story when and where he pleased. When he did tell it, it was with absolute accuracy. The first letters to the newspapers, meanwhile, drew out from the grosser and more ignorant of the medical profession, and also from some who ought to have been above exposing themselves to be so classified, speculations, comments, and narratives, not only foolish and utterly false in regard to facts, but so offensive that it was absolutely necessary to take some step, as no one intervened for my protection from a persecution most odious to a woman. After much consideration, it seemed to me best to send to (not a newspaper, but) a scientific journal, a simple narrative of the facts,—making no allusion to any thing already published, but so offering the story as to lift it out of the professional mire into which it had been dragged, and to place it on its right ground as a matter of scientific observation. This was the act which was called ' rushing into print.'

The conduct of the editor who accepted and profited by my 'Letters on Mesmerism' is so capital an illustration of the mode in which I and my coadjutors were treated on this occasion, and of that in which persons concerned in any new natural discovery are usually treated, that it may be profitable to give a brief statement of the facts as a compendium of the whole subject.—I wrote to one of the staff of the *Athenæum*, saying that I found it necessary to write my experience; and that I preferred a periodical like the Athenæum to a newspaper, because I wanted to lift up the subject out of the dirt into which it had been plunged, and to place it on a scientific ground, if possible. I said that I was aware that the editor of the Athenæum was an unbeliever in mesmerism; but that this was no sufficient reason for my concluding that his periodical would be closed against a plain story on a controverted subject. I begged, at the outset, to say that I could take no money for my articles, under the circumstances; and that, if it was the rule of the Athenæum, as of some publications, to take no contributions that were not paid for, perhaps the editor might think fit to give the money to some charity. What I did require, I said, was, that my articles should appear unaltered, and that they and I should be treated with the respect due to the utterance and intentions of a conscientious and thoughtful observer. I hold the reply, in the hand-writing of the editor, who eagerly accepted the proposed articles, and agreed without reserve to my conditions. The six 'Letters' that I sent carried six numbers of the Athenæum through three editions. Appended to the last was a string of comments by the editor, insult-

ing and slanderous to the last degree. For a course
of weeks and months from that time, that periodical
assailed the characters of my mesmeriser and of my
fellow-patient, the excellent girl whom I before described. It held out inducements to two medical men
to terrify some of the witnesses, and traduce others,
till the controversy expired in the sheer inability of
the honest party to compete with rogues who stuck at
no falsehoods : and finally, the Athenæum gave public
notice that it would receive communications from our
adversaries, and not from us. Meantime, Mr. Moxon
wrote to ask me to allow him to reprint the ' Letters '
as a pamphlet ; and I gave permission, declining to
receive any profit from the sale. While the ' Letters '
were reprinting, the editor of the Athenæum actually
wrote, and then sent his lawyer, to forbid Mr. Moxon
to proceed, declaring that he claimed the property of
the ' Letters,' by which he had already pocketed so
large a profit. Of course the claim was absurd,—
nothing having been paid for the articles,—which I
had also told the editor it was my attention to allow
to be reprinted. The editor finally stooped to say
that I did not know that he had not given money on
account of the ' Letters ' to some charity : but,
when we asked whether he had, there was no reply
forthcoming. Mr. Moxon of course proceeded in his
re-publication, and the editor gained nothing by his
move but the reputation, wherever the facts were
known, of having achieved the most ill-conditioned
transaction in regard to principle, temper and taste,
known to any of those who read his letters, public
and private, or heard the story.—As for me, what I
did was this. When I found that a conscientious

witness has no chance against unscrupulous informers, I ceased to bandy statements in regard to the characters of my coadjutors: (nobody attacked mine*) but I took measures which would avail to rectify the whole business, if it should ever become necessary to any of the injured parties to do so. I sent my solicitor to one of the unscrupulous doctors, to require from him a retractation of his original statement. This retractation, obtained in the presence, and under the sanction, of the doctor's witness (his pastor) I now

* The only doubtful point, as far as I know, about my own accuracy is one which is easily explained. I explained it in private letters at the time, but had no opportunity of doing more. My medical attendant charged me with first desiring that he should publish my case, and then being wroth with him for doing so. The facts are these. He spoke to me about sending an account of the case to a Medical Journal. I could not conceive why he consulted me about it; and I told him so: saying that I believed the custom was for doctors to do what they thought proper about such a proceeding; and that, as the patients are not likely ever to hear of such a use of their case, it does not, in fact, concern them at all. Some time after, he told me he was going to do it; and the very letter in which he said so enclosed one of the many very disagreeable applications at that time sent both to him and me from medical men,—requesting to know the facts of the case. My reply was that I was glad he was going to relieve me of such correspondence by putting his statement where medical men could learn what they wanted better than from me.—He then or afterwards changed his mind, forgetting to tell me so; and published the case,—not in a Medical Journal, where nobody but the profession would ever have seen it, and where I should never have heard of it,—but in a shilling pamphlet,—not even written in Latin,—but open to all the world! When, in addition to such an act as this, he declared that it was done under my sanction, I had much ado to keep any calmness at all. But the sympathy of all the world, —even of the medical profession,—was by this act secured to me: and the whole affair presently passed from my mind. The only consequence was that I could never again hold intercourse with one from whom I had so suffered.

hold, in the slanderer's own hand-writing: and it
effectually served to keep him quiet henceforward.   I
hold also an additional legal declaration which esta-
blishes the main fact on which the somnambule's story
of the shipwreck was attempted to be overthrown.
The whole set of documents has been shown to a
great variety of people,—lawyers and clergymen,
among others: and all but medical men have declared,
under one form of expression or another, that the
evidence is as strong as evidence can be on any
transaction whatever.   One eminent lawyer told me
that the twelve Judges would be unanimous in regard
to the truth of the parties concerned, and the certainty
of the facts from the documents which were offered
to the public, and the two or three which I have held
in readiness to fill up any gaps of which we were
not in the first instance aware.—Such a persecution
could hardly be repeated now, in regard to the particular subject,—after the great amount of evidence
of the facts of mesmerism which the intervening
years have yielded; but it will be repeated in regard
to every new discovery of a power or leading fact in
nature.   Human pride and prejudice cannot brook
discoveries which innovate upon old associations, and
expose human ignorance; and, as long as any thing
in the laws of the universe remains to be revealed,
there is a tolerable certainty that somebody will yet
be persecuted, whatever is the age of the world.   We
may hope, however, that long before that, men will
have become ashamed of allowing rapacity and bad
faith to make use of such occasions, as the Athenæum
did in the year 1844.—I may just mention that the
editor was an entire stranger to me.   I had never

had any acquaintance with him then ; and I need not
say that I have desired none since.

I was as familiar as most people with the old story
of the unkindly reception of new truth in natural or
moral science. I had talked and moralized, like every
body else, on the early Christians, on Galileo, on
Harvey and his discovery, and so forth : but it all
came upon me like novelty when I saw it so near, and
in a certain degree, though slightly, felt it myself. It
is a very great privilege to have such an experience ;
and especially to one who, like me is too anxious for
sympathy, and for the good opinion of personal friends.
That season of recovery was one of most profitable
discipline to me. At times my heart would swell
that people *could* be so cruel to sufferers, like poor
Jane and myself, recovering from years of hopeless
pain ; and again my spirit rose against the rank
injustice of attempting to destroy reputations in a
matter of scientific inquiry. But, on the whole, my
strength kept up very well. I kept to myself my
quiverings at the sight of the postman, and of newspapers and letters. After the first stab of every new
insult, my spirit rose, and shed forth the *vis medicatrix*
of which we all carry an inexhaustible fountain within
us. I knew, steadily, and from first to last, that we
were right,—my coadjutors and I. I knew that we
were secure as to our facts and innocent in our
intentions : and it was my earnest desire and endeavour to be no less right in temper. How I
succeeded, others can tell better than I. I only know
that my recovery and the sweet sensations of restored
health disposed me to good-humour, and continually
reminded me how much I had gained in comparison

with what I had to bear.   I owed much to the fine
example of poor Jane.   That good girl, whose health
was much less firmly established, at that time, than
mine, was an orphan, and wholly dependent on her
own industry,—that industry being dependent on
her precarious health, and on the character which two
or three physicians first, and two or three journalists
after them, strove by the most profligate plotting, *

* I think I ought to relate the anecdote alluded to, to show
what treatment medical men inflict on women of any rank who
have recourse to mesmerism.—A girl called on my mesmeriser
(the widow of a clergyman) to say that a physician of Shields,
who had enjoined her not to tell his name, had desired her to
ask my friend to mesmerise her for epilepsy.   We took time to
consider, and found on inquiry that the patient belonged to a
respectable family, her brother, with whom she lived, being a
banker's clerk, and living in a good house in Tynemouth, with
his name on a brass plate on the door.   We allowed her to come,
attended by her sister ; and she was mesmerised with obvious
benefit.   On the second occasion, two gentlemen from Newcastle
were at tea with us.   She had been introduced by the name of
Ann ; and Ann we called her.   One of the gentlemen said, in an
odd rough way, ' Jane : her name is Jane : ' and she said her
name was Jane Ann.   The next morning, he called, and very
properly told us that the girl had been seduced at the age of
fifteen, and had been afterwards too well known among the
officers of the garrison.   On inquiry, we found that she had long
been repentant and reformed, so that she was now an esteemed
member of the Methodist body ; so we did not dismiss her to
disease and death, but, with the sanction of my landlady, let
her come while we remained at Tynemouth,—taking care so to
admit her as that our own Jane should not see her again.—Some
weeks after I had left Tynemouth, I was written to by a clergyman at Derby, who thought I ought to know what was doing by
the ' first-physician in Derby.'   He was driving about, telling
his patients, as by authority, about our Tynemouth proceedings.
Among other things, he related that he was informed *by a physician at Shields,* that those proceedings of ours were most dis-
reputable, as ' Jane of Tynemouth was a girl of loose character,

to deprive her of.   They tried to confound her with a
woman of loose character; they bullied and threatened her; they tried to set her relations against her.
But she said cheerfully that people ought not to
grumble at having some penalty to pay for such
blessings as rescue from blindness and restoration to
health by a new method ; and, moreover, that they
should be glad to tell the truth about it, under any
abuse, and to spread the blessing if they could.   So
she bore her share very quietly, and with wonderful
courage resisted the bullies who waited for my separation from her to frighten her into concessions : and,
from that day to this, her healing hand, her time
and her efforts have ever been at the service of the
sick, to not a few of whom she has been a bene-
factress in their time of need.   She has long been
valued as she deserved ; and she has probably forgotten
that season of trial of her temper: but I felt at
the time that I should never forget it ; and I never
have.

I was much aided and comforted during the five
months that my recovery was proceeding by the visits
of friends who knew more about mesmerism than I
did, and who entirely approved my recourse to it.
Among others came a gentleman and his wife whose
name and connexions were well known to me, but
whom I had not chanced ever to meet. The gentleman
was one of the very earliest inquirers into mesmerism
in England in our time; and he was a practiced
operator.   He came out of pure benevolence, at the

too well known among the officers there.' The plot was now
clear: and surely the story needs no comment. What were my
wrongs, in comparison with my good Jane's ?

suggestion of a mutual friend who saw, and who told
him, that this was a case of life and death, which
might terminate according to the preponderance of
discouragement from my own neighbouring family, or
encouragement from those who understood the subject
better.   He came, bringing his wife ; and their visit
was not the less pleasant for the urgent need of it
being almost past.   They found me going on well
under the hands of the kind lady who was restoring
me.   But it is clear that even then we were so
moderate in our hopes as not to expect any thing like
complete restoration.   When they bade us farewell,
we talked of meeting again at Tynemouth,—having
no idea of my ever leaving the place ; and in truth a
journey did then appear about the most impossible of
all achievements.   A few weeks later, however, we
had agreed that I should confirm my recovery by
change of scene, and that the scene should be Windermere, on the shores of which my new friends were
then living.   They kindly urged their invitation on
the ground that I must not give up being mesmerised
suddenly or too soon, and that in their house there
would be every facility for its daily use.   So, early in
January, 1845, my mesmeriser and I left Tynemouth,
little thinking that I should never return to it.   I had
no sooner left my late home, however, than the evil
spirit broke out so strongly, in the medical profession
and in the discontented part of the family, that the
consideration was forced upon me—why I should go
back.   There was indeed no attraction whatever but
the sea ; and if there had been every thing that there
was not,—society, books, fine scenery, &c.,—they
could have been no compensation for non-intercourse

with the relations who were disconcerted at my mode
of recovery.

My first anxiety was to ascertain whether, in the
opinion of the family, my mother should be left undisturbed in her present arrangements at Liverpool, or
whether I had further services to render to her. To
allow time for the fullest understanding on this head,
I resolved to spend six months or more in visiting
those of my family who had approved my proceedings,
and in lodgings near Windermere; after which, I
would determine on my course of life.

One wintry morning, while walking to Waterhead
with my host, we said 'what wonderful things do
come to pass!' We looked back to that day twelve-
months, when I was lying, sick and suffering for life,
as every body supposed, on my couch at Tynemouth;
and we wondered what I should have said if any
prophet had told me that that day twelve months I
should be walking in a snow storm, with a host whom
I had then never seen, looking for lodgings in which
to undergo my transformation into a Laker!

SIXTH PERIOD.

SECTION I.

My life, it has been seen, began with winter. Then
followed a season of storm and sunshine, merging in
a long gloom.   If I had died of that six years' illness,
I should have considered my life a fair average one,
as to happiness,—even while thinking more about
happiness, and caring more for it, than I do now.
I did not know, ten years ago, what life might be, in
regard to freedom, vigour, and peace of mind ; and,
not knowing this, I should have died in the persuasion
that I had been, on the whole, as happy as the conditions of human existence allow.   But the spring,
summer, and autumn of life were yet to come.   I have
had them now,—all rapidly succeeding each other,
and crowded into a small space, like the Swedish
summer, which bursts out of a long winter with the
briefest interval of spring.   At past forty years of
age, I began to relish life, without drawback ; and for
ten years I have been vividly conscious of its delights,
as undisturbed by cares as my anxious nature, and my
long training to trouble could permit me ever to be.
I believe there never was before any time in my life

when I should not have been rather glad than sorry to lay it down. During this last sunny period, I have not acquired any dread or dislike of death; but I have felt, for the first time, a keen and unvarying relish of life. It seems to be generally supposed that a relish of life implies a fear or dislike of death, except in the minds of those shallow and self-willed persons who expect to step over the threshold of death into just the same life that they have quitted,—with the same associates, employments, recreations,—the same every thing, except natural scenery. But this does not at all agree with my experience. I have no expectation of that kind,—nor personal expectation of any kind after death; and I have a particularly keen relish of life,—all the keener for being late: yet now, while in daily expectation of death, I certainly feel no dislike or dread of it; nor do I find my pleasant daily life at all overshadowed by the certainty that it is near its end. If this seems strange to people who hold other views than mine, their baseless conclusions,—that I must dread death because I enjoy life,—appear no less strange to me. They surely do not refuse to enjoy any other pleasure because it must come to an end; and why this? And if they feel sad as the end of other pleasures draws near, it is because they antici-pate feeling the absence and the blank. Thus, we grieve, and cannot but grieve, at the death of a friend, whose absence will leave a blank in our life: but the laying down our own life, to yield our place to our successors, and simply ceasing to be, seems to me to admit of no fear or regret, except through the corrup-tion introduced by false and superstitious associations. I suppose we must judge, each for ourselves, in such

matters; but I cannot but remember that I have gone
through the Christian experience in regard to the
expectation of death, and feel that I understand it,
while Christians have not experienced, and I perceive
do not understand, my present view and feeling in the
expectation of death.   But if they care to have my
own statement, they are welcome to it.   It is what I
have said :—that for ten years I have had as keen a
relish of life as I believe my nature to be capable of;
and that I feel no reluctance whatever to pass into
nothingness, leaving my place in the universe to be
filled by another.   The very conception of *self* and
other is, in truth, merely human, and when the self
ceases to be, the distinction expires.

I remember that when the prospect of health and
prolonged life opened before me, there was a positive
drawback, and a serious one, in the dread of having
the whole thing to go over again, some time or other.
I had recourse to desperate comforts under this
apprehension.   I hoped I might die by a railway
crash, or some other sudden accident; or that I
might sink away in mere old age; or I trusted that
time might somehow make some change.   I little
thought how short a time would make so vast a
change !   I little thought that in ten years I should
find myself far more fatally ill, without the slightest
reluctance, and with the gayest feeling that really it
does not matter whether I feel ill or well,—(short of
acute and protracted pain, of which I have still a
great dread) if only other people are not made
unhappy.   All the solemn, doleful feeling about my
sufferings, which seemed right and appropriate, if not
religious, a dozen years ago, now appears selfish, and

low, and a most needless infliction on myself and
others. Once become aware of how little consequence
it is, and how the universe will go on just the same,
whether one dies at fifty or seventy, one looks gaily
on the last stage of one's subjection to the great laws
of nature,—notes what one can of one's state for the
benefit of others, and enjoys the amusement of watching the course of human affairs from one's fresh and
airy point of view, above the changes of the elements
with which one has no further personal concern. The
objective and disinterested contemplation of eternity
is, in my apprehension, the sublimest pleasure that
human faculties are capable of; and the pleasure is
most vivid and real when one's disinterestedness is
most necessary and complete,—that is, when our
form of its life is about to dissolve, to make way
for another.

After spending a month on the shores of Windermere, I went for a long visit to my dear elder
brother's, some of whose children had grown up from
infancy to youth during my illness. He and his wife
had attached me to them more than ever by their
recent conduct. Thinking me right in my effort to
recover health, and wronged in much of the treatment
I had received, they upheld me steadily and effectually,
while, at the same time, they saw how the wrong was
mainly owing to prejudice and want of the knowledge
pertinent to the case ; and they therefore did not find
it necessary to quarrel with any body. I thought
then, and I think now, that they were just and kind
all round ; and I am sure they were no small assistance
to me in keeping my temper. They took a great
interest in the subject of mesmerism, and enjoyed

seeing its operation in cases similar to my own, and in many others, in which sufferers, pronounced incurable by the doctors, were restored as I had been. One amusement to us all at that time was the pity with which the doctors regarded me. I could quote several medical men who reasoned that, *as* my disease was an incurable one, I could not possibly be radically better; that I was then in a state of exhilaration, infatuation, and so forth; and that in six months (or three months or a year, as might be) I should be as ill as ever, and mourning over my having been duped by the mesmerists. Now and then we heard, or saw in the newspapers, that I *was* as ill as ever, and mourning my infatuation,—though I was walking five or seven miles at a time, and giving every evidence of perfect health. The end of it was that I went off to the East,—into the depths of Nubia, and traversing Arabia on a camel; and then the doctors said I had never been ill! It is very curious, —this difficulty of admitting evidence about any new, or newly revived, fact in nature. I remember Mr. Hallam (the last man open to the charge of credulity) telling me at Tynemouth a story which struck me very much. He told me how he and his friend Mr. Rogers had had the privilege of witnessing that very rare spectacle, ‘the reception by a great metropolis, of the discovery of a pregnant natural fact.’ He told me,—and he has so manfully told plenty of other people, that I am betraying no confidence in repeating the story once more,—that Mr. Rogers and he had, many years before, seen some mesmeric facts in Paris which convinced and impressed them for life. When they returned, they told what they had seen, and were met by such insulting ridicule that they were compelled to be silent, or to quarrel with some of their pleasantest friends. One physician in particular he named, who treated them at his own table in a way which prevented their ever again communicating their knowledge to him, if they wished to remain on civil terms with him. By degrees, in course of years, facts became known; higher scientific authorities on the continent declared themselves convinced, or in favour of that genuine inquiry which has always ended in conviction; and the tone of London society began to change. The physician referred to ceased to gibe and jeer, and sat silent and embarrassed while the subject was discussed; and at length began to ask questions, and show a desire to learn : ' and now,' continued Mr. Hallam, ' we can say that we are acquainted with nobody who has attended to the subject with any earnestness who does not consider certain facts of mesmerism to be as completely established as any facts whatever in the whole range of science.' He added, ' this reception of a great truth is a great thing to have seen.'—In a note I had from Mr. Hallam before I left Tynemouth, he declared his view to be this. ' I have no doubt that mesmerism, and some other things which are not mesmerism properly so called, are fragmentary parts of some great law of the human frame which we are on the verge of discovering.' It appears to be the method of the London doctors now to admit the facts (being unable longer to suppress them) and to account for them, each according to his own favourite physiological view; and thus the truth is near its full admission. When the facts are admitted in London, the medical men in the provinces will not long continue to scoff and perpetrate slander: and when a score of commentators on a single class of facts offer a score of explanations, the true solution is so much needed that it must soon be obtained.

Amidst the happiness of my visit at my brother's, I felt a really painful longing to see verdure and foliage. On leaving Newcastle, I had been carried swiftly past a railway embankment covered with broom; and the dark green of that bank made my heart throb at the time, and bred in me a desperate longing to see more. I did not think I could have wished so much for any thing as I did to see foliage. I had not seen a tree for above five years, except a scrubby little affair which stood above the haven at Tynemouth, exposed to every wind that blew, and which looked nearly the same at midsummer and Christmas. It was this kind of destitution which occasioned some of the graceful acts of kindness which cheered my Tynemouth sojourn. An old friend sent me charming coloured sketches of old trees in Sherwood Forest: and an artist who was an entire stranger to me, Mr. McIan, stayed away from a day's excursion at a friend's house in the country, to paint me a breezy tree. For months the breezy tree was pinned up on the wall before me, sending many a breeze through my mind. But now I wanted to see a real tree in leaf; and I had to wait sadly long for it. The spring of 1846 was the latest I remember, I think,—unless it be the present one (1855). My impatience must have been very apparent, for my sister-in-law 'fooled' me, when I came down to breakfast on the 1st of April, with lamentations about the snow under the acacia.' There was no snow there ; but the hedges seemed dead for ever : and there was scarcely a tinge of green on them when I left Edgbaston for Nottingham, on the second of May.

There,—at Lenton, near Nottingham,—new pleasures awaited me. Spring is always charming on the Trent meadows at Nottingham, where the clear shoaly river runs between wide expanses of meadow, where crocuses almost hide the grass for a few weeks of the year. It was an unspeakable pleasure to me to move freely about blossoming gardens ; but no one but a restored invalid can conceive what it was to ramble for miles, to Clifton woods, or to Woollaton, drinking in the sunshine in the fields, and the cool shade under the green avenues. Now, at the end of ten years, I do not find my thirst for foliage fully quenched, after the long absence at Tynemouth. There were excursions from Nottingham to Newstead and elsewhere,— all delightful ; but I don't know that I had not more pleasure from the common lawn, with the shadows of the trees flickering upon it, than from any change of objects. The surprise to my friends, and also to myself, was that I was so little nervous,—so capable of doing like other people, as if I had not led a sick and hermit life for so many years. This exemption from the penalties of long illness I believe I owe to mesmerism being the means of cure. I had left off all drugs for ten months, except the opiates, which had been speedily reduced from the outset of the experiment, and now discontinued for half a year. I had not therefore to recover from the induced illness and constitutional poisoning caused by drugs ; and

my nerves had been well strung by the mesmerism
which I had now discontinued.   I certainly felt at
first, when at the Lakes and at Edgbaston, by no
means sure that I knew how to behave in society;
but old associations soon revived, and I fell into the
old habit of social intercourse.   It was not very long
indeed before we proposed,—my friends and I,—to
ignore altogether the five years at Tynemouth,—to
call me 38 instead of 43, and proceed as if that awful
chasm had never opened in my path which now
seemed closed up, or invisible as it lay behind.   There
were things belonging to it, however, which I should
have been sorry to forget, or to lose the vivid sense
of; and chief among these was the kindness of a host
of friends.   I have observed, however, at intervals
since, that though the sense of that kindness is as
vivid as ever, the other incidents and interests of that
term of purgatory have so collapsed as to make the
period which seemed in experience to be an eternity,
like a momentary blank,—a night of uneasy dreams,
soon forgotten between the genuine waking interests
of two active days.

With this new day of activity arose a strong fresh
interest.   It was at Lenton, near Nottingham, that I
first saw Mr. Atkinson, whose friendship has been the
great privilege of the concluding period of my life.   I
have told above that Mr. and Mrs. Basil Montagu
mentioned him to me in the letter in which they besought me to try mesmerism.   I had never heard of
him before, as far as I know.   I have often said, as I
am ready to say again, that I owe my recovery mainly
to him,—that my ten last happy years have been his
gift to me : but it is not true, as many people have

supposed and led others to believe, that I was mesmerised by him at Tynemouth. I am careful in explaining this, because many persons who think it necessary to assign some marvellous reason for my present philosophical views, and who are unwilling to admit that I could have arrived at them by my own means and in my own way, have asserted that Mr. Atkinson was my mesmeriser, and that he infused into me his own views by the power he thus gained over my brain. I might explain that I never was unconscious,—never in the mesmeric sleep,—during the whole process of recovery; but the simplest and most incontestible reply is by dates. I was first mesmerised on the 22nd of June, 1844; I was well in the following November: I went forth on my travels in January, 1845, and first saw Mr. Atkinson on the 24th of May of that year. The case was this. Mr. and Mrs. Montagu, earnest that I should try mesmerism, brought about a meeting at their house, in June, 1844, between Mr. Atkinson and an intimate friend of mine who had visited me, and was about to go to me again. They discussed the case: and from that time Mr. Atkinson's instructions were our guidance. He, too, obtained for me the generous services of the widow lady mentioned above, when my maid's operations were no longer sufficient; and we followed his counsel till I was well. As for the share he had in the ultimate form assumed by my speculations, on their becoming opinions,—he himself expressed it in a saying so curiously resembling one uttered by a former guide and instructor that it is worth quoting both. The more ancient guide said, when I was expressing gratitude to him, ' O! I only

helped you to do in a fortnight what you would have
done for yourself in six weeks.' Mr. Atkinson said
' I found you out of the old ways, and I showed you
the shortest way round the corner—that's all.' I
certainly knew nothing of his philosophical opinions
when we met at Lenton; and it was not till the close
of 1847, when, on my setting about my book on
Egypt, I wrote him an account of *my* opinions, and
how I came by them, and he replied by a somewhat
similar confidence, that I had any clear knowledge
what his views were. I shall probably have more
to say about this hereafter. Meantime, this is the
place for explaining away, a prevalent mistake as to
my recovery having been wrought by the mesmerising
of a friend whom I had, in fact, never seen.

I vividly remember the first sight of him, when
one of my hostesses and I having gone out to meet
him, and show him the way, saw him turn the corner
into the lane, talking with the gardener who was con-
veying his carpet-bag. He also carried a bag over
his shoulder. He looked older than I expected, and
than I knew he was. His perfect gentlemanliness is
his most immediately striking and uncontested attribute. We were struck with this; and also with a
certain dryness in his mode of conversation which
showed us at once that he was no sentimentalist; a
conviction which was confirmed in proportion as we
became acquainted with his habit of thought. We
could not exactly call him reserved; for he was willing
to converse and ready to communicate his thoughts;
yet we felt it difficult to know him. It was years
before I, in particular, learned to know him, certainly
and soundly, though we were in constant corre-

spondence, and frequently met : but I consider myself no rule for others in the matter.   All my faults, and all my peculiarities, were such as might and did conspire to defer the time when I might understand my friend as he was perfectly willing to be understood. One of the bad consequences of my deafness has been the making me far too much of a talker : and, though friends whom I can trust aver that I am also a good listener, I certainly have never allowed a fair share of time and opportunity to slower and more modest and considerate speakers.   I believe that amidst the stream of talk I poured out upon him, it was impossible for him to suppose or believe how truly and earnestly I really did desire to hear his views and opinions ; and as, in spite of this, he did tell me much which I thought over, and talked over when he was gone, it is plain that he was not reserved with me. A yet greater impediment to our mutual understanding was that I, hitherto alone in my pursuit of philosophy, had no sufficient notion of other roads to it than that which I had found open before me ; and Mr. Atkinson's method was so wholly different that it took me, prepossessed as I was, a very long time to ascertain his route and ultimate point of view.   I had, for half my life, been astray among the metaphysicians, whose schemes I had at my tongue's end, and whose methods I supposed to be the only philosophical ones.   I at first took Mr. Atkinson's disregard of them and their methods for ignorance of what they had done, as others who think themselves philosophers have done since.   Let it not be supposed that I set this down without due shame. I have much to blush for in this matter, and in worse. I now and then

proffered him in those days information from my
metaphysical authors, for which he politely thanked
me, leaving me to find out in time how he knew
through and through the very matters which the
metaphysicians had barely sketched the outside of. In
truth, he at his Baconian point of view, and I at my
metaphysical, were in our attempts to understand each
other something like beings whose reliance is on a
different sense,—those who hear well and those who
see well,—meeting to communicate. When the
blind with their quick ears, and the deaf and dumb
with their alert eyes meet, the consequences usually are desperate quarrels. In our case, I was
sometimes irritated; and when irritated, always conceited and wrong; but my friend had patience with
me, seeing what was the matter, and knowing that
there were grand points of agreement between us
which would secure a thorough understanding, sooner
or later. If, amidst my metaphysical wanderings, I
had reached those points of agreement, there was
every reason to suppose that when I had found the
hopelessness of the metaphysical point of view, with
its uncertain method and infinite diversity of conclusions,—corresponding with the variety of speculators,—I should find the true exterior point of view,
the positive method, and its uniform and reliable conclusions. In this faith, and in wonderful patience,
my friend bore with my waywardness and occasional
sauciness, till at length we arrived at a complete
understanding. When our book,—our 'Letters on
Man's Nature and Development,'—came out, and
was abused in almost every periodical in the kingdom,
it amused me to see how very like my old self the

metaphysical reviewers were ;—how exclusively they fastened on the collateral parts of the book, leaving its method, and all its essential part, wholly untouched. It is a curious fact that, of all the multitude of adverse reviews of our book that we read, there was not one that took the least notice of its essential part,—its philosophical Method. Scarcely any part of it indeed was touched at all, except the anti-theological portion, which was merely collateral.

Such was my method of criticism of Mr. Atkinson, on the first occasion of our meeting. As we walked up and down a green alley in the garden, he astonished and somewhat confounded me by saying how great he thought the mistake of thinking so much and so arti-ficially as people are for ever striving to do about death and about living again. Not having yet by any means got out of the atmosphere of selfishness which is the very life of Christian doctrine, and of every theological scheme, I was amazed at his question,—what it could signify whether we, with our individual consciousness, lived again? I asked what could possibly signify so much,—being in a fluctuating state then as to the natural grounds of expectation of a future life, (I had long given up the scriptural) but being still totally blind to the selfish instincts involved in such anxiety as I felt about the matter. I was, however, in a certain degree struck by the nobleness of his larger view, and by the good sense of the doctrine that our present health of mind is all the personal concern that we have with our state and destiny : that our duties lie before our eyes and close to our hands ; and that our business is with what we know, and have it in our charge to do, and not at all with a future which is, of its own nature, impenetrable. With grave interest and an uneasy concern, I talked this over afterwards with my hostess. At first she would not credit my account of Mr. Atkinson's view; and then she was exceedingly shocked, and put away the subject. I, for my part, soon became able to separate the uneasiness of contravened associations from that of intellectual opposition. I soon perceived that this outspoken doctrine was in full agreement with the action of my mind for some years past, on the particular subject of a future life ; and that, when once Christianity ceases to be entertained as a scheme of salvation, the question of a future life becomes indeed one of which every large-minded and unselfish person may and should say,—' What does it signify?' Amidst many alternations of feeling, I soon began to enjoy breathings of the blessed air of freedom from superstition,—which is the same thing as freedom from personal anxiety and selfishness ;—that freedom, under a vivid sense of which my friend and I, contrasting our superstitious youth with our emancipated maturity, agreed that not for the universe would we again have the care of our souls upon our hands.

At length, the last day of May arrived, and my longings for my Lake lodgings were to be gratified. The mossy walls with their fringes of ferns ; the black pines reflected in the waters : the amethyst mountains at sunset, and the groves and white beaches beside the lake had haunted me almost painfully, all spring ; and my hosts and hostesses must have thought my unconcealable anticipations somewhat unmannerly. They could make allowance for me, however : and they sent much sympathy with me. It was truly a

gay life that was before me now. My intention was
not to work at all; an intention which I had never
been able to fulfil when in health, and which soon
gave way now, before a call of duty which I very
grudgingly obeyed. On the day of my arrival at
Waterhead, however, I had no idea of working; and
the prospect before me was of basking in the summer
sunshine, and roving over hill and dale in fine weather,
and reading and working beside the window overlooking the lake (Windermere) in rainy hours, when lakes
have a beauty of their own. My lodging, taken for
six months, was the house which stands precisely at
the head of the lake, and whose grassplat is washed
by its waters. The view from the windows of my
house was wonderfully beautiful,—one feature being
a prominent rock, crowned with firs, which so projected
into the lake as to be precisely reflected in the crimson,
orange, and purple waters when the pine-crest rose
black into the crimson, orange, and purple sky, at
sunset. When the young moon hung over those
black pines, the beauty was so great that I could
hardly believe my eyes. On the day of my arrival,
when I had met my new maid from Dublin (my Tynemouth nurse being unable to leave her mother's neighbourhood), and when I had been welcomed by a dear
old friend or two, I found an intoxicating promise of
bliss whichever way I turned. I was speedily instructed
in the morality of lakers,—the first principle of which
is (at least, so they told me) never to work except in
bad weather. The woods were still full of wild ane-
mones and sorrel, and the blue bells were just coming
out. The meadows were emerald green, and the oaks
were just exchanging their May-golden hue for light

green, when the sycamores, so characteristic of the
region, were growing sombre in their massy foliage.
The friends whom I had met during my winter visit
were kind in their welcome; and many relations and
friends came that summer, to enjoy excursions with me.
It was all very gay and charming; and if I found the
bustle of society a little too much,—if I felt myself
somewhat disappointed in regard to the repose which
I had reckoned on, that blessing was, as I knew, only
deferred.

As to this matter,—of society. There is a perpetual change going on in such neighbourhoods in
the Lake District as that of Ambleside. Retired
merchants and professional men fall in love with the
region, buy or build a house, are in a transport with
what they have done, and, after a time, go away. In
five or six years, six houses of friends or acquaintance
of mine became inhabited by strangers. Sorry as I
was, on each occasion, to lose good friends or pleasant
acquaintances, I did not call on their successors,—nor
on any other new-comers: nor did I choose, from the
beginning, to visit generally in Ambleside. When I
made up my mind to live there, I declined the dinner
and evening engagements offered to me, and visited at
only three or four houses; and very sparingly at those.
It did not suit me to give parties, otherwise than in
the plainest and most familiar way; and I had some
idea of the mischiefs and dangers of such society as is
found promiscuously cast into a small neighbourhood
like this. I had not time to waste in meeting the
same people,—not chosen as in London, but such as
chanced to be thrown together in a very small country
town,—night after night: I was aware how nearly

impossible it is to keep out of the gossip and the quarrels which prevail in such places; and there was no adequate reason for encountering them. I foresaw that among a High-church squirearchy, and Low-church evangelicals, and the moderate-church few, who were timid in proportion to their small numbers, I might be tolerated, and even courted at first, on account of my reputation, but must sooner or later give deadly offence by some outbreak of heresy or reforming tendency stronger than they could bear. I therefore confined my visiting to three or four houses, merely exchanging calls with others: and it is well I did. Of those three or four, scarcely one could endure my avowal of my opinions in 1851. Even with them, I had before ceased, or did then cease to exchange hospitalities. As they had sought me, and even urgently pressed themselves upon me (one family in particular, whose mere name I had never heard when I arrived), they were especially in need of my compassion at the plight they found them-selves in,—with goodness of heart enough to remember that our acquaintance was all of their seeking, but with too much narrowness and timidity to keep up intercourse through such opprobrium as my opinions brought on me among their High-church neighbours. They had the shame (which I believe them to be capable of feeling) of being aware, and knowing that *I* was aware, that they sought me, as they are wont to seek and flatter all celebrities, for my fame, and to gratify their own love of excitement; and that their weakness stood confessed before the trial of my plain avowal of honest opinions. It made no difference that, after a time, when the gossip had

blown over, and my neighbours saw that I did not
want them, and did not depend on their opinions in
any way, they came round, and began to be attentive
and kind:—their conduct at a moment of crisis
proved to me that I had judged rightly in declining
Ambleside visiting from the beginning; and their
mutual quarrelling, fierce and wide and deep, certainly
confirmed my satisfaction with my independent plan
of life.   My interests lay among old friends at a distance; and I had as much social intercourse as I at all
desired when they came into the district.   I was
amused and instructed by the words of an ingenuous
young friend, who, taking leave of me one winter
afternoon at her own gate, said : 'Ah! now,—you
are going home to a comfortable quiet evening by
your own fire!   Really, I think it is quite hypocritical
in us!—We dress and go out, and seem to be so
pleased, when we are longing all the time to be at
home!   We meet the same people, who have only the
same talk; and we get *so* tired!'   It was not long
before that family withdrew from the Ambleside
visiting which I had always declined.   A very few
faithful friends, whose regard did not depend on the
popular nature of my opinions, remained true and
dear to me; and thus I found that book,—the
'Atkinson Letters,'—do me the same good and
welcome service in my own valley that it did in the
wide world;—it dissolved all false relations, and confirmed all true ones.   Finally, now that that business
has long been settled, and that all my other affairs
are drawing near their close, I may make my declaration that I have always had as much society as I
wished for, and sometimes a great deal more.   And

this leads me to explain why I came to live where I am ;—a prodigious puzzle, I am told, to the great majority of my London acquaintance.

When I had been thoroughly and avowedly well for half a year, I found my family had made up their minds, as I had scarcely a doubt that they would, that my mother's settlement at Liverpool had better not be disturbed. She was among three of her children settled there, and she was suited with a companion better adapted to aid her in her nearly blind condition than any deaf person could be. It would have been a most serious and injurious sacrifice to me to live in a provincial town. The choice for me, in regard to my vocation, was between London and a purely country residence. I was partly amused and partly shocked at the amazement of some of my really intimate friends, to whom I supposed my character fully known, at my choosing the latter. One of these friends wrote to me that she could not at all fancy me ‘ a real country lady ’; and another told Mr. Atkinson that she did not believe I had any genuine love of natural scenery. Mr. Hallam told me, some years afterwards, that he and others of my friends had considered my retreat from London, after having known the delights of its society, ‘a most doubtful and serious experiment,— a *most* doubtful experiment’; but that they found, by the testimony of mutual friends who had visited me, that it had ‘ answered completely.’—My reasons are easily told. I was now, when at liberty to form my own plan of life, past the middle of its course. I had seen the dangers and moral penalties of literary life in London for women who had become accustomed to its excite-

ments ; and I knew that I could not be happy if I
degenerated into ' a hackney-coach and company life.'
No true woman, married or single, *can* be happy
without some sort of domestic life ;—without having
somebody's happiness dependent on her ; and my own
ideal of an innocent and happy life was a house of my
own among poor improvable neighbours, with young
servants whom I might train and attach to myself ;
with pure air, a garden, leisure, solitude at command,
and freedom to work in peace and quietness. When
to all this could be added fine natural scenery, the
temptations were such as London could not rival. If
I had country, I would have the best ; and my mind
was made up at once,—to live at the Lakes,—as
soon as I was sure of my liberty to choose. I began
to look about in the neighbourhood at cottages to let
or on sale. The most promising was one at Clappers-
gate, at the head of Windermere, which was offered
me for £20 a year. It had more rooms than I wanted,
and an exceedingly pretty porch ; and a little garden,
in which was a tempting copper-beech. But the
ceilings were too low for my bookcases, and the house
was old ; and it commanded no great beauty, except
from the attic windows. A friend who went with me
to view it said that £20 was the interest of £500 ;
and that for £500 I could build myself a cottage after
my own heart. This was strikingly true : and thus the
idea of having at once a house of my own was suggested.
By the necessity of the case, the matter was soon
settled. A dissenting minister, an opulent man who
had built a chapel and school, and bought a field for
cottage-building, found life too hard for a dissenter
among the orthodox at Ambleside, and especially after

he had proposed to supply the want of cottages which
is there the screw which the rich put upon the labour-
ing classes; and, after his health had sunk under the
treatment he encountered, he was obliged to leave the
place to save his life. My house-viewing friend
brought me, on the 27th of June, the plan of this
minister's field, which was to be sold in lots the next
day but one. The time was short; but land was
becoming rare in the neighbourhood ; and I went to
see the field. One of the lots was a rocky knoll, com-
manding a charming view. I knew no one whom I
could ask to go and bid; and I could not feel sure of
a due supply of water ; not knowing then that wherever there is rock, there is a tolerable certainty of
water. The other lots appeared to me to lie too low
for building ; and I, in my simplicity, concluded that
the pretty knoll would be the first and surest to sell.
Next day, I found that that lot, and the one at the
foot of the rise, remained unsold. I went to the minister for a consultation. His wife satisfied me about
the water-supply ; and she moreover said that as the
other unsold slip, valued at £70, would not sell by
itself, if I would buy the knoll, I should have the
other for £20. I agreed on the spot. There was one
other three-cornered piece, lying between these and
the meadows which were entailed land, certain never
to be built on : and this bit had been bought at the
sale by an exciseman, to graze his pony when he came
his rounds. My friends all agreed in lamenting over
that sale, and said the exciseman would soon be running up some hideous structure, to make me pay
' through the nose' for his nook. I replied that I
must stop somewhere ; and that the matter seemed

settled by the land having been sold. It makes me grateful now to think what pains my friends took on my behalf. Mrs. Arnold consulted the Wordsworths : and they all came to exhort me to try to get the nook, for the sake of myself and my heirs ; and my original adviser found up the exciseman, and came back with the news that no conveyance had yet been made out, and that the man would let me have the land for a bonus of £5. I whipped out my five sovereigns ; and the whole was mine. It may seem that I have gone into much detail about a trifle : but I am giving an account of myself ; and there have been few things in my life which have had a more genial effect on my mind than the possession of a piece of land. Those who consider what some scenes of my life had been,—my being left with a single shilling at the time of our losses, my plodding through London mud when I could not get my Series published, and my five years' confinement at Tynemouth, may conceive what it was to me to go, in the lustrous days of that summer, to meditate in my field at eventide, and anticipate the healthful and genial life before me. The kind cousin whom I have mentioned as always at my elbow in all time of need, or when a graceful service could be rendered, came with his family to the Lakes at that precise time. Knowing my affairs,—of which he generously took the management,—he approved my scheme ; and he did more. I asked him plainly whether he thought me justified in building a house of the kind I explained, and of which I showed him the builder's estimate. He called on me alone one morning,—on business, as he said ; and his ' business ' was this. He told me that he considered me abun-

dantly justified; he added that there could be no
difficulty in obtaining, on such securities as I could
offer, whatever additional money would be requisite
for finishing the house (the land was already paid
for,) but that, to save trouble and speculation, I had
better send in the bills to him: and he would, to save
me from all sense of obligation, charge me with
interest till I had paid off the whole. The transaction of which this was the graceful beginning, was
no less gracefully carried on and ended. The amount
was (as always happens in such cases) more than we
expected; and I was longer, owing to the failure of
one of my plans, in repaying the loan; but my cousin
cheered me by his approbation and sympathy; and at
last presented me with the final batch of interest, to
purchase something for the house to remember him by.

Then came the amusement of planning my house,
which I did all myself. It was the newest of enterprises to me; and seriously did I ponder all the requi-
sites,—how to plan the bedrooms so that the beds
should not be in a draught, nor face the window nor
the fireplace, &c. I did not then know the importance
of placing beds north and south, in case of illness,
when that position may be of the last consequence to
the patient: but it so happens that all my beds stand
or may stand so. The whole scheme was fortunate
and charming. There is not a single blunder or
nuisance in my pretty house; and now that it is
nearly covered with ivy, roses, passion flowers, and
other climbers, and the porch a bower of honeysuckles,
I find that several of my neighbours, and not a few
strangers, consider my knoll,—position and house
together,—the prettiest dwelling in the valley;—

airy, gay, and 'sunny within and without,' as one family are pleased to say. 'It is,' said Wordsworth, 'the wisest step in her life; for' ... ... and we supposed he was going on to speak of the respectability, comfort, and charm of such a retreat for an elderly woman; but not so. 'It is the wisest step in her life; for the value of the property will be doubled in ten years.'

One of those London friends whom I have mentioned as doubting my discretion in settling here, was paying me a morning visit at my lodgings when I was planning my house; and, while taking a kind interest in looking over the plan and elevation, she thought it right to make a remonstrance which she has since recalled with a generous amusement. 'Now, my dear friend,' said she, 'I take a real interest in all this: but,—do be persuaded,—sell your field, and stay where you are, in this nice lodging. Do, now! Why should you not stay here?'

'First,' said I, 'because it costs me more to live here in three rooms than it would in a whole house of my own.

'Second: there is no room here for my bookcases; and I want my library.

'Third: I am paying for house-room for my furniture at Tynemouth.

'Fourth: this house stands low, and is apt to be flooded and damp in winter.

'Fifth: this house was a barn; and the dust lies a quarter of an inch thick, in some weathers, on every thing in the sitting-room.

'Sixth: the chimney smokes so that I could not have a fire without keeping a window open.

'Seventh : Being close on the margin of the lake, the house is swarming with rats.

'Eighth : ... ...'

'O! stop—stop!' cried my friend, now quite ready to leave my own affairs in my own hands. She long after spent some days with me at the knoll, and pronounced my house and my scheme of life perfect for me.

SECTION II.

THE whole business of the house-building went off without a difficulty, or a shadow of misunderstanding throughout. The contractor proposed his own terms; and they were so reasonable that I had great pleasure in giving him all his own way. It is the pernicious custom of the district to give very long credit, even in the case of workmen's wages. One of my intentions in becoming a housekeeper was to discountenance this, and to break through the custom in my own person. I told all the tradesmen that I would not deal with them on any other terms than ready money payments, alleging the inconvenience to persons of small income of having all their bills pouring in at Candlemas. At first I was grumbled at for the 'inconvenience'; but, before I had lived here two years, I was supplicated for my custom, my reputation being that of being 'the best paymaster in the neighbourhood.' I began with the house itself, offering to pay down £100 every alternate month, on condition that the workpeople were paid weekly. At the end, when the contractor received his last £100, I asked him whether he and all his people were fully satisfied, saying that if there was any discontent, however slight, I wished to hear of it there and then. His answer was, ' Ma'am, there has not been a rough word spoken from beginning to end.' ' Are *you* satisfied ?' I asked. 'Entirely,' he replied. ' I underrated the cost of the terrace; but you paid me what I asked; a bargain is a bargain : and I gained by other parts, so as to make up for it and more; and so I am satisfied,—entirely.' When I afterwards designed to build a cottage and cow-stable, he came to beg the servants to help to get the job for him,—complimenting my mode of payment. I mention this because the poor man, whom I greatly esteemed, got his head turned with subsequent building speculations, fell into drinking habits, and died of a fever thus brought on,—leaving debts to the amount of £1,000 : and I wish it to be clearly understood that I was in no degree connected with his misfortunes.

The first sod was turned on the 1st of October, by Mr. Seymour Tremenheere, in the presence of my elder brother and myself. There was only one tree on the summit of the knoll ; and that was a fine thorn, which the builder kindly managed to leave, to cover a corner; and I seldom look at it, powdered with blossom in May and June, without thinking of the consideration of the poor fellow who lies in the church-yard, so miserably cut off in the vigour of his years. The winter of 1845–6 was (as the potato-rot makes us all remember) the rainiest in the experience of our generation : but the new house was not injured by it ; and it was ready for occupation when April arrived. If I am to give an account of my most deep-felt pleasures, I may well mention that of my sunset walks, on the few fine days, when I saw from the

The Small
Anblecide
as it appeared in 1846.
Sketched by Flemmersley; drawn on wood by Harvey;
and engraved by Harriet R. Clarke.

—

opposite side of the valley the progress of my house.
One evening I saw the red sunset glittering on the
windows, which I did not know were in.   Another
day, I saw the first smoke from the chimney; —the
thin blue smoke from a fire the workmen had lighted,
which gave a home-like aspect to the dwelling.—
When the garden was to take form, new pleasures
arose.   The grass was entirely destroyed round the
base of the knoll by the carts which brought the stone
and wood; and I much wished for some sods.   But
the summer had been as dry as the winter and spring
were wet; and no sods were to be had for love or
money,— every gardener assured me.   In riding over
Loughrigg terrace, I saw where large patches of turf
had been cut; and I asked Mr. Wordsworth whether
one might get sods from the mountain.   He told me
that the fells were the property of the dalesmen, and
that it takes 100 years to replace turf so cut.   So I
made up my mind to wait till grass-seed would grow,
and wondered how I was to secure the seed being
good.   One morning, the servants told me that there
was a great heap of the finest sods lying under the
boundary wall; and that they must have been put
over during the night.   It was even so : and, though
we did our best to watch and listen, the same thing
happened four times,—the last load being a very
large one, abundantly supplying all our need.   A dirty
note, wafered, lay under the pile.   It pretended to
come from two poachers, who professed to be grateful
to me for my Game Law Tales, and to have rendered
me this service in return for my opinion about wild
creatures being fair game.   The writing and spelling
were like those of an ignorant person ; and I supposed

that the inditing was really so, at the bidding of some neighbour of higher quality. The Archbishop of Dublin, who was at Fox How at the time, offered me the benefit of his large experience in the sight of anonymous letters : (not the reading of them, for he always burns unread, before the eyes of his servants, all that come to him) and he instantly pronounced that the note was written by an educated person. He judged by the evenness of the lines, saying that persons who scrawl and misspell from ignorance never write straight. Every body I knew declared to me, sooner or later, in a way too sincere to be doubted, that he or she did not know any thing whatever about my sods : and the mystery remains unsolved to this day. It was a very pretty and *piquant* mystery. Several friends planted a young tree each on my ground. Some of the saplings died and some lived : but the most flourishing is one of the two which Wordsworth planted. We had provided two young oaks : but he objected to them as not remarkable enough for a commemorative occasion. We found that the stone pine suited his idea : and a neighbour kindly sent me two. Wordsworth chose to plant them on the slope under my terrace wall, where, in my humble opinion, they were in the extremest danger from dogs and cats, —which are our local nuisance. I lay awake thinking how to protect them. The barriers I put up were broken down immediately; but I saved one by making a parterre round it : and there it flourishes,— so finely that my successor will have to remove my best pear-tree ere long, to leave room for the forest tree.

The planting-scene was characteristic. Wordsworth

had taken a kindly interest in the whole affair; and
where my study now is, he had thrown himself down,
among the hazel bushes, and talked of the meadows,
and of the right aspect and disposition of a house,
one summer day when he and his wife and daughter
had come to view the site, and give me the benefit
of their experience; and long after, when I had
begun to farm my two acres, he came to see my first
calf. On occasion of the planting of his pine, he
dug and planted in a most experienced manner,—
then washed his hands in the watering-pot, took my
hand in both his, and wished me many happy years
in my new abode,—and then proceeded to give me
a piece of friendly advice. He told me I should find
visitors a great expense, and that I must promise him,
—(and he laid his hand on my arm to enforce what
he said) I must promise him to do as he and his
sister had done, when, in their early days, they had
lived at Grasmere.

  ‘ When you have a visitor,’ said he, ‘ you must do
as we did;—you must say “ if you like to have a cup
of tea with us, you are very welcome : but if you
wan't any meat,—you must pay for your board.”
Now, promise me that you will do this.’ Of course,
I could promise nothing of the sort. I told him I
had rather not invite my friends unless I could make
them comfortable. He insisted: I declined promising;
and changed the subject. The mixture of odd eco-
nomies and neighbourly generosity was one of the
most striking things in the old poet. At tea there,
one could hardly get a drop of cream with any ease
of mind, while he was giving away all the milk that
the household did not want to neighbouring cottagers,

who were perfectly well able to buy it, and would have been all the better for being allowed to do so.— It was one of the pleasures of my walks, for the first few years of my residence here, to meet with Wordsworth when he happened to be walking, and taking his time on the road. In winter, he was to be seen in his cloak, his Scotch bonnet, and green goggles, attended perhaps by half-a-score of cottagers' children,—the youngest pulling at his cloak, or holding by his trowsers, while he cut ash switches out of the hedge for them. After his daughter's death, I seldom saw him except in his phaeton, or when I called. He gave way sadly (and inconsiderately as regarded Mrs. Wordsworth) to his grief for his daughter's loss ; and I heard that the evenings were very sad. Neither of them could see to read by candle-light ; and he was not a man of cheerful temperament, nor of much practical sympathy. Mrs. Wordsworth often asked me to 'drop in' in the winter evenings : but I really could not do this. We lived about a mile and a half apart ; I had only young girls for servants, and no carriage ; and I really could not have done my work but by the aid of my evening reading. I never went but twice ; and both times were in the summer. My deafness was a great difficulty too, and especially when his teeth were out, as they were in the evenings, when the family were alone. He began a sentence to me, and then turned his head away to finish it to somebody on the other side : so that I had no chance with him unless we were *tête-à-tête*, when we got on very well.—Our acquaintance had begun during the visit I paid to the Lakes in January 1845, when he and Mrs. Wordsworth had requested a conversation with me about mesmerism, which they thought might avail in the case of a daughter-in-law, who was then abroad, mortally ill. After a very long consultation, they left me, much disposed for the experiment : but I supposed at the time that they would not be allowed to try; and I dare say they were not.   They invited me to Rydal Mount, to see the terrace where he had meditated his poems ; and I went accordingly, one winter noon.   On that occasion, I remember, he said many characteristic things, beginning with complaints of Jeffrey and other reviewers, who had prevented his poems bringing him more than £100, for a long course of years, —up to a time so recent indeed that I will not set it down, lest there should be some mistake.   Knowing that he had no objection to be talked to about his works, I told him that I thought it might interest him to hear which of his poems was Dr. Channing's favourite.   I told him that I had not been a day in Dr. Channing's house when he brought me 'the Happy Warrior'—(a choice which I thought very characteristic also).   'Ay,' said Wordsworth: 'that was not on account of the *poetic conditions* being best fulfilled in that poem : but because it is ' (solemnly) 'a chain of extremely *valooable* thoughts.—You see,— it does not best fulfil the conditions of poetry : but it is' (solemnly) 'a chain of extremely valooable thoughts.'   I thought this eminently true : and by no means the worse for the description being given by himself.—He was kind enough to be very anxious lest I should overwalk myself.   Both he and Mrs. Wordsworth repeatedly bade me take warning by his sister, who had lost first her strength, and then her

sanity by extreme imprudence in that way, and its
consequences. Mrs. Wordsworth told me what I could
not have believed on any less trustworthy authority,—
that Miss Wordsworth had—not once, but frequently,
—walked forty miles in a day.   In vain I assured
them that I did not meditate or perpetrate any such
imprudence, and that I valued my recovered health
too much to hazard it for any self-indulgence whatever.
It was a fixed idea with them that I walked all day
long.   One afternoon Mr. Atkinson and I met them
on the Rydal road.   They asked where we had been;
and we told them.   I think it was over Loughrigg
terrace to Grasmere; which was no immoderate walk.
'There, there!' said Wordsworth, laying his hand on
my companion's arm.   'Take care! take care! Don't
let *her* carry you about.   She is killing off half the
gentlemen in the county!'   I could not then, nor
can I now, remember any Westmoreland gentleman,
except my host on Windermere, having taken a walk
with me at all.

There had been a period of a few years, in my
youth, when I worshipped Wordsworth.   I pinned up
his likeness in my room; and I could repeat his poetry
by the hour.   He had been of great service to me at
a very important time of my life.   By degrees, and
especially for ten or twelve years before I saw him, I
found more disappointment than pleasure when I turned
again to his works,—feeling at once the absence of
sound, accurate, weighty thought, and of genuine
poetic inspiration.   It is still an increasing wonder
with me that he should ever have been considered
a *philosophical* poet,—so remarkably as the very
basis of philosophy is absent in him, and so thoroughly

self-derived, self-conscious and subjective is what he himself mistook for philosophy. As to his poetic genius, it needs but to open Shelley, Tennyson, or even poor Keats, and any of our best classic English poets, to feel at once that, with all their truth and all their charm, few of Wordsworth's pieces are poems. As eloquence, some of them are very beautiful; and others are didactic or metaphysical meditations or speculations poetically rendered; but, to my mind, this is not enough to constitute a man a poet. A benefactor, to poetry and to society, Wordsworth undoubtedly was. He brought us back out of a wrong track into a right one;—out of a fashion of pedantry, antithesis and bombast, in which thought was sacrificed to sound, and common sense was degraded, where it existed, by being made to pass for something else. He taught us to say what we had to say in a way,— not only the more rational but the more beautiful; and, as we have grown more simple in expression, we have become more unsophisticated and clear-seeing and far-seeing in our observation of the scene of life, if not of life itself. These are vast services to have rendered, if no more can be claimed for the poet. In proportion to our need was the early unpopularity of the reform proposed; and in proportion to our gratitude, when we recognised our benefactor, was the temporary exaggeration of his merits as a poet. His fame seems to have now settled in its proper level. Those who understand mankind are aware that he did not understand them; and those who dwell near his abode especially wonder at his representation of his neighbours. He saw through an imagination, less poetic than metaphysical; and the heart element was in him not strong. He had scarcely any intercourse with other minds, in books or in conversation ; and he probably never knew what it was to have anything to do. His old age suffered from these causes ; and it was probably the least happy portion of a life too self-enclosed to be very happy as a whole. In regard to politics, however, and even to religion, he grew more and more liberal in his latter years. It is in that view, and as a neighbour among the cottagers, that he is most genially remembered : and considering the course of flattery he was subjected to by his blue-stocking and clerical neighbours, who coaxed him into monologue, and then wrote down all he said for future publication, it is wonderful that there is any thing so genial to record. His admirable wife, who, I believe, never suspected how much *she* was respected and beloved by all who knew them both, sustained what was genial in him, and ameliorated whatever was not so. Her excellent sense and her womanly devotedness,—(especially when she grew pale and shrunk and dim-eyed under her mute sorrow for the daughter whom *he* mourned aloud, and without apparent consideration for the heart-sufferer by his side) made her by far the more interesting of the two to me. But, while writing these recollections, the spring sunshine and air which are streaming in through my open window remind me of the advent of the ' tourist season,' and of the large allowance to be made for a ' lake poet,' subject to the perpetual incursions of flatterers of the coarsest order. The modest and well-bred pass by the gates of celebrated people who live in the country for quiet, while the coarse and selfish intrude,—as hundreds of strangers

intruded every year on Wordsworth. When I came
into the district, I was told that the average of utter
strangers who visited Rydal Mount in the season was
five hundred! Their visits were not the only penalty
inflicted. Some of these gentry occasionally sent
letters to the newspapers, containing their opinions of
the old man's state of health or of intellect: and then,
if a particularly intrusive lion-hunter got a surly
reception, and wrote to a newspaper that Wordsworth's
intellects were failing, there came letters of inquiry
from all the family friends and acquaintances, whose
affectionate solicitudes had to be satisfied.

For my part, I refused, from the first, to introduce
any of my visitors at Rydal Mount, because there
were far too many already. Mrs. Wordsworth repeatedly acknowledged my scrupulosity about this:
but in time I found that she rather wished that I
would bear my share in what had become a kind of
resource to her husband. I never liked seeing him
go the round of his garden and terraces, relating to
persons whose very names he had not attended to,
particulars about his writing and other affairs which
each stranger flattered himself was a confidential communication to himself. One anecdote will show how
the process went forward, and how persons fared who
deserved something better than this invariable treatment. In the first autumn of my residence,—while
I was in lodgings,—Mr. Seymour Tremenheere and
his comrade in his Educational Commissionership, Mr.
Tufnell, asked me to obtain lodgings for them, as they
wished to repose from their labours beside Windermere.
When they came I told them that I could not take
them to Rydal Mount. They acquiesced, though

much wishing to obtain some testimony from the old poet on behalf of popular education. In a week or two, however, I had to call on Mrs. Wordsworth, and I invited the gentlemen to take their chance by going with me. We met Mr. and Mrs. Wordsworth just coming out of their door into the garden. I twice distinctly named both gentlemen; but I saw that he did not attend, and that he received them precisely after his usual manner with strangers. He marched them off to his terraces; and Mrs. Wordsworth and I sat down on a garden seat. I told her the state of the case; and she said she would take care that, when they returned, Mr. Wordsworth should understand who his guests were. This was more easily promised than done, however. When they appeared, Mr. Wordsworth uncovered his grey head as usual, wished the gentlemen improved health and much enjoyment of the lake scenery, and bowed us out. My friends told me (what I could have told them) that Mr. Wordsworth had related many interesting things about his poems, but that they doubted whether he had any idea who they were; and they had no opportunity of introducing the subject of popular education. That evening, when a party of friends an I were at tea, an urgent message came, through three families, from Rydal Mount, to the effect that Mr. Wordsworth understood that Mr. Seymour Tremenheere was in the neighbourhood; and that he was anxious to obtain an interview with Mr. Tremenheere for conversation about popular education!—Mr. Tremenheere called at the Mount the next day. He told me on his return that he had, he hoped, gained his point. He hoped for a sonnet at least. He observed, 'Mr. Wordsworth discoursed to me about Education, trying to impress upon me whatever I have most insisted on in my Reports for seven years past: but I do not expect him to read Reports, and I was very happy to hear what he had to say.' The next time I fell in with Mr. Wordsworth, he said, ' I have to thank you for procuring for me a call from that intelligent gentleman, Mr. Tremenheere. I was glad to have some conversation with him. To be sure, he was bent on enlightening me on principles of popular education which have been published in my poems these forty years: but that is of little consequence. I am very happy to have seen him.'

In no aspect did Wordsworth appear to more advantage than in his conduct to Hartley Coleridge, who lived in his neighbourhood. The weakness,—the special vice,—of that poor, gentle, hopeless being, is universally known by the publication of his life; and I am therefore free to say that, as long as there was any chance of good from remonstrance and rebuke, Wordsworth administered both, sternly and faithfully: but, when nothing more than pity and help was possible, Wordsworth treated him as gently as if he had been—(what indeed he was in our eyes)—a sick child. I have nothing to tell of poor Hartley, of my own knowledge. Except meeting him on the road, I knew nothing of him. I recoiled from acquaintanceship,—seeing how burdensome it was in the case of persons less busy than myself, and not having, to say the truth, courage to accept the conditions on which his wonderfully beautiful conversation might be enjoyed. The simple fact is that I was in company with him five times; and all those five times

he was drunk. I should think there are few solitary
ladies, whose time is valuable, who would encourage
intercourse with him after that. Yet I quite understood the tenderness and earnestness with which he
was tended in his last illness, and the sorrow with
which he was missed by his personal friends. I witnessed his funeral; and as I saw his grey-headed old
friend Wordsworth bending over his grave, that
winter morning, I felt that the aged mourner might
well enjoy such support as could arise from a sense of
duty faithfully performed to the being who was too
weak for the conflicts of life. On his tombstone,
which stands near Wordsworth's own, is the cross
wreathed with the thorny crown, and the inscription,
so touching in this case, 'By thy Cross and Passion,
Good Lord, deliver me!'

One of my objects during this summer was to
become acquainted with the Lake District, in a complete and orderly manner. It has been a leading
pleasure and satisfaction of mine, since I grew up, to
compass some one department of knowledge at a time,
so as to feel a real command of it, succeeding to a
misty ignorance. The first approach to this was
perhaps my acquaintance with the French and Latin
languages; and the next my study of the Metaphysical schools of Mental Philosophy. But these pursuits
were partly ordained for me in my educational course;
and they belonged to the immature period of my
mind. Perhaps my first thorough *possession* was of
the doctrine of Necessity, as I have explained in its
place. Then, there was the orderly comprehension of
what I then took to be the science of Political

Economy, as elaborated by the Economists of our time : but I believe I should not have been greatly surprised or displeased to have perceived, even then, that the pretended science is no science at all, strictly speaking; and that so many of its parts must undergo essential change, that it may be a question whether future generations will owe much more to it than the benefit (inestimable, to be sure) of establishing the grand truth that social affairs proceed according to great general laws, no less than natural phenomena of every kind. Such as Political Economy was, however, I knew what it meant and what it comprehended.—Next came my study of the United States republic : and this study yielded me the satisfaction I am now referring to in full measure. Before I went, I actually sat down, on the only spare evening I had, to learn how many States there were in the American Union.—I am not sure that I knew that there were more than thirteen : and in three years after, one of the first constitutional lawyers in America wrote me the spontaneous assurance that there was not a single mistake in my ' Society in America,' in regard to the political constitution of the republic. I really had learned something thoroughly :—not the people, of course, whom it would take a lifetime to understand : but the social system under which they were living, with the geography and the sectional facts of their country.—The next act of mastery was a somewhat dreary one, but useful in its way. I understood sickness and the prospect of death, with some completeness, at the end of my five years at Tynemouth.—Now, on my recovery, I set myself to learn the Lake District, which was still a *terra incognita,*

veiled in bright mists before my mind's eye : and by
the close of a year from the purchase of my field, I
knew every lake (I think) but two, and almost every
mountain pass. I have since been complimented
with the task of writing a Complete Guide to the
Lakes, which was the most satisfactory testimony on
the part of my neighbours that they believed I understood their beloved District.—After that, there was
the working out for myself of the genealogy of the
faiths of the East, as represented in my 'Eastern
Life.' Lastly, there was the history of the last
half century of the English nation, as shown in my
' History of the Peace,' and in my articles for the
' Daily News,' at the beginning of the present war.
I need not say that I feel now, as I have ever felt,
hedged in by ignorance on every side : but I know
that we must all feel this, if we could live and learn
for a thousand years : but it is a privilege, as far as
it goes, to make clearings, one at a time, in the
wilderness of the unknown, as the settler in the Far
West opens out his crofts from the primeval forest.
Of these joyous labours, none has been sweeter than
that of my first recovered health, when Lake-land
became gradually disclosed before my explorations, till
it lay before me map-like, as if seen from a mountain
top.

I had not been settled many days in my lodging
at Waterhead before I was appealed to by my landlady and others, on behalf of sick neighbours, to know
whether mesmerism would serve them, and whether I
would administer it. After what I owed to mesmerism, I could not refuse to try ; and, though my
power has always been very moderate, I found I could

do some good. Sometimes I had seven patients asleep
at one time in my sitting-room ; and all on whom I
tried my hand were either cured or sensibly benefited.
One poor youth who was doomed to lose both arms,
from scrofulous disease in the elbows, was brought to
me, and settled beside me, to see what could be done
till it could be ascertained whether his lungs were or
were not hopelessly diseased. I mesmerised him
twice a day for ten weeks, giving up all engagements
which could interfere with the work. He obtained
sleep, to the extent of thirteen hours in twenty-four.
He recovered appetite, strength, and (the decisive
circumstance) flesh. In six weeks, his parents hardly
knew him, when they came over to see him. He lost
his cough, and all his consumptive symptoms ; we
made him our postman and errand-boy; and he
walked many miles in a day. But alas ! my house
was not built : he could not remain in the lodging
when the weather broke up : his return to his father's
cottage for the winter was inevitable ; and there he
fell back : and the damps of February carried him off
in rapid decline. None who knew him doubt that his
life was lengthened for several months, and that those
were months of ease and enjoyment, through the mesmeric treatment. The completest case under my
hands was one which I always think of with pleasure.
My landlady came up one day to ask my good offices
on behalf of a young nursemaid in the service of some
ladies who were lodging on the ground floor of the
house. This girl was always suffering under sick headache, so that her life was a burden to her, and she
was quite unfit for her place. I agreed to see her ;
but her mistress declared that she could not spare her,

as she was wanted, ill or well, to carry the baby out.
One day, however, she was too ill to raise her head at
all; and, as she was compelled to lie down, her
mistress allowed her to be brought to my sofa.   In
seven minutes, she was in the mesmeric trance.   She
awoke well, and never had a headache again.   The
ladies were so struck that they begged I would mesmerise her daily.   They came, the second day, to see
her asleep, and said she looked so different that they
should not have known her; and they called her the
' little Nell,' of Dickens.   In a few days she went
into the trance in seven seconds: and I could do what
I pleased with her, without her being conscious that
I sent her all over the house, and made her open
windows, make up the fire, &c., &c.   She began to
grow fast, became completely altered, and was in full
health, and presently very pretty.   Her parents came
many miles to thank me; and their reluctant and
hesitating request was that I would not mesmerise
her in the presence of any body who would tell the
clergy, on account of the practice of unbelievers of
traducing the characters of all who were cured by
mesmerism.   I was sorry, because Professor Gregory
and his lady, and some other friends, were coming for
the purpose of pursuing the subject; and this girl
would have been valuable to us in the inquiry: but, of
course, I could not resist the wish of the parents,
which I thought perfectly reasonable.—This reminds
me of an incident too curious not to be related.   There
is at Ambleside a retired surgeon, confined to the sofa
by disease.   A former patient of his, an elderly woman,
went to him that summer, and told him that the
doctors so completely despaired of her case that they

would give her no more medicine. Mr. C—— was very
sorry, of course ; but what could be said ? The
woman lingered and hesitated, wanting his opinion.
There *was* a lady,—she was lodging at Waterhead,
—and she did wonderful cures. What did Mr.
C—— think of an application to that lady ? ' Why
not ? ' asked Mr. C——, if the doctors would do
nothing more for the patient ? He advised the
attempt. After more hesitation the scruple came out.
' Why, Sir, they *do* say that the lady does it through
the Old 'Un.' The sick woman feared what the
clergy would say : and, in spite of Mr. C——'s
encouragement, she never came.

My own experience that year was an instructive
one. I have mentioned that, during my recovery, I
was never in the mesmeric sleep,—never unconscious.
From the time that I was quite well, however, I fell
into the sleep,—sometimes partially and sometimes
wholly : though it took a long while to convince me
that I was ever unconscious. It was only by finding
that I had lost an hour that I could be convinced that
I had slept at all. One day, when mesmerised by two
persons, I had begun to speak ; and from that time,
whenever I was thus double mesmerised, I discoursed
in a way which those who heard it call very remarkable. I could remember some of the wonderful things
I had seen and thought, if questioned immediately on
my waking ; but the impressions were presently gone.
A short-hand writer took down much of what I said ;
and certainly those fragments are wholly unlike any
thing I have ever said under any other circumstances.
I still believe that some faculties are thus reached
which are not, as far as can be known, exercised at any

other time; and also that the conceptive and imaginative faculties, as well as those of insight and of
memory, are liable to be excited to very vigorous
action. When consciousness is incomplete,—or, rather,
when unconsciousness is all but complete,—so that
actual experience is interfused with the dreams of the
mesmeric condition, there is danger of that state of
mind which is not uncommon under mesmeric treatment, and which renders the superintendence of an
experienced and philosophical mesmeriser so desirable
as we see it to be,—a state of exaltation almost
amounting to delusion, when imaginative patients are
concerned. Nobody would consider me, I think, a
particularly imaginative patient: and nothing could be
more common-place and safe than the practice while
I was either wide awake or so completely asleep as to
remember nothing of my dreams afterwards: but, in
the intermediate case, I was subject to a set of impressions so strong that,—having seen instances of
the *clairvoyant* and prophetic faculty in others,—it
was scarcely possible to avoid the belief that my constant and highly detailed impressions were of the same
character. It is impossible to be absolutely certain,
at this moment, that they were not: but the strongest
probability is that they were of the same nature with
the preachments and oracular statements of a host of
mesmeric patients who give forth their notions about
'the spiritual world' and its inhabitants.*   It is

---

* An eminent literary man said lately that he never was
afraid of dying before; but that he now could not endure the
idea of being summoned by students of spirit-rapping to talk
such nonsense as their ghosts are made to do. This suggests to
me the expediency of declaring my conviction that if any such
students should think fit to summon me, when I am gone hence,

observed, in all accounts of spirit-rappings and mesmeric speculation, that, on the subject of religion, each speaker gives out his own order of opinions in the form of testimony from what he sees. We have all the sects of Christendom represented in their mesmerised members,—constituting, to the perplexity of inexperienced observers, as remarkable a Babel in the spiritual world as on our European and American soil ; and, when there is no hope of reconciling these incompatible oracles, the timid resort to the supposition of demoniacal agency. There is no marvel in this to persons who, like myself, are aware, from their own experience, of the irresistible strength of the impressions of mesmeric dreaming, when more or less interfused with waking knowledge ; nor to philosophical observers who, like my guardian in this stage of my experience, have witnessed the whole range of the phenomena with cool judgment, and under a trained method of investigation. Under different management, and without his discouragements and cool exposure of the discrepancies of dreaming, I might have been one of the victims of the curiosity and half-knowledge of the time, and my own trust in my waking faculties, and, much more, other people's trust in them, might have been lost ; and my career of literary action might have prematurely

they will get a visit from,—not me,—but the ghosts of their own thoughts : and I beg beforehand not to be considered answerable for any thing that may be revealed under such circumstances.— I do not attempt to offer any explanation of that curious class of phenomena, but I do confidently deny that we can be justified in believing that Bacon, Washington, and other wise men are the speakers of the trash that the ' spiritual circles ' report as their revelations.

come to an end.   Even before I was quite safe, an incident occurred which deeply impressed me.—Margaret
Fuller, who had been, in spite of certain mutual
repulsions, an intimate acquaintance of mine in
America, came to Ambleside while Professor and Mrs.
Gregory and other friends were pursuing the investigations I have referred to.   I gave her, and the excellent
friends with whom she was travelling, the best welcome
I could.   My house was full : but I got lodgings for
them, made them welcome as guests, and planned
excursions for them.   Her companions evidently
enjoyed themselves ; and Margaret Fuller as evidently
did not, except when she could harangue the drawing-
room party, without the interruption of any other
voice within its precincts.   There were other persons
present, at least as eminent as herself, to whom we
wished to listen ; but we were willing that all should
have their turn : and I am sure I met her with every
desire for friendly intercourse.   She presently left off
conversing with me, however ; while I, as hostess, had
to see that my other guests were entertained, according
to their various tastes.   During our excursion in
Langdale, she scarcely spoke to any body ; and not at
all to me ; and when we afterwards met in London,
when I was setting off for the East, she treated me
with the contemptuous benevolence which it was her
wont to bestow on common-place people.   I was therefore not surprised when I became acquainted, presently
after, with her own account of the matter.   She told
her friends that she had been bitterly disappointed in
me.   It had been a great object with her to see me,
after my recovery by mesmerism, to enjoy the exaltation and spiritual development which she concluded I

must have derived from my excursions in the spiritual
world : but she had found me in no way altered by it ;
no one could have discovered that I had been mesmerised at all; and I was so thoroughly common-place
that she had no pleasure in intercourse with me.—
This was a very welcome confirmation of my hope that
I had, under Mr. Atkinson's wise care, come back
nearly unharmed from the land of dreams ; and this
more than compensated for the unpleasantness of dis-
appointing the hopes of one whom I cordially respected
for many fine qualities, intellectual and moral, while I
could not pretend to find her mind unspoiled and her
manners agreeable.   She was then unconsciously
approaching the hour of that remarkable regeneration
which transformed her from the dreaming and haughty
pedant into the true woman.   In a few months more,
she had loved and married ; and how interesting and
beautiful was the closing period of her life, when
husband and child concentrated the powers and affections which had so long run to waste in intellectual and
moral eccentricity, the concluding period of her memoirs has shown to us all.   Meantime, the most
acceptable verdict that she could pronounce upon me
in my own function of housekeeper and hostess, while
the medical world was hoping to hear of my insanity,
was that I was ' common-place.'

Some members of that medical world were, in that
summer at Waterhead (1845), demonstrating to me
what my duty was in regard to poor Jane, at Tynemouth,—usually called my maid, but not yet so, nor
to be so till the spring of 1846.   The sudden cessation
of mesmerism was disastrous to the poor girl.—Her

eyes became as bad as ever; and the persecution of
the two doctors employed by Dr. Forbes fell upon her
alone,—her ignorant and selfish aunt refusing to let
her be mesmerised, and permitting her rather to go
blind.   When she was blind, these two men came to
her with a paper which they required her to sign,
declaring that she had been guilty of imposture
throughout; and they told her that she should
be taken to prison if she did not, then and
there, sign their paper.   She steadily refused
not only to sign, but to answer any of their questions,
saying that they had set down false replies for both
her aunts; and in this her aunts took courage to support her, in the face of threats from the doctors that
they would prevent these poor widows having any
more lodgers.   An Ambleside friend of mine, calling
on Jane at Tynemouth, found her in this plight, and
most kindly brought over from South Shields a benevolent druggist, accustomed to mesmerise.   The aunt
refused him admission to her house; and he therefore
went to the bottom of the garden, where Jane was
supported to a seat.   At the end of the *séance*, she
could see some bright thing on her lap; and she had
an appetite, for the first time for some weeks.   The
aunt could not resist this appeal to her heart and her
self-interest at once; and she made the druggist
welcome.   As soon as I heard all this, I begged my
kind aunts to go over from Newcastle, and tell Jane's
aunt that if she could restore Jane so far as to undertake the journey to Ambleside, I would thenceforth
take charge of her.   It was a fearful undertaking,
under the circumstances; but I felt that my protection
and support were due to the poor girl.   The aunt had

her mesmerised and well cared for; and in two or three weeks she said she could come. I had, as yet, no house; and there was no room for her in my lodging; so I engaged a cottager near Ambleside to receive the girl and board her for her services in taking care of the children till my house should be habitable. She was so eager to reach me that when she found the Keswick coach full, she walked sixteen miles, rather than wait, and presented herself to me tearful, nervous, in sordid clothes (for her aunt had let the poor girl's wardrobe go to rags while she was too blind to sew), and her eyes like those of a blind person, looking as if the iris was covered with tissue paper. My heart sank at the sight. I told her that I had not mentioned mesmerism to her hostess, because, after all she had gone through, I thought the choice should be hers whether to speak of it or not. I had simply told the woman that I wished Jane to take a walk to my lodgings, three or four times a week. Jane's instant reply was that she did not wish for any secret about the matter; and that she thought she ought not to mind any ill-treatment while God permitted sick people to get well by a new means, whether the doctors liked it or not. I soon found that she was mesmerising a diseased baby in the cottage, and teaching the mother to do it;—whereby the child lived for months after the medical man declined visiting it any more because it was dying. I mesmerised Jane three times a week: and in ten days her eyes were as clear as my own. When, henceforth, I saw any doubtful appearance in them, I mesmerised her once or twice; and that set all right. She never had any more trouble with them, except during my long absence in the East. They looked ill when I returned; when again, and finally, a few *séances* cured them. She lived with me seven years, and then went, with my entire approbation, to Australia. She immediately became cook in the family of the High Sheriff of Melbourne, where she is still. The zeal with which she assisted in furnishing and preparing my new house may be imagined; and how happy she was in those opening spring days when we met at the house early in the mornings and stayed till nine at night, making all ready in the new house which we longed to occupy. The first night (April 7th, 1846) when we made our beds, stirred up the fires, and locked the doors, and had some serious talk, as members of a new household, will never be forgotten, for its sweetness and solemnity, by my maids or myself.

Many persons, before doubtful or adverse, began to take a true view of this girl and her case when I was in the East. When they saw that, instead of accepting large sums of money to go about as a *clair voyante*, with lecturers on mesmerism, she remained at her post in my house, during the long fourteen months of my absence, they were convinced that she was no notoriety-seeker, or trickster, or speculator for money. She practised the closest economy, and invested her savings carefully, because she doubted her eyes, and wished to provide against accidents; and, when she emigrated, she had money enough for a good outfit, and to spare. But she might have had ten times as much if she had been tempted to itinerate as a *clair-voyante*. With these facts I close her history. I have given it fully, because it happened repeatedly during the seven years that she lived with me, that reports

appeared in the newspapers, or by applications to myself through the post, that I had dismissed her in
disgrace.   My reply always was that if I had seen
reason to doubt her honesty in the matter of the mesmerism, or in any other way, I should have felt myself bound to avow the fact in print, after all that had
happened.   My final declaration is that I have never
known a more truthful person than my Jane; and I
am confident that, among all the neighbours to whom
she was known for seven years, and among her
Tynemouth neighbours, who knew her for the nineteen preceding years of her life, there are none who
would dissent from my judgment of her.

My notion of doing no work during the gladsome
year 1845 soon gave way,—not before inclination,
(for I was sorely reluctant) but duty.   When the
potato famine was impending, and there was alarm
for the farming interest, Mr. Bright's Committee on
the Game-laws published the evidence laid before
them; and it appeared that there could not be a
better time for drawing public attention to a system
more detrimental to the farming class, and more
injurious to the production of food than any of the
grievances put forth by the complaining 'agricultural
interest.'   I was told that I ought to treat the
subject as I had treated the topics of Political Economy
in my Series; and I agreed that I ought.   Mr. Bright
supplied me with the evidence ; I collected historical
material; and I wrote the three volumes of ' Forest
and Game-Law Tales' in the autumn of 1845.
Above 2,000 copies of these have sold ; but, at the
time, the publication appeared to be a total failure ;—

my first failure.   The book came out, as it happened, precisely at the time when Sir R. Peel was known to be about to repeal the Corn-laws.   It was said at the time that for three weeks no publisher in London sold anything, with the one exception of Wordsworth's new and last edition of his works, wherein he took his farewell of the public.   Nearly 1,000 copies of my book were sold at once; but, reckoning on a very large sale, we had stereotyped it; and this turned out a mistake, —the stereotyping more than cutting off the profits of the sale.   From that work I have never received a shilling.   On my own account I have never regretted doing the work,—reluctant as I was to work that happy autumn.   I know that many young men, and some of them sure to become members of the legislature, have been impressed by those essentially true stories to a degree which cannot but affect the destination and duration of the Game-laws; and this is enough.   That the toil was an encroachment on my fresh pleasures at the time, and has proved gratuitous, is of no consequence now, while it is certain that a few young lords and gentry have had their eyes opened to the cost of their sport, and to their duty in regard to it.   If I could but learn that some of the 2,000 copies sold had gone into the hands of the farmers, and had put any strength into their hearts to assert their rights, and resist the wrongs they have too tamely submitted to, I should feel that the result deserved a much greater sacrifice. As it was, I set down the gratuitous labour as my contribution to, or fine upon, the repeal of the Corn-laws.

That repeal was now drawing nigh.   I was in the

November and December of that year that Lord John Russell condescended to that struggle for power with Sir R. Peel which will damage his fame in the eyes of posterity, and which reflected disgrace at the time on the whole Whig party, as it waned towards dissolution. During the struggle, and the alternate 'fall' of the two statesmen, much wonder was felt by people generally, and, it is believed, especially by Sir R. Peel, that the great middle-class body, including the Anti-corn-law League, showed so little earnestness in supporting Peel; so that when the matter was placed in Peel's hands by his restoration to power, it did not seem to *get on.* I had occasion to know where the hitch was; and, as it appeared to me, to act upon that knowledge, in a way quite new to me,—indisposed as I have always been to meddle in matters which did not concern me.—While I was ill at Tynemouth, Colonel Thompson and Mr. Cobden called on me; and we had a long talk on League affairs, and the prospect of a repeal of the Corn-laws. Mr. Cobden told me that he and his comrades were so incessantly occupied in lecturing, and in showing up to multitudes the facts of a past and present time, that they had no leisure or opportunity to study the probable future; and that the opinions or suggestions of a person like myself, lying still, and reading and thinking, might be of use to the leaders of the agitation; and he asked me to write to him if at any time I had any thing to criticise or suggest in regard to League affairs. I had not much idea that I could be of any service; but I made the desired promise.

In the autumn of 1845, when Sir R. Peel retired from the government to make way for Lord J. Russell,

Mr. Cobden made a speech to his Stockport con-
stitutents, in which he spoke in terms of insult of Peel.
I saw this with much regret; and, recalling my
promise, I wrote to Mr. Cobden, telling him that it
was as a member of the League, and not as a censor
that I wrote to him.   It was no business of mine to
criticise his temper or taste in addressing his constituents; but I reminded him that his Stockport
speech was read all over the kingdom; and I asked
him whether he thought the object of the League
would be furthered by his having insulted a fallen
Minister;—whether, indeed, anything had ever
been gained, since society began, by any man having
insulted any other man.   Before my letter reached
Mr. Cobden, he had spoken in yet more outrageous
terms of Peel, at a crowded meeting in Covent Garden
theatre, leaving himself without the excuse that, in
addressing his constituents, he had lost sight of her
consideration of the general publicity of his speech.
Mr. Cobden's reply was all good-humour and candour
as regarded myself; but it disclosed the depth of
the sore in his mind in regard to his relations with
Sir R. Peel.   There is no occasion to tell at length
the sad story of what had passed between them in
February 1843, when Peel charged Cobden with
being answerable for assassination, and Cobden, losing
his presence of mind, let the occasion turn against
him.   It was the worst act of Peel's public life, no
doubt; and the moment was one of such anguish to
Cobden that he could never recall it without agitation.
He referred to it, in his reply to me, in extenuation of
his recent outbreak,—while declining to justify himself.   I wrote again, allowing that Peel's conduct

admitted of no justification ; but showing that there
were extenuating circumstances in his case too.   Of
these circumstances I happened to know more than
the public did ; and I now laid them before my correspondent,—again saying that I did not see why
the cause should suffer for such individual griefs.   In
the course of two or three weeks, plenty of evidence
reached me that the great manufacturing classes were
holding back on account of this unsettled reckoning
between Peel and their leader ; and also that Cobden
had suffered much and magnanimously, for a course of
years, from the remonstrances and instigations of
Liberal members, who urged his seeking personal
satisfaction from his enemy. Mr. Cobden had steadily
refused, because he was in parliament as the representative of the bread-eaters, and had no right, as he
thought, to consume the time and attention of parliament with his private grievances.   It struck me that
it was highly important that Sir R. Peel should know
all this, as he was otherwise not master of his own
position.   I therefore wrote to a neutral friend of his
and mine, laying the case before him.   He was a
Conservative M.P., wholly opposed to the repeal of
the Corn-laws ; but I did not see that that was
necessarily an obstacle.   I told him that he must see
that the Corn-laws must be repealed, and that there
would be no peace and quiet till the thing was done;
and I had little doubt that he would be glad of the
opportunity of bringing two earnest men to a better
understanding with each other.   My friend did not
answer my letter for three weeks : and when he did,
he could send me nothing but fierce vituperation of
his abjured leader.   Time was now pressing; and I

had not felt it right to wait. The whole move would
have failed but for the accident that Mr. Cobden had
sat in a draught, and suffered from an abscess in the
ear which kept him from the House for three weeks
or so.   What I did was this.

As I sat at breakfast on New Year's day, (1846)
thinking over this matter, it struck me that no harm
could be done by my writing myself to Sir R. Peel.
He would probably think me meddlesome, and be
vexed at the womanish folly of supposing that, while
the laws of honour which are so sacred in men's eyes
remain, he could make any move towards a man who
had insulted him as Mr. Cobden had recently done.
But it was nothing to me what Sir R. Peel thought
of the act. He was a stranger to me; and his
opinion could not weigh for an instant against the
remotest chance of abridging the suspense about the
Corn-laws. I frankly told him this, in the letter
which I wrote him after breakfast. I laid the case
before him; and, when I came to the duelling considerations, I told him what a woman's belief is in
such a case,—that a devoted man can rise above
arbitrary social rules; and that I believed him to be
the man who could do it. I believed him to be
capable of doing the impossible in social morals, as
he was proving himself to be in politics. I told him
that my sole object was to put him in possession of a
case which I suspected he did not understand; and
that I therefore desired no answer, nor any notice
whatever of my letter, which was written without anybody's knowledge, and would be posted by my own
hand. By return of post came a long letter from Sir
R. Peel which moved me deeply. Nothing could be

more frank, more cordial, or more satisfactory. It
was as I suspected.   He had not had the remotest
idea that what he had said in the House by way of
amende, the next (Monday) evening after the insult,
had not been considered satisfactory.   He wrote
strongly about the hardship of being thus kept
in the dark for years,—neither Mr. Cobden nor any
other member on either side of the House having
hinted to him that the matter was not entirely settled.
—Now that it was clear that Sir R. Peel would act
on his new knowledge in one way or another, the
question occurred to me,—what was to be done with
Mr. Cobden, whose want of presence of mind had
aggravated the original mischief.   The same defi-
ciencies might spoil the whole business now.—I had
told Sir R. Peel, whilst praising Mr. Cobden, that of
course *he* knew nothing of what I was doing.   I now
wrote to Mr. Cobden the most artful letter I ever
penned.   It really was difficult to manage this, my
first intrigue, all alone.   I told Mr. Cobden that the
more I pondered the existing state of the Corn-law
affair, the more sure I felt that Sir R. Peel must
become aware of the cause of the backwardness of the
Manchester interest ; and also, that my view of
certain unconspicuous features of the Minister's cha--
acter led me to expect some magnanimous offer of an
amende : and I ventured to observe what a pity it
would be if Mr. Cobden should be so taken by surprise as to let such an occasion of reconciliation be
lost.   I also wrote to Sir R. Peel, telling him that,
however it might appear to him, Mr. Cobden was of
a relenting nature, likely to go more than half way
to meet an adversary ; and that, though he knew

nothing of my interference, I had a confident hope
that he would not be found wanting, if an occasion
should present itself for him finally to merge his
private grief in the great public cause of the day.

The next morning but one, the post brought me a
newspaper directed by Sir R. Peel, and autographed
by him ; and, as usual, the ' Times.'   There was also
a note from Mr. Cobden which prepared me for something interesting in the report of the Debates.   His
note was scrawled in evident feebleness, and expressive
of the deepest emotion.   He dated at 3 A. M., and
said he had just returned from the House, and that
he could not lay his head on his pillow till he had sent
me the blessing on the peace-maker.   He declared
that his mind was eased of a load which had burdened
it for long and miserable years ; and now he should
be a new man.   The ' Times ' told me how immediately Sir R. Peel had acted on his new information,
and that that union of effort was now obtained under
which the immediate repeal of the Corn-laws was
certain.   How well the hostile statesmen acted together thenceforth, every body knows.   But scarcely
any body knows (unless Sir R. Peel thought proper
to tell) how they came to an understanding.   Mr.
Cobden has told his friends that it was somehow my
doing ; but he never heard a word of it from or
through me.—He wrote, after some time, to beg me
to burn any letters of his which contained his former
opinion of Sir R. Peel.   I had already done so.   I
wished to preserve only what all the parties implicated
would enjoy seeing twenty years later : and I should
not have related the story here if I had not considered
it honourable to every body concerned.

I little dreamed during that winter how I should
pass the next. The months slipped away rapidly,
amidst the visits of family and friends, writing, study,
house-building, and intercourse with the few neighbours whom I knew. A young nephew and niece
came late in the autumn, and others in the spring;
and we went little journeys on foot among the
mountains, carrying knapsack or basket, and making
acquaintance among the small country inns. In the
spring, there was the pleasure of bringing home
basketsful of the beautiful ferns and mosses of the
district, and now and then a cartful of heather, to
cover my rocks; and primroses and foxgloves and
daffodils and periwinkle for the garden; and wood-
sorrel for the copses, where the blue-bells presently
eclipsed the grass. A friend in London, who knew
my desire for a sundial, and heard that I could not
obtain the old one which had told me so important a
story in my childhood, presented me with one, to
stand on the grass under my terrace wall, and above
the quarry which was already beginning to fill with
shrubs and wild flowers. The design of the dial is
beautiful,—being a copy of an ancient font; and in
grey granite, to accord with the grey-stone house
above it. The motto was an important affair. A
neighbour had one so perfect in its way as to eclipse
a whole class;—the class of bible sayings about the
shortness of life and the flight of time. 'The night
cometh.' In asking my friends for suggestions, I
told them of this; and they agreed that we could not
approach this motto, in the same direction. Some
good Latin ones, to which I inclined, were put aside
because I was besought, for what I considered good

reasons, to have nothing but English. It has always been my way to ask advice very rarely, and then to follow it. But on this occasion, I preferred a motto of my own to all that were offered in English ; and Wordsworth gave it his emphatic approbation. ' Come, Light ! visit me !' stands emblazoned on my dial : and it has been, I believe, as frequent and impressive a monitor to me as ever was any dial which bore warning of the fugacious nature of life and time.

Summer brought a succession of visitors,—very agreeable, but rather too many for my strength and repose. I began to find what are the liabilities of Lake residents in regard to tourists. There is quite wear and tear enough in receiving those whom one wishes to see ; one's invited guests, or those introduced by one's invited friends. But these are fewer than the unscrupulous strangers who intrude themselves with compliments, requests for autographs, or without any pretence whatever. Every summer they come and stare in at the windows while we are at dinner, hide behind shrubs or the corner of the house, plant themselves in the yards behind or the field before ; are staring up at one's window when one gets up in the morning, gather handfuls of flowers in the garden, stop or follow us in the road, and report us to the newspapers. I soon found that I must pay a serious tax for living in my paradise : I must, like many of my neighbours, go away in ' the tourist season.' My practice has since been to let my house for the months of July, August and September,—or for the two latter at least, and go to the sea, or some country place where I could be quiet.

I do not know that a better idea of the place could

be given than by the following paragraphs from a palpable description of our little town (under the name of Hauksidc,—a compound of Hawkshead and Ambleside) which appeared some time since in ' Chambers's Journal.'

' The constitution of our town suffers six months of the year from fever, and the other six from collapse. In the summer-time, our inns are filled to bursting; our private houses broken into by parties desperate after lodgings; the prices of every thing are quadrupled ; our best meat, our thickest cream, our freshest fish, are reserved for strangers; our letters, delivered three hours after time, have been opened and read by banditti assuming our own title ; ladies of quality, loaded with tracts, fusillade us ; savage and bearded foreigners harass us with brazen wind instruments; coaches run frantically towards us from every point of the compass; a great steam-monster ploughs our lake, and disgorges multitudes upon the pier; the excursion-trains bring thousands of curious vulgar, who mistake us for the authoress next door, and compel us to forge her autograph ; the donkeys in our streets increase and multiply a hundredfold, tottering under the weight of enormous females visiting our water-falls from morn to eve ; our hills are darkened by swarms of tourists; we are ruthlessly eyed by painters, and brought into foregrounds and backgrounds, as "warm tints" or "bits of repose;" our lawns are picnicked upon by twenty at a time, and our trees branded with initial letters ; creatures with introductions come to us, and can't be got away ; we have to lionise poor, stupid, and ill-looking people for weeks, without past, present, or future recompense;

Sunday is a day of rest least of all, and strange clergy-men preach charity-sermons every week with a perfect kaleidoscope of religious views.

‘ The fever lasts from May until October.

‘ When it is over, horses are turned out to grass, and inn-servants are disbanded ; houses seem all too big for us ; the hissing fiend is “ laid ” upon the lake ; the coaches and cars are on their backs in outhouses, with their wheels upwards ; the trees get bare, the rain begins to fall, grass grows in the streets, and Haukside collapses.

‘ Our collapse lasts generally from November to May. During this interval, we residents venture to call upon each other. Barouches and chariots we have none, but chiefly shandrydans and buggies ; we are stately and solemn in our hospitalities, and retain fashions amongst us that are far from new ; we have evening-parties very often, and at every party—whist ! Not that it is our sole profession : not that it is our only amusement ; it is simply an eternal and unalterable custom—whist ! We have no clubs to force it into vigour : the production is indigenous and natural to the place. It is the attainment of all who have reached years of maturity ; the dignity of the aged, and the ambition of the young ; a little whirling in the dance, a little leaning over the piano, a little attachment to the supper-table, a little flirting on both sides—all this is at Haukside as elsewhere ; but the end, the bourne to which male and female alike tend at last after experiencing the vanity of all things else, and from which none ever returns, is—the whist-table.’

The autumn of 1846 had been fixed on for a series

of visits to some of my family, and to London; and
I let my house to a young couple of my acquaintance
for their honeymoon, and went to Liverpool, to my
younger sister's, on the last day of August, little
dreaming how long it would be before I came back
again. I should have gone away even more sad than
I was, if I had known.

SECTION III.

WHILE at Liverpool, I was the guest of my old friends, the Misses Yates, for a few days; on one of which days, Miss E. Yates and I went out to dinner, while Miss Yates paid a family visit. On our return, she looked very bright and happy; but it did not strike me that it was from any hidden secret. Mr. Richard V. Yates came to breakfast the next morning; and he was placed next to me,—and next to my best ear. The conversation soon turned on his projected Eastern journey, about which I had before had some talk,—remarkably free in regard to the dangers and disagreeables,—with Mrs. R. V. Yates, as we afterwards remembered with much amusement. Mr. Yates now renewed that conversation, consulting me about turning back at the first cataract of the Nile, or going on to the second. From 'Would you go on to the second?' Mr. Yates changed his question to 'Will you go on to the second?' and, after a few moments of perplexity to me, he said 'Now, seriously, —will you go with us? Mrs. Yates will do every thing in her power to render the journey agreeable to you; and I will find the piastres.' At first, I felt and said, while deeply gratified, that I could not go;

and for hours and days it seemed impracticable. I
was engaged to write a new series of ' The Playfellow ' for Mr. Knight, and had sent him the MS.
of the first (' The Billow and the Rock.') I had just
begun housekeeping, and had left home without any
other idea than returning for the winter: and the
truth was, I had the strongest possible inclination to
return, and indisposition to wander away from the
repose and beauty of my home. But the way soon
cleared so as to leave me no doubt what I ought to
do. My family urged my accepting an opportunity
too fine ever to recur: Mr. Knight generously proposed to put my story into his ' Weekly Volume,' and
wait for more ' Playfellows,'—sending the money at
once, to make my outfit easy; and my neighbours at
Ambleside promised to look after my house and servant, and let the house if possible. Tenants were in
it for a part of the time, and Jane was well taken care
of for the rest; so that nothing could turn out better
than the whole scheme. We were joined *en route* by
Mr. J. C. Ewart, the present representative of Liverpool; and he remained with us till we reached Malta
on our return. He thence wrote to his sister about
our parting,—he to go to Constantinople, and we
homewards; saying that our experience was, he feared,
a very rare one ;—that of a travelling party who had
been in the constant and close companionship imposed
by Nile and Desert travelling, for eight months, and
who, instead of quarrelling and parting, like most
such groups, had travelled in harmony, were separating
with regret, and should be more glad to meet in future
than we were before we set out. It is worth mentioning this, because I heard, a year or so afterwards, that

a report was abroad that our party had quarrelled immediately,—in France,—and that I had prosecuted my eastern journey alone. My book, however, must have demolished that fiction, one would think: but such fictions are tenacious of life. In my preface to that book, I related the kindness of my companions in listening to my journal, and in authorising me to say that they bore testimony to the correctness of my facts, to the best of their judgment, while disclaiming all connexion with the resulting opinions. I have a letter from Mr. Yates, in acknowledgement of his copy of the book, in which he bears the same testimony, with the same reservation, and adds an expression of gratification, on Mrs. Yates's part and his own, at the manner in which they are spoken of throughout the work. Some idle reports about this matter, injurious to those excellent friends of mine, are probably extinct already: and if not, this statement will extinguish them.

My travelling companions and I met in London in October, after I had secured my outfit there, and run down into Norfolk to see old Norwich again. We had had hopes that Mr. Atkinson could go with us; and the plan had been nearly arranged; but he was prevented at the last, and could accompany us no further than Boulogne. We traversed France to Marseilles, resting for two days at Paris, where, strange to say, I had never been before. We were quite late enough at best; but the evil chance which sent us on board the mail-packet Volcano caused a most vexatious delay. We were detained, at the outset, for the mails. The captain started with a short supply of coal, because it was dear at Marseilles, and soon found that

he had been 'penny wise and pound foolish.' The
engines of the vessel were too weak for her work; and
the wind was dead against us.   The captain forsook
the usual route, and took the northerly one, for I
forget what reason; and thus we were out of the way
of succour.   The vessel swarmed with cockroaches;
two ill-mannered women shared the cabin with Mrs.
Yates and me; the captain was so happy flirting with
one of them as to seem provokingly complacent under
our delays.   It was really vexatious to see him and
the widow sitting hand-in-hand, and giggling on the
sofa, while our stomachs turned at the sea-pie to which
we were reduced, and our precious autumn days were
slipping away, during which we ought to have been at
Cairo, preparing for our ascent of the Nile.   It was
worse with others on board,—gentlemen on their way
to India, whose clothes and money were now sure to
have left Malta before they could arrive there.   One
of these gentlemen was to meet at Malta a sister
from Naples, whom he had not seen for twenty years,
and who must either be in agony about his fate, or
have given up the rendezvous as a failure.   This
gentleman, whose good manners and cheerfulness in
company never failed, told me on deck, when no one
was within hearing, that the trial was as much as he
could bear.   Some passengers were ill,—some angry,
—some alarmed; and the occasion was a touch-stone
of temper and manners.   All our coal was consumed,
except enough for six hours,—that quantity being
reserved to carry us into port.   Every morning, the
captain let us sail about a little, to make believe that
we were on our way; but every evening we found
ourselves again off Pantellaria, which seemed as much

an enchanted island to us as if we had seen Calypso
on its cliffs. Now and then, Sicily came provokingly
into view, and the captain told us he was bound not
to touch there or any where till we were in extremity;
and we should not be in extremity till he had burned
the cabin wainscot and furniture, and the stairs and
berths, and there was nothing whatever left to eat.
We now had cheese and the materials for plum-
pudding. Every thing else on table began to be too
disgusting for even sea-appetites. A young lieutenant offered us a receipt for a dish which he said we
should find palatable enough when we could get
nothing better,—broiled boot leather, well seasoned.
—As for me, I was an old sailor; and, when the
sickness was once over, I kept on deck and did very
well. The weather was dreary,—the ship sticky and
dirty in every part,—and our prospect singularly
obscure; but there was clearly nothing to be done
but to wait as good-humouredly as we could.

One afternoon, just before dinner, the fellow-passenger who pined for his sister, hastily called the captain,
who, looking towards the southern horizon, was in
earnest for once. A thread of smoke was visible
where all had been blank for so many days; and it
was astonishing to me that the wise as well as the
foolish on board jumped to the conclusion that it was
a steamer sent from Malta in search of us. They
were right; and in another hour we were in tow of
our deliverer. There had been time for only two or
three questions before we were on our course. I left
the dinner-table as soon as I could, and went to the
bows, to see how her Majesty's mail-steamer looked
in tow. The officers of the two vessels wanted to

converse; but the wind was too high. 'Try your trumpet,' was written on a black board in the other vessel. 'Have not got one,' was our Lieutenant's reply; to which the black board soon rejoined, 'Why, that lady has got it.' They actually took my special trumpet for that of the ship. When in sight of Malta, we burned our remnant of coal; and at midnight a gun in Valetta harbour told the inhabitants that the Volcano was safe in port. Our party remained on board till the morning; but the brother and sister met that night; and we saw them on the ramparts next day, arm-in-arm, looking as happy as could be. I was made uneasy about my own family by hearing that Valetta newspapers had gone to England the day before, notifying the non-arrival of the Volcano, and the general belief that she was gone to the bottom, with the addition that I was on board. My first business was to close and dispatch the journal-letter which I had amused myself with writing on board. Before it arrived, some of my relatives had been rendered as uneasy as I feared by the inconsiderate paragraph in the Valetta paper.

At Malta I began to feel (rather than see) the first evidences of the rivalry then existing between the English and French at the Egyptian court. I could not conceive why Captain Glasscock, whose ship was then in the port, made so much of me; but his homage was so exaggerated that I suspected some reason of policy. He came daily, bringing his lady, and all his officers in parties; he loaded me with compliments, and seized every occasion of enforcing certain views of his own. which I was glad to hear in the way of

guidance in a new scene; and his most emphatic
enforcement of all was in regard to the merits of a
certain Englishman who was waiting, he intimated,
to worship us on our landing at Alexandria. Captain
Glasscock insisted on sending my party in his man-
of-war's boat to the Ariel, in which we were to proceed to Egypt. We saw his friend at Alexandria,
and received the promised homage, and, really, some
agreeable hospitality, but not the impressions of the
gentleman's abilities of which we had been assured.
By degrees it became apparent to me that what was
wanted was that I should write a book on Egypt, like
Mrs. Romer, who had preceded me by a year or two ;
and that, like Mrs. Romer, I should be flattered into
advocating the Egyptian Railway scheme by which
the English in Egypt hoped to gain an advantage
over the French, and for which the Alexandrian
gentleman had already imported the rails. There they
lay, absorbing his capital in a very inconvenient
manner ; and he seized every chance of getting his
scheme advocated. With Mrs. Romer he succeeded,
but not with me. At Cairo I had the means of
knowing that much more was involved in the scheme,
—much difficulty with the Bedoueens and others
besides the French,—than I had been told at Alexandria. I knew what would be the consequences of
my treatment of the matter in my book ; and I learned
them in an amusing way. An acquaintance of mine
in London told me, a day or two after publication,
that the brother of the Alexandrian gentleman, and
part-owner of the rails, had got a copy of the book
already. 'And he does not like it,' said I : 'he
tells you it is damned humbug.' My friend burs

into a fit of laughter, shouting out, ' Why, that is
exactly what he did say.'

The greater was my reluctance to go this journey
under my new and happy domestic circumstances, the
stronger is the evidence of my estimate of its advantages. I should not have gone but for the entire
conviction that it would prove an inestimable privilege.
Yet, I had little idea what the privilege would turn
out to be, nor how the convictions and the action of
the remnant of my life would be shaped and determined by what I saw and thought during those all-
important months that I spent in the East. I need
say nothing here of the charms of the scenery, and
the atmosphere, and the novelty, and the associations
with hallowed regions of the earth. The book I
wrote on my return gives a fresher impression of all
that enjoyment than any thing I could write now :
but there were effects produced on my own character
of mind which it would have been impertinent to
offer there, even if the lapse of years had not been
necessary to make them clear to myself. I never
before had better opportunity for quiet meditation.
My travelling companions, and especially the one
with whom I was the most inseparably associated,
Mrs. Yates, had that invaluable travelling qualification,—the tact to leave me perfectly free. We were
silent when we chose, without fear of being supposed
unmannerly; and I could not have believed beforehand that so incessant and prolonged a companionship
could have entailed so little restraint. My deafness
which would, in the opposite case, have imposed a
most disabling fatigue, was thus rather an advantage.
While we had abundance of cheerful conversation at

meals and in the evenings, and whenever we were
disposed for it, there were many hours of every day
when I was virtually as much alone as I could have
been in my own house; and, of the many benefits
and kindnesses that I received from my companions,
none excited my lasting gratitude more than this.
During the ten weeks that we were on the Nile, I
could sit on deck and think for hours of every morning; and while we were in the desert, or traversing
the varied scenery in Palestine, or winding about in
the passes of the Lebanon, I rode alone,—in
advance or in the rear of the caravan, or of our own
group, without a word spoken, when it was once
understood that it was troublesome and difficult to me
to listen from the ridge of my camel, or even from my
horse. I cannot attempt to give an idea what I learned
during those quiet seasons. All the historical hints I
had gained from my school days onward now rose up
amidst a wholly new light. It is impossible for even
erudite home-stayers to conceive what is gained by
seeing for one'sself the scenes of history, after any
considerable preparation of philosophical thought.
When, after my return, the Chevalier Bunsen told me
that he would not go to Egypt, if he had the leisure,
because he already knew every thing that could be
learned about it, I could not but feel that this was a
matter which could be judged of nowhere but on the
spot; and that no use of the eyes and mind of Lepsius
could avail him so well as the employment of his own.
Step by step as we proceeded, evidence arose of the
true character of the faiths which ruled the world;
and my observations issued in a view of their genealogy and its results which I certainly did not carry

out with me, or invent by the way side. It was not till we had long left the Nile, and were leaving the desert, that the plan of my book occurred to me. The book itself had been determined on from the time when I found the influx of impressions growing painful, for want of expression; and various were the forms which I imagined for what I had to say; but none of them satisfied me till that in which it afterwards appeared struck me, and instantly approved itself to me. It happened amidst the dreariest part of the desert, between Petra and Hebron,—not far from the boundary of Judea. I was ill, and in pain that day, from the face-ache; which troubled me in the dryest weather, amidst the hottest part of the desert; and one of our party rode beside me, to amuse me with conversation. I told him that I had just been inspired with the main idea of my book about the East. 'That is,' said he, ' you think it the best scheme till you prefer another.' ' No, I replied; ' there can be but one perfect one; and this completely answers to my view. My book will illustrate the genealogy, as it appears to me, of the old faiths,—the Egyptian, the Hebrew, the Christian and the Mohammedan.' After my life-long study of the Hebrew and Christian, our travels in Palestine brought a rich accession of material for thought; and the Syrian part of the journey was the more profitable for what had gone before. The result of the whole, when reconsidered in the quiet of my study, was that I obtained clearness as to the historical nature and moral value of all theology whatever, and attained that view of it which has been set forth in some of my subsequent works. It was evident to me, in a way which it could never have been if I had not wandered amidst the old monuments and scenes of the various faiths, that a passage through these latter faiths is as natural to men, and was as necessary in those former periods of human progress, as fetishism is to the infant nations and individuals, without the notion being more true in the one case than in the other. Every child, and every childish tribe of people, transfers its own consciousness, by a supposition so necessary as to be an instinct, to all external objects, so as to conclude them all to be alive like itself; and passes through this stage of belief to a more reasonable view: and, in like manner, more advanced nations and individuals suppose a whole pantheon of Gods first, —and then a trinity,—and then a single deity ;— all the divine beings being exaggerated men, regarding the universe from the human point of view, and under the influences of human notions and affections. In proportion as this stage is passed through, the conceptions of deity and divine government become abstract and indefinite, till the indistinguishable line is reached which is supposed, and not seen to separate, the highest order of Christian philosopher from the philosophical atheist. A future point of my narrative will be the proper one for disclosing how I reached the other point of view for which I was now exchanging the theological and metaphysical. What I have said will indicate the view under which I set about relating what I had seen and thought in the birthplaces of the old family of faiths.

I have said thus much, partly to show how I came by the views which I have been absurdly supposed to derive, in some necromantic way, from Mr. Atkinson. The fact is, our intercourse on these subjects had as yet hardly amounted to any thing. It may be dated, I think, from a letter which I wrote him in November 1847, and his reply   I had returned from the East in June 1847, after an absence of eight months.   I had then paid the visits which had been intercepted by my eastern travel, and had returned home early in October. After settling myself, and considering the plan and materials of my book, I consulted Mr. Atkinson as to whether honesty required that I should avow the total extent of my dissent from the world's theologies.   I thought *not*, as my subject was the mutual relation of those theologies, and not their relation to science and philosophy.   I had no desire to conceal, as my subsequent writings have shown, my total relinquishment of theology; but it did not seem to me that this book was the natural or proper ground for that kind of discussion.   The birthplaces of the four faiths had been my study; and the four faiths were my specific subject: and it seemed to me that it would spoil the book to intrude any other.   Thus it was settled; and the consideration of the point led to my writing the following letter to Mr. Atkinson.   I give it here that it may be seen how my passage from theology to a more effectual philosophy was, in its early stages, entirely independent of Mr. Atkinson's influence.   It is true, these letters exhibit a very early stage of conviction,—before I had attained firmness and clearness, and while a large leaven of the old anxiety and obscurity remained.   I was, as Mr. Atkinson said, out of the old ways; and he was about to show me the shortest way round the corner.

'Sunday evening, Nov. 7th, 1847.

'My dear friend.

'I seem to have much to say; but I waited to hear from you, because, when people's letters once cross, as ours did last time, they generally continue to do so.   How I pity you for your yellow fog! Here it is grey mist, hanging or driving about the mountain ridges. In the early morning I love to see it rising from the lake. I always go out before it is quite light; and in the fine mornings I go up the hill behind the church—the Kirk-stone road—where I reach a great height, and see from half way along Windermere to Rydal. When the little shred of moon that is left, and the morning star, hang over Wansfell, among the amber clouds of the approaching sunrise, it is delicious. On the positively rainy mornings, my walk is to Pelter Bridge and back. Sometimes it is round the south end of the valley. These early walks (I sit down to breakfast at half-past seven) are good, among other things, in preparing me in mind for my work. It is *very serious* work. I feel it so, more and more. The more I read (and I am reading a good deal) and the more I am struck with the diversity of men's views, and the weakness, in some point or other, of all, in the midst of great learning, the more presumptuous it appears in me to speak at all. And yet, how are we to learn, if those who have travelled to the birth-places of the old world do not tell what they think, in consequence of what they have seen? I have felt a good deal depressed,—or rather, say oppressed,—today about this. To-morrow morning I begin upon my (necessary) sketch of the history of Egypt; and in preparation I have been to-day reading again Heeren and Warburton. While I value and admire their accumulation of facts, I cannot but dissent from their inferences; that is, some of the most important of them. For instance, Warburton declares that rulers have ever strenuously taught the people the doctrines of a future life, and reward and punish-ment, without believing them; admits that some of the Egyp-tian priests believed in the Unity of God, and that Moses knew their opinions; and then argues that it is a proof that Moses' legation was divine that he did not teach a future life, but a protracted temporal reward and punishment, extending to future generations. The existence, on the temple walls, of represen-tations of judgment scenes, from the earliest times, and the presumption that the Egyptian priests believed in One (national) God,—Moses being in their confidence,—are inestimable facts to me; but *my* inference from the silence of Moses about a future life is that he was too honest to teach what he did not know to be true. But no more of this.

' The depressing feeling is from the conflict of opinions among people far wiser than myself about points which I do not believe at all; points which they believe, but in different ways. I am

pretty confident that I am right in seeing the progression of
ideas through thousands of years,—a progression advanced by
every new form of faith (of the four great forms)—every one of
these faiths being beset by the same corruptions. But I do not
know of any one who has regarded the matter thus: and it is
an awful thing to stand alone in ;—for a half-learned person at
least. But I cannot decline speaking about it. We cannot
understand the old Egyptians and Arabians through any other
channel of study. I must speak as diffidently as I truly feel,
and as simply as possible. One thing (which I am to work out
tomorrow) I cannot be wrong in;—in claiming for the old
heathens the same rule we claim to be judged by. If we refuse
to have our faith judged by our state of society, we must not
conclude on theirs by *their* state of society. If we estimate our
moral ideas by the minds of our best thinkers, we must estimate
theirs by their philosophers, and not by the commonalty. Insisting on this, I think I can show that we have no right to
despise either their faith or their best men. I must try, in
short, to show that Men's faculties exist complete, and pretty
much alike, in all ages; and that the diversity of the objects
on which they are exercised is of far less consequence than the
exercise itself.—Do you not feel strangely alone in your views
of the highest subjects ? I do. I really know of no one but you
to whom I can speak freely about mine. To a great degree, I
always did feel this. I used to long to be a Catholic, though I
deeply suspected that no reliance on authority would give me
peace of mind.· Now, all such longings are out of the question ;
for I feel that I never *could* believe on any ground of reasoning
that I once took for granted in prejudice. But I do feel sadly
lonely, for this reason,—that I could not, if I tried, communicate
to any one the *feeling* that I have that the theological belief of
almost every body in the civilised world is baseless. The very
statement between you and me looks startling in its presumption. And if I could, I dare not, till I have more assurance
than I have now that my faith is enough for my own self-government and support. I know, as well as I ever knew anything,
that for support I really need nothing else than a steady desire
to learn the truth and abide by it ; and, for self-government,
that it is enough to revere my own best nature and capabilities :
but it will require a long process of proof before I can be sure
that these convictions will avail me, under daily pressure, instead
of those by which I have lived all my life. At my age, when the
season of moral resolution, and of permanent fervour from the

reception of new ideas is pretty well over, one's goodness must be, I fear, more the result of habit than of new inspiration.— And yet there is hope that some youthfulness is left in me, too. I trust so from my interest in the subjects I am now writing about : and I have lately fairly broken the only two bad habits that ever had much power over me. ... ...

'I quite enjoy your letter. I am always pleased to have your thoughts on your present subjects of study,—as I show by sending you mine. I agree emphatically with you about philosophers inventing methods instead of learning from nature how to teach.

' My house is so pretty, now it is finished! I hope Emerson is coming. Would you like to come and meet him or not? I don't know whether he interests you. ... ...'

Mr. Atkinson's reply was delightful to me at the time ; and it is so now, in remembrance of that time, —the beginning of my free communication to him of my views and studies. It is no fair specimen of his letters when I rose to a more equal reciprocity of intercourse, and when the comfort and satisfaction which I derived from standing firm on a higher standpoint than I had at this time reached rendered unnecessary the kind of encouragement which I derived from the following letter :

'November 13, 1847,
'18, Upper Gloucester Place.

' My dear friend,

' Your letter has interested me *extremely*.—Most certainly we must judge the tree by its fruit, and the doctrine by its influence; calculating, of course, the whole circumstances and material in which that doctrine has to operate : and it would appear that all opinions with regard to a God and a future life had much the same fruits and sustaining influence, though producing results in proportion to the grossness and immorality of the times. But we must consider each view as a stage in the progress of knowledge and reason, and so, perhaps, essential to the circumstances of the times in which it existed. I would strongly urge a full consideration of this view ; that Man cannot interfere with truth or nature; but that himself and his opinions are evolved in due course,—not in a perceptible direct line, but necessarily so, as regards the whole; so that in a wide view of the question, whatever is, is right, in its general and ultimate bearing, and ever must be so. That legislators have ever given forth certain views from motives of policy, and not from conviction of their truth, seems to me a most unwarrantable assertion, and certainly not agreeing with facts of the present times which we are able to recognise; though doubtless it was and is often so. You will do a great and good thing if you can trace the origin and progress of opinion in Egypt. I had designed to do this in a general and philosophical sense in the Introduction to my contemplated work, and to wage war, tooth and nail, as they say, against the assumptions of natural theology. Philosophers, with hardly an exception, cling to the idea of a God creator: Bacon at the head of them, saying that he would rather believe in all things most gross and absurd, than that creation was without a mind. How unphilosophical —I had almost said contemptible!* I recognised a godhead long after I rejected a revelation; but I can now perceive no tittle of evidence, in the mind or out of the mind, so to speak, —for such a belief, but that all evidence, reason and analogy are against it ; and that the origin of the idea is traceable to the errors (and necessary errors) of the mind striving in ignorance.

'I delight in the tone of mind in which you enter on the inquiry with regard to Egypt's Faith. That noble feeling— faith, how sadly is it cramped and misapplied,—though never to be considered sad in its position in the chain of progress, any more than pain or death is sad, as essential to the progress of life, and the fulfilment of the law. It is well that men feel loneliness in advancing in truth, for it holds them back to instruct and bring others forward, and gives them a mission to perform, to save their fellows from that to which they cannot return. For knowledge, to the truthful and earnest, is a mistress to whom you are wedded for life: and in confidence and constancy must you seek your self-respect and happiness, whatever may be the peril and disaffection of the world. 'I place a sword in the world,' said Christ, 'and set brother against brother.'—' But blessed are those who are persecuted for righteousness' sake.' I see no pleasure in martyrdom: but I feel it

* See in explanation of this, ' Letters on the Laws of Man's Nature and Development,' pp. 180, 182, 183.

necessary to die if it must be, in maintaining what I believe—
earnestly, and in reason and faith believe,—to be true : to sacrifice friendship and every other thing to maintain this predomi-
nating impulse and want. You feel, nevertheless, a sense of
loneliness now ; and so do I ; and have done more than I do
now. But this is passing away, and one friend in truth is a
host against the world assembled. The time may come when
you, and perhaps I, may be pointed at and despised by
thousands. Pshaw ! what matter ? I have more fear of an east
wind or a November fog, than of all the hubbub they can make.
But we may reasonably hope that it will not be so. There are
too many believing as we believe on vital questions, and many
more who are indifferent ; and others may be convinced. Yet,
still, the sense of loneliness will accompany you more or less
through much of your social intercourse ; and friends may grow
cold, and you may be misrepresented and misunderstood. But
out of this sense of loneliness shall grow your strength, as the
oak, standing alone, grows and strengthens with the storm ;
whilst the ivy, clinging for protection to the old temple wall,
has no power of self-support. Be sure that you will find sufficient, if you hold to the truth, and are true to yourself. How well
does the great philosopher speak of the pleasure of standing
fortified in truth watching the wandering up and down of other
minds, and in pity and charity bending over their weakness !
Strong in the faith and knowledge of good intentions, we must
endeavour to fix the good, true, and noble impulses, and obliterate
the evil ones. Thus we shall be strong in resignation and gratitude, enjoying all things that we may ; indifferent as to the end,
seeing that it is of no more consequence that we should live
again, than that the pebble-stones should rise and become living
beings. The difficulty is not in the condition of self-reliance,
but in the want of sympathy under the pressure of adverse
opinion, and the mass of our prejudices which still encumber
the brain's action, and the soil where better thoughts and habits
should have been early sown. Lesser minds will hereafter float
easily and merrily down the stream where you find impediments ;
but the necessity of self-support will give you strength, and
pleasures which they shall not feel ; and so the balance and
opportunity are more even than would at first appear. A noble
path lies before you, and stern necessity bids you accept un-
moved what was "designed "—for you from all time,—that link
of being in which you exist and act. Not alone are we, but
bound in the eternal laws of the whole. Let us unindividu-

alise ourselves ;—merge our personality in the infinite ;—raise
the ideal in our mind ;—see each as but a part of that ideal ;—
and we lose the sense of imperfection—the sense of individual
opinions and character, and rise into a new life of god-like conceptions—active, practical, and earnest ; but above the accidents,
of life : not altogether separate from, but superior to them ;
enjoying all the harmonious action of mind and body ; loving
with all our heart and in spirit, all that is good and noble and
most beautiful ;—casting out and destroying every wrong action
of the mind, as we would the pains and ills of the body :—
warming with affection and interest for every human being ;
untouched except by pity for their ill thoughts of us :—such are
aspirations which may live in the breast which has rejected its
Man-God, and lost all faith in consciousness revived in the same
shape and being from the grave. At least we lose the fear (if we
have not the hope), and the curse of a cruel uncertainty, and are
left free to enjoy the present in seeking our best and highest
happiness and exaltation. The highest minds will still impress
the world with the sense of what is right ; and the religion of
morals and philosophy will advance, until theology is in the
grave, and man will be free to think, and, morally expanded,
will be more free to act than perhaps has yet entered into many
brains to conceive ; because men, in their fears and ignorance,
look into the darkness and not into the light, and cannot measure
beyond their knowledge. But this is too much of a preachment,
—so I say stop !

  ' I should like, indeed, very much to see Emerson if it could
be, you may be sure. I think you have a very high opinion of
him. I fear I have filled up my letter with nothing, when I
have so much in my thoughts to say that has engaged my attention.

  ' Well, well,—all in time. I am glad to hear Mr. —— ——
is talking over such important questions with you. I hope you
will find him free and wise. Pray remember me to them, will
you ? and to that cheerful, dear woman, Mrs. ——. You have
not told me what is to be the motto of your dial. Never mind
but you should differ from the world ; and, with that wise doubt
of self which you express, you need not fear ; for that will
lead you to dwell on evidence, and on the cause of your oppo-
nent's errors, and how you should be satisfied if your convictions
be indeed the truth.

                              ' Adieu, &c., &c.,
                                        ' H. G. ATKINSON.

'P.S.—A friend just writes to me that he cannot understand the consciousness of doing wrong, if we have no free will, and are not accountable. This is at the root of the errors of philosophers, who take a particular state of feeling for the simple and essential condition of an innate sense. They argue a God from a similar error. Conscience arises from a sense of right, with the desire that the right should be done. But what is felt to be right depends much on the state of opinion and society. The sense of sinning is a mere condition and habit of thinking, arising from a belief in free will—a deifying of the mind.

'Much of the manner that has been thought pride in me, has arisen from a sense of loneliness and non-sympathy with the opinions of others, and that they would dislike my opinions if they fully knew them. But I am passing over this barrier, in losing the care and thought of sympathy, in a livelier interest and care for the happiness of all, and in the thought of the ultimate glory and triumph of all truth—when the wrong shall prove right, and the right shall become wrong.'

My reply will close, for the present, the subject of my anti-theological views, at the beginning of my intimate correspondence with Mr. Atkinson.

'Ambleside, November 21, 1847.

'My dear friend,

'It was very kind of you to write that last letter to me. I agree in, and like, almost every word of it: but I was especially pleased to see your distinct recognition of the good of the old superstitions in their day. As a necessarian, you are of course bound to recognise this : but the way in which you point it out pleases me, because it is the great idea I have before me in my book. I have found the good of those old superstitions in my day. How it might have been with me (how much better) if I had had parents of your way of thinking, there is no saying. As it was, I was *very* religious (far beyond the knowledge and intentions of my parents) till I was quite grown up. I don't know what I should have done without my faith ; for I was an unhealthy and most unhappy child, and had no other resource. Yet it used to strike me often, and most painfully ever relief and comfort my religion gave to my feelings, it did not help me much against my faults. Certainly, my belief in a future life never was either check or stimulus to me in the matter of self-government. Five-and-twenty years ago I became a thoroughly grounded necessarian. I have never wavered for an hour on that point since; and nothing ever gave me so much comfort. Of course this paved the way for the cessation of prayer. I left off praying however, less from seeing the absurdity (though I did see it) of petitioning about things already ordained, than from a keen sense of the impiety of prayer. First, I could not pray for daily bread, or for any outward good, because I really did not wish to ask for them,—not knowing whether they would be good for me or not. So, for some years, I prayed only for good states of mind for myself and others. Of course, the feeling grew on me that true piety required resignation about spiritual matters as much as others. So I left off express prayer : and without remorse. As for Christ's example and need of prayer,—I felt that he did not mean what we mean by prayer : and I think so still. I think he would condemn our prayers as much as he did those of the Pharisees of his time : and that with him prayer was contemplation and aspiration chiefly.—Next, I saw very painfully (I mean with the pain of disgust) how much lower a thing it is to lead even the loftiest life from a regard to the will or mind of any other being, than from a natural working out of our own powers. I felt this first as to resignation under suffering, and soon after as to moral action. Now, I do know something of this matter of resignation. I know it to the very bottom. I have been a very great sufferer, —subject to keen miseries almost all my life till quite lately ; and never, I am pretty confident, did any one acquiesce in God's will with a more permanent enthusiasm than I did;—because this suited the bent of my nature. But I became ashamed of this ;—ashamed of that kind of support when I felt I had a much higher ground of patience in myself. (Only think how shocked the orthodox would be at this, and how they would talk of the depravity of our nature, and of my awful presumption ! I saw a sort of scared smile on Mrs. ———'s face the other day, when, in talking about education, I said we had yet to see what could be done by a direct appeal to our noble human nature. She, liberal as she is, thinks we have such active bad tendencies, such interior corruption, that we can do nothing without—not effort, or toil, but—Help. Yet she, and Mrs. ——— too, devour

my Household Education papers, as if she had never met with
any thing true before on that subject. She says I most certainly
have been a mother in a pre-existent state: and yet, if she
knew that these papers were founded on 'infidel' and phreno-
logical principles, she would mourn over me with deep grief.)—
Well but,—you see now, how long a preparation I have had;
and how gradual, for my present freedom.—As to what my
present views are, when clearly brought to the point of expression, they are just these. I feel a most reverential sense of
something wholly beyond our apprehension. Here we are, in
the universe ! this is all we know: and while we feel ourselves
in this isolated position, with obscurity before and behind, we
must feel that there is something above and beyond us. If that
something were God (as people mean by that word, and I am
confident it is not), he would consider those of us the noblest
who must have evidence in order to belief;—who can wait to
learn, rather than rush into supposition. As for the whole series
of Faiths, my present studies would have been enough, if I had
not been prepared before, to convince me that all the forms of
the higher religions contain (in their best aspect) the same
great and noble ideas, which arise naturally out of our own
minds, and grow with the growth of the general mind; but
that there is really *no* evidence whatever of any sort of revelation, at any point in the history. The idea of a future life, too,
I take to be a necessary one (I mean necessary for support) in
its proper place, but likely to die out when men better understand their nature and the *summum bonum* which it incloses. At
the same time, so ignorant as I am of what is possible in nature,
I do not deny the possibility of a life after death: and if I believed
the desire for it to be as universal as I once thought it, I should
look upon so universal a tendency as some presumption in favour
of a continuous life. But I doubt the desire and belief being so
general as they are said to be: and then, the evidence in favour
of it is nothing;—except some unaccountable mesmeric stories.
—As for your correspondent's very young question, about why
we should do right,—how such remarks show that we neglect
our own nature while running after the supposed pleasure of
another ! I am sure I never felt more desirous of the right than
I do now, or more discomposed when it flashes across me that I
have done wrong. But I need not write about this to you, of all
people.—What a long confession of faith I have written you !
Yes, it *is* faith, is it not?—and not infidelity, as ninety-nine

hundredths of the world would call it.—As for the loneliness I
spoke of, I don't generally mind it: and there is abundant
ground of sympathy between me and my best friends, as long as
occasion does not require that I should give names to my
opinions. I have not yet had any struggle with my natural
openness or indiscretion. I never could conceal any opinion I
hold, and I am sure I never would: and I know therefore that I
am at the mercy (in regard to reputation and some of my friendships) of accident, which may at any hour render an avowal
necessary. But I do not fear this. I have run so many inferior
risks, and suffered so little in my peace by divers avowals and
heresies, that I am not likely to tremble now. What does give
me a qualm sometimes, is thinking what such friends as ———
and as ——— will suffer, whenever they come to know that I
think their 'Christian hope' baseless. They are widows, and
they live by their expectation of a future life.* I seriously
believe that ——— would go mad or die, if this hope was shaken
in her: and my opinions are more to her than any others since
her husband's death. But I say to myself as you would say,—
that these matters must take care of themselves. If the truth
comes to me, I must believe it.—Yes, I should not wonder if
there is a prodigious clamour against me, some day, as you say;
—perhaps after this book comes out. But I don't think I should
care for that, about a matter of opinion. I should (or might)
about a matter of conduct; for I am sadly weak in my love of
approbation: but about a matter of opinion, I can't and don't
believe what I once did; and there's an end. It is a thing
which settles itself;—for there is no going back to discarded
beliefs. It is a great comfort to me to have you to speak to,
and to look to for sympathy. It is a delightful indulgence and
refreshment: but if you were to die, or to be engrossed by other
interests and occupations, so as to diverge from me, I think I
could do without sympathy, in a matter so certain as my inability
to believe as I once did.—But enough and too much. There will
surely never be occasion to write you such a letter again. But
I have written, not so much about *my* mind, as about *a* mind,

---

* I need not have feared. The one was offended and the
other grieved; but neither understood me. The one behaved ill
and the other well; and both presently settled down into their
habitual conceptions.

which you, as a philosopher, may like to see into, as well as to sympathise with as a friend.   ...   .

          ...   .

I walk every morning, never stopping for weather.   I shall have the young moon now for ten days.   Emerson is engaged (lecturing) deep at present, but hopes to come by and by.   He is free, if any man is.   So I hope you can come when he does.—The motto of the dial is, ' Come, light ! Visit me ! ' Old Wordsworth likes this much.

          ' O ! your letter was very pleasant to me.   We rarely agree as completely as I do in that.

          'Good night !—it is late.   Ever yours truly,

                                             'H. MARTINEAU.'

Mr. Emerson did come.   He spent a few days in February with me; and, unfavourable as the season was for seeing the district,—the fells and meadows being in their dunnest hay-colour instead of green,— he saw in rides with a neighbour and myself some of the most striking features in the nearer scenery.   I remember bringing him, one early morning, the first green spray of the wild currant, from a warm nook. We met soon after in London, where Mr. Atkinson made acquaintance with him.   It was a great pleasure to me to have for my guest one of the most honoured of my American hosts, and to find him as full as ever of the sincerity and serenity which had inspired me with so cordial a reverence twelve years before.

The mention of ' Household Education ' in the letter just quoted reminds me of some work that I was busy about when invited to go to the East. ' The People's Journal ' was then in the hands of Mr. Saunders, who has since shown more of his quality than he had scope for in that periodical, but who engaged my respect by the spirit in which he carried

on his enterprise. He was a perfect stranger to me
before; but we soon became friends on the ground of
that enterprise of his; and I wrote a good deal for
him;—a set of papers called 'Surveys from the
Mountain,' and many on desultory subjects : I
forget when it was that he suggested the subject of
' Household Education' to me, as one which required
different treatment from any that it had hitherto met
with : but it was certainly after my return from the
East, and after his discontinuance of the 'People's
Journal,' that I planned the volume,—the first
chapters of which had been written at his request.
When I was entirely independent of him, and had
nothing to consider but the best use to make of my
opportunity, I resolved to write the book for the
Secularist order of parents. It had been conveyed to
me, before this time, that there was a great want of
juvenile literature for the Secularists, who could obtain
few story-books for their children which were not
stuffed with what was in their eyes pernicious superstition. People of all beliefs can see the hardship of
this; and I was forcibly struck by it. If the age of
fiction-writing had not been over with me, so that I
felt that I *could not* write good stories, I should have
responded to the appeal by writing more children's
tales. The next best thing that I could do was to
write for the Secularists a familiar book on 'Household Education.' Two surprises awaited me, on the
appearance of that volume :— the bulk of the Secularist body, and the cordial reception of the book
by Christian parents. After the publication of the
' Atkinson Letters,' I had reason to know how very
different was the state of opinion in England from

anything that I had supposed when I had felt lonely
in my views. I then found that I was, as far as I
can discover, actually on the side of the majority of
sensible and thoughtful persons; and that the Christians, who are apt to look on a seceder as, in some sort,
a fallen person, are in fact in a minority, under that
mode of reckoning. The reception of my book, when
its qualities came to be understood, prepared me for
the welcome discovery of the actual condition of the
Secularists, and their daily extending prospects; while
it proved that there are a good many Christian parents
who can accept suggestion and aid from one who will
not pronounce their Shibboleth; and that they can
enter into moral sympathy with one who finds aspiration to be wholly unconnected with notions of inherent human corruption, free will, and the immortality of the soul. The book was published in 1848;
and it must be published again; for it has been for
some time out of print.

The winter of 1847-8 passed delightfully in the
preparation of my book. I doubt whether there is
any higher pleasure, in which intellectual and moral
enjoyment are commingled, than in writing a book
from the heart;—a book of one's own conception,
and wrought out all alone: and I doubt whether any
author could feel more satisfaction, (in proportion to
individual capacity for pleasure, of course) in the production of a book than I did in regard to ' Eastern
Life.' I wrote on in entire security about its publication; for I had made an agreement with Mr.
Murray in the autumn. His father had wished to
publish for me, and had made more than one overture;
and I wished to try whether there was advantage, in

point of circulation, in being published by Murray.
After the failure of the ' Game Law Tales,' I considered myself fully authorised to do the best I could
for my next work, and especially for one so considerable as ' Eastern Life.' I had every desire that Mr.
Murray should know precisely what he was undertaking; and I explained to him, in the presence of a
witness, as distinctly as possible, and even with
reiteration, what the plan and agreement of the book
were designed to be. He seemed so entirely satisfied,
and offered his terms afterwards with so much good
will, that I never dreamed of difficulty, and sent him
the MS. of the two first volumes when finished.
After a note of acknowledgment and compliment,
the MS. was immediately returned, with a curt note
which afforded no explanation. Mr. Murray could not
publish the book; and that was all. The story goes
that Mr. Murray was alarmed by being told,—what
he then gave forth as his plea for breach of contract,
—that the book was a ' conspiracy against Moses.'
Without crediting this joke in full, we may suppose
that his clerical clients interfered to compel him to
resign the publication; and I understood, on good
authority, long after, when the success of the book
was secure, that he heartily regretted the mischance.
I wrote by the same day's post to Mr. Moxon, to tell
him the facts of the case, and to offer him the publication, which he accepted by return of post,—on the
usual terms; viz., that Mr. Moxon should take the
risk, and give me two-thirds of the profits. The first
year's proceeds made my house and its contents my
own. I declined all interest in the second edition,
desiring that my share of the proceeds should go to

the cheapening of the book.   I had got all I wanted from it, in the way of money, and I had an earnest desire that it should circulate widely among the less opulent class who were most likely to sympathise with its contents.   I do not know why I should not relate an incident, in connection with this matter, which it gratifies me to recall.   One day in the desert, when some hostile Arabs waylaid our party, my camel-leader trotted me away, against my will, from the spectacle of the fight which was to ensue.   The same thing happened to Mr. and Mrs. Yates ; and we three found ourselves near a clump of acacias where we were to await the event of the feud, and the rest of our caravan.   We alighted, and sat down in the scanty shade.   Mr. Yates observed that this encounter would be a picturesque incident for my book : and this led us to talk of whether there should be a book or not.   I told Mr. Yates that this was a good opportunity for mentioning my chief scruple about writing the book at all.   I knew he and Mrs. Yates would not sympathise in it; but yet it was best to utter it frankly.   I scrupled about making money by a journey which was his gift.   The surprise expressed in his countenance was really amusing.   ' O, dear !' said he : 'I am sure Mrs. Yates and I shall be very happy indeed if you should be able so soon to make your house completely your own.   It will be, indeed, *another* pleasant consequence of this journey, that we had not thought of.'   It gave me hearty satisfaction, after this, to write to them that, through this book, their kind wish was fulfilled.

SECTION IV.

The same mail which brought back my MS. from Mr. Murray brought the news of the flight of Louis Philippe. My petty interests seemed unworthy of mention, even to myself, in the same day with that event. Mine were rearranged in three days, while the affairs of the Continent became more exciting from hour to hour. Towards the end of March, when my book was finished, and nearly ready for publication, letters came in, in increasing numbers, appealing to me for help, in one form or another, for or against popular interests, so far as they were supposed to be represented by Chartism. Of these letters, one was from the wife of a Cabinet Minister, an old acquaintance, who was in a terrible panic about Feargus O'Connor and the threatened Chartist outbreak of the tenth of April, then approaching. She told me that she wrote under her husband's sanction, to ask me, now that they saw my book was advertised for publication, to use my power over the working-classes, to bring them to reason, &c., &c. The letter was all one tremor in regard to the Chartists, and flattery to myself. I replied that I had no influence, as far as I knew, with the Chartists; and that, as a matter of fact, I agreed with them in some points of doctrine while thinking them sadly mistaken in others, and in their proposed course of action. I told her that I had seen something in the newspapers which had made me think of going to London : and that if I did go, I would endeavour to see as many political leaders (in and out of parliament) as possible, and would, if she pleased, write her an account of what should seem to me the state of things, and the best to be done, by myself and others. It was an advertisement in the newspapers which had made me think of going ;— the advertisement of a new periodical to be issued by Mr. Knight, called 'The Voice of the People.' It was pointed out to me by several of my friends, as full of promise in such hands at such a time. The day after my letter to Lady —— was sent, I heard from Mr. Knight. He desired to see me so earnestly that he said, if I could not go to town, he would come to me,—ill as he could just then spare the time : or, he would come and fetch me, if I wished it. Of course, I went immediately ; and I helped to the extent Mr. Knight wished, in his new periodical. But I saw immediately, as he did, that the thing would never do. The Whig touch perished it at once. The Whig officials set it up, and wished to dictate and control its management in a way which no literary man could have endured, if their ideas and feelings had been as good as possible. But the poverty and perverseness of their ideas and the insolence of their feelings were precisely what might be expected by all who really knew that remarkably vulgar class of men. They proposed to lecture the working-classes, who were by far the wiser party of the two, in a jejune, coaxing,

dull, religious-tract sort of tone, and criticised and
deprecated everything like vigour, and a manly and
genial tone of address in the new publication, while
trying to push in, as contributors, effete and exhausted writers, and friends of their own who knew
about as much of the working-classes of England as
of those of Turkey. Of course the scheme was a
complete and immediate failure. On the insertion
of an article by a Conservative Whig (which was certainly enough to account for the catastrophe), the
sale fell to almost nothing at all; and Mr. Knight,
who had before stood his ground manfully against
the patrons of the scheme, threw up the business.

Meantime, the tenth of April arrived (while I was
near London) and passed in the way which we all
remember. Lady —— wrote to me in a strain of
exultation, as vulgar, to say the least, as Feargus
O'Connor's behaviour, about the escape of the government. She told of O'Connor's whimpering because
his toes were trodden on; and was as insolent in her
triumph about a result which was purely a citizen
work as she had been abject when in fear that the
Chartists would hold the metropolis. I felt the more
obliged to write the promised letter, when I had seen
several leading politicians of the Liberal party; and
I did it when I came home. I did it carefully; and
I submitted my letter to two ladies who were judges
of manners, as well as of politics; and they gave it
their sanction —one of them copying it, with entire
approbation. Lady —— 's reply was one of such
insolence as precluded my writing to her again. She
spoke of the 'lower classes' (she herself being a
commoner by birth) as comprising all below the

peerage; so that she classed together the merchants and manufacturers with 'cottagers' and even paupers; and, knowing me to be a manufacturer's daughter, she wrote of that class as low, and spoke of having been once obliged to pass a week in the house of a manufacturer, where the governess was maltreated with the tyranny which marks low people. My two consultees reddened with indignation at the personal insolence to myself; which I had overlooked in my disgust at the wrong to my 'order,' and to the 'cottagers' with whom she classed us. By their advice, I wrote a short note to this lady's husband, to explain that my letter was not a spontaneous address, as his lady now assumed, but written in answer to her request. This little transaction confirmed the impression which I had derived from all my recent intercourse with official Whigs;—that there was nothing to be expected from them now that they were spoiled by the possession of place and power. I had seen that they had learned nothing by their opportunities: that they were hardened in their conceit and their prejudices, and as blind as bats to the new lights which time was introducing into society. I expected what became apparent in the first year of the war, when their incapacity and aristocratic self-complacency disgraced our administration, and lowered our national character in the eyes of the world, and cost their country many thousands of lives and many millions of treasure. I have seen a good deal of life and many varieties of manners; and it now appears to me that the broadest vulgarity I have encountered is in the families of official Whigs, who conceive themselves the cream of society, and the lights and rulers of the world of our

empire. The time is not far off, though I shall not
live to see it, when that coterie will be found to have
brought about a social revolution more disastrous to
themselves than anything that could have been ra-
tionally anticipated from poor Feargus O'Connor and
his Chartist host of April 10th, 1848.

What Mr. Knight wanted of me at that time was
not mainly my assistance in his new periodical, but to
carry on an old enterprise which had been dropped.
The ' History of the Thirty Years' Peace ' had been
begun long before ; but difficulties had occurred which
had brought it to a stand for two years past. That
his subscribers should have been thus apparently
deserted, and left with the early numbers useless on
their hands, was a heavy care to my good friend ; and
he proposed to me to release him from his uncomfortable position by undertaking to finish the work. I
felt tempted ; but I did not at all know whether I
could write History. Under his encouragement I promised to try, if he could wait three months. I was
writing ' Household Education,' and I had promised
him an account of the Lake District, for the work
he was publishing, called ' The Land we Live in.'
It was on or about the 1st of August that I opened,
for study, the books which Mr. Knight had been
collecting and forwarding to me for the sources of
my material.

This year was the beginning of a new work which
has afforded me more vivid and unmixed pleasure
than any, except authorship, that I ever undertook ;—
that of delivering a yearly course of lectures to the
mechanics of Ambleside and their families. Nothing
could have been further from my thoughts, at the

outset, than such an extension of the first effort. On my return from the East, I was talking with a neighbour about the way in which children, and many other untravelled persons, regard the Holy Land. When Dr. Carpenter taught me in my youth, among his other catechumens, the geography of Palestine, with notices from Maundrell's travels there, it was like finding out that a sort of fairy land was a real and substantial part of our everyday earth; and my eagerness to learn all about it was extreme, and highly improving in a religious sense. I remarked now to my neighbour that it was a pity that the school-children should not learn from me something of what I had learned in my youth from Maundrell. She seized upon the idea, and proposed that I should give familiar lectures to the monitors and best scholars of the national school,—sometimes, when convenient, to escape visitation, called the Squire's school. I was willing, and we went to the school-mistress, whose reception of the scheme amused us much. She said she knew, and had taught the children, ' all about the sources of the Nile;' but that she should be glad to hear anything more that I had to tell. We could hardly refrain from asking her to teach *us* ' all about the sources of the Nile :' but we satisfied ourselves with fixing the plan for my addressing the children in the school-house. I was more nervous the first time than ever after,—serious as was the extension of the plan. After the first lecture, which was to two or three rows of children and their school-mistress, a difficulty arose. The incumbent's lady made a speech in School Committee, against our scheme, saying that the incumbent had found so much discontent in the

parish from a dissenter having been allowed to set
foot in the school-house, that its doors must be closed
against me. She added some compliments to me and
the lectures, which she expressed a great wish to hear,
and so on. My neighbour immediately took all the
blame on herself, saying that I had not even known
where the school-house was till she introduced me to
it; and that what I had done was at her request. She
went straight to the authorities of the chapel which
stands at the foot of my rock, and in an hour obtained
from them in writing an assurance that it would give
them 'the greatest pleasure' that I should lecture in
their school-rooms. Armed with this, and blushing
all over, my neighbour came, and was relieved to find
that I was not offended but amused at the transaction.
I proposed to have the children in my kitchen,
which would hold them very well; and that we should
invite the incumbent's lady to be present. My neighbour said 'No, no : she does not deserve that,' and
produced the Methodists' gracious letter. I may add
here that last year the incumbent's lady said, in a
railway carriage, in the hearing of a friend of mine,
that there was great alarm among the clergy when I
first came to live at Ambleside ; but that it had died
away gradually and completely (even after the publication of the Atkinson Letters) from their finding that,
while I thought it right to issue through the press
whatever I thought, I never meddled with anybody's
opinions in private. I may add, too, that I have been
treated with courtesy and kindness, whenever occasion
brought us together.

It occurs to me also to add an anecdote which
diverted me and my friends at the time, and which

seems more odd than ever, after the lapse of a few years. There is a book-club at Ambleside, the members of which are always complaining to outsiders of the dullness of the books, and the burdensomeness of the connection. I had had hints about the duty of neighbours to subscribe to the book-club; and when one or two books that I wished to see were circulating, I told a member that I was not anxious to join, at an expense which could hardly be compensated,—judging by what I heard about the choice of books : but that, if I ever joined, it should be then. She mentioned this to another member; and it was agreed that I should be proposed and seconded. But the gentleman she spoke to—always a friendly neighbour to me—called on her to communicate, with much concern, his apprehension that I might possibly be black-balled. He was entirely uncertain ; but he had some notion that it might be so. The lady came, very nervous, to ask whether I would proceed or not. I had half a mind to try the experiment,—it would have been such a rich joke,—so voluminous a writer, and one so familiar in literary society in London, being black-balled in a country book-club ! But I thought it more considerate not to thrust myself into any sort of connection with anybody who might be afraid of me. I profited by an invitation to join a few families in a subscription to a London library, by which, for less money, I got a sight of all the books I wished to see,—and no others ; for my friends and I are of the same mind in our choice of reading.

At the second lecture, some of the parents and elder brothers and sisters of the children stole in to listen ; and before I had done, there was a petition that I would deliver the lectures to grown people. I saw at once what an opportunity this was, and nerved myself to use it. I expanded the lectures, and made them of a higher cast; and before another year, the Mechanics of Ambleside and their families were eager for other subjects. I have since lectured every winter but two; and with singular satisfaction. The winter was the time chosen, because the apprentices and shop-keepers could not leave their business in time, when the days lengthened. No gentry were admitted, except two or three friends who took tea with me, and went as my staff,—in order to help me, if any difficulty arose, and to let me know if I spoke either too loud or too low; a matter of which, from my deafness, I could not judge. It is rather remarkable that, being so deaf, and having never before spoken in any but a conversational tone, I never got wrong as to loudness. I placed one of my servants at the far end of the room; and relied on her to take out her handerchief if she failed to hear me; but it always went well. I made notes on half-a-sheet of paper, of dates or other numbers, or of facts which might slip my memory; but I trusted entirely to my power at the time for my matter and words. I never wrote a sentence; and I never once stopped for a word. —The reasons why no gentry were admitted were, first, because there was no room for more than the ' workies '; and next, that I wished to keep the thing natural and quiet. If once the affair got into the newspapers, there would be an end of the simplicity of the proceeding. Again, I had, as I told the gentry, nothing new to tell to persons who had books at home, and leisure to read them.—My object was to give rational amusement to men whom all circumstances seemed to conspire to drive to the public-house, and to interest them in matters which might lead them to books, or at least give them something to think about. My lectures were maliciously misrepresented by a quizzer here and there, and especially by a lawyer or two, who came this way on circuit, and professed to have been present ; but they were welcome to their amusement, as long as it was an indisputable matter that they had *not* been present.

The second course was on Sanitary matters; and it was an effectual preparation for my scheme of instituting a Building Society. In a place like Ambleside, where wages are high, the screw is applied to the working men in regard to their dwellings. The great land-owners, who can always find room to build mansions, have never a corner for a cottage : and not only are rents excessively high, but it is a serious matter for a working man to offend his landlord, by going to chapel instead of church, for instance, when he may be met by the threat—' If you enter that chapel again, I will turn your family out of your cottage ; and you know you can't get another.' When the people are compelled to sleep, ten, twelve, or fourteen in two rooms, there can be little hope for their morals or manners; and one of the causes of the excessive intemperance of the population is well known to be the discomfort of the crowded dwellings. When the young men come home to bad smells and no room to turn, they go off to the public-house. The kind-hearted among the gentry tend the sick, and pray with the disheartened, and reprove the sinner ; but I have found it singularly difficult to persuade them that, however good may be wine and broth, and prayers and admonition, it is better to cut off the sources of disease, sin and misery by a purer method of living. My recourse was to the ' workies ' themselves, in that set of lectures; in which I endeavoured to show them that all the means of healthy and virtuous living were around them,—in a wide space of country, slopes for drainage, floods of gushing water, and the wholesomest air imaginable. I showed them how they were paying away in rent, money enough to provide every head of a household with a cottage of his own in a few years; and I explained to them the principle of such a Building Society as we might have,—free from the dangers which beset such societies in large towns, where the members are unknown to each other, and sharp lawyers may get in to occasion trouble. They saw at once that if twenty men lay by together, instead of separately, a shilling a week each, they need not wait twenty weeks for any one to have the use of a pound; but the twentieth man may have his pound, just the same, while the other nineteen will have had earlier use of theirs and be paying interest for it. Hence arose our Building Society; the meeting to form it being held in my kitchen. A generous friend of mine advanced the money to buy a field, which I got surveyed, parcelled out, drained, fenced, and prepared for use. The lots were immediately purchased, and paid for without default. Impediments and difficulties arose, as might be expected. Jealousy and ridicule were at work against the scheme. Some who might have helped it were selfish, and others timid. Death (among a population where almost every man drinks) and

emigration, and other causes impeded an increase of
members; and the property was less held by working
men, and more by opulent persons, than I had desired
and intended ; but the result is, on the whole, satisfactory, inasmuch as thirteen cottages have arisen
already ; and more are in prospect : and this number
is no small relief in a little country town like Ambleside.   The eye of visitors is now caught by an upland
hamlet, just above the parsonage, where there are two
good houses, and some ranges of cottages which will
stand, as the builders say, ' a thousand years,'—so
substantial is the mode of building the grey stone
dwellings of the district.   I scarcely need add that
I made no reference, in the lectures or otherwise, to
the form of tyranny exercised by the owners of
land and houses.   My business was to preclude the
tyranny, by showing the people that their own
interests were in their own hands, and by no means
to excite angry feelings about grievances which I
hoped to mitigate, or even extinguish.

The generous friend who enabled me to buy the
land declined to receive the money back.   She is the
proprietress of two of the cottages and their gardens ;
and she placed the rest of the money at my disposal,
for the benefit of the place, as long as it was wanted.
Since my illness began, three months ago, I have
transferred the trust to other hands; and there is
reason to hope that the place will be provided with a
good Mechanics' Institute, and Baths,—which are
now the next great want.

In the two last lectures of the Sanitary course,
there was an opportunity for dealing with the great
curse of the place,—its intemperance.   Those two

lectures were on the Stomach and Brain. I drew the
outline of the stomach on a large expanse of paper,
which was fixed in front of the desk; and I sent round
the coloured prints, used in Temperance Societies,
of the appearances of progressive disease in the
drunkard's stomach,—from the first faint blush of
inflammation to the schirrous condition. It was a
subject which had long and deeply engaged my
attention; and my audience, so closely packed as that
the movement of one person swayed the whole, were
as much interested as myself; so that my lecture
spread out to an hour and twenty minutes, without
my being at all aware of the time. The only stir,
except when the prints were handed round, was made
by a young man who staggered out, and fainted at
the door. He was a recent comer to the place, and
had lately begun to tipple, like his neighbours. After
that night, he joined my Building Society, that he
might have no money for the public-house. Many
told me afterwards that they were sick with pain of
mind during that lecture; and I found, on inquiry,
that there was probably hardly a listener there, except
the children, who had not family reasons for strong
emotion during an exposure of the results of intemper-
ate habits.

The longest course I have given was one of twenty
lectures on the History of England, from the earliest
days of tradition to the beginning of the present
century. Another was on the History of America,
from its discovery by Columbus to the death of
Washington. This was to have been followed by a
course which I shall not live to offer;—the modern
History of the United States,—with a special view

to recommend the Anti-slavery cause. Last November
and December, I addressed my neighbours for the last
time,—On Russia and the War. At the close, I
told them that if I were alive and well next winter,
we would carry on the subject to the close of the
campaign of 1855. I should be happy to know that
some one would take up my work, and not allow my
neighbours to suffer by my departure. I found myself fatigued and faint during the two last lectures;
and I spoke seriously when making my conditional
promise for another season; but I had no clear notion
how ill I was, even then, and that I should never meet
that array of honest, earnest faces again.

There was some fear that the strong political
interests of the spring of 1848 would interfere with
the literary prosperity of the season. Whether they
did or not, I do not know. For my own part I cared
more for newspapers than books in that exciting year;
but my own book had an excellent sale. The remembrance of the newspaper reading of those revolu-
tionary times recalls a group of circumstances in my
own experience which may be worth recording,—to
show how important a work it is to give an account
of the constitution and politics of a foreign nation.
—Ten years before this,—(I think it was the year
before my long illness began) a gentleman was brought
to a *soirée* at my mother's house, and introduced to
me by a friend, who intimated that the stranger had a
message to deliver to me. The gentleman had been
for some time resident in Sweden, where he was
intimately acquainted with the late Prime Minister.
The Crown Prince Oscar of that day (the present

King) was earnestly desirous of introducing constitutional reforms on a large scale, many of which, as
we all know, he has since achieved. The retired
Prime Minister desired my guest of that evening to
procure an introduction to me, and to be the bearer of
an invitation to me to spend a Swedish summer at
the Minister's country-house, where his lady and
family would make me welcome. His object was, he
said, to discuss some political topics of deep interest to
Sweden ; and he conceived that my books on America
showed me to be the person whom he wanted ; —to
be capable, in fact, of understanding the working of
the constitutions of foreign nations. He wanted to
talk over the condition and prospects of Sweden in
the light of the experiments of other countries. I
could not think of going ; and I forgot the invitation
till it was recalled to memory by an incident which
happened in April 1839. I was then going to
Switzerland with three friends, and our passage to
Rotterdam was taken, when a friend of my family,
the English representative of an Irish county, called
on me with an earnest request that I would suspend
my scheme, for reasons which he would assign in a
few days. I explained that I really could not do so,
as I was pledged to accompany a sick cousin. In a
day or two, my friend called, to insist on my dining
at his house the next Wednesday, to meet Mr.
O'Connell on business of importance. Mr. O'Connell
could not be in town earlier, because the freedom of
some place (I forget what) was to be presented to
him on Tuesday ; and travelling all night would
bring him to London only on Wednesday afternoon.
I could not meet him, as we were to go on board the

packet on Wednesday evening.—My friend, hoping still to dissuade me, told me what Mr. O'Connell wanted. He had private reasons for believing that ' Peel and the Tories' would soon come into power : (in fact, the Bedchamber Question occurred within a month after) and he feared more than ever for the liberties of Ireland, and felt that not a day must be lost in providing every assistance to the cause that could be obtained. He had long been convinced that one of the chief misfortunes of Ireland was that her cause was pleaded in print by authors who represented only the violent, and vulgar, and factious elements of Irish discontent ; by Irish people, in fact, who could not speak in a way which the English were willing to listen to. He considered that my American books established my capacity to understand and represent the political and social condition of another country ; and what he had to request was that I would study Irish affairs on the spot, and report of them. He offered introductions to the best-informed Catholic families in any or every part of Ireland, and besought me to devote to the object all the time I thought needful,—either employing twelve months or so in going over the whole of Ireland, or a shorter time in a deeper study of any particular part,—publishing the results of my observations without interference from anybody, or the expression of any desire from any quarter that my opinions should be of one colour rather than another.

It was impossible for me to say anything to this scheme at the time : but my family and friends were deeply impressed by it. It was frequently discussed by my comrades and myself during our continental journey; and one of them, — the same generous friend to whom I have had occasion to refer in connexion with my Ambleside schemes,—offered to accompany me, with a servant, to help and countenance me, and *hear* for me, and further the object in every possible way; and she was not the only one who so volunteered. It stood before my mind as the next great work to be undertaken: but, in another month, not only were ' Peel and the Tories' sent to the right-about for the time, but I was prostrate in the illness which was to lay me aside for nearly six years. On our return from Italy, we fell in with the family of Lord Plunket, to whom, in the course of conversation about Ireland, we related the incident. Miss Plunket seemed as much struck with the rationality of the scheme as we were ; and, after some consultation apart, Miss Plunket came to me with an express offer of introductions from Lord Plunket to intelligent Protestants, in any or every part of Ireland where this business might carry me. My illness, however, broke up the scheme.

This incident, again, was recalled to my memory by what happened the next time I was abroad. It occurred in the spring of 1847. Our desert party agreed, at Jerusalem, to make an excursion of three days to the Jordan and the Dead Sea. On the eve of the trip, three European gentlemen sent a petition to Lady Harriet K——, that they might be allowed to ride with our party, on account of the dangerous state of the road to Jericho. They joined our troop in the Valley of Jehosaphat, and rode among us all day. It did not occur to me to ask who they were. In the course of the next morning, when the ladies of the

party were going through the wood on the bank of
the Jordan, to bathe northwards, while the gentlemen
went southwards, we met one of these strangers; and
I told him where he might find his companions. I
never doubted his being English,—he looked so like
a country squire, with his close-cropped, rather light
hair, and sunburned complexion. He appeared to be
somewhere about five-and-thirty. On leaving the
Jordan, we had to traverse an open tract, in excessive
heat, to the margin of the Dead Sea. The hard
sand looked trustworthy; and I put my horse to a
gallop, for the sake of the wind thus obtained. I
soon heard other horses coming up; and this gentleman, with two others, appeared : and he rode close by
my side till an accident to one of the party obliged
him to dismount and give help. I was among those
who rode on when we found that no harm was done;
and presently after I was asked by Lady Harriet
K—— whether I would allow Count Porro to be
introduced to me,—he being desirous of some conversation with me. For Silvio Pellico's sake, as well as
Count Porro's father's and his own, I was happy to
make his acquaintance; and I supposed we should
meet at our halting place,—at Santa Saba. But
Count Porro and his companions were to strike off
northwards by the Damascus road; and they were
gone before I was aware.—A few weeks afterwards,
when we four, of the Nile party, rode up to our hotel
at Damascus, Count Porro was awaiting us; and he
helped us ladies down from our horses. He had
remained some days, in order to see me. He desired
some conversation with me at a convenient time ; and
that convenient time proved to be the next morning,

when he joined me on the divan, in the alcove in
the quadrangle. He was so agitated that he could
scarcely speak. His English, however, was excellent.
He told me that in what he was going to say he was
the mouth-piece of many of his countrymen, as well
as of his own wishes ; and especially of several fellow-
citizens of Milan. What he said was as nearly as
could be a repetition of O'Connell's plea and request.
He said it was the misfortune of his country to be
represented abroad by injured and exasperated patriots,
who demanded more than the bulk of the people
desired, and gave forth views which the citizens in
general disclaimed. It was believed by the leading
men in Lombardy that the changes which were really
most essential might be obtained from Austria, if
sought in a temperate and rational manner ; and that
the best way of obtaining these changes would be by
means of a report on the condition of affairs by some
traveller of reputation, who had shown, as they considered that I had done by my work on the United
States, a capacity to understand and report of a
foreign state of society. He was therefore authorised to
request that I would reside in Milan for six months or
a year, and to say that every facility should be afforded
for my obtaining information, and all possible respect
shown to my liberty of judgment and representation.
All they wanted was that I should study their condition, and report it fully, on my return to England.
He told me (in consideration of my deafness, which
disabled me for conversation, though not, of course,
for reading, in a foreign language) that every educated
Milanese speaks English ; and that every thing should
be done to render my abode as pleasant as possible ;

and so forth.—I positively declined, being, in truth, heartily home-sick,—longing for my green, quiet valley, and the repose of my own abode. My duties there seemed more congenial and natural than investigating the politics of Lombardy; and I did not therefore think it selfish to refuse. With increasing agitation, Count Porro declared that he would take no refusal. He asked how much time these home duties would occupy; said, in spite of all my discouragements, that he should go to England the next spring; and declared, when taking his leave next day, that, on landing at Southampton, his first step would be to put himself into the train for Ambleside, whence he would not depart without my promise to go to Milan.

When that 'next spring' arrived,—the anniversary of those conversations of ours at Damascus,—Count Porro was a member of the Provisional Government at Milan, telling Austria by his acts and decrees what it was that Lombardy required. The mention, in my narrative, of the revolutions of 1848 brought up these three stories at once to my recollection; and their strong resemblance to each other seems to show that there must be something in them which makes them worth the telling.

I began my great task of the History under much anxiety of mind. My mother was known to be dying from the spring onwards; and she died in August. She was removed, while yet able, to the house of her eldest surviving son, at Edgbaston; and there, amidst the best possible tendance, she declined and died. Her life hung upon perfect quiet; and therefore, as all

her children had seen her not long before, it was
considered best to leave her in the good hands of one
of the families. I saw her at Liverpool, on my return
home from the East. By evil offices, working on her
prejudice against mesmerism, she had been prevented
from meeting me after my recovery : but such a cause
of separation was too absurd to be perpetual. I knew
that the sound of my voice, and my mere presence for
five minutes, would put to flight all objections to my
mode of recovery : and we did meet and part in comfort and satisfaction. I did hope to have had the
pleasure of a visit from her that summer, though I
proposed it with much doubt. She was now blind ;
and she could not but be perpetually hearing of the
charms of the scenery. She could walk only on
smooth and level ground ; and walking was essential
to her health : and it is not easy to find smooth level
ground in our valley. Yet, as one main inducement
to my building and settling here was that there might
be a paradise for any tired or delicate members of my
family to rest in, I did wish that my mother should
have tried it, this first practicable summer : but she
was too ill to do more than go to Edgbaston, and find
her grave there. She was in her seventy-sixth year,—
I have never felt otherwise than soundly and substan-
tially happy, during this last term of my life : but
certainly those months of July and August 1848
were the most anxious of the whole ten years since I
left Tynemouth. The same faithful old friend to
whom I have often referred, must come into my history again here. She came to me when I was becoming most anxious, and remained above two
months,—saving me from being overwhelmed with

visits from strangers, and taking me quiet drives, when my work was done;—a recreation which I have always found the most refreshing of all. Some of my own family came before the event, and some after; and a few old and dear friends looked in upon me in the course of the season.

When I had laid out my plan for the History, and begun upon the first portion, I sank into a state of dismay. I should hardly say 'sank;' for I never thought of giving up or stopping; but I doubt whether, at any point of my career, I ever felt so oppressed by what I had undertaken as during the first two or three weeks after I had begun the History. The idea of publishing a number of my Political Economy series every month was fearful at first: but that was only the quantity of work. The Discontented Pendulum comforted me then,—not only because every month's work would have its own month to be done in, but because there was a clear, separate topic for each number, which would enable the work to take care of itself, in regard to subject as well as time. In America, I was overwhelmed with the mass of material to be dealt with; but then, I was not engaged to write a book; and by the time I had made up my mind to do so, the mass had become classified. Now, the quantity and variety of details fairly overpowered my spirits, in that hot month of August. I feel my weakness,—more in body than (consciously) in mind—in having to deal with many details. The most fatiguing work I ever have to do is arranging my library; and even packing my trunks for a journey, or distributing the contents when I come home, fatigues me more than it seems to do other people.

In this case, I fear I afflicted my friend by my discouragement,—the like of which she had never seen
in me. At times, she comforted me with assurances
that the chaos would become orderly; but, on the
whole, she desired that I should throw up the work,
—a thing which I could not even meditate for a moment, under the circumstances in which Mr. Knight
found himself. No doubt, the nervous watching of
the post at that time had much to do with my anxiety.
My habit was to rise at six, and to take a walk,—
returning to my solitary breakfast at half-past seven.
For several years, while I was strong enough, I found
this an excellent preparation for work. My household
orders were given for the day, and all affairs settled,
out of doors and in, by a quarter or half-past eight,
when I went to work, which I continued without
interruption, except from the post, till three o'clock,
or later, when alone. While my friend was with me,
we dined at two; and that was, of course, the limit of
my day's work. The post came in at half-past ten;
and my object was to keep close to my work till the
letters appeared. When my mother became so ill that
this effort was beyond my power, I sent to meet the
coach, and got my letters earlier; but the wear and
tear of nerve was very great. One strong evidence of
the reality of my recovery was that my health stood
the struggle very well. In a few weeks, I was in full
career, and had got my work well in hand. My first
clear relief came when I had written a certain passage
about Canning's eloquence, and found in the course
of it that I really was interested in my business. Mr.
Knight, happily, was satisfied; and I was indebted to
him for every kind of encouragement. By the 1st of

February, the last MS. of the first volume was in
the hands of the printer.   I mention this because a
contemporary review spoke of 'two years' as the
time it had occupied me,—calling it very rapid work ;
whereas, from the first opening of the books to study
for the History to the depositing of the MS. of the
first volume at press was exactly six months.   The
second volume took six months to do, with an interval
of some weeks of holiday, and other work. I delivered
the last sheets into Mr. Knight's hands in November
1849.

During the year 1849,-—the dismal cholera year,
—I found that I had been overworking ; and in the
autumn I accepted Mrs. Knight's invitation to join
their family at St. Leonards for a month, and then
to stay with them for the remaining weeks which were
necessary to finish the History.   The Sunday when I
put the last batch of MS. into Mr. Knight's hands
was a memorable day to me.   I had grown nervous
towards the end ; and especially doubtful, without any
assignable reason, whether Mr. Knight would like the
concluding portion.   To put it out of my mind, I
went a long walk after breakfast with Mr. Atkinson
to Primrose Hill (where I had never been before) and
Regent's park.   My heart fluttered all the way ; and
when I came home, to meet a farewell family party
at lunch, I could not eat.   Mr. Knight looked at me,
with an expression of countenance which I could not
interpret ; and when he beckoned me into the drawing-room, I was ready to drop.   I might have spared
myself the alarm.   His acknowledgments were such
as sent me to my room perfectly happy; and I returned

to my Knoll with a light heart.   I was soon followed
by an invitation from Mr. Knight to write the introductory period, from the opening of the century to the
Peace, to be followed by the four years to 1850, if we
should live to see the close of that year, so as to make
a complete 'History of the Half Century.'   The
work would be comparatively light, from the quantity
of material supplied by the Memoirs of the statesmen
now long dead.   I was somewhat disappointed in
regard to the pleasure of it from Mr. Knight's
frequent changes of mind as to the form in which it
was to be done.   I imagine he had become somewhat
tired of the scheme ; for, not only was I kept waiting
weeks, and once three months, for a promised letter
which should guide me as to space and other particulars; but he three times changed his mind as to the
form in which he should present the whole.   He approved, as cordially as ever, what I wrote; but finally
decided to print the portion from 1800 to the Peace
as an Introductory volume, relinquishing the project
of completing the Half Century by a History of the
ast four years.   I state these facts because it was
afterwards believed by many people, who quoted his
authority, that he broke off the scheme, to his own
injury, from terror at the publication of the Atkinson
Letters,—as if he had been taken by surprise by that
publication.   I can only say that it was as far as
possible from being my intention to conceal our plan
of publishing those Letters.   I not only told him of
it while at his house in the autumn of 1849, and
received certain sarcasms from him on our 'infidel'
philosophy; but I read to Mrs. Knight two of he
boldest of Mr. Atkinson's letters : and it was after

this that Mr. Knight invited me to write the Introductory volume.   Moreover, it was after some of his
changes of plan that he stayed at my house (May 1850)
with Mr. Atkinson and Mr. Jerrold, and considerately
took Mr. Jerrold for a walk, on the last day of their
visit, to leave Mr. Atkinson and me at liberty to read
our manuscript.   He was certainly panic-stricken
when the volume appeared, in January 1851 ; but, if
he was surprised, it was through no fault of mine, as
the dates show.   In July 1851, half-a-year after the
' Letters' appeared, when he paid me for my work
at his own house, he expressed himself more than
satisfied with the Introductory History, and told me
that, though the Exhibition had interfered with the
publishing season, he had sold two-thirds of the
edition, and had no doubt of its entire success in the
next.   Before the next season opened, however, he
sold off the whole work.   With his reasons for doing
so I have no concern, as the preceding facts show.
In regard to him, I need only say,—which · I do
with great pleasure,—that he has continued to show
me kindness and affection, worthy of our long friendship.   In regard to the History,—it has passed into
the hands of Messrs. Chambers of Edinburgh, who
invited me, last summer, to bring the History of the
Peace down to the War.   I agreed to do so ; and the
scheme was only broken off by my present illness,
which, of course, renders the execution of it impossible.

SECTION V.

On the last evening of my stay at Mr. Knight's a parcel arrived for me, enclosing a book, and a note which was examined as few notes ever are. The book was 'Shirley;' and the note was from 'Currer Bell.' Here it is:

> ' Currer Bell offers a copy of "Shirley" to Miss Martineau's acceptance, in acknowledgment of the pleasure and profit she (sic) he has derived from her works. When C. B. first read " Deerbrook " he tasted a new and keen pleasure, and experienced a genuine benefit. In his mind, " Deerbrook " ranks with the writings that have really done him good, added to his stock of ideas, and rectified his views of life.'
>
> ' November 7th, 1849.'

We examined this note to make out whether it was written by a man or a woman. The hand was a cramped and nervous one, which might belong to any body who had written too much, or was in bad health, or who had been badly taught. The erased ' she ' seemed at first to settle the matter; but somebody suggested that the ' she ' might refer to me under a form of sentence which might easily have been changed in the penning. I had made up my mind, as

I had repeatedly said, that a certain passage in 'Jane
Eyre,' about sewing on brass rings, could have been
written only by a woman or an upholsterer. I
now addressed my reply externally to 'Currer Bell,
Esq.,' and began it 'Madam.'—I had more reason
for interest than even the deeply-interested public
in knowing who wrote 'Jane Eyre;' for, when it
appeared, I was taxed with the authorship by more
than one personal friend, and charged by others, and
even by relatives, with knowing the author, and
having supplied some of the facts of the first volume
from my own childhood.   When I read it, I was convinced that it was by some friend of my own, who
had portions of my childish experience in his or her
mind.   'Currer Bell' told me long after, that she
had read with astonishment those parts of 'Household
Education' which relate my own experience.   It was
like meeting her own fetch,—so precisely were the
fears and miseries there described the same as her
own, told or not told in 'Jane Eyre.'

A month after my receipt of 'Shirley,' I removed,
on a certain Saturday, from the house of a friend in
Hyde Park Street to that of a cousin in Westbourne
Street, in time for a dinner party.   Meanwhile, a
messenger was running about to find me, and reached
my cousin's when we were at dessert, bringing the
following note :

                                        'December 8th, 1849.
  My dear Madam,
        'I happen to be staying n London for a few days; and
having just heard that you are likewise in town, I could not help
feeling a very strong wish to see you.   If you will permit me to
call upon you, have the goodness to tell me when to come.. Should
you prefer calling on me, my address is   ...   .

'Do not think this request springs from mere curiosity. I hope it has its origin in a better feeling. It would grieve me to lose this chance of seeing one whose works have so often made her the subject of my thoughts.

                    'I am, my dear Madam,
                              'Yours sincerely,
                                        'CURRER BELL.'

My host and hostess desired me to ask the favour of C. B.'s company the next day, or any subsequent one. According to the old dissenting custom of early hours on Sundays, we should have tea at six the next evening:—on any other day, dinner at a somewhat later hour. The servant was sent with this invitation on Sunday morning, and brought back the following reply:

'My dear Madam,

    'I hope to have the pleasure of seeing you at six o'clock to-day:—and I shall try now to be patient till six o'clock comes.

                              'I am, &c., &c.'

'That is a woman's note,' we agreed. We were in a certain state of excitement all day, and especially towards evening. The footman would certainly announce this mysterious personage by his or her right name; and, as I could not hear the announcement, I charged my cousins to take care that I was duly informed of it. A little before six, there was a thundering rap:—the drawing-room door was thrown open, and in stalked a gentleman six feet high. It was not 'Currer,' but a philanthropist, who had an errand about a model lodging-house. Minute by minute I, for one, wished him away; and he did go

before anybody else came. Precisely as the time-piece
struck six, a carriage stopped at the door; and after
a minute of suspense, the footman announced ' Miss
Brogden;' whereupon, my cousin informed me that
it was Miss Brontë; for we had heard the name before,
among others, in the way of conjecture.—I thought
her the smallest creature I had ever seen (except at a
fair) and her eyes blazed, as it seemed to me.   She
glanced quickly round; and my trumpet pointing me
out, she held out her hand frankly and pleasantly.   I
introduced her, of course, to the family; and then came
a moment which I had not anticipated.   When she
was seated by me on the sofa, she cast up at me such
a look,—so loving, so appealing,—that, in connexion
with her deep mourning dress, and the knowledge that
she was the sole survivor of her family, I could with
the utmost difficulty return her smile, or keep my
composure.   I should have been heartily glad to cry.
We soon got on very well; and she appeared more at
her ease that evening than I ever saw her afterwards,
except when we were alone.   My hostess was so considerate as to leave us together after tea, in case of
C. B. desiring to have private conversation with me.
She was glad of the opportunity to consult me about
certain strictures of the reviewers which she did not
understand, and had every desire to profit by.   I did
not approve the spirit of those strictures; but I
thought them not entirely groundless.   She besought
me then, and repeatedly afterwards, to tell her, at
whatever cost of pain to herself, if I saw her afford any
justification of them. I believed her, (and I now believe
her to have been) perfectly sincere: but when the
time came (on the publication of ' Villette,' in regard

to which she had expressly claimed my promise a week
before the book arrived) she could not bear it.   There
was never any quarrel, or even misunderstanding,
between us. She thanked me for my sincere fulfilment
of my engagement; but she could not, she said, come
' at present ' to see me, as she had promised : and
the present was alas! all that she had to dispose of.
She is dead, before another book of hers could (as I
hoped it would) enable her to see what I meant, and
me to re-establish a fuller sympathy between us.—
Between the appearance of ' Shirley ' and that of
' Villette,' she came to me;—in December, 1850.
Our intercourse then confirmed my deep impression of
her integrity, her noble conscientiousness about her
vocation, and her consequent self-reliance in the moral
conduct of her life.   I saw at the same time tokens
of a morbid condition of mind, in one or two directions ;—much less than might have been expected, or
than would have been seen in almost any one else
under circumstances so unfavourable to health of body
and mind as those in which she lived; and the one
fault which I pointed out to her in ' Villette ' was so
clearly traceable to these unwholesome influences that
I would fain have been spared a task of criticism
which could hardly be of much use while the circumstances remained unchanged.   But she had exacted
first the promise, and then the performance in this
particular instance ; and I had no choice. ' I know,'
she wrote (January 21st, 1853) ' that you will give
me your thoughts upon my book,—as frankly as if
you spoke to some near relative whose good you preferred to her gratification. I wince under the pain of
condemnation—like any other weak structure of flesh

and blood; but I love, I honour, I kneel to Truth.
Let her smite me on one cheek—good! the tears may
spring to the eyes; but courage! There is the other
side—hit again — right sharply!' This was the
genuine spirit of the woman. She might be weak
for once; but her permanent temper was one of
humility, candour, integrity and conscientiousness.
She was not only unspoiled by her sudden and prodigious fame, but obviously unspoilable. She was
somewhat amused by her fame, but oftener annoyed;
—at least, when obliged to come out into the world to
meet it, instead of its reaching her in her secluded
home in the wilds of Yorkshire. There was little
hope that she, the frail survivor of a whole family
cut off in childhood or youth, could live to old age;
but, now that she is gone, under the age of forty, the
feeling is that society has sustained an unexpected,
as well as irreparable loss.

I have often observed that, from the time I wrote
the Prize Essays, I have never come to a stand for
work;—have never had any anxiety as to whether
there would be work for me;—have, in short, only
had to choose my work. Holiday I have never had,
since before that time, except in as far as my foreign
travels and a few months of illness could be called
such : and it had now been a weight on my mind for
some years that I had not got on with my autobiography,—which I felt to be a real duty. I find that I
wrote this to Mr. Atkinson, when under uneasiness
about whether Murray would hold to his engagement
to publish 'Eastern Life' (February 1848.) 'It is
a very great and pressing object with me to go on

with my own Life ; lest it should end before I have
recorded what I could trust no one to record of it. I
always feel this a weight upon my mind, as a duty yet
undone ; and my doing it within a moderate time
depends on my getting this book out now.' It was
got out; but then came the History, which could not
be delayed, and which I should have done wrong to
refuse. Now that those three great volumes were
nearly done, Mr. Dickens sent me an invitation to
write for 'Household Words.' That kind of work
does not, in my own opinion, suit me well ; and I
have refused to write for Magazines by the score ;
but the wide circulation of 'Household Words' made
it a peculiar case ; and I agreed to try my hand,—
while I was yet a good way from the end of my
History. I did this with the more ease because a
scheme was now rising to the light which would relieve
me of much of the anxiety I felt about recording the
later experiences of my life. The Atkinson Letters
were by this time in preparation.

The publication of those letters was my doing.
Having found, after some years of correspondence
with Mr. Atkinson, that my views were becoming
broader and clearer, my practice of duty easier and
gayer, and my peace of mind something wholly unlike
what I had ever had experience of before ; and, being
able to recognize and point out what fundamental
truths they were that I had thus been brought to
grasp, I thought that much good might be done by
our making known, as master and pupil, what truths
lay at the root of our philosophy. If I had known
—what I could not know till the reception of our
volume revealed it to me,—how small is the proportion

of believers to the disbelievers in theology to what I imagined,— I might have proposed a different method; or we might have done our work in a different way. In regard to disbelief in theology, much more had already taken place than I, at least, was aware of. But there is an essential point,—the most essential of all,—in regard to which the secular and the theological worlds seem to need conviction almost equally: viz., the real value of science, and of philosophy as its legitimate offspring. It seems to us, even now, the most impossible, or, speaking cautiously, the rarest thing in the world to find any body who has the remotest conception of the indispensableness of science as the only source of, not only enlightenment, but wisdom, goodness and happiness. It is, of course, useless to speak to theologians or their disciples about this, while they remain addicted to theology, because they avowedly give their preference to theology over the science with which it is incompatible. They, in the face of clear proof that science and theology are incompatible, embrace theology as the foundation of wisdom, goodness and happiness. They incline, all the while, to what they call philosophy;—that is, to theologico-metaphysics, from which they derive, as they say, (and truly) improvement in intellectual power, and confirmation of their religious faith in one direction, nearly equivalent to the damage inflicted on it in another. The result must be, when the study is real and earnest, either that the metaphysics must dwindle away into a mere fanciful adornment of the theology, or the theology must be in time stripped of its dogmatic character, exhausted thereby of its vitality, and reduced to a mere name and semblance.

Examples of the first alternative are conspicuous in the argumentative preachers and writers of the Church of England, and other Christian sects; and, we may add, in the same functionaries of the Romish Church, who thus unconsciously yield to the tendencies of their age so far as to undermine the foundations of their own ' everlasting ' Church.   Examples of the second alternative are conspicuous, in our own country and in America, in the class of metaphysical Deists,—who may be, by courtesy, called a class because they agree in being metaphysical, and, in one way or another, Deists; but who cannot be called a sect, or a body, because it is scarcely possible to find any two of them who agree in anything with any approach to precision.   One makes the Necessarian doctrine his chief reliance, while another denounces it as Atheistic. One insists on the immortality of the soul, while another considers a future life doubtful, and a matter of no great consequence.   Others belong, amid an unbounded variety of minor views, to one or another of the five sorts of Pantheism.   All these claim to be philosophers, and scientific in the matter of mental philosophy; while observers discover that all are wandering wide of the central point of knowledge and conviction,—each in his own balloon, wafted in complacency by whatever current he may be caught by, and all crossing each other, up and down, right or left, all manner of ways, hopeless of finding a common centre till they begin to conceive of, and seek for, a firm standpoint.

The so-called scientific men, who consider themselves philosophers, are, for the most part, in a scarcely more promising condition.   Between their endless

subdivision as labourers in the field of research, before
they have discovered any incorporating principle ; and
the absorbing and blinding influence of exclusive
attention to detail; and some remaining fear of casting
themselves loose from theology, together with their
share of the universal tendency to cling to the old
notions even in their own department,—the men of
science are almost as hopelessly astray, as to the discovery of true wisdom, as the theologians. Well read
men, who call themselves impartial and disinterested,
as they stand aloof and observe all these others, are
no nearer to the blessed discovery or conviction. They
extol philosophy, perhaps ; but it is merely on the
ground that (conceiving metaphysics to be philosophy)
it is a fine exercise of the subtle powers of the intellect.
As to science, they regard it either as a grave and
graceful pastime, or they see no use in it, or they
consider it valuable for its utilitarian results. As for
the grand conception,—the inestimable recognition,
—that science (or the knowledge of fact inducing
the discovery of laws) is the sole and the eternal basis
of wisdom,—and therefore of human morality and
peace,—none of all these seem to have obtained any
view of it at all. For my part, I must in truth say
that Mr. Atkinson is the only person, of the multitude I have known, who has clearly apprehended this
central truth. He found me searching after it ; and
he put me in clear possession of it. He showed me
how all moral evil, and much, and possibly all, physical evil arises from intellectual imperfection,—from
ignorance and consequent error. He led me to sympathise in Bacon's philosophy, in a truer way than the
multitude of Bacon's theological and metaphysical

professed adorers; and to see how a man may be
happier than his fellows who obey Bacon's incitements
to the pursuit of truth, as the greatest good of man.
There is plenty of talk of the honour and blessedness
of the unflinching pursuit of truth, wherever it may
lead; but I never met any one else who lived for that
object, or who seemed to understand the nature of
the apostleship. I have already told where I was in
(or in pursuit of) this path when Mr. Atkinson found
me. Learning what I could from him, and meditating
for myself, I soon found myself quite outside of my
old world of thought and speculation,—under a new
heaven and on a new earth; disembarrassed of a load
of selfish cares and troubles; with some of my difficulties fairly solved, and others chased away, like bad
dreams; and others, again, deprived of all power to
trouble me, because the line was clearly drawn between
the feasible and the unknowable. I had got out of
the prison of my own self,* wherein I had formerly
sat trying to interpret life and the world,— much as
a captive might undertake to paint the aspect of
Nature from the gleams and shadows and faint
colours reflected on his dungeon walls. I had learned
that, to form any true notion whatever of any of the
affairs of the universe, we must take our stand in the

* 'Fear only has its seat,' says Schiller, 'where heavy and shape-
less masses prevail, and the gloomy outlines waver between uncertain boundaries. Man rises superior to every terror of Nature
as soon as he is able to give it a form, and can make it a definite
object. When he begins to assert his independence against
Nature as an appearance, he also asserts his dignity against
Nature as a power, and in all freedom stands up boldly before
his gods. He tears away the masks from the spectres which
terrified his childhood; and they surprise him with his own
image; for they are merely his own imaginations.'

external world,—regarding man as one of the products and subjects of the everlasting laws of the universe, and not as the favourite of its Maker; a favourite to whom it is rendered subservient by divine partiality. I had learned that the death-blow was given to theology when Copernicus made his discovery that our world was not the centre and shrine of the universe, where God had placed man 'in his own image,' to be worshipped and served by all the rest of creation. I had learned that men judge from an inverted image of external things within themselves when they insist upon the Design argument, as it is called,—applying the solution from out of their own peculiar faculties to external things which, in fact, suggest that very conception of design to the human faculty. I had learned that whatever conception is transferred by 'instinct' or supposition from the human mind to the universe cannot possibly be the true solution, as the action of any product of the general laws of the universe cannot possibly be the original principle of those laws. Hence it followed that the conceptions of a God with any human attributes whatever, of a principle or practice of Design, of an administration of life according to human wishes, or of the affairs of the world by the principles of human morals, must be mere visions,—necessary and useful in their day, but not philosophically and permanently true. I had learned, above all, that only by a study of the external and internal world in conjunction can we gather such wisdom as we are qualified to attain; and that this study must be *bonâ fide*,—personal and diligent, and at any sacrifice, if we would become such as we hint to ourselves in our highest and truest aspirations.

The hollowness of the popular views of philosophy
and science,—as good intellectual exercise, as harmless, as valuable in a utilitarian sense, and even as
elevating in their mere influence,—was, by this time,
to me the clearest thing I ever saw : and the opposite
reality,—that philosophy founded upon science is the
one thing needful,—the source and the vital principle of all intellectuality, all morality, and all peace
to individuals, and goodwill among men,—had
become the crown of my experience, and the joy of
my life.

One of the earliest consequent observations was, of
course, that the science of Human Nature, in all its
departments, is yet in its infancy. The mere principle
of Mental Philosophy is, as yet, very partially recognised ; and the very conception of it is new. It is so
absolutely incompatible with theology that the. remaining prevalence of theology, circumscribed as it is,
sufficiently testifies to the infant state of the philosophy
of Man. I have found Mr. Atkinson's knowledge of
Man, general and particular, physical, intellectual and
moral, theoretical and practical, greater than I ever
met with elsewhere, in books or conversation ; and I
immediately discovered that his superior knowledge
was due to his higher and truer point of view, whereby
he could cast light from every part of the universe
upon the organisation and action of Man, and use and
test the analogies from without in their application to
the world within. I had long desired that the years
should not pass over his head without the world being
the better, as I felt myself, for his fresh method of
thought, and conscientious exercise of it. I wished
that some others besides myself should be led by him

to the true point of view which they were wandering
in search of; and I therefore went as far as I dared in
urging him to give the world a piece of his mind.
At length he consented to my scheme of publishing
a set of 'Letters on Man's Nature and Development.'
Certainly I have reason to congratulate myself on
my pertinacity in petitioning for this. I do not often
trouble my friends with requests or advice as to their
doings: and in this case, I was careful not to intrude
on my friend's independence. But I succeeded; and
I have rejoiced in my success ever since,—seeing and
hearing what that book has done for others, and
feeling very sensibly what a blessing it has been to
myself.

Once embarked in the scheme, my friend was
naturally anxious to get on; but he was wonderfully
patient with the slowness to which the pressure of my
other work condemned us. I have mentioned that I
read two of his letters to my hostess in the autumn of
1849. The book did not appear till January 1851.
My literary practice indicated that I ought to copy
out the whole of Mr. Atkinson's portion in proper
order for press; and this was the more necessary
because Mr. Atkinson's hand-writing is only not so
bad as Dr. Parr's and Sydney Smith's. When I
began, I supposed I must alter and amend a little, to
fit the expression to the habit and taste of the reading
world; but, after the first letter, I did not alter a
single sentence. The style seems to me,—as it does
to many better judges than myself,—as beautiful as
it is remarkable. Eminent writers and readers have
said that they could not lay the book down till they
had run it through,—led on through the night by

the beauty of the style, no less than by the interest
of the matter. Such opinions justify my decision not
to touch a sentence. (I speak of the volume without
scruple, because, as far as its merits are concerned, it
is Mr. Atkinson's. The responsibility was mine, and
a fourth or fifth part of its contents ; but my letters
were a mere instigation to his utterance.)

It appears, by the dates above, that nearly the
whole of 1850 elapsed during my copying. I was
writing the Introductory volume of the History, and
was in the midst of a series of papers, (the title of
which I cannot recal) for an American periodical,
whereby I wanted to earn some money for the
Abolition cause there. I sent off the last of them
in April. By that time, my season guests began to
arrive ; and my evenings were not at my own disposal.
I had engaged myself to 'Household Words' for a
series of tales on Sanitary subjects ; and I wrote this
spring the two first, — 'Woodruffe the Gardener'
and 'The People of Bleaburn.'

I spent a fortnight at Armathwaite, a beautiful
place between Penrith and Carlisle ; (departing, I remember, on the day of Wordsworth's funeral) and,
though I carried my work, and my kind friends
allowed me the disposal of my mornings, I could not
do any work which would bear postponement.   I
looked forward hopefully to a ten weeks' sojourn at a
farm-house near Bolton Abbey, where I went to escape
the tourist-season ; and there I did get on. My house
had been full of guests, from April till the end of
July, with little intermission : and the greater the
pleasure of receiving one's friends, the worse goes
one's work. Among the guests of that spring were

three who came together, and who together made an
illustrious week,—Mr. Charles Knight, Mr. Douglas
Jerrold, and Mr. Atkinson.   Four days were spent in
making that circuit of the district which forms the
ground-plan of my 'Complete Guide:' and memorable days they were.   We were amused at the way in
which some bystander at Strands recorded his sense
of this in a Kendal paper.   He told how the tourists
were beginning to appear for the season, and how I
had been seen touring with a party of the *élite* of the
literary world, &c., &c.   He declared that I, with
these *élite*, had crossed the mountains 'in a gig' to
Strands, and that wit and repartee had genially flowed
throughout the evening;—an evening, as it happened,
when our conversation was rather grave.   I was so
amused at this that I cut out the paragraph, and sent
it to Mr. Jerrold, who wrote back that, while the
people were about it, they might as well have put us
into a howdah on an elephant.   It would have been
as true as the gig, and far grander.—I owed the
pleasure of Mr. Jerrold's acquaintance to Mr. Knight;
and I wish I had known him more.   My first impression was one of surprise,—not at his remarkable
appearance, of which I was aware;—the eyes and the
mobile countenance, the stoop and the small figure,
reminding one of Coleridge, without being like him,
—but at the gentle and thoughtful kindness which
set its mark on all he said and did.   Somehow, all his
good things were so dropped as to fall into my
trumpet, without any trouble or ostentation.   This
was the dreaded and unpopular man who·must have
been hated (for he *was* hated) as 'Punch' and not
as Jerrold,—through fear, and not through reason or

feeling. His wit always appeared to me as gentle as
it was honest,—as innocent as it was sound. I could
say of him as of Sydney Smith, that I never heard
him say, in the way of raillery, any thing of others
that I should mind his saying of me. I never feared
him in the least, nor saw reason why any but knaves
or fools should fear him.—The other witty journalist
of my time, Mr. Fonblanque, I knew but little, having
met him only at Mr. Macready's, I think. I once
had the luck to have him all to myself, during a long
dinner; and I found his conversation as agreeable for
other qualities as for its wit. The pale face, the lank hair,
the thin hands, and dimmed dark eye, speaking of ill
health, made the humour of his conversation the more
impressive, as recommended by patience and amiability.

But to return to my summer of 1850. At
Bolton I was not by any means lonely; for tourists
came there too; and relations and friends gave me
many a pleasant day and evening. But, on the
whole, the History got on very well in the mornings,
and the transcribing of the Letters in the evening;
and, but for the relaxing air of the place, which
injured my health, that Bolton sojourn would have
been a season of singular enjoyment. With the same
dear, faithful old friend whom I have so often referred
to, I saw Ilkley and Benrhydding, and some of the
finest parts of the West of Yorkshire. I found time
to write another long story for ' Household Words,'
(' The Marsh Fog and the Sea Breeze ') and engaged
to make my subscription to the new weekly journal,
the ' Leader ' (which has lagged terribly, instead of
leading) in the form of twelve ' Sketches from Life,'
which I began before the Atkinson Letters were well

off my hands. Another small piece of authorship which interposed itself was really no fault of mine. In 1848 (I think it was) I had begun an experiment of very small farming, which I never intended to become an affair of public interest. My field, let to a neighbour, was always in such bad condition as to be an eyesore from my windows. I found myself badly and expensively served with cream and butter, and vegetables, and eggs. In summer there was no depending on the one butcher of the place for meat, even though joints had been timely ordered and promised,—so great and increasing was the pressure of the tourist multitude. In winter, when I was alone, and did not care what came to table, I could have what I liked: but in summer, when my house was full, it was frequently an anxiety how to get up a dinner when the butcher was so set fast as to have to divide the promised joint between three houses. All the while, I had to pay an occasional gardener very high, to keep the place in any order at all,—over and above what my maids and I could do. A more serious consideration was the bad method of farming in the Lake District, which seemed to need an example of better management, on however humble a scale. My neighbours insisted on it that cows require three acres of land apiece; whereas I believed that, without emulating Cobbett, I could do better than that. I procured an active, trustworthy married labourer from Norfolk, and enlisted his ambition and sympathy in the experiment. We have since kept about a cow and a half on my land, with the addition of half an acre which I rent from the adjoining field; and the purchase of a fourth part of the food is worth while, because I am thus kept constantly supplied with milk, while able to sell the surplus; besides that the stable may as well hold a second cow; and that two cows are little more trouble than one. My whole place is kept in the highest order: I have the comfort of a strong man on the premises (his cottage being at the foot of the knoll) for the protection of my household and property; and I have always had the satisfaction of feeling that, come who may, there are at all times hams, bacon and eggs in the house. The regular supply of fresh vegetables, eggs, cream and butter is a substantial comfort to a housekeeper. A much greater blessing than all these together is that a plentiful subsistence for two worthy people has been actually created out of my field; and that the spectacle has certainly not been lost on my neighbours. At first, we were abundantly ridiculed, and severely condemned for our methods; and my good servant's spirits were sometimes sorely tried: but I told him that if we persevered good-humouredly, people would come round to our views. And so they did. First, I was declared deluded and extravagant: next, I was cruel to my live stock; then, I petted them so that they would die of luxury; and finally, one after another of our neighbours admitted the fine plight of my cows; and a few adopted our methods. At the end of a year's experience, I wrote a letter, by request, to an Assistant Poor-law Commissioner, who was earnest in his endeavours to get workhouses supplied with milk and vegetables, by the labour of the inmates on the land. To my amazement, I found my letter in the 'Times,' one day while I was at Bolton. How it got there, I know not. Other papers quoted portions of it which, separated from the rest, gave rise to wrong impressions; so that I found it necessary to write a second letter, giving the result of the second year's tillage; and to issue the two as a small pamphlet. I need say nothing here about our method of farming, as the whole story is told in that pamphlet. I may simply add that we go on with it very comfortably, and that my good farm-servant is a prosperous man. Strangers come every summer to see the place as a curiosity; and I am assured that the invariable remark is that not a foot of ground is lost, and not a sign of neglect appears in any corner. I have added a little boiling-house, a root-house, and a capital manure-pit, since those letters were written; and I have put up a higher order of fences,—to the improvement at once of the appearance and the economy of my little estate. All this, with the growth of the shrubs and little copses, and the spread of roses and evergreen climbers over the house, makes my Knoll dwelling, to say the truth, a charming spectacle to visitors;—though not half so much as to me. Some have called it 'a perfect poem:' and it is truly that to me: and so, speaking frankly, is the life that I have passed within it.

SECTION VI.

With all the writing that I have particularised on my hands, it is not to be wondered at that November arrived before Mr. Atkinson was wanted, to finish off our work for press: and by that time, my winter course of lectures was due. So much for the 'leisure,' and the 'dulness' which distant friends have attributed to my life at the Lakes. This winter's course was the arduous one of twenty lectures on the History of England,—the first of which was delivered on the fifth of November, and the last on the first of April, 1851. Amidst the undeniable overwork of that winter, I had a feeling, which I remember expressing to one friend at least, that this might probably be the last season of work for me. It seemed to me probable that, after the plain-speaking of the Atkinson Letters, I might never be asked, or allowed, to utter myself again. I had, on four previous occasions of my life, supposed the same thing, and found myself mistaken; but the 'audacity,' (as a scientific reader called my practice of plain avowal) was so much greater in appearance (though not in reality) in the present case than ever before, that I anticipated excommunication from the world of literature, if not from society.

This seems amusing enough, now, when I have enjoyed more prosperity since the publication of that volume, realised more money, earned more fame of a substantial kind, seen more of my books go out of print, and made more friendships and acquaintance with really congenial people than in any preceding four years of my life. But the anticipation was very sincere at the time; and I took care that my comrade in the work knew what my anticipation was.—There was to me, I must observe, no choice about making known, in this form or some other, my views at this period. From the time when, in my youth, I uttered my notions and was listened to, I had no further choice. For a quarter of a century past I had been answerable to an unknown number of persons for a declaration of my opinions as my experience advanced; and I could not stop now. If I had desired it, any concealment would have been most imprudent. A life of hypocrisy was wholly impracticable to me, if it had been endurable in idea; and disclosure by bits, in mere conversation, could never have answered any other purpose than misleading my friends, and subjecting me to misconception. So much for the necessity and the prudence of a full avowal. A far more serious matter was the duty of it, in regard to integrity and humanity. My comrade and I were both pursuers of truth, and were bound to render our homage openly and devoutly. We both care for our kind; and we could not see them suffering as we had suffered without imparting to them our consolation and our joy. Having found, as my friend said, a spring in the desert, should we see the multitude wandering in desolation, and not show them our refreshment? We never had a moment's doubt or misgiving; though we anticipated (or I did, for I ought only to speak for myself) all manner of consequences which never ensued.

Just as I am writing on this subject, an old letter of mine to Mr. Atkinson is put before my eyes. It was written before the publication of 'Eastern Life;' and I will insert a part of it, both because it indicates the kind of difficulty I had to deal with, on these occasions, and because it is an honest comfort to see what I had gained in courage, strength and cheerfulness in the three years which intervened between the publication of the two books.

'I am not afraid of censure,' I wrote in February 1848, 'from individuals or from the world. I don't feel, at present, any fear of the most thorough pulling to pieces that I suppose can ever befall me. The book once out, I am in for it, and must and will bear every thing. ... ... The fact is, however, —this book is, I believe, the greatest effort of courage I ever made. I only hope I may not fail in the proof. Some people would think the Population number of my Political Economy, and the Women and Marriage and Property chapters in my American books, and the Mesmerism affair, bolder feats: but I know that they were not. I was younger and more ardent then; and now the forecast and love of ease belonging to age are coming upon me. Then, I believed in a Protector who ordered me to do that work, and would sustain me under it: and, however I may now despise that sort of support, I had it then, and have none of that sort now. I have all that I want, I believe, in the absolute necessity of saying what I really believe, if I speak at all, on those Egyptian and Mosaic subjects;

and I would not exchange my present views, imperfect. and doubtful as they are,— I had better say, I would not exchange my freedom from old superstition, if I were to be burned at the stake next month, for all the peace and quiet of orthodoxy, if I must take the orthodoxy with the peace and quiet.   Nor would I, for any exemption, give up the blessing of the power of appeal to thoughtful minds.   There was —— ——, the other day, at the reading of the Sinai part of my book.   I should have expected her to be purely shocked at so much of it as to carry away a bad impression of the whole : but she was beyond all measure interested,—beyond anything ever seen in her.   So I would not have anything otherwise than as it is, as to my fate in consequence of my opinions, or absence of belief.   What I dread is being silenced, and the mortification and loss of the manner of it : (from a refusal to publish the book).   Yet, if it happens, I dare say it will become clear to me what I ought to do ; and that is the only really important thing...   ...

...   ...   Well : I have had plenty of painful enterprises to go through, and found support from the two considerations that I could not help being so circumstanced, and that I believed myself right.   ...

...   .   I will tell you of a terrible pain I have had about this matter of religious opinion. When I was at —— in September, I was told about a Town Missionary, Mr. ——, who desired particularly to see me.   He came to the house, when it appeared (—no, we knew it before ; but, however,) he had formed himself upon my books,—the more serious ones particularly,—and we found, had taken up that notion of me which we know to be idealism,

—all but idolatry. In every thing else he seemed a
rational, as he certainly was a very interesting young
man. Such a face! so full of life and happiness,—
all made up of benevolence. He was delicate; and
so was his young wife. He was then thinking of
undertaking the ———— City Mission. He did so:
and soon sank;—had influenza, and fell into rapid
consumption. A friend of his at Birmingham wrote
me that he declared himself dying, in his letter to her
received that day: and she immediately wrote to suggest to me that a letter from me would gratify him.
There was scarcely any thing I would not rather have
done: but it was impossible to refuse. I wrote at
once; and every word was as true to my own state of
mind as what I write to you now: but I feared it
would be taken for a Christian letter. There was not
a word about the future, or of God, or even Christ.
It was a letter of sympathy in his benevolent and
happy life, and also, of course, in his present weakness.
It reached him on the last day of his life. It was
read to him. When a little revived, he asked for it,
and read it himself; and then desired his wife to tell
all who loved him of ' this last flush on his darkness.'
This is dreadful pain to me. I feel as if I had told
him a lie for my last words to him. I cannot now see
how I could have acted otherwise. It would have
been hard and unkind not to write: and it was impossible to disturb his life at the last. Yet I feel that
that letter did not carry my real mind to him, and
does not to the many who are reading it. His poor
delicate young widow is strong in heart; but she has
two young infants to maintain, and not a shilling in
the world. But missionaries' widows are, I believe,

always cared for,—as I am sure they ought to be.'

It is cheering to read this letter now, and feel how much clearer and stronger my mind had become before the time arrived for the far greater enterprise which caused me so much less apprehension, and which was to release me for ever from all danger of misleading missionaries, or any body else, by letters of sympathy under solemn circumstances, which they would interpret by their preconceptions. I can write such letters now to all kinds of sufferers, in full assurance that, whether they satisfy or not, they are not misapprehended.

On the nineteenth of November, my friend and I revised his last letter, I wrote my preface, and we tied up our MS. for press; and on the twentieth, he went away. As we were going to the coach he said, 'I am glad we have done this work. We shall never repent it.' We next met in London, in the summer, when our book had run the gauntlet of all the reviews, and we found ourselves no worse for the venture we had made, and well satisfied that we had borne our testimony to the truth,—not in vain,—for many who had sorely needed the support and blessing which our philosophy had long afforded to ourselves.

When Mr. Atkinson was gone, the printing began; and I highly enjoyed the proof-correcting. That is always the time when I begin to relish any book that I have part in. The conception I enjoy, of course, or I should not write the book; but during the work, I am doubtful, and the manuscript disgusts me. Then come the proofs, when one sees exactly, and in order, what one has really said; and the work appears to that time is shown by a sad piece of weakness of mine, which I have sorely repented since;—trusting to the printing-office the proof-correcting of the Appendix. Almost three-fourths of the Appendix being sent in print to the office, and the rest in the remarkably good handwriting of a helpful neighbour, I did hope that errors might be avoided; and I inquired about it, and was assured that I might trust the printer. But never did I see such a shameful mess as those sheets; and never could I have conceived of such an ignorant sort of blunders being allowed to pass. I have never forgiven myself for my laziness in letting any part of the business out of my own hands.

The neighbour who helped me kindly in getting up the Appendix was a sickly retired clerk living close by my gate,—a man of good tastes and fond of reading. I, as I thought, hired him for a succession of evenings to write for me; and, by working together, we soon finished the business. He would not have supper, nor any refreshment whatever; and, to my consternation, (and admiration too) he declined all remuneration in such a way that I could only accept his gift of his time and labour. Since that time he has had the loan, daily, of my newspaper :—his wife buys milk of my dairy; and he sends me many a dish of trout; and I lend books to his good son. Thus we go on; and very pleasant it is.

It was while our evenings were thus filled up, that Mr. Quillinan, Wordsworth's son-in-law, called one day, full of kindly pleasure, to tell me that I must dine with him next Thursday; and sadly blank he looked when I told him I was engaged every evening that week. Could I not put off my engagement?—No: Miss

Brontë was coming on Monday; and I had business which must be finished first. His disappointment was great; for he had a benevolent scheme of bringing me into the favourable acquaintance of certain clergy of the neighbourhood, and of a physician whose further acquaintance I by no means desired. I have before mentioned that, from the first, I avoided visiting among all my neighbours, except a very few intimates; and, of course, I had no intention of beginning now, when a book was in the press which would make them gnash their teeth at me in a month or two. Mr. Quillinan had ascertained from the whole party that they should be happy to meet me; and he enjoyed, as he told me, ' bringing neighbours together, to like each other.' It had never occurred to him that I might not like to meet them; and sadly disconcerted he was. However, I promised to take Miss Brontë with me, one day, if he would dine early enough to enable my delicate guest to return before nightfall. That was a truly pleasant day,— no one being there, in addition to the family, but Mr. Arnold, from Fox How, and ourselves. And when ' Currer ' and I came home, there were proof-sheets lying; and I read her Mr. Atkinson's three letters about the distribution of the brain. She was exceedingly impressed by what she called ' the tone of calm power in all he wrote; ' moreover, she insisted on having the whole book, when it came out; and no one, so little qualified by training to enter into its substance and method, did it more generous justice. She was very far indeed from sympathising in our doctrine; and she emphatically said so; but this did not prevent her doing justice to us, under our different

view. In a preceding letter, she had said, 'I quite
expect that the publication of this book will bring
you troublous times. Many who are beginning to
draw near to you will start away again affrighted.
Your present position is high. Consequently there
are many persons, very likely, precisely in the
mood to be glad to see it lower. I anticipate a
popular outcry which you will stand much as the Duke
of Wellington would;—and in due time, it will die
round you; but I think not soon.' A month afterwards she wrote, ' Having read your book, I cannot
now think it will create any outcry. You are tender
of others :—you are serious, reverent and gentle.
Who can be angry?' This appreciation, from one
who declared (as she did to me) that our doctrine was
to her ' vinegar mingled with gall,' was honourable
to her justice and candour. And so was the readiness
with which she admitted and accepted my explanation
that I was an atheist in the vulgar sense,—that of
rejecting the popular theology,—but not in the philosophical sense, of denying a First Cause. She had
no sympathy whatever with the shallow and foolish
complaint that we were ' taking away people's faith.'
She thought that nobody's faith was worth much
which was held, more or less, because I held it too ;
and of course she saw that truth and Man would
never advance if they must wait for the weak, who
have themselves no means of progression but by the
explorations of the strong, or of those more disposed
for speculation than themselves. As I have had occasion to say to some people who seem to have forgotten
all they knew of the history of Opinion, and as
Luther and many others greater than I have had to

say, ' If your faith is worth anything, it does not depend on me : and if it depends on me, it is not worth anything.' This reminds me of an incident perhaps worth relating, in connexion with this absurd plea for standing still, which, under the laws of the mind, means retrogression.

When I was publishing ' Eastern Life,' I rather dreaded its effects on two intimate friends of mine, widows, both far removed from orthodoxy, and zealous all their lives long for free thought, and an open declaration of it. If I might judge by their profession of principle, I should become more dear to them in proportion to my efforts or sacrifices in the discovery and avowal of truth : but I knew that they could not be so judged, because neither of them had encountered any serious trial of their principle. They bore ' Eastern Life ' better than I expected,—not fully perceiving, perhaps, the extent of the speculation about belief in a future life. In the ' Atkinson Letters,' the full truth burst upon them ; and it was too much for them. They had been accustomed to detail to me their visions of that future life, which were curiously particular,—their ' heaven ' being filled with the atmosphere of their respective homes, and framed to meet the sufferings and desires of their own individual minds. I never pretended to sympathise in all this, of course ; but neither had I meddled with it, because I never meddle, except by invitation, with individual minds. After ' Eastern Life,' they must have been thoroughly aware that they had not my sympathy ; but, while they insisted (against my wish) in reading the ' Atkinson Letters,' which was altogether out of their way, they blamed

me excessively,—wholly forgetting their professions
in favour of free-thought and speech. One partially
recovered herself: the other had not power to do so.
She went about every where, eloquently bemoaning
my act, as a sort of fall, and doing me more mischief (as far as such talk can do damage) than any
enemy could have done; and, by the time she began
to see how she stood, she had done too much for entire
reparation,—earnestly as I believe she desires it. As
for the other, an anecdote will show how considerable
her self-recovery was. The very woman who had
taken on herself to inform me that God would forgive
me was not long in reaching the point I will show.
—She came to stay with me a year afterwards; and
when she departed, I went down to the gate, to put
her into the coach, when an old acquaintance greeted
me,—an aged lady living some miles off. The two
fellow-passengers talked me over, and the aged one
related how fierce an opinionated old lady of the
neighbourhood was against me,—without having
read the book;—the narrator confessing that she
herself thought I was 'exceedingly wrong to take
away people's faith.' Did not my friend think so?
She replied that if I was wrong on that ground,—in
seeking truth, and avowing it in opposition to the
popular belief, so was every religious reformer, in all
times, mounting up through Luther to St. Paul.
'Why, that's true!' cried the old lady. 'I will
remember that and tell it again.' 'And as to the
moral obligation of the case,' continued my friend,
'we must each judge by our own conscience: and
perhaps Harriet is as able to judge as Mrs. ——.'
'Yes, indeed, and a great deal better,' was the reply.

I certainly had no idea how little faith Christians have in their own faith till I saw how ill their courage and temper can stand any attack upon it. And the metaphysical deists who call themselves free-thinkers are, if possible, more alarmed and angry still. There were some of all orders of believers who treated us perfectly well: and perhaps the settled orthodox had more sympathy with us than any other class of Christians. They were not alarmed,—safely anchored as they are on the rock of authority; and they were therefore at leisure to do justice to our intentions, and even to our reasoning. Having once declared our whole basis to be wrong,—their own being divine,—they could appreciate our view and conduct in a way impossible to persons who had left the anchorage of authority, and not reached that of genuine philosophy. Certainly the heretical,—from reforming churchmen to metaphysical deists,—behaved the worst. The reviews of the time were a great instruction to us. They all, without one exception, as far as we know, shirked the subject-matter of the book, and fastened on the collateral, anti-theological portions. In regard to these portions, the reviewers contradicted each other endlessly. We had half a mind to collect their articles, and put them in such juxtaposition as to make them destroy one another, so as to leave us where they found us. It is never worth while, however, to notice reviews in their bearing upon the books they discuss. When we revert to reviews, so-called, it is for their value as essays; for it is, I believe, a thing almost unknown for a review to give a reliable account of the book which forms its text, if the work be of any substance at all. This is not the place for an essay on reviewing. I will merely observe that the causes of this phenomenon are so clear to me, and I think them so nearly unavoidable, that I have declined reviewing, except in a very few instances, since the age of thirty; and in those few instances, my articles have been avowedly essays, and not, in any strict sense, reviews.

As for the ' outcry' which ' Currer Bell' and many others anticipated, I really do not know what it amounted to,—outside of the reviewing world. If I knew, I would tell: but I know very little. To the best of my recollection, we were downright insulted only by two people;—by the opinionated old lady (above eighty) above referred to, and by one of my nearest relations;—the former in a letter to me (avowing that she had not seen the book) and the latter in print. Another old lady and her family, with whom I was barely acquainted, passed me in the road thenceforth without speaking,—a marriage into a bishop's family taking place soon after. Others spoke coldly, for a time; and one family, from whom more wisdom might have been expected, ceased to visit me, while continuing on friendly terms. I think this is all, as regards my own neighbourhood. My genuine friends did not change; and the others, failing under so clear a test, were nothing to me. When, in the evening of that spring, I went out (as I always do, when in health) to meet the midnight on my terrace, or, in bad weather, in the porch, and saw and felt what I always do see and feel there at that hour, what did it matter whether people who were nothing to me had smiled or frowned as I passed them in the village in the morning? When I experienced the still new joy of feeling myself to be a portion of the universe, resting on the security of its everlasting laws, certain that its Cause was wholly out of the sphere of human attributes, and that the special destination of my race is infinitely nobler than the highest proposed under a scheme of 'divine moral government,' how could it matter to me that the adherents of a decaying mythology,—(the Christian following the heathen, as the heathen followed the barbaric-fetish) were fiercely clinging to their Man-God, their scheme of salvation, their reward and punishment, their arrogance, their selfishness, their essential pay-system, as ordered by their mythology? As the astronomer rejoices in new knowledge which compels him to give up the dignity of our globe as the centre, the pride, and even the final cause of the universe, so do those who have escaped from the Christian mythology enjoy their release from the superstition which fails to make happy, fails to make good, fails to make wise, and has become as great an obstacle in the way of progress as the prior mythologies which it took the place of nearly two thousand years ago. For three centuries it has been undermined, and its overthrow completely decided,* as all true interpreters of the Reformation very well know. To the emancipated, it is a small matter that those who remain imprisoned are shocked at the daring which goes forth into the sunshine and under the stars, to study and enjoy, without leave asked, or fear of penalty. As to my neighbours, they

---

* As Comte pithily puts it, the three reformers who were all living at the same time, provided among them for the total demolition of Christianity,—Luther having overthrown the discipline, Calvin the hierarchy, and Socinus the dogma.

came round by degrees to their former methods of
greeting. They could do no more, because I was
wholly independent of all of them but the few intimates on whom I could rely. As one of these last
observed to me,—people leave off gossip and impertinence when they see that one is independent of them.
If one has one's own business and pleasure and near
connexions, so that the gossips are visibly of no consequence to one, they soon stop talking. Whether it
was so in my case, I never inquired. I am very civilly
treated, as far as I see; and that is enough.

As to more distant connexions, I can only say the
same thing. I had many scolding letters; but they
were chiefly from friends who were sure to think better
of it, and who have done so. For a time there was
a diminution of letters from mere acquaintances, and
persons who wanted autographs, or patronage, or the
like: but these have increased again since. I went to
London the summer after the publication of the book,
and have done so more than once since; and my
friends are very kind. I think I may sum up my
experience of this sort by saying that this book has
been an inestimable blessing to me by dissolving all
false relations, and confirming all true ones. No
one who would leave me on account of it is qualified
to be my friend; and all who, agreeing or disagreeing
with my opinions, are faithful to me through a trial
too severe for the weak, are truly friends for life. I
early felt this; and certainly no ardent friendships of
my youthful days have been half so precious to me as
those which have borne unchanged the full revelation
of my heresies. As to my fortunes,—I have already
said that my latest years have been the most pros-

perous since the publication of my Political Economy
Series.

When my friends in Egypt and I came down from,
and out of, the Great Pyramid, we agreed that no
pleasure in the recollection of the adventure, and no
forgetfulness of the fatigue and awfulness of it, should
ever make us represent the feat as easy and altogether
agreeable. For the sake of those who might come
after us, we were bound to remember the pains and
penalties, as well as the gains. In the same way, I
am endeavouring now to revive the faded impressions
of any painful social consequences which followed the
publication of the 'Atkinson Letters,' that I may
not appear to convey that there is no fine to pay for
the privilege of free utterance. I do not remember
much about a sort of pain which was over so long ago,
and which there has been nothing to revive ; but I am
aware, in a general way, that the nightly mood which
yields me such lofty pleasure, under the stars, and
within the circuit of the solemn mountains, was not
always preserved : and that if I had not been on my
guard in advance, and afterwards supported by Mr.
Atkinson's fine temper, I might have declined into a
state of suspicion, and practice of searching into
people's opinion of me. To renew the impressions
of the time, I have now been glancing over Mr.
Atkinson's letters of that spring, which I preserved
for some such purpose : and I am tempted to insert
one or two, as faithful reflexions of his mood at the
time, which was the guide and aid of mine. This
reminds me that one of our amusements at the time
was at the various attempts,—in print, in letters, and
in conversation,—to set us at variance. One of our
literary magnates, who admires the book, said that

this was the first instance in history of an able man joining a woman in authorship ; and the novelty was not likely to be acquiesced in without resistance. In print, Mr. Atkinson was reproached,—in the face of my own preface,—with drawing me into the business, and making me his ' victim,' and so forth, by persons who knew perfectly well that, so far from wanting any aid in coming forward, he had lectured, and published his lecture, containing the same views, both physiological and anti-theological, before we had any acquaintance whatever : and, on the other hand, I was scolded for dragging forth a good man into persecution which I had shown I did not myself care for. On this sort of charge, which admitted of no public reply, (if he had replied to any thing) Mr. Atkinson wrote these few words,—after reading the one only review which stooped to insult,—insult being, in that instance, safe to the perpetrator by accident of position. ' The thing that impressed me, in reading that review was,—how ingenious men are in seeking how to poison their neighbours, and how men themselves do just what they accuse others of doing. Honest scorn I don't at all mind : but I don't like a wrong or undue advantage being taken. I don't like a cabman to charge a shilling extra when one is with ladies, thinking you won't dispute it. All our principles of honour and justice and benevolence seem to me to be implicated in questions of truth; and in this, I certainly feel firm as a rock, and with the courage of the lion : —that the position is to be maintained, and the thing to be done, and there's an end of it,—be the consequences what they may.' Then came a letter to him, candidly advising' him to do himself justice, as

speedily as might be, by publishing something alone,
to repair the disadvantage of having let a woman
speak under the same cover : and on the same day,
came a letter to me, gently reproving my good-nature
in lending my literary experience to any man's objects.
Sometimes the volume was all mine, and sometimes all
his,—each taking the advantage of the other's name.
There was a good deal of talk to the same purpose ;
and Mr. Atkinson's comment on this policy was,—
' the aim is evident,—to stir up jealousy between us.
But it won't do. They don't know the man,—nor
the woman either.'

The following morsel may serve to show our view
of the large class of censors who, believing nothing
themselves, of theology or any thing else, were
scandalised at our ' shaking the faith ' of other
people. A lawyer of this class, avowing that he had
not read the book, launched ' a thunderbolt ' at me,
—possibly forgetting how many ' thunderbolts ' I
had seen him launch at superstitions, like that of a
future life, and at those who teach them. Mr.
Atkinson's remark on this will not take up much
space. ' Bravo——! A pretty lawyer he, to give
judgment before he has read his brief! What a
Scribe it is ! lawyer to the backbone ! I wish he
would tell us what truths we may be allowed to utter,
and when. Certainly it seems a pity to hurt any
one's feelings : but Christianity was not so tender
about that : nor does Nature seem very particular.
It is all very fine, talking about people's religious
convictions ; but what is to become of those who
have no such convictions,— that increasing crowd
filling up the spaces between the schisms of the

churches? The Church is rotting away daily. Convictions are losing their stability. Men are being scattered in the wilderness. Shall we not hold up a light in the distance, and prepare them a shelter from the storm? The religious people, you will see, will respect us more than the infidels, who have no faith in truth, no light but law, no hope for Man but his fancies ("convictions"). No, I don't feel any thing at "thunderbolts" of this kind, I assure you. I think it more like the squash of a rotten apple. Let such thunderbolts come as thick as rain; and they will not stir a blade of grass.' On April eleventh, my friend wrote, in reply to some accounts of excursions with two nieces, who were staying with me:

'Here is a nice packet of letters from you. It is delightful to read your account of your doings. You have no time to be miserable and repent,—have you? no time to be thinking of your reputation or your soul. Your cheerful front to the storm and active exertions will make you respected ; and remember, the Cause requires it. It would be hard for a Christian to be brave and cheerful in a Mahomedan country, with any amount of pitying and abusing; and so you have not a fair chance of the effect of your faith on your happiness in life,—as it will be for all when the community think as you do, and each supports each, and sympathy abounds.   ...   .
As for Dr. B. and the rest,—when men don't like the end, of course they find fault with the means. How *could* it be logical and scientific if it leads to a different conclusion from them :—*them*—yes, all of them thinking differently! F. in "Fraser" does not think any thing of a future life from instinct, or a

God from design : but these points are just what the
others insist on. To my mind F.'s article and the
one in the " Westminster " are full of sheer assertion
and error and bad taste. I think *they* want logic,
science, or whatever they may term it. If I am
wrong and unscientific, why do they not put me
right ?—taking the " Letters " as a mere *sketch*, of
course, and presenting only a few points of the subject.
It is but a slight sketch of the head, leaving the
whole figure to be completed. The fact is, these
reviewers skip over the science to the theology, and
talk nonsense when they *feel* uncomfortably opposed,
—perhaps insulted. I don't mean in the least to
argue that I am not wrong ; only, those who think so
ought to show how and why. Mr. F. reasons from
analogy when my chief argument is in opposition to
those analogical reasonings. The *analogy* with Christ
is curious, as showing how minds are impressed
with resemblances. Some see a man with the slightest
curve of the nose, and say, " How like the Duke of
Wellington ! " or with a club-foot, and say, " How
like Byron ! " I am certainly well contented with
F.'s praise ; for one reason only ; that people won't
think you so foolish in bringing me forward in the
way you have. As for the book, it is left by the
critics just where it was ; nothing disproved,—neither
the facts nor the method, nor Bacon ; and after all,
if mine is " a careless sketch " (and I dare say it is),
the question is the truth of what it contains. If these
men are such good artists, they will read the fact out
of a rough sketch. F. throws out that idea about
Bacon again, and calls it a *moral* fault in me. I
cannot see it, especially as I am supported by others

well acquainted with Bacon. The sin was of a piece with the rest of his doings,—in a measure essential at the time for getting a hearing at all for his philosophy: and F. forgets that if Bacon was an atheist, there was no offence against sacred matters, seeing that he did not consider them sacred, but " the delirium of phrenetics; " and thus it was rather a showing of respect and yielding. I do not see that this can spoil him as an authority, any more than Macaulay spoils him: and if it did, he had better be no authority at all than an authority *against* science. Lord Campbell says Bacon was accustomed in his youth to ridicule religion, thinks the Paradoxes were his, but that in riper years he probably changed his opinion; the only reason given for which is a sentence in the Advancement of Learning,—his *earliest* great work. The passage there is, " A little or superficial knowledge of philosophy may incline the mind of man to atheism, &c.; " which is absurd, if it were insisted on by Campbell. (I suppose Pope's " A little learning is a dangerous thing," is taken from this passage.) Of course, people will say I am wrong; *but let them show it*, with all their logic; and we shall see who has the best of it.—So you think the storm is at its height. It shows how little I know of it,—I thought it was all over. The organ now playing a wretched tune before my windows is more annoyance than all their articles put together. If they generally speak so of it, methinks there must be something in it, and they are not indifferent to it. Your American correspondent is quite a mystic. What curious turns and twists the human mind takes, before it gets into the clear road of true philosophy, walking through the midst of the facts of Nature, the view widening and clearing at every step! Men like —— and —— don't like our book because it makes so little of theirs and all their study, by taking a more direct line to the results. I can't think what —— can have to say that has not been said. So he is reading Comte, is he? I hope it will do him good.—Make Dr. ——understand that repetition of the general fact was not the thing required or intended. I had other things to say, and to press into a mere notice. It is this very fact of incompleteness, &c., &c., that I believe Bacon would have praised. There is nothing cut and dried. There are facts; and in a certain order; a form for thinking men to work upon,—not to satisfy superficial men with a show of completeness. There are "particulars not known before for the use of man," which is better than all their logic: the one is mere measure and music,—the other "for future ages,"—the grain of mustard seed only, perhaps, but a germ full of life. The first letters are a sketch expository of my views on mental science and the means of discovery; and the following letters merely an *example* (like Bacon's Natural History) of the kind of fact that will throw light on the nature of the mind's action, out of which, when *extended and arranged in order*, inductions are to be made of the laws of action. The rest is little more than conversational replies to your questions.'

Another of these letters was written when I was ill under an attack of influenza, which disabled me from duly enjoying a visit I was paying in the north of the district, and from getting on with my next great scheme. After telling me how ill every body was at that time, he says:

'It is sad to be making your visit now. As to our concerns,—there is no saying how the next post may alter every thing. There really is no place for an ill feeling, or a disturbed one, if we could but keep it so in view. It seems to me that life is either too holy, or a matter too indifferent to be moved by every silly thought or angry feeling. With regard to what they say about us, it is only precisely what you anticipated they would say: and it seems to me that after all is said, our facts and position remain untouched. It seems that we ought to have something to bear. I value this more every day. If I can be safe from flatterers and inducements to indulgence, I will be thankful for all the rest, and smile at all their scandal, and their great discovery that I am not allwise. It all presents some new matter for contemplation; and if we cannot absolutely love our enemies, at least we may thank them for showing us our faults, which flattering friends hide from us. It seems all kinds of things must happen to us before we can become at all wise. First, we must become disenchanted of many delusions, that we may discover the pure gold through all the alloy which passes with it in the current coin of life. The Idols of the Market are inveterate; but down they must go, if we would be in the least wise: and the process must be healthful when one does not become soured, but feels one's heart rather expanding and warming than cooling with years; and more thankful for every kindness, and not exacting as formerly.—I have been staying a few days in the country. We went over to a charming place, one day. Such a common! Perfectly beautiful! Acres of cherry-blossom, and splendid furze, like heaps of living gold; and the dark pine-trees rising from the midst! But one can't describe such things. I walked about there alone while the others were shooting young rooks,—the parson at the head of them. I had a little volume which pleased me much. It was never published ...   .   There does not seem to be any chance of my having got at Comte's ideas through any indirect channel; and I know nothing of him directly. Knight's volume by Lewes is the whole of my acquaintance with him. What I do think is by labour in the fields or wild commons, and on the bench in the Regent's Park.—That unqualified condemnation of us in regard to Bacon looks rather like a condemnation by prejudiced and ignorant divines which Bacon grieves over. The whole matter is not worth wasting good feelings upon: but it should rather bring them forth, not injured, but strengthened. If, from being ill, we cannot depend on our forces, we can only make the best of it. I will soon tell you what I think I can best do now, in furtherance of our subject. All before us seems clear and sure, and the prospect even full of gaiety, if only I knew that you were quite well again. We must have our sad moments that we may have our wise ones.'

Here is his Good Friday letter, written amidst the ringing of church bells. It begins with a comment on an unhappy aged person,—of whom we have been speaking:

'Age is a sad affair. If men went out of life in the very fulness of their powers, in a flash of lightning, one might imagine them transferred to heaven: but when the fruit fails, and then the flower and leaf, and branch after branch rots by our side while we yet live, we can hardly wish for a better thing than early death. Yes; it is true;—we do good to those to whom we have done good: we insult those we have insulted. Goodness is twice blessed; but hatred cankers the soul; and there is no relief, no unction, but in hating on. But of all the sad effects of age, the saddest is when as in this case a person reverses the noble principle of his life, —like the insane mother who detests the child she has so tenderly nurtured and loved. Every thing is flimsy, wrong, illogical, which does not confirm such an one in his own opinions: as a lady declared last evening who had been accusing *me* of not giving a fair consideration to the other side of the question, while I was recommending *her* to read so and so. "Well," said she, "it does not signify talking: in plain truth, I do not care to know about any body's views or reasons which will not confirm me in my own faith." This was a sudden burst of honest pride, and eagerness, in the midst of the confusion, to hold tight where she had got footing. Notions are worth nothing which are uttered in irritation partly, and in ignorance greatly, and in the spirit of old age,—not of Christ or of Paul. If what I have said is wrong in logic or in fact, it is no use abusing us: the thing is to exhibit the error; and I am sure none will be more thankful for the correction than I. F—— is the only one who has tried to do this; and I thank him for it, though I think him wholly wrong on matters of fact.—The book is objected to on religious grounds. Now, what is the use of all the millions spent, of all the learning of the colleges, and of all the parsons,—as thick as

crows over the land,—if they cannot correct what is
"shallow" and "superficial ?" No; they feel otherwise
than as they assert. They fear that however arrogant
or superficial the book may be, there is substance in the
midst of it; there is danger to the existing state of
things; and they dare not honestly face the facts, and
meet the argument which they declare to be too superficial to deceive any one. They dare not honestly and
fairly do it. Shame upon the land! With that skulk-
ing phantom of a dressed-up faith that dares not face
the light in broad day: with God upon their lips, and
preaching Christ crucified, they fear to encounter
God's truth by the way side! Why does Gavazzi
waste his breath upon the Pope? Let him face the
wide world, and denounce its false faith, and show
them how God walks with them in Nature as he did
by Adam in Eden, and they hide away in shame,
worship the Devil, and feed on the apple of sin every
day of their lives. Men are subdued by *fear*. There
is no faith in change, in progress, in truth, in virtue,
in holiness. It is a terror-stricken age; and men fly
to God to save them, and God gives them truth in his
own way; and they receive it not. There is every
kind of stupid terror got up about the Great Exhibition. F. is in terror about phreno-mesmerism: he
would drown himself,—go out of the world if the
thing were true. They like "Deerbrook"—yes,
as a picture: but the spirit of "Deerbrook" is not in
them, or they would love the spirit of the author of
"Deerbrook." Well! it is not so bad as Basil
Montagu used to say, "My dear Atkinson, they will
tear you to pieces." It is something then to say
what we have said, and remain in a whole skin.

...   .   The world is ripe if there were but the towering genius that would speak to it. We are all dead asleep. We want rousing from a lethargy, that we may listen to the God of Heaven and of earth who speaks to us in our hearts. The word of God is in every man, if he will listen. God is with us in all Nature, if we will but read the written law; written not on tables of stone, but on the wide expanse of nature. Yes, the savage is more right. God is in the clouds, and we hear him in the wind. Yes : and in the curse of ignorance, and the voice of reprobation, there too is God,—warning us of ignorance,—of unbelief of temper,—putting another law in our way, that we may read and interpret the book of fate. O ! that some great teacher would arise, and make himself heard from the mountain top ! The man whom they crucified on this day gave a Sermon on a mount. It is in every house, in every head ; it is known, passage after passage : but in how few has it touched the heart, and opened the understanding ! Men are but slowly led by pure virtue or by pure reason. They require eloquence and powerful persuasion ; deep, solemn, unceasing persuasion. The Bible is a dead letter. Men worship the air and call it God. God is truth, law, morals, noble deeds of heroism, conscience, self-sacrifice, love, freedom, and cheerfulness. Men have no God. It is yet to be given them. They have but a log, and are croaking and unsatisfied ; and to-morrow they try King Hudson or the Devil.'

The looking over these letters has revived my recollection of the really critical time at which they were written,—the trials of which I had forgotten as completely as the fatigues of the outside, and the

gloomy horror of the inside of the pyramid.—I shall
say nothing of the counterpart of the experience; of
the vast discoveries of sympathy, the new connexions,
the pleasant friendships, and the gratitude of disciples
which have accrued to us, from that time to the
present hour.   The act was what I had to give an
account of, and not its consequences.   The same
reasons which have deterred me from exhibiting the
praises awarded to other works are operative here.—
I will conclude the whole subject with observing that
time shows us more and more the need there is of
such testimony as any of us can give to the value of
philosophy, and of science as its basis.   Those who
praised us and our book, in print or in conversation,
seem to have no more notion than those who condemned us of the infinite importance of philosophy,
—not only to intellectual wisdom, but to goodness
and happiness; and, again, that, in my comrade's
words, 'the only method of arriving at a true
philosophy of Mind is by the contemplation of Man
as a whole,—as a creature endowed with definite
properties, capable of being observed and classified
like other phenomena resulting from any other portion
of Nature.'   The day when we agreed upon bearing
our testimony, (in however imperfect a form) to these
great truths was a great day for me, in regard both
to my social duty and my private relations.   Humble
as was my share in the book, it served to bring me
into a wide new sphere of duty; and, as to my
private connexions, it did what I have said before;—
it dissolved all false relations, and confirmed all true
ones.   Its great importance to me may excuse, as
well as account for, the length to which this chapter
of my life has extended.

SECTION VII.

IT appears, from two or three notices above, that
Comte's philosophy was at this time a matter of
interest to me. For many months after, his great
work was indeed a means of singular enjoyment to
me. After hearing Comte's name for many years,
and having a vague notion of the relation of his
philosophy to the intellectual and social needs of the
time, I obtained something like a clear preparatory
view, at second-hand, from a friend, at whose house
in Yorkshire I was staying, before going to Bolton,
in 1850. What I learned then and there impelled
me to study the great book for myself; and in the
spring of 1851, when the 'Atkinson Letters' were
out, and the History was finished, and I intended to
make holiday from the pen for awhile, I got the book,
and set to work. I had meantime looked at Lewes's
chapter on Comte in Mr. Knight's Weekly Volume,
and at Littré's epitome; and I could thus, in a
manner, see the end from the beginning of the complete and extended work. This must be my excuse
for the early date at which I conceived the scheme of
translating the *Philosophie Positive*.

My course of lectures on English History finished

on the first of April: and on the eighth, I sent off
the last proof-sheet of my history. On the fourteenth,
my nieces left me; and there was an interval before
my spring visits which I employed in a close study of
the first volume of Comte's work. On the twenty-
fourth, the book arrived from London; and I am
amazed, and somewhat ashamed to see by my Diary,
that, on the twenty-sixth, I began to 'dream' of
translating it; and on the next night (Sunday the
twenty-seventh) sat up late,—not dreaming, but
planning it. On the second of May, I was in such
enthusiasm that I wrote to one of the best-informed
men on this matter in the kingdom, (an old friend) to
ask his opinion on my scheme. He emphatically
approved my design,—of introducing the work to
the notice of a wide portion of the English public
who could never read it in the original; but he proposed a different method of doing it. He said that
no results could compensate to me for the toil of
translating six volumes in a style like Comte's, and
in the form of lectures, whereby much recapitulation
was inevitable. He proposed that I should give an
abstract of Comte's philosophy, with illustrations of
my own devising, in one volume; or, at most, in two
of a moderate size. I was fully disposed to do this;
and I immediately began an analysis, which would, I
thought, be useful in whatever form I might decide
to put forth the substance. I know no greater luxury,
after months of writing, than reading, and making
an analysis as one goes. This work I pursued while
making my spring visits. On the eighth of May, I
went for a fortnight to stay with some friends,
between whom and myself there was cordial affection,

though they were Swedenborgians, of no ordinary
degree of *possession* (for I will not call it fanaticism
in people so gentle and kind). Their curiosity about
Comte rather distressed me; and certainly it is not in
the power of the most elastic mind to entertain at
once Swedenborg and Comte. They soon settled the
matter, however. My host kept aloof,—going out
to his fishing every morning, while I was at work,
and having very different matters to talk about in
the evenings. It was his lady who took up the
matter; and I was amused to see how. She came to
my writing-table, to beg the loan of the first volume,
when I was going out for a walk. When her
daughter and I returned from our walk, we met her
in the wood; and the whole affair was settled. She
knew 'all about it,' and had decided that Comte
knew nothing. I inquired in amazement the grounds
of this decision. She had glanced over the first
chapter, and could venture to say she now 'knew all
about it.' There was mere human science (which,
for that matter, Swedenborg had also); and such
science bears no relation to the realities which concern
men most. This was all very well: and I was rejoiced
that the thing had passed over so easily, though
marvelling at the presumption of the judgment in one
whom I consider nearly the humblest of women
where her own qualities are concerned. A year later,
however, she sent me a letter of rebuke about my
work, which had less of the modesty, and more of the
presumption, than I should have expected. I reminded
her of what we had often agreed upon, with remarkable
satisfaction,—the superiority of the Swedenborgians
to all other religious sects in liberality. Not only

does their doctrine in a manner necessitate this
liberality, but the temper of its professors responds
to the doctrine more faithfully than that of religious
professors in general. I was sorry, as I told my
friend, to see this liberality fail, on a mere change of
the ground,—from that of religious controversy to
that of the opposition between science and theology.
I claimed my liberty to do the work which I thought
best for the truth, for the same reason that I rejoiced
in seeing her and her excellent family doing what they
thought best for what they regarded as truth. I have
had no more censure or remonstrance from any of the
family, and much kindness,—the eldest daughter
even desiring to come and nurse me, when she heard
of my present illness : but I have no doubt that all
the heresy I have ever spoken and written is tolerable
in their eyes, in comparison with the furtherance given
to science by the rendering of Comte's work into a
tongue which the multitude can read; and which
they will read, while the young men should be seeing
visions and the old men dreaming dreams.

During other visits, and a great press of business
about cottage-building, and of writing for 'Household
Words' and elsewhere, I persevered in my study and
analysis,—spending the evenings in collateral reading,
—the lives and the history of the works of eminent
mathematicians, and other scientific men. This went
on till the twenty-sixth of June, when tourists began
to fill the place and every body's time, and I must be
off to London and into Norfolk, and leave my house
to my tenant for three months. My first visit was to
some beloved American friends in London, by whom I
was introduced to the Great Exhibition. I attended

the last of Mr. Thackeray's lectures of that season,
and paid evening visits, and saw many old friends.
But I was now convinced that I had lost my former
keen relish for London pleasures. The quiet talks late
at night with my hostesses were charming; and there
was great pleasure in meeting old acquaintances: but
the heat, and the glare, and the noise, and the superficial bustle, so unlike my quiet life of grave pursuit
and prevailing solitude at home, showed me that my
knoll had in truth spoiled me for every other abode.

The mention of Mr. Thackeray's name here reminds me that it does not occur in my notes of literary
London twenty years ago. At that time I saw him,
if I remember right, only once. It was at Mr.
Buller's, at dinner ;—at a dinner which was partly
ludicrous and partly painful. Mrs. Buller did not
excel in tact ; and her party was singularly arranged
at the dinner-table. I was placed at the bottom of the
table, at its square end, with an empty chair on the
one hand, and Mr. Buller on the other,—he being
so excessively deaf that no trumpet was of much use to
him. There we sat with our trumpets,—an empty
chair on the one hand, and on the other, Mr. J. S.
Mill, whose singularly feeble voice cut us off from
conversation in that direction. As if to make another
pair, Mrs. Buller placed on either side of her a gentleman with a flattened nose,— Mr. Thackeray on her
right, and her son Charles on the left. It was on
this day only that I met either Mr. Dickens or Mr.
Thackeray during my London life. About Mr.
Thackeray I had no clear notion in any way, except
that he seemed cynical ; and my first real interest in
him arose from reading M. A. Titmarsh in Ireland,

during my Tynemouth illness.   I confess to being unable to read ' Vanity Fair,' from the moral disgust it occasions ; and this was my immediate association with the writer's name when I next met him, during the visit to London in 1851.   I could not follow his lead into the subject of the Bullers (then·all dead), so strong was my doubt of his real feeling.   I was, I fear, rather rough and hard when we talked of ' Vanity Fair ;' but a sudden and most genuine change of tone,—of voice, face, and feeling,—that occurred on my alluding to Dobbin's admirable turning of the tables on Amelia, won my trust and regard more than any thing he had said yet.   ' Pendennis ' much increased my respect and admiration ; and ' Esmond ' appears to me *the* book of the century, in its department.   I have read it three times ; and each time with new wonder at its rich ripe wisdom, and at the singular charm of Esmond's own character.   The power that astonishes me the most in Thackeray is his fertility, shown in the way in which he opens glimpses into a multitudinous world as he proceeds.   The chief moral charm is in the paternal vigilance and sympathy which constitute the spirit of his narration.   The first drawback in his books, as in his manners, is the impression conveyed by both that he never can have known a good and sensible woman.   I do not believe he has any idea whatever of such women as abound among the matronage of England,—women of excellent capacity and cultivation applied to the natural business of life. It is perhaps not changing the subject to say next what the other drawback is.   Mr. Thackeray has said more, and more effectually, about snobs and snobbism than any other man ; and yet his frittered life, and his obedience to the call of the great are the observed of all observers. As it is so, so it must be; but ' O! the pity of it! the pity of it!' Great and unusual allowance is to be made in his case, I am aware; but this does not lessen the concern occasioned by the spectacle of one after another of the aristocracy of nature making the ko-tow to the aristocracy of accident. If society does not owe all it would be thankful to owe to Mr. Thackeray, yet it is under deep and large obligations to him; and if he should even yet be seen to be as wise and happy in his life and temper as he might be any day, he may do much that would far transcend all his great and rising achievements thus far; and I who shall not see it would fain persuade myself that I foresee it. He who stands before the world as a sage *de jure* must surely have impulses to be a sage *de facto*.

Of Mr. Dickens I have seen but little in face-to-face intercourse; but I am glad to have enjoyed that little. There may be, and I believe there are, many who go beyond me in admiration of his works,—high and strong as is my delight in some of them. Many can more keenly enjoy his peculiar humour,—delightful as it is to me; and few seem to miss as I do the pure plain daylight in the atmosphere of his scenery. So many fine painters have been mannerists as to atmosphere and colour that it may be unreasonable to object to one more: but the very excellence and diversity of Mr. Dickens's powers makes one long that they should exercise their full force under the broad open sky of nature, instead of in the most brilliant palace of art. While he tells us a world of things that are natural and even true, his personages are generally, as I suppose is undeniable, profoundly unreal. It is a curious speculation what effect his universally read works will have on the foreign conception of English character. Washington Irving came here expecting to find the English life of Queen Anne's days, as his ' Sketchbook' shows; and very unlike his preconception was the England he found. And thus it must be with Germans, Americans, and French who take Mr. Dickens's books to be pictures of our real life.—Another vexation in his vigorous erroneousness about matters of science, as shown in ' Oliver Twist' about the new poor-law (which he confounds with the abrogated old one) and in ' Hard Times,' about the controversies of employers. Nobody wants to make Mr. Dickens a Political economist; but there are many who wish that he would abstain from a set of difficult subjects, on which all true sentiment must be underlain by a sort of knowledge which he has not. The more fervent and inexhaustible his kindliness (and it is fervent and inexhaustible), the more important it is that it should be well-informed and well-directed, that no errors of his may mislead his readers on the one hand, nor lessen his own genial influence on the other.

The finest thing in Mr. Dickens's case is that he, from time to time, proves himself capable of progress, —however vast his preceding achievements had been. In humour, he will hardly surpass ' Pickwick,' simply because ' Pickwick ' is scarcely surpassable in humour: but in several crises, as it were, of his fame, when every body was disappointed, and his faults seemed running his graces down, there has appeared something so prodigiously fine as to make us all joyfully exclaim

that Dickens can never permanently fail. It was so
with ' Copperfield : ' and I hope it may be so again
with the new work which my survivors will soon have
in their hands.—Meantime, every indication seems to
show that the man himself is rising. He is a virtuous
and happy family man, in the first place. His glowing
and generous heart is kept steady by the best domestic
influences; and we may fairly hope now that he will
fulfil the natural purpose of his life, and stand by
literature to the last; and again, that he will be an
honour to the high vocation by prudence as well as
by power: so that the graces of genius and generosity
may rest on the finest basis of probity and prudence;
and that his old age may be honoured as heartily as
his youth and manhood have been admired.—Nothing
could exceed the frank kindness and consideration
shown by him in the correspondence and personal
intercourse we have had; and my cordial regard has
grown with my knowledge of him.

When I left London, it was for the singular contrast of spending the next night in a workhouse.
Two of my servants (brother and sister) had been sent
to me from Norfolk,—the maid by my own family,
and the man by the excellent master of the Union
Workhouse near Harling. The girl (now married to
the master of the Ragged School at Bristol) had a
strong inclination to school-keeping, and had pursued
it in this workhouse and elsewhere with such assiduity
as to lose her health. During the five years that she
lived with me (beloved like a daughter by me, and
honoured by all who knew her) she in a great measure
recovered her health ; and when she married from my
house, at Christmas 1852, she went to resume her

vocation, in which she is now leading the most useful
life conceivable. We went to Harling, she and I, in
this July 1851, to see her old friends, and the old
school, and her old parents, and the success of the
agricultural part of the management of this Guiltcross
Union. Thus it was that I went from London to
sleep in a workhouse. Very comfortable and agreeable
I found it.

The next weeks were spent in the neighbourhood of
Norwich, and at Cromer, where I was joined by my
younger sister and her children. It was at Cromer
that a strange impulse on my part,—an impulse of
yielding chiefly,—caused me to go into an enterprise
which had no result. It put me, for a time, in the
difficulty of having too many irons in the fire; but
that was not my fault; for I could have no conception
of the news which was awaiting me in London, on my
return. While at Cromer, I was justified in feeling
that I might take as much time as I pleased about
Comte. It depended wholly on myself: but before I
got home, the case was changed, as I shall presently
have to tell. The intervening anecdote has been
hitherto a profound secret, by my own desire;—
perhaps the only secret of my own that I ever had :
and this was part of the amusement. One reason
why I tell it now is because it affords a confirmation
out of my own experience of what many of my
friends have wondered to hear me say;—that one
cannot write fiction, after having written (*con amore*,
at least) history and philosophy.

Ever since the ' Deerbrook ' days, my friends had
urged me to write more novels. When ' Currer Bell '
was staying with me, the winter before the time I

have arrived at, she had spoken earnestly to me
about it, and, as it appeared to us both, wholly in vain.
While at Cromer, however, I read 'Pendennis'
with such intense enjoyment, and it seemed so much
the richer from its contrast with 'The Ogilvies,' and
some other metaphysical, sentimental novels that had
fallen in my way, that the notion of trying my hand
once more at a novel seized upon me; and I wrote to
Charlotte Brontë, to consult her as to the possibility
of doing it secretly, and getting it out anonymously,
and quite unsuspected,—as a curious experiment.
She wrote joyously about it, and at once engaged her
publisher's * interest in the scheme.   She showed the
most earnest friendliness throughout.   She sent me a
packet of envelopes directed by herself to her publisher; and she allowed his letters to me to come
through her hands.   When I reached home, on the
first of October, I was somewhat scared at what I
had undertaken,—the case of Comte having so
changed, as I will tell; and the matter was not made
easier by my inability to tell Mr. Chapman, who was
to publish Comte, or Mr. Atkinson, who was in
almost daily correspondence with me, what was delay-
ing the progress of the philosophical half of my
work.   The difficulty was at an end before Christmas
by the scheme of the novel being at an end.   It was
on an odd plan.   It was no oddness in the plan,
however, which discouraged me; but I doubted from
the first whether I could ever again succeed in fiction,
after having completely passed out of the state of
mind in which I used to write it.   In old days, I had

* Mr. G. Smith, of the firm of Smith, Elder, & Co.

caught myself quoting the sayings of my own personages, so strong was the impression of reality on
myself; and I let my pen go as it would when the
general plan of the story, and the principal scenes,
were once laid down.   Now I read and pondered, and
arranged, and sifted, and satisfied myself, before I
entered upon any chapter, or while doing it :—carrying, in fact, the methods and habits of historical
composition into tale-telling.   I had many misgivings
about this; but, on the whole, I thought that the
original principle of the work, and some particular
scenes, would carry it through.   At Christmas, I sent
the first volume to Charlotte Brontë, who read it
before forwarding it to the publisher.   She wrote
gloriously about it: and three days after came a
pathetic letter from the publisher.   He dared not
publish it on account of some favourable representa-
tions and auguries on behalf of the Catholics.   That
was a matter on which C. Brontë and I had perpetual controversy,—her opinion being one in which
I could by no means agree ; and thus expressed, after
I had claimed credit for the Catholics, as for every
body else, as far as their good works extended :—
'Their good deeds I don't dispute ; but I regard
them as the hectic bloom on the cheek of disease.   I
believe the Catholics, in short, to be always doing evil
that good may come, or doing good that evil may
come.'   Yet did my representation of the Catholics
in no way shake her faith in the success of my novel;
and her opinion, reaching the publisher the day after
he had written his apprehensions to me, aggravated,
as he said, his embarrassment and distress.   He
implored me to lay aside this scheme, and send him a

novel 'like "Deerbrook."' That was no more in my
power now than to go back to thirty years of age.
C. Brontë entreated me merely to lay aside my novel.
if I would not finish it on speculation, saying that
some things in it were equal to, or beyond, any thing I
had ever written. I did intend at first to finish it:
but other works pressed; the stimulus, and even the
conception, passed away; and I burned the MS. and
memoranda, a few months since, not wishing to leave
to my survivors the trouble of an unfinished MS.
which they could make no use of, and might scruple
to burn. I told Mr. Atkinson and my Executor
the facts when the scheme was at an end; and I
hereby record the only failure of the sort I had
experienced since the misleading I underwent about
the Life of Howard, at the outset of my career. I
may add that the publisher behaved as well as possible,
under the circumstances. He showed me civility in
various ways, was at all times ready to negotiate for
another novel 'like "Deerbrook,"' and purchased the
copy-right of 'Deerbrook' itself, in order to bring
it out in a cheap series, with the novels of Mr.
Thackeray and 'Currer Bell.'

While I write, I recal, with some wonder, the fact
that I had another literary engagement on my hands,
at that very time. On recurring to my Diary, I find
it was even so; and I wonder how I could justify it
to myself. It was at Cromer, as I have said, that
this scheme of the novel was framed, after I had
consulted Mr. Chapman in London about publishing
Comte's 'Positive Philosophy.' We had a clear
understanding that it was to be done; but I was
then wholly free in regard to time. On my return,

I spent a week in London (then 'empty, according to the London use of the word) with a cousin, in a lodging, for the sole object of seeing the Exhibition in our own way, and in peace and quiet. On the last day, Mr. Chapman, who had been trying to track me, overtook me with a wonderful piece of news. Mr. Lombe, a Norfolk country gentleman, and late High Sheriff of the county, had for many years been a disciple of Comte, and had earnestly wished to translate the 'Positive Philosophy,' but had been prevented by ill health. He was a perfect stranger to me, and residing in Florence; but, hearing from Mr. Chapman what I was doing, he sent me, by him, a draft on his bankers for 500*l*. His obvious intention was to give me the money, in recompense for the work; but I preferred paying the expenses of paper, print, and publication out of it, taking 200*l*. for my own remuneration. To finish now about the money part of the affair,—I took advice how to act, in regard to so important a trust; and, in accordance with that advice, I immediately invested the whole amount in the Three per Cents., and, on the death of Mr. Lombe, in the next winter, I added a codicil to my will, appointing two trustees to the charge and application of the money, in case of my dying before the work was completed and published. Just when Mr. Lombe died, I was proposing to send him a portion of my MS., to see whether my method and execution satisfied him. When the whole sum was distributed, and the work out, I submitted the accounts and vouchers to two intimate friends of Mr. Lombe, both men of business, and obtained their written assurance of their entire approbation of what

I had done,—with the one exception that they thought I ought to have taken more of the money myself. As to the profits of the sale,—it seemed to me fair that M. Comte should have a portion; and also Mr. Chapman, through whom Mr. Lombe had become interested in the scheme.   The profits have therefore been, up to this time, and will be henceforward, divided among the three,—M. Comte, Mr. Chapman and myself or my legatees.—My engagement to Mr. Chapman was to deliver the MS. entire within two years of my return home; that is, in October, 1853; and this was precisely the date at which I delivered the last sheets.   The printing had been proceeding during the summer; so that the work appeared at the beginning of November 1853.

The additional work to which I have referred, as upon my hands at the same time, was this.   I returned home, in the autumn of 1851, by Birmingham, where I spent a month at my brother Robert's house, at Edgbaston.   The proprietors of ' Household Words ' had all this time been urgent with me to write stories for them.   I found myself really unable to do this with any satisfaction,—not only because of the absurdity of sending fiction to Mr. Dickens, but because I felt more and more that I had passed out of that stage of mind in which I could write stories well.   It struck me that a full, but picturesque account of manufactures and other productive processes might be valuable, both for instruction and entertainment : and I proposed to try my hand on two or three of the Birmingham manufactures, under the advantage of my brother's introduction, in the first place, and, in the next, of his correction, if I

should fall into any technical mistakes. The proposal
was eagerly accepted ; and I then wrote the papers on
Electro-plating, Papier-mâché and the Nail and Screw
manufacture,—which stand in ' Household Words '
under the titles of ' Magic Troughs at Birmingham,'
' Flower-shows in a Birmingham Hot-house,' and
' Wonders of Nails and Screws.' These succeeded
so well that I went on at home with such materials as
the neighbourhood afforded,—the next papers which
appeared being ' Kendal Weavers,' and.' The Bobbin-
mill at Ambleside.' Moreover, it was presently
settled that I should spend a month at Birmingham
after Christmas, to do another batch. Thereby hangs
a pretty little tale:—at least, so it appears to me.
My brother and sister having taken for granted that
I should go to their house. I begged them not to take
it amiss if I preferred going to a lodging, with my
maid. My reasons were that I was going for business
purposes, which would occupy all the daylight hours
at that time of year ; that I must therefore dine late ;
that I should be going about among the manu-
factories, with my maid to *hear* for me ; and that I
really thought my family and I should enjoy most of
one another's society by my lodging near enough to
go to tea with them every evening, and spend the
Sundays at their house. They appeared to acquiesce
at once,—saying, however, that I ought to be very
near, on account of the highway robberies, with
violence, which were at that time taking place at
Edgbaston almost every evening. My sister wrote
me an account of the rooms she had secured. I was
rather struck by her recommendations about leaving
terms and arrangements to my landlady, and by an

odd bit of deprecation about not expecting the charms
of my beautiful home. The next letter from one of
my nephews at first dispersed a nascent doubt whether
they were not intending to take me in,—in both senses.
He wrote, ' Your rooms are in one of those houses
near Mrs. F——'s, in the Highfield Road ; so that
you will not have so far to go to our tea-table but
that you will be very safe from thieves. Your landlady is a very trustworthy person. She lived with us
when we lived in the Bristol road ; and she left that
place, not for any fault, but for a better situation.'
On a second reading, it struck me that this was all
true of his mother, and of their house ; and I was not
therefore wholly surprised when the nephew who met
us at the station directed the car to my brother's
house. I was surprised, however, when I saw what
preparation they had made for me and my work.
They had taken down a bed in one of the prettiest
rooms in the house, and had put in a writing-table, a
sofa, a lamp, and all possible conveniences. As one
of my nephews had to dine late, there was no difficulty about that ; and my sister and nieces went every
where with me, one at a time, to listen with and
for me, make notes, and render all easy. It really
was charming. I then wrote ten more papers, as
follows :

' The Miller and his Men,'—The Birmingham
Flour-mills.

' Account of some treatment of Gold and Gems,
—Gold refining, Gold Chains and Jewellery.

' Rainbow-Making,'—Coventry Ribbons.

' Needles,'—the Redditch Manufacture.

' Time and the Hour,'—Coventry Watches.

'Guns and Pistols,'---Birmingham Gun-manufacture.

'Birmingham Glass-works,'—Messrs. Chances and Messrs. Oslers.

'What there is in a Button,'—Birmingham buttons.

'Tubal Cain,'—Brass-founding.

'New School for Wives,'—Evening School for Women.

Invitations were sent me, when the authorship of these papers got abroad, from various seats of manufacture; but the editors and I agreed that our chief textile manufactures were already familiar to every body's knowledge; and I therefore omitted all of that kind except Kendal carpets, Coventry ribbons, and Paisley shawls.   This last was done the next summer, when I was in Scotland, at the same time with Paper-hangings ('Household Scenery') and 'News of an old Place,'—the Lead works at 'Leadhills.'   From Scotland, my niece and I passed into Ireland, as I shall have to tell; and there I wrote, at the Giant's Causeway, 'the Life of a Salmon;' and afterwards 'Peatal Aggression,'—the Peat Works near Athy : the 'English Passport System,' — Railway ticket manufacture; 'Triumphant Carriages.' — Messrs. Hutton's Coach factory at Dublin : 'Hope with a Slate Anchor,'—the slate quarries in Valentia : 'Butter,' 'the Irish Union,' a workhouse picture; and 'Famine-time,' a true picture of one of the worst districts, at the worst time of the visitation.   I have done only two more of the same character,—of the productive processes;—'Cheshire Cheese,' and 'How to get Paper,' --both last year, (1854).—It

will be seen that I need have entertained no apprehension of enforced idleness in consequence of the
publication of the ' Atkinson Letters.' It appears
that, at the close of the same year, I was over-burdened
with work ; and I will add, for truth's sake, that I
was uneasy, and dissatisfied with myself for having
undertaken so much. The last entry in my Diary
(a mere note-book) for 1851 is on the thirtieth of
December. ' As I shall be travelling to Birmingham
to-morrow, I here close my journal of this remarkable
year :—רא improving and happy one, little as the
large wo ld would believe it. I have found it full of
blessings.'

All this time, my study of Comte was going on ;
and I continued the analysis for some weeks; but at
length I found that I had attained sufficient insight
and familiarity to render that work unnecessary. The
first day on which I actually embodied my study of it
in writing,—the first day on which I wrote what
was to stand,—was June 1st. 1852 : and a month
before that, the greatest literary engagement of my
life had been entered upon, of which I shall have to
speak presently. After my return from Birmingham,
I had had to give my annual course of lectures to the
Mechanics ; and my subject, the History of the United
States, from Columbus to Washington, required some
study. Before I left home for the tourist season, I
had got into the thick of the mathematical portion of
Comte : and there I had to stop till my return in the
middle of October. I had then to write an article on
Ireland for the ' Westminster Review,' and other
matters; so that it was the first of December before
I opened Comte again, and Christmas day when I

finished the first of the six volumes. After that, the
work went on swimmingly. All the rest was easy. I
finished Astronomy in the middle of January, and
Biology on the twenty-third of April; so that I had
five months for the last three volumes, which were by
far the easiest to do, though half as long again as the
first three. I had a perpetual succession of guests,
from April till the end of September; but I did not
stop work for them; nor did I choose to leave home
till I had fulfilled my engagement. It was on the
eighth of October that I put the finishing stroke to
the version: on the ninth I wrote the Preface; and
on the tenth, I had the pleasure of carrying the last
packet of MS. to the post. Some cousins who were
staying with me at the time went on an excursion for
the day; and when they returned, they sympathised
with me on the close of so long and so arduous a
task. I was much·exhausted,—after a summer of
abundant authorship in other ways, as well as of social
engagement from the number and variety of guests,
and the absence of my usual autumn retirement to
the sea, or some other quiet place: but the gain
was well worth the toil. I find in my Diary some
very strong expressions of rapture about my task;
and I often said to myself and others, in the course
of it, that I should never enjoy any thing so much
again. And I believe that if I were now to live and
work for twenty years, I could never enjoy any thing
more. The vast range of knowledge, through which
one is carried so easily, is a prodigious treat; and yet
more, the clear enunciation, and incessant application
of principles. The weak part of the book,—the
sacrifices made to system and order,—happens just

to fall in with my weak tendency in that direction;
so that it required some warning from others, and
more from within, to prevent my being carried away
altogether by my author. After all deductions made,
on the score of his faults as a teacher, and my weakness as a learner, the relation was a blessed one. I
became 'strengthened, stablished, settled' on many
a great point; I learned much that I should never
otherwise have known, and revived a great deal of
early knowledge which I might never otherwise have
recalled : and the subdued enthusiasm of my author,
his philosophical sensibility, and honest earnestness,
and evident enjoyment of his own wide range of views
and deep human sympathy, kept the mind of his
pupil in a perpetual and delightful glow. Many a
passage of my version did I write with tears falling
into my lap ; and many a time did I feel almost stifled
for want of the presence of some genial disciple of my
instructor, to whom I might speak of his achievement, with some chance of being understood.

As for my method of working at my version, about
which I have often been questioned,—it was simple
enough.—I studied as I went along, (in the
evenings, for the most part) the subjects of my author,
reviving all I had ever known about them, and
learning much more. Being thus secure of what I was
about, I simply set up the volume on a little desk
before me, glanced over a page or a paragraph, and
set down its meaning in the briefest and simplest way
I could. Thus, my work was not mere translation :
it involved quite a different kind of intellectual
exercise ; and, much as I enjoy translating,—pleasant
as is the finding of equivalent terms, and arranging

them harmoniously,—it is pleasanter still to combine with this the work of condensation. To me, in truth, nothing was ever pleasanter : and I had no sympathy with the friends who hoped, as I proceeded, that I should not again occupy myself with translation. I told them that it was like going to school again while doing the useful work of mature age; and that I should relish nothing better than to go on with it as long as I lived. As for the average amount of my daily work, (four or five days in the week) I was discontented if it was under twenty pages of my author, and satisfied if it was any where from twenty-five to thirty. The largest day's work, in the whole course of the business, was forty-eight pages : but that was when I had breakfasted before seven, to dismiss a guest; and on a Saturday, when there was no post to London, and I had set my mind on finishing a volume. I worked nearly all day, and finished after midnight. I find fifty pages set down on another occasion ; but in that case there was an omission of a recapitulatory portion. In saying what was tl.e daily amount done, I ought to observe that it was really *done*. I finished as I went along; and I looked at my work no more till it came in the shape of proof-sheets.—I have stated in my Preface to the work that, on my expressing my intention to obtain a revision of the three first Books, (Mathematics, Astronomy and Physics) by a scientific man, Professor Nichol kindly offered his services. His revision of that portion (in which he found, he said, no mistakes) and the few notes and observations which he inserted, made me easy about the correctness of what I was putting forth ; and I did not run the risk of spoiling the freshness of what I had done so enjoyably by any re-touching. It came out precisely as I wrote it, day by day.

One part of my enjoyment was from the hope that the appearance of a readable English version would put a stop to the mischievous, though ludicrous, mistakes about Comte's doctrine and work put forth by men who assumed, and might be expected, to know better. The mistakes were repeated, it is true ; but they were more harmless after my version had appeared. When I was studying the work I was really astonished to see a very able review article open with a false statement about Comte, not only altogether gratuitous, but so ignorant that it is a curious thing that it could have passed the press. It alleged that a man called Auguste Comte, who assumed in 1822 to be a social prophet, had declared the belief and interest in theology to be at an end ; whereas, here was the whole kingdom, thirty years later, convulsed with theological passion, about Papal aggression and the Gorham controversy. Now, this was a treble blunder. In the first place, Comte has never said that theology and the popular interest in it are over. In the next, he has written largely on the social turmoil which this generation is in, and generations to come will be in, from the collision between the theological passion of one social period, and the metaphysical rage of another, with the advance of the positive philosophy which is to supersede them both. If there is one thing rather than another reiterated to weariness in Comte's work, it is the state of turmoil, and its causes, of which the Gorham controversy was an admirable exemplification. In the third place, Comte's doctrine is that theology can be extinguished only by a true Science of Human

Nature; that this science is as yet barely initiated; and that therefore theology is very far from being yet popularly superseded.

At a later time, in October 1851, when an eminent philosopher from Scotland was my guest for a few days, I invited to meet him at dinner a friend of his, who was in the neighbourhood, and that friend's lady, and another guest or two. I was before slightly acquainted with this couple, and knew that the gentleman was highly thought of, by himself and others (by the late Dr. Arnold, among the rest) as a scholar and writer. When he was taking me in to dinner, he asked me whether I had heard that M. Comte was insane. I replied that it was not true,—M. Comte being perfectly well the week before; and I told him that I was engaged on his work. My guest replied that he had heard the whole story,—about Mr. Lombe's gift and all,—from another gentleman, then present. He asked me an insulting question or two about the work, and made objections to my handling it, which I answered shortly, (the servants being present) and put down my trumpet, to help the fish. While I was so engaged, he asked questions which I could not hear, across me, of my philosopher guest; and then, with triumph and glee, reported to me my friend's replies, as if they were spontaneous remarks, and with gross exaggeration. During the whole of dinner, and in the presence of my servants, he continued his aspersions of Comte, and his insults to me as his translator; so that, as it came to my knowledge long afterwards, my other guest wondered that I put up with it, and did not request him to leave the house. I saw, however, that he knew nothing of what he was talking about; and I then merely asked him if he had read the portion of the work that he was abusing. Being pressed, he reluctantly answered—No; but he knew all about it. When the dessert was on the table, and the servants were gone, he still continued his criticisms. I looked him full in the face, and again inquired if he had read that portion of the *Philosophie Positive:*— 'N—n—o:' but he knew all about it. I said I doubted it; and asked if he had read the book at all. 'N—n—o:' but he knew all about it. 'Come,' said I, 'tell me,—have you ever seen the book?' —'No: I can't say I have;' he replied, 'but I know all about it.' 'Now,' said I, 'look at the bookshelves behind you. You see those six volumes in green paper? Now you can say that you have *seen* the book.' I need not say that this was the last invitation that this *gentleman* would ever have from me.

Again,—a lady, younger than myself, who shrinks from the uncomfortable notion that there is any subject which she is not qualified to lay down the law upon, folded her hands on her knees, and began in an orderly way to reprehend me for translating a book which had such shocking things in it as Comte's work. I made the usual inquiry,—whether she had read it. She could not say she had; but she too 'knew all about it,' from a very clever man; a *very* clever man, who was a great admirer of Comte, and on my 'side.' She was sorry I could introduce into England the work of a man who said in it that he could have made a better solar system than the real one;—who declared that he would have made it always moonshine at night. I laughed, and told her she was the victim of her clever friend's moonshine. She ended, however, with a firm faith in her clever friend, in preference to reading the book for herself. She will go on to the end of her days, no doubt, regarding the 'Positive Philosophy' as a receipt for making permanent moonshine, in opposition to the nineteenth Psalm.

Once more, (and only once, though I might fill many pages with anecdotes of the blunders about Comte made by critics who assume to understand their subject:)—a professor of Mental Philosophy has, even since the publication of my version, asserted, both in print, and repeatedly in his lectures in London, that Positive philosophers declare that ' we *can* know nothing but phenomena :' and the lecturer fancies that he has confuted the doctrine by saying that the knowledge of phenomena would occupy Man's observing faculties only, and leave the reasoning and other faculties without exercise. In this case, the lecturer has taken half Comte's assertion, and dropped the other half,—' *and their laws.*' This restoration, of course, overthrows the lecturer's argument, even if it were not otherwise assailable. It is true that Mr. Atkinson and I, and many others, have made the assertion as the lecturer gives it ;—that ' we *can* know nothing but phenomena,'—the laws being themselves phenomena : but in that view, as in the case of the restoration of Comte's text, the lecturer's argument about the partial use of the human faculties is stultified. Some of his pupils should have asked him what we can know but phenomena. The *onus* of showing that certainly rests with him. Such are, at present, the opponents of Comte among us, while his work is heartily and profitably studied by wiser men, who choose to read and think and understand before they scoff and upbraid.

A letter of Mr. Atkinson's in my possession seems
to me to give so distinct an account of what Man
'can know,' and of the true way of obtaining the
knowledge, that I am tempted to insert a part of it
here as settling the question with our incompetent
critics, as to what we declare that we can and cannot
know.

' Man cannot know more than has been observed of
the order of Nature,—he himself being a part of that
nature, and, like all other bodies in nature, exhibiting
clear individual effects according to particular laws.
The infinite.character and subtlety of Nature are
beyond his power of comprehension; for the mind of
Man is no more than (as it were) a conscious mirror,
possessing a certain extent of interreflexion.   In a
rude state, as before it has become reduced to a proper
focus, and cleansed and purified by knowledge, it is
subject to all manner of spectral illusions, presumptuous and vain conceits, which may be well termed a
kind of normal or infantine madness; a kind of disease like the small-pox or the measles: conditions to
which all children are subject; and it is well if the
child can be helped through these strange malignant
conditions in early youth, and be then and there
cleansed from them for ever.

' If we study the formation of the globe, and the
history of nations or of individuals, or glance at the
progress of knowledge in the human mind, we shall
perceive that difficulties have been overcome and
advances achieved in the early stages through violent
means; that that which we call evil has always in
effect been working for the general good; and that, in
the very nature of things, that good could not have

come about by any other means : and thus, whatever is is good, in its place and season.   Concluding thus, I think we may henceforth dispense with that very popular gentleman in black, the Devil. Indeed, once for all, we may sign ourselves Naturalists, as having no knowledge, or having no means of knowing any thing, beyond Nature.   To advance by the acquiring of knowledge and by reason is the high privilege and prerogative of Man : for, as glorious as it is to possess a just, candid, and truth-loving nature, essential as it is that we know what is true,—yet must we be content that in the first instance, and for some short space, the progress should be slow and devious : for the errors and imperfections of the mind itself prevent men from attaining that knowledge which is almost essential to the cure of those very errors, imperfections, and impediments.   Thus, mankind have had to rely upon a genius springing up here and there,—great men who have had the strength to overleap the diffi-culties, and the sense to see what was before them ; and the honesty to declare what they have seen.

'The power of knowledge is in the knowledge of causes ; that is, of the material conditions and circum-stances under which any given effect takes place. These conditions we have termed Second Causes : but of the primitive matter which is *sui generis* we know nothing : for knowledge is limited by the senses.   The knowledge of a thing includes a sense of its material cause or conditions,—its relative or distinguishing qualities, — the laws of form and quantity implicated in the case, and the laws of action in sequence and duration.—The higher laws are dis-covered in the analogy of knowledge : but of the

primitive or fundamental cause or matter,—that
" cause of causes itself without a cause,"—we know
and can know absolutely nothing.   We judge it to be
something positive : to so much the nature of the
mind compels assent : but we do not know what this
positive something is in itself, in its absolute and real
being and presence.   We must rest content to take it
as we find it, and suppose it inherently capable of
performing or flowing into all those effects exhibited
throughout nature.   We only recognise a primitive
matter as a required cause and necessary existence
implied in the sensational phenomena which appear to
include it in their embraces.   But the existence of
matter cannot be proved ; nor can we form any conception of its real nature, because we can only divine
by similitudes; and our similitudes cannot press
beyond sensational phenomena and the simple inference.   " So that all the specious meditations, speculations, and theories of mankind (in regard to the
nature of nature) are but a kind of insanity."   " But
those who resolve not to conjecture and divine, but to
discover and know ; not to invent buffooneries and
fables about worlds, but to inspect, and, as it were,
dissect the nature of this real world, must derive all
from things themselves : nor can any substitution or
compensation of wit, meditation, or argument (were
the whole wit of all combined in one) supply the place
of this labour, investigation, and personal examination of the world; our method then must necessarily
be-pursued, or the whole for ever abandoned."

' The intellect, in a general sense, is simply· an
observing faculty.   The highest efforts of reason and
of imagination are but an extension of observation.

A law is but the observed form of a fact; and, in truth, the entire conscious mind may be termed a faculty of observation. To deny this is only to make a quibble about distinctions not really essential. The most important fact which the experienced mind observes is the fixed order in nature: and the trained philosopher instinctively concludes, and I may say perceives, the necessity of this order, just as he acknowledges the existence of objects in their objective or material appearance: (and this in spite of all that Bishop Berkeley and others have said). The human mind by the constitution of its nature recognises the necessity of a determinate order in nature,—dependence in causes, and form or law in effects; and on this faith we build all our confidence that similar results will always flow, as a necessary consequence, from similar causes. In this fact we have the reason of reason, and the power of knowledge over nature, applying the principles of nature by art to the wants of Man. The instinct or sense of Man acknowledges a fundamental cause in the primitive matter, and the necessity of a particular form and order in objects and their effects: and that it is absolutely impossible that things should be different from what they are found to be. Now, until a man clears his mind, and abstracts it from all fanciful causes, to rest upon the true and fundamental cause in the primitive matter, perceiving at the same time that this cause must be positive, and capable of producing all the effects and variety of nature, and in a form and order absolutely fixed in "an adamantine chain of necessity"—until, I say, a man is fully and deeply impressed with this law of laws, this form of forms, evolved from the inherent nature of the ultimate fact and cause (this primitive matter and cause being fundamental, neither depending upon nor requiring any other cause) he is not a philosopher, but a dreamer of dreams, a poor wanderer on a false scent, seeking for a cause out of nature, and in a magnified shadow of himself. " If," says Bacon,* " any man shall think, by view and inquiry into these sensible and material things, to attain to any light for the revealing of the nature or will of God, he shall dangerously abuse himself."— " And this appeareth sufficiently in that there is no proceeding in invention of knowledge but by similitude; and God is only self-like, having nothing in common with any creature, otherwise than as in shadow and trope." † These remarks of Bacon in regard to the "invention" of a cause out of nature apply equally to the " invention " of the nature of the cause in nature: for all the knowledge we can have of the primitive matter is by way of negatives and exclusions.

'I hold, then, with Democritus, Heraclitus, Empedocles, Anaxagoras, Anaximenes and others, that matter is eternal, possessing an active principle, and being the source of all objects and their effects: for you may as well suppose time and space to have a beginning, and to have been created, as that matter should have been brought out of nothing, and have had a beginning. The active principle and the properties of matter are essential to our very conception of matter: and the necessary form of the effects we term Laws:—laws, not to be considered in a political sense, as rules laid down by a ruler, and

* Interpretation of Nature.   Chapter I.   † Interpretation of Nature.   Chapter I.

capable of alteration and change; but the rule of rules;—the essential and necessary form and life and mind, so to speak, of what is in fact not a ruling power at all, but simply the principle or form of the result,—just as grammar exhibits the form of language.

'The belief in the freedom of the will, or that any thing is free in any other way than as being unimpeded and at liberty to move according as it is impelled by that which determines its motion or choice, is absolutely nonsense: and the doctrine of chance is as absurd as would be the belief that Nature arose from a rude mob of lawless atoms, arranging themselves by chance; a notion which is clearly nonsense,—a weak and unmitigated atheism, to escape from which men impose upon themselves a despotism in the shape of a King Log or a King Stork, as the case may be. That which they suppose to be divine and most holy is but a presumptuous, shallow, and ridiculous assumption. It is a folly built upon a shifting sand-bank, which the tide will presently carry away, exhibiting the true stronghold of the understanding built upon the solid granite rock of Nature: —that Nature which is no despotism, but a pure and free republic, and a law unto itself,—an eternal, unalterable law unto itself: for two and two will never become five; nor will the three angles of a triangle ever be less than two right angles; nor will the great law of gravity be changed, nor the Atomic rule in chemical effects; nor the material conditions essential to thought and feeling be reversed. The world may come to an end,—become worn out, and dissolve away, or explode; but the nature of the particles of matter cannot change : the principles of truth will hold the same, and a new world will rise out of the dust.

'With regard to the origin of the mind itself,— it is clearly a consequence or result of the body evolved under particular laws :—as much so as a flower is a consequence of the growth of a tree,—instinct of the lower animal body,—light of a tallow candle. The light and heat of a candle may set light to other candles, or react upon its own body, as mental conditions may, when they cause the heart to beat, and the face to flush, and tears to flow, and the whole frame to be convulsed by laughter. So may the bile, or any other secretion, react on the body : but not the less is the mind the effect and consequent of the body, dependent on the condition of the body, and the proper supply of air and food. To suppose otherwise is to give up all hope and all philosophy, and to desert common sense and universal experience. The mind proper is simply the conscious phenomenon which is not a power at all, but the representative or expression of an unconscious power and condition of which it is a concomitant. Strictly speaking, there are but two conditions in nature ; matter the *physique*, and the conscious mind, or the *metaphysique*,—the positive and the negative. The conscious mind is purely phenomenal : it is not therefore the mind proper which acts upon the body, but that force which underlies the mind, of which the mind is simply the result, expression or exponent. The mind's unconscious working power or sphere is evident in almost every act of the body, as well as in almost every fact of the mind. It may be studied in the higher pheno-

mena of *clairvoyance* and prophecy,—higher, only as
an extending of experience by another and a clearer
sense. We spring up from the earth like a flower.
We live, love, and look abroad on the wide expanse of
heaven, wondering at the night which lies behind,
and at the dim shadows and flickering lights which
coming events cast before them : and then we expire,
and give place, as others have given place to us. We
have but a glance at existence; yet the laws we discover are eternal truths. Knowledge is not infinite.
A few simple principles or elements are fundamental
to the whole; as a few simple primitive sounds form
into glorious music, and all the languages which
exist : and therefore knowledge is not infinite, and
progress has its limit.   .   .   .   .   .

Still, " the mighty ocean of truth lies before us," and
its advance is irresistible ; and it will be well to
remember King Canute, and take the hint in time ;
—to look abroad upon the expanse, and up to the
multitude of stars; and to listen to the deep-speaking
truths which are now making themselves heard in
society ; and not to seek to resist what is inevitable.
That the new day will be bright and glorious when
Man will know his own power and nature, and rise
into his new dignity as a rational human being, is
enough for us now to prophesy.'

SECTION VIII.

I HAVE referred, some pages back, to a great opening
for work, of a delightful kind, which offered while I
was busy about Comte. As I have explained, the
whole version, except half of Comte's first volume
(that is, about a sixteenth part) was done between
Christmas 1852 and the following October : and it
remains to be told what else I had to do while engaged
on that version. In April 1852 I received a letter
from a literary friend in London, asking me, by desire
of the Editor of 'Daily News,' whether I would
'send him a "leader" occasionally.' I did not know
who this editor was ; had hardly seen a number of the
paper, and had not the remotest idea whether I could
write 'leaders :' and this was my reply. I saw that
this might be an opening to greater usefulness than
was likely to be equalled by anything else that I could
undertake ; so I was not sorry to be urgently invited
to try. The editor, my now deeply-mourned friend,
Mr. Frederick Knight Hunt, and I wrote frank and
copious letters, to see how far our views and principles
agreed ; and his letters gave me the impression which
all my subsequent knowledge of him confirmed, that
he was one of the most upright and rational of men,

and a thorough gentleman in mind and manners. I
sent him two or three articles, the second of which
(I think it was) made such a noise that I found that
there would be no little amusement in my new work,
if I found I could do it. It was attributed to almost
every possible writer but the real one. This ' hit '
sent me forward cheerily: and I immediately promised
to do a ' leader ' per week, while engaged on Comte.
Mr. Hunt begged for two ; and to this I agreed when
I found that each required only two or three hours in
an evening, and that topics abounded. I had sufficient
misgiving and uncertainty to desire very earnestly to
have some conversation with Mr. Hunt ; and I offered
to go to London (on my way to Scotland) for the
purpose. He would not hear of this, but said he
would come to me, if public affairs would allow of his
leaving the office. Then Parliament was dissolved ;
and the elections kept him at home ; so that I looked
for him in vain by every train for ten days before my
niece and I started for Edinburgh. He came to us at
Portobello ; and for two half days he poured out so
rich a stream of conversation that my niece could not
stand the excitement. She went out upon the shore,
to recover her mind's breath, and came in to enjoy
more. It was indeed an unequalled treat ; and when
we parted, I felt that a bright new career was indeed
opened to me. He had before desired that I should
write him letters from Ireland ; and he now bespoke
three per week during our travels there. This I
accomplished ; and the letters were afterwards, by his
advice and the desire of Mr. Chapman, published in a
volume. It was on occasion of that long journey,
which extended from the Giant's Causeway to Bantry

Bay, and from the Mullet to Wexford, that I first felt
the signs of failure in bodily strength which I now
believe to have been a warning of my present fatal
malady. My companion was an incomparable help.
It was impossible to be more extensively and effectually aided than I was by her. She took upon herself all the fatigue that it was possible to avert from
me ; and I reposed upon her sense and spirit and
watchfulness like a spoiled child. Yet I found, and
said at the time, that this must be my last arduous
journey. The writing those Letters was a pure
pleasure, whether they were penned in a quiet chamber
at a friend's house, or amidst a host of tourists, and
to the sound of the harp, in a *salon* at Killarney ;
but, in addition to the fatigue of travelling and of
introductions to strangers, they were too much for me.
I had some domestic griefs on my mind, it is true.
During the spring, my neighbours had requested me
to deliver two or three lectures on Australia ; and one
consequence of my doing so was that my dear servant
Jane resolved to emigrate (for reasons which I thought
sound), and she was to sail in November : and now at
Cork, the news met me that the other servant, no less
beloved, was going to marry the Master of the Ragged
School at Bristol, who had been her coadjutor in the
Norfolk Workhouse School before mentioned.   I
wrote to advise their marriage at Christmas ; but it
was with the sense of a heavy misfortune having
befallen me. I did not believe that my little household could ever again be what it had been since I
built my house : and I should have been thankful to
have foreseen how well I should settle again,—to
change no more. I did not fully recover my strength

till our pretty wedding was over, and I was fairly settled down, in winter quiet, to Comte and my weekly work for 'Daily News.'—The wedding was truly a charming one. My dear girl had the honour of having Miss Carpenter for her bridesmaid, and the Revd. Philip P. Carpenter to perform the ceremony,—the Bristol Ragged School being, as every body knows, the special care of Miss Carpenter. I told the bride, the week before the bridegroom and guests arrived, that, as I could not think of sending the former to the kitchen table, nor yet of separating them, it would be a convenience and pleasure to me if she would be my guest in the sitting-rooms for the few days before the marriage. She did it with the best possible grace. She had worked hard at her wedding clothes during my absence, that she might be free for my service after my return : and now, after instructing her young successor, she dressed herself well, and dined with us, conversing freely, and, best of all, making a good dinner, while watching that every body was well served. A more graceful lady I never saw. She presented me with a pretty cap of her own making for the wedding morning ; and would let nobody else dress me. The evening before, when Mr. Carpenter delivered a Temperance lecture, Miss Carpenter and I sent the entire household to the lecture ; and we set out the long table for the morning, dressed the flowers (which came in from neighbouring conservatories) and put on all the cold dishes ; covered up the whole, and shut up the cat. The kitchen was the only room large enough for the party ; and there, after the ceremony, we had a capital breakfast, with good speaking, and all manner of good feeling. When all were gone

and my new maids had dried their sympathetic tears,
and removed the tables, and given away the good
things which that year served my usual Christmas day
guests for dinner at home instead of here; and when
I had put off my finery, and sat down, with a bursting
headache, to write the story to the bride's family, and
the Carpenters' and my own, I felt more thoroughly
down-hearted than for many a year.—All went well,
however.   The good couple are in their right place,
honoured and useful; and 'our darling,' as Miss
Carpenter called my good girl, is beloved by others
as by me.   There have been no more changes in my
household ; and, as for me, I soon recovered entirely
from my griefs in my delectable work.

When summer was coming on, and Comte was
advancing well, I agreed to do three leaders per week
for Mr. Hunt.   All the early attempts at secrecy were
over.   Within the first month, I had been taxed with
almost every article by somebody or other, who ' knew
me by my style,' or had heard it in omnibuses, or
somehow ; and, after some Galway priests had pointed
me out by guess, in the Irish papers, as the writer of
one of the Irish Letters, and this got copied into the
English papers, Mr. Hunt wrote me that all concealment was wholly out of the question, and that I need
not trouble myself further about it.   In the summer
he came to see me ; and we settled that I should send
him four articles per week when Comte was out of my
hands.   During that visit of his, we went by the lake
one day, to pay a visit a few miles off,—he rowing me
in one of the lake skiffs.   A windy rain overtook us
on our return.   I had no serious idea of danger, or I
should not have talked as I did, about drowning being

an easy death, and my affairs being always settled, even to the arrangement of my papers, &c. We came home to dinner without his giving me (experienced boatman as he was) any idea of our having had a serious adventure.   I found afterwards that he had told his friends in London that we had been in extreme danger from the swell on the lake ; and that when I was talking of the ease of drowning, in comparison with other deaths, he was thinking of his wife and children.   He requested me to write an article, at the opening of the next season, on the criminal careless-ness of our boatkeepers in letting those little skiffs to strangers, on a lake subject to gusts and sudden storms : and this I did.   How little did he imagine that before the beginning of yet another season, he would have been months in his grave, and I standing on the verge of mine !

Immediately on the publication of my ' Positive Philosophy,' I went to London and Birmingham for nearly three months. I visited so many hosts, and saw so much society that I became fully and finally satisfied that my settling myself at Ambleside was, as Wordsworth had said, the wisest step of my life. It is true, I was at work the whole time.   Besides the plentiful assistance which I desired to give the ' Daily News,' while on the spot, and some papers for ' Household Words,' a serious piece of business required my attention.   The impending war rendered desirable an earnest and well-studied article on England's Foreign Policy, for the ' Westminster Review ;' and I agreed to do it.   I went to the Editor's house, for the purpose, and enjoyed both my visit and my work.—On taking possession of my

room there, and finding a capital desk on my table,
with a singularly convenient slope, and of an admirable
height for writing without fatigue, it struck me that,
during my whole course of literary labour,—of nearly
five-and-thirty years, it had never once occurred to me
to provide myself with a proper, business-like desk.
I had always written on blotting-paper, on a flat table,
except when, in a lazy mood in winter, I had written
as short-sighted people do (as Mrs. Somerville and
'Currer Bell' always did) on a board, or something
stiff, held in the left hand. I wrote a good deal of
the 'Political Economy' in that way, and with steel
pens ; and the method had the effect, advantageous or
not, of making the writing more upright, and thereby
increasing the quantity in a page. But it was radically
uncomfortable ; and I have ever since written on a
table, and with quill pens. Now, on occasion of this
visit at my friend's, Mr. Chapman's, I was to begin on
a new and most luxurious method,—just, as it happens, at the close of my life's work. Mr. Chapman
obtained for me a first-rate regular Chancery-lane
desk, with all manner of conveniences, and of a proper
sanitary form : and, moreover, some French paper of
various sizes, which has spoiled me for all other paper :
ink to correspond ; and a pen-maker, of French work-
manship, suitable to eyes which were now feeling the
effects of years and over-work. I had before me the
prospect of more moderate work than for a quarter of
a century past, with sure and sufficient gain from it ;
work pleasant in itself, and recommended by all
agreeable appliances. Never was I more home-sick,
even in the wilds of Arabia, than I now was,
amidst the high civilisation of literary society in

London.—I came home very happy ; and well I might.

Mr. Hunt escorted me part of the way to my host's, on our last meeting for that time, for the sake of some conversation which he, very properly, called serious. He told me that he had something to say which he begged me to consider well. He told me that he had been looking back through my connexion with ' Daily News ; ' and he found that of nearly 300 articles that I had sent him, only eight had not been used ; and that (I think) six of those eight had been. sent during the first few weeks, before I had got into the ways of the paper. I had now written four or five per week for a considerable time, without one rejection. His advice was that I should henceforth do six per week,—under the liability, of course, of a few more being unused, from the enhanced chances of being intercepted by recent news, when my communications were daily. If I should agree to this, and continue my other literary connexion, he thought I ought to lay out money freely in books, and in frequent visits to London, to keep up with the times. This scheme suited me exactly ; for my work, under his guidance, had become thoroughly delightful.

His recourse to me was avowedly on account of the ' History of the Peace ; ' and now that war was beginning, my recent study of the politics of the last half-century *was* a fair qualification. We were precisely agreed as to the principle of the war, as to the character of the Aberdeen Ministry, as to the fallaciousness and mischievousness of the negotiations for the Austrian alliance, and as to the vicious absurdity of Prussia, and the mode and degree in which Louis

Napoleon was to be regarded as the representative of
the French nation. For some time past, the historical
and geographical articles had been my charge; together with the descriptive and speculative ones, in
relation to foreign personages and states. At home,
the agricultural and educational articles were usually
consigned to me; and I had the fullest liberty about the
treatment of special topics, arising anywhere. With
party contests, and the treatment of ' hot and hot '
news, I never had any concern,—being several
hundred miles out of the way of the latest intelligence. Mr. Hunt thought my distance from London
no disadvantage; and he was quite plain-spoken about
the inferiority of the articles I wrote in London and
Birmingham to those I sent him from home.—I
followed his suggestions with great satisfaction,—his
wife and family having already made a compact with
me for an exchange of visits when I wanted London
news, and they needed country refreshment. So I
bought books to the amount of above £100, under his
guidance, and came home exceedingly happy,—little
dreaming that in one year from that time, he would
be in his grave, his wife a broken-spirited widow, and
I myself under sentence of death, and compelled to
tell her that we should never meet again.

That eventful year, 1854, began most cheerily to us
all. Mr. Hunt had raised the paper to a condition of
high honour and prosperity. He enjoyed his work
and his position, and was at ease about his affairs and
his beloved family, after years of heroic struggle, and
the glorious self-denial of a man of sensitive conscience and thoroughly domestic heart. He had to
bear the wear and tear which a man of his order of

conscience has to endure in a post of such responsibility as his; and this, we all believe, was a pre-
disposing cause of his inability to resist an attack of
disease. But at the opening of the year, he was in
his usual health, and had every reason to be very
happy. As for me,—my life was now like nothing
that I had ever experienced. I had all the benefits
of work, and of complete success, without any of the
responsibility, the sense of which has always been the
great drawback on my literary satisfactions, and
especially in historical writing,—in which I could
have no comfort but by directing my readers to my
authorities, in all matters of any importance. Now,
while exercising the same anxious care as to correctness, and always referring Mr. Hunt to my sources of
information, I was free from the responsibility of
publication altogether. My continued contributions
to the 'Westminster Review' and elsewhere preserved
me from being engrossed in political studies; and I
had more leisure for philosophical and literary pursuits
than at any time since my youth. Two or three
hours, after the arrival of the post (at breakfast time
now) usually served me for my work; and when my
correspondence was done, there was time for exercise,
and the discharge of neighbourly business before
dinner. Then,—I have always had some piece of
fancy-work on hand,—usually for the benefit of the
Abolition fund in America; and I have a thoroughly
womanish love of needle-work,—yes, even ('I own
the soft impeachment') of wool-work, many a square
yard of which is all invisibly embossed with thoughts of
mine wrought in, under the various moods and experiences of a long series of years. It is with singular

alacrity that, in winter evenings, I light the lamp, and unroll my wool-work, and meditate or dream till the arrival of the newspaper tells me that the tea has stood long enough.   Before Mr. Rowland Hill gave us a second post delivery at Ambleside, Mr. Hunt had made arrangements by which I received the paper of the day at tea time.   After tea, if there was news from the seat of war, I called in my maids, who brought down the great atlas, and studied the chances of the campaign with me.   Then there was an hour or two for Montaigne, or Bacon, or Shakspere, or Tennyson, or some dear old biography, or last new book from London,—historical, moral or political.   Then, when the house and neighbourhood were asleep, there was the half-hour on the terrace, or, if the weather was too bad for that, in the porch,—whence I seldom or never came in without a clear purpose for my next morning's work.   I believe that, but for my country life, much of the benefit and enjoyment of my travels, and also of my studies, would have been lost to me. On my terrace, there were two worlds extended bright before me, even when the midnight darkness hid from my bodily eyes all but the outlines of the solemn mountains that surround our valley on three sides, and the clear opening to the lake on the south.   In the one of those worlds, I saw now the magnificent coast of Massachusetts in autumn, or the flowery swamps of Louisiana, or the forests of Georgia in spring, or the Illinois prairie in summer; or the blue Nile, or the brown Sinai, or the gorgeous Petra, or the view of Damascus from the Salahiey; or the Grand Canal under a Venetian sunset, or the Black Forest in twilight, or Malta in the glare of noon, or

the broad desert stretching away under the stars, or
the Red Sea tossing its superb shells on shore, in the
pale dawn.   That is one world, all comprehended
within my terrace wall, and coming up into the light
at my call.—The other and finer scenery is of that
world, only beginning to be explored, of Science.
The long study of Comte had deeply impressed on me
the imagery of the glorious hierarchy of the sciences
which he has exhibited.   The time was gone by when
I could look at objects as mere surface, or separate
existences; and since that late labour of love, I had
more than ever seen the alliance and concert of the
heavenly bodies, and the mutual action and interior
composition of the substances which I used to regard
as one in themselves, and unconnected in respect to
each other.   It is truly an exquisite pleasure to dream,
after the toil of study, on the sublime abstractions of
mathematics;   the transcendent scenery unrolled by
astronomy;   the mysterious, invisible forces dimly
hinted to us by Physics;   the new conception of the
constitution of Matter originated by Chemistry;   and
then, the inestimable glimpses opened to us, in regard
to the nature and destiny of Man, by the researches
into vegetable and animal organisation, which are at
length perceived to be the right path of inquiry into
the highest subjects of thought.   All the grandeur
and all the beauty of this series of spectacles is
deepened by the ever-present sense of the smallness of
the amount of discovery achieved.   In the scenery of
our travels, it is otherwise.   The forest, the steppe,
the lake, the city. each filled and sufficed the sense of
the observer in the   ld days when, instead of the
Western Continents, there were dreams of far Cathay;

and we of this day are occupied for the moment with
any single scene, without caring whether the whole
globe is explored.   But it is different in the sphere
of science.   Wondrous beyond the comprehension of
any one mind is the mass of glorious facts, and the
series of mighty conceptions laid open ; but the
shadow of the surrounding darkness rests upon it all.
The unknown always engrosses the greater part of the
field of vision ; and the awe of infinity sanctifies both
the study and the dream.   Between these worlds, and
other interests, literary and political, were my evenings
passed a short year ago.   Perhaps no one has had a
much more vivid enjoyment than myself of London
society of a very high order ; and few, I believe, are
of a more radically social nature than myself : yet, I
may say that there has never been, since I had a home
of my own, an evening spent in the most charming
intercourse that I would not have exchanged (as far
as the mere pleasure was concerned) for one of my
ordinary evenings under the lamp within, and the
lights of heaven without.

I did not at once, however, sit down in comparative
leisure on my return.   I had before promised, most
unwillingly, and merely for neighbourly reasons, to
write a guide to Windermere and the neighbourhood ;
and this, and an article on the Census (requiring much
care) for the 'Westminster Review' for April, were
pressing to be done, as soon as I could sit down on
my return home.   Then there was a series of articles
(on Personal Infirmities,—the treatment of Blindness,
Deafness, Idiotcy, &c.) promised for 'Household
Words.'

I must pause a moment here to relate that these

papers were the last I sent to 'Household Words,' except two or three which filled up previous schemes. I have observed above that Magazine writing is quite out of my way: and that I accepted Mr. Dickens's invitation to write for his, simply because its wide circulation went far to compensate for the ordinary objections to that mode of authorship. I did not hesitate on the ground on which some of my relations and friends disapproved the connexion; on the ground of its being *infra dig.*: for, in the first place, I have never stopped to consider my own dignity in matters of business; and in the next, Mr. Dickens himself being a contributor disposed of the objection abundantly. But some time before the present date, I had become uneasy about the way in which 'Household Words' was going on, and more and more doubtful about allowing my name to be in any way connected with it: and I have lately finally declined Mr. Wills's invitation to send him more papers. As there is no quarrel concerned in the case, I think it is right to explain the grounds of my secession. My disapproval of the principles, or want of principles, on which the Magazine is carried on is a part of my own history; and it may be easily understood that feelings of personal friendliness may remain unaffected by opposition of views, even in a matter so serious as this. I think the proprietors of 'Household Words' grievously inadequate to their function, philosophically and morally; and they, no doubt, regard me as extravagant, presumptuous and impertinent. I have offered my objections as a reply to a direct request for a contribution; and Mr. Wills has closed the subject. But on all other ground, we are friends.

In the autumn of 1849, my misgivings first became
serious. Mr. Wills proposed my doing some articles
on the Employments of Women (especially in connexion with the Schools of Design and branches of
Fine-Art manufacture), and was quite unable to see
that every contribution of the kind was necessarily
excluded by Mr. Dickens's prior articles on behalf of
his view of Woman's position; articles in which he
ignored the fact that nineteen-twentieths of the
women of England earn their bread, and in which he
prescribes the function of Women; viz., to dress well
and look pretty, as an adornment to the homes of
men. I was startled by this; and at the same time,
and for many weeks after, by Mr. Dickens's treatment
in his Magazine of the Preston Strike, then existing,
and of the Factory and Wages controversy, in his tale
of ' Hard Times.' A more serious incident still
occurred in the same autumn. In consequence of a
request from Mr. Dickens that I would send him a
tale for his Christmas Number, I looked about for
material in real life; for, as I had told him, and as I
have told every body else, I have a profound contempt
of myself as a writer of fiction, and the strongest
disinclination to attempt that order of writing. I
selected a historical fact, and wrote the story which
appears under the title of ' The Missionary ' in
my volume of ' Sketches from Life.' I carried
it with me to Mr. Wills's house; and he spoke
in the strongest terms of approbation of it to me,
but requested to have also ' a tale of more domestic
interest,' which I wrote on his selection of the ground-
work (also fact). Some weeks afterwards, my friends
told me, with renewed praises of the story, that they

mourned the impossibility of publishing it,—Mrs.
Wills said, because the public would say that Mr.
Dickens was turning Catholic; and Mr. Wills and
Mr. Dickens, because they never would publish any
thing, fact or fiction, which gave a favourable view of
any one under the influence of the Catholic faith.
This appeared to me so incredible that Mr. Dickens
gave me his 'ground' three times over, with all
possible distinctness, lest there should be any mistake:
—he would print nothing which could possibly dispose any mind whatever in favour of Romanism, even
by the example of real good men.   In vain I asked
him whether he really meant to ignore all the good
men who had lived from the Christian era to three
centuries ago: and in vain I pointed out that Père
d'Estélan was a hero as a man, and not as a Jesuit, at
a date and in a region where Romanism was the only
Christianity. Mr. Dickens *would* ignore, in any publication of his, all good Catholics; and insisted that
Père d'Estélan was what he was as a Jesuit and not
as a man; —which was, as I told him, the greatest
eulogium I had ever heard passed upon Jesuitism.   I
told him that his way of going to work,—suppress-
ing facts advantageous to the Catholics,—was the
very way to rouse all fair minds in their defence; and
that I had never before felt so disposed to make
popularly known all historical facts in their favour.—
I hope I need not add that the editors never for a
moment supposed that my remonstrance had any connexion with the story in question being written by
me. They knew me too well to suppose that such
a trifle as my personal interest in the acceptance or
rejection of the story had anything to do with my

final declaration that my confidence and comfort in
regard to 'Household Words' were gone, and that
I could never again write fiction for them, nor any
thing in which principle or feeling were concerned.
Mr. Dickens hoped I should 'think better of it';
and this proof of utter insensibility to the nature of
the difficulty, and his and his partner's hint that the
real illiberality lay in not admitting that they were
doing their duty in keeping Catholic good deeds out
of the sight of the public, showed me that the case
was hopeless. To a descendant of Huguenots, such
total darkness of conscience on the morality of opinion
is difficult to believe in when it is before one's very eyes.

I need not add that my hopes from the influence of
'Household Words' were pretty nearly annihilated
from that time (the end of 1853) forwards : but there
was worse to come. I had supposed that the editors
would of course abstain from publishing any harm of
Catholic priests and professors, if they would admit no
good ; but in this I have recently found myself mistaken : and great is my concern. I had just been
reading in an American advertisement a short account
of the tale called the 'Yellow Mask,' with its
wicked priest, when I received from the editor of
'Household Words' another request for an article.
I had not read 'The Yellow Mask'; but a guest
then with me related the story so fully as to put me
in complete possession of it. I will cite the portion
of my letter to Mr. Wills which contains my reply to
his request. It is abundantly plain-spoken ; but we
were plain-spoken throughout the controversy ; and
never did occasion more stringently require the utmost
plainness of remonstrance on the side of the advocate

of religious liberty and social justice, and any clearness of reply that might be possible on the opposite
side.—Here is my letter, as far as relates to Mr.
Wills's petition:—

' ...   .   Another paper from
me? you ask.   No—not if I were to live twenty
years,—if the enclosed paragraph from an American
paper be no mistake; and except, of course, in case of
repentance and amendment.

'"The 'Yellow Mask,' in Twelve Chapters:
Philadelphia.

'"This pamphlet is a reprint from Dickens's
'Household Words.' The story is ingenious, and
fraught with considerable interest. The despicable
course of 'Father Rocco' pursued so stealthily for
the pecuniary benefit of 'holy mother church' shows
of what stuff priestcraft is made."

'The last thing I am likely to do is to write for an
anti-catholic publication; and least of all when it is
anti-catholic on the sly.   I have had little hope of
"Household Words" since the proprietors refused to
print a historical fact (otherwise approved of) on the
ground that the hero was a Jesuit: and now that they
follow up this suppression of an honourable truth by
the insertion of a dishonouring fiction (or fact,—no
matter which) they can expect no support from advocates of religious liberty or lovers of fair-play: and so
fond are English people of fair-play, that if they knew
this fact, you would soon find your course in this
matter ruinous to your publication.—As for my
writing for it,—I might as well write for the
"Record" newspaper; and, indeed, so far better, that
the "Record" avows its anti-catholic course.   No one

wants "Household Words" to enter into any theological implication whatever :--but you choose to do it, and must accept accordingly the opinions you thereby excite. I do not forget that you plead duty ; and I give you credit for it,—precisely as I do to the Grand Inquisitor. He consecrates his treatment of heretics by the plea of the dangers of Protestantism : and you justify your treatment of Catholics by the plea of the dangers of Romanism. The one difference that there is, is in his favour ;—that *he* does not profess Protestant principles while pursuing the practices of Jesuitry. —No, I have no more to say to "Household Words"; and you will prefer my telling you plainly why, and giving you this much light on the views your course has occasioned in one who was a hearty well-wisher to " Household Words," as long as possible. ... ...
... ... ' H. MARTINEAU.'

Mr. Wills replied that he felt justified in what he had done ; that we should never agree on the matter ; and that, agreeing to differ, we would drop the subject.—Such are the grounds, and such was the process, of my secession from the corps of Mr. Dickens's contributors.

When I fancied I was going to do what I pleased till I left home in July 1854, the proprietor of the Windermere Guide made an irresistible appeal to me to do the whole district, under the form of a ' Complete Guide to the Lakes.' Still in hope that leisure would come at last, and feeling that I should enjoy it the more for having omitted no duty, I gave up my holiday evenings now. I made the tour of the district once more with a delightful party of friends, —reviving impressions and noting facts, and then came home, resigned to work 'double tides' for the remaining weeks before my summer absence,—dining early, after my morning's work, and writing topography in the evenings. I received much aid in the collection of materials from the publisher, and from the accomplished artist, Mr. Lindsey Aspland, who illustrated the volume: and I finished my work, and went forth on a series of visits which were to occupy the tourist season,—my house being let for that time. I little imagined when I left my own gate, that the ease and light-hearted pleasure of my life,—I might almost say my life itself,—were left behind me;—that I was going to meet sickness and sorrow, and should return to sorrow, sickness, and death.

If I had been duly attentive to my health, I might have become aware already that there was something wrong. Long after, I remembered that, from about March, I had been kept awake for some little time at night by odd sensations at the heart, followed by hurried and difficult breathing: and once, I had been surprised, while reading, to find myself unable to see more than the upper half of the letters, or more of that than the word I was reading. I laid aside my book; and if I thought at all of the matter it was to suppose it to be a passing fit of indigestion,—though I had no other sign of indigestion. While at Liverpool, I found myself far less strong than I had supposed; and again in Wales and at Shrewsbury; but I attributed this to the heat. Mr. Hunt met me and my maid at the station in London, and took us over to his house at Sydenham, giving us bad news by the way of the spread of cholera. A poor carpenter had, the week before, died of cholera while at work in

Mr. Hunt's house,—the seizure being too sudden to admit of his removal to his own unhealthy home,—from whence, no doubt, he brought the disease. On our way from the Sydenham station to Mr. Hunt's house, he pointed out to me an abominable pond, covered with slime and duckweed, which he had tried in vain to draw official attention to. During my short visit, and just after it, almost all of us were ill, —my host and hostess, some of the children, a servant, and myself: and after my removal to an airy lodging at Upper Norwood, opposite the Crystal Palace fence, I had repeated attacks of illness, and was, in fact, never well during the five weeks of my residence there.—It was a time of anxiety and sorrow. My good friend and publisher, Mr. Chapman, had just failed,—in consequence of misfortunes which came thick upon him, from the time of Mr. Lombe's death, which was a serious blow to the 'Westminster Review.' Mr. Chapman, never in all our intercourse, asked me to lend him money; yet the 'Westminster Review' was by this time mortgaged to me. It was entirely my own doing; and I am anxious, for Mr. Chapman's sake, that this should be understood. The truth of the case is that I had long felt, as many others had professed to do, that the cause of free-thought and free-speech was under great obligations to Mr. Chapman; and it naturally occurred to me that it was therefore a duty incumbent on the advocates of free-thought and speech to support and aid one by whom they had been enabled to address society. Thinking, in the preceding winter, that I saw that Mr. Chapman was hampered by certain liabilities that the Review was under, I offered to assume the mort-

gage,—knowing the uncertain nature of that kind of
investment, but regarding the danger of loss as my
contribution to the cause. At first, after the failure,
there was every probability, apparently, that Mr.
Chapman's affairs would be speedily settled,—so
satisfied were all his creditors who were present with
his conduct under examination, and the accounts he
rendered. A few generous friends and creditors made
all smooth, as it was hoped ; but two absent discontented creditors pursued their debtor with (as some
men of business among the creditors said) 'a cruelty
unequalled in all their experience.' One of their
endeavours was to get the Review out of Mr.
Chapman's hands ; and one feature of the enterprise
was an attempt to upset the mortgage, and to drive
Mr. Chapman to bankruptcy, in order to throw the
Review into the market, at the most disadvantageous
season, when London was empty, and cholera prevalent,—that these personages might get it cheap.
One of them made no secret of his having raised a
subscription for the purpose. It was the will of the
great body of the creditors, however, that Mr.
Chapman should keep the Review, which he had edited
thus far with great and rising success ; and his two
foes were got rid of by the generosity of Mr.
Chapman's guaranteeing supporters. The attempt to
upset the mortgage failed, of course. I had an intimation in twenty-four hours that I was 'not to be
swindled out of the Review ': but the whole anxiety,
aggravated by indignation and pain at such conduct
on the part of men who had professed a sense of
obligation to Mr. Chapman, extended over many
weeks. The whole body of the creditors were kept

waiting, and the estate was deteriorating for those weeks, during which the two persecutors were canvassing for subscriptions for the Review which one of them endeavoured to drive into a bad market, at my expense, and to the ruin of its proprietor. The business extended over my residence at Sydenham. I had long before promised an article, involving no small labour, for the next number of the Review ('Rajah Brooke'); and, when I was reckoning on my return home, two misfortunes occurred which determined me to stay another week, and work. A relative of Mr. Chapman's, his most valued friend and contributor, was struck down by cholera in the very act of writing an article of first-rate consequence for the forthcoming number: and, while my poor friend was suffering under the first anguish of this loss, another contributor, wrought on by evil influences, disappointed the editor of a promised article at the time it ought to have been at press. I could not but stay and write another; and I did so,—being bound, however, to be at home on the nineteenth of September, to receive the first of a series of autumn guests. On the night of my arrival at home, after a too arduous journey for one day, I was again taken ill; and next morning, the post brought the news of the death of another of my dear aunts,—one having died during my absence from home. I had left Mr. Hunt in a very poor state of health—as, indeed, everybody seemed to be during those melancholy months; but we hoped that a shooting excursion would restore him to business in his usual vigour. It appeared to do so; but cholera was making such ravage among the corps of the paper that those who could work

were compelled to over-work; and the editor slept
at the office during the most critical time. Every
circumstance was against him; and we began to be
uneasy, without having any serious apprehension of
what was about to befal.

There was great enjoyment in that Sydenham
sojourn, through all its anxieties. During the first
half of the time that I was in lodgings, a dear young
niece was with me; and for the other half, a beloved
cousin—my faithful friend for forty years. Some
whole days, and many half holidays, I spent with
them in the Crystal Palace, with great joy and delight.
I dwell upon those days now with as much pleasure as
ever,—the fresh beauty of the summer morning,
when we were almost the first to enter, and found the
floors sprinkled, and the vegetation revived, and the
tables covered with cool-looking viands, and the rus-
tics coming in and venting their first amazement in a
very interesting way:—and again, our steady duties
in the courts in the middle of the day; and again,
the walk on the terrace, or the lingering in the nave
when the last train was gone, and the exhibitors were
shutting up for the day. There were also merry parties,
and merry plans at Mr. Hunt's. We went, a carriage-
full, to the prorogation of parliament, when I had a
ticket to the peeresses' gallery, where, however, we
were met by the news (which encountered us everywhere) of a mournful death from cholera,—Lord
Jocelyn having died that afternoon. We had a plan
for going, a party of fifteen, in the next April
to Paris, for the opening of the Exhibition on
May-day. May-day has passed without the opening
of the Exhibition: Mr. Hunt has been above five

months in his grave; and I have been above three
months in daily expectation of death. In November,
when Mr. Hunt was ill, but we knew not how ill, I
wrote to him that, on consideration, it seemed to me
that the party to Paris would be better without me
(for political reasons): and Mr. Hunt's message (the
last to me) was that it would be time enough to settle
that when April came. I suspect that he foresaw his
fate.—In November, my correspondence was with the
sub-editor, because Mr. Hunt was ill. The cashier
told me next of his 'alarm' about his beloved
friend: but the sub-editor wrote that *he* was not
alarmed like the rest. Then the accounts were worse;
there was one almost hopeless: and then, he was dead.
I did not think that such capacity for sorrow was left
in me. He was so happy in life; and the happiness of
so many was bound up in him! He was only forty;
and he had fairly entered on a career of unsurpassed
usefulness and honour, and was beginning to reap the
natural reward of many years of glorious effort! But
he was gone; and I had not known such a personal
sorrow since the loss of Dr. Follen, in 1840, by the
burning of a steamer at sea. I certainly felt very ill;
and I told my family so; but I thought I could go to
London, and work at the office during the interval till
his place could be filled. I offered to do so; but the
proprietors assured me that I could help them best by
working daily at home. The cousin, who had been my
companion at Sydenham, wrote that she was glad I
had not gone: for she believed, after what she had
seen in September, that it would have killed me. I
believe she was right, though it seemed rather extravagant at the time.

SECTION IX.

By December I felt somewhat better; but I was not able to write my usual New Year's letters to my family. The odd obliteration of words and half letters when I read returned once or twice when there was certainly no indigestion to account for it; and a symptom which had perplexed me for months grew upon me,—an occasional uncertainty about the spelling of even common words. I had mentioned this, as an odd circumstance, to a Professor of Mental Philosophy, when he was my guest in October : and his reply was, ' there is some little screw loose somewhere ' : and so indeed it proved. Throughout December and the early part of January, the disturbance on lying down increased, night by night. There was a *creaking* sensation at the heart (the beating of which was no longer to be felt externally) ; and, after the creak, there was an intermission, and then a throb. When this had gone on a few minutes, breathing became perturbed and difficult ; and I lay till two, three, or four o'clock, struggling for breath. When this process began to spread back into the evening, and then forward into the morning, I was convinced that there was something seriously wrong ; and with the appro-

bation of my family, I wrote to consult Dr. Latham;
and soon after, went to London to be examined by
him. That honest and excellent physician knew
beforehand that I desired, for reasons which concerned others more than myself, to know the exact
truth; and he fulfilled my wish.—I felt it so probable that I might die in the night, and any night,
that I would not go to the house of any of my nearest
friends, or of any aged or delicate hostess: and I
therefore declined all invitations, and took rooms
at Mr. Chapman's, where all possible care would be
taken of, me, without risk to any one. There Dr.
Latham visited and examined me, the day after my
arrival, and frankly told me his 'impression,'—
observing that it could not yet be called an opinion.
The impression soon became an opinion, as I knew it
would, because he would not have told me of such an
impression without the strongest ground for it. He
requested me to· see another physician; and Dr.
Watson's opinion, formed on examination, without
prior information from Dr. Latham or me, was the
same as Dr. Latham's. Indeed the case appears to be
as plain as can well be. It appears that the substance
of the heart is deteriorated, so that 'it is too feeble
for its work'; there is more or less dilatation; and
the organ is very much enlarged. Before I left London, the sinking-fits which are characteristic of the
disease began to occur; and it has since been perfectly
understood by us all that the alternative lies between
death at any hour in one of these sinking-fits, or by
dropsy, if I live for the disease to run its course.

Though I expected some such account of the case,
I was rather surprised that it caused so little emotion

in me.   I went out, in a friend's carriage, to tell her
the result of Dr. Latham's visit; and I also told a
cousin who had been my friend since our school-days.
When I returned to my lodgings, and was preparing
for dinner, a momentary thrill of something like
painful emotion passed through me,—not at all
because I was going to die, but at the thought that
I should never feel health again.   It was merely
momentary; and I joined the family and Mr. Atkinson,
who dined with us, without any indisposition to the
merriment which went on during dinner,—no one
but my hostess being aware of what had passed since
breakfast.   In the course of the evening, I told them ;
and I saw at once what support I might depend on
from my friend.   I did not sleep at all that night ;
and many were the things I had to think over ; but I
never passed a more tranquil and easy night.   As
soon as my family heard the news, a beloved niece,
who had repeatedly requested to be allowed to come
to me, joined me in London, and gave me to understand, with her parents' free consent, that she would
not leave me again.   I sent for my executor, made
a new will, and put him in possession of my affairs,
my designs and wishes, as fully as possible, and
accepted his escort home to Ambleside.   As there
was but one possible mode of treatment, and as that
could be pursued in one place as well as another,
I was eager to get home to the repose and freshness
of my own sweet place.   It was not only for the
pleasure of it, but for the sake of my servants ; and,
because, while prepared, in regard to my affairs, to go
at any time, there were things to be done, if I could
do them, to which the quiet of home was almost

Engraved by Benka Edw?

The Knoll, Ambleside
March 5th, 1856.

My dear friend

I have looked out
the various accounts, & I
think you will find the
version of the story in the
Biographie Universelle
the truest & best. But
judge for yourself, of course.

Yours affectionately
Harriet Martineau.

indispensable. The weather was at that time the worst of a very bad winter; and it was a very doubtful matter whether I could perform the journey. By the kindness of a friend, however, the invalid carriage of the North Western Railway was placed at my disposal; and we four,—my niece, my executor, my maid and myself, travelled in all possible comfort. The first thing I saw in my own house,—the pale, shrunk countenance of the servant I had left at home, — made me rejoice that I had returned without further delay. I found afterwards that she had cried more than she had slept from the time that she had heard how ill I was, and what was to happen.—That was three months ago : and during those three months, I have been visited by my family, one by one, and by some dear friends, while my niece has been so constantly with me as to have, in my opinion, prolonged my life by her incomparable nursing. The interval has been employed in writing this Memoir, and in closing all my engagements, so that no interest of any kind may suffer by my departure at any moment. The winter, after long lingering, is gone, and I am still here, — sitting in the sun on my terrace, and at night going out, according to old custom, to look abroad in the moon or star-light. We are surrounded by bouquets and flowering plants. Never was a dying person more nobly ' friended,' as the Scotch have it. My days are filled with pleasures, and I have no cares; so that the only thing I have to fear is that, after all the discipline of my life, I should be spoiled at the end of it.

When I learned what my state is, it was my wish (as far as I wish anything, which is indeed very slightly and superficially) that my death might take place before long, and by the quicker process : and such is, in an easy sort of way, my wish still. The last is for the sake of my nurse, and of all about me; and the first is mainly because I do not want to deteriorate and get spoiled in the final stage of my life, by ceasing to hear the truth, and the whole truth : and nobody ventures to utter any unpleasant truth to a person with ' a heart-complaint.' I must take my chance for this ; and I have a better chance than most, because my nurse and constant companion knows that I do not desire that anybody should ' make things pleasant' because I am ill. I should wish, as she knows, to live under complete and healthy moral conditions to the last, if these can be accommo-dated, by courage and mutual trust, with the physical conditions.—As to the spoiling process, — I have been doubting, for some years past, whether I was not undergoing it. I have lived too long to think of making myself anxious about my state and prospects in any way ; but it has occurred to me occasionally, of late years, whether I could endure as I formerly did. I had become so accustomed to ease of body and mind, that it seemed to me doubtful how I might bear pain, or any change ;—for it seemed as if any change must be for the worse, as to enjoyment. I remember being struck with a saying of Mrs. Wordsworth's, uttered ten years ago, when she was seventy-six,—that the beauty of our valley made us too fond of life,—too little ready to leave it. Her domestic bereavements since that time have doubtless altered this feeling entirely ; but, in many an hour of intense enjoyment on the hills, I have recalled that saying; and, in wonder at my freedom from care, have speculated on whether I should think it an evil to die, then and there. I have now had three months' experience of the fact of constant expectation of death; and the result is, as much regret as a rational person can admit at the absurd waste of time, thought, and energy that I have been guilty of in the course of my life in dwelling on the subject of death. It is really melancholy that young people (and, for that matter, middle-aged and old people) are exhorted and encouraged as they are to such waste of all manner of power. I romanced internally about early death till it was too late to die early; and, even in the midst of work and the busiest engagements of my life, I used to be always thinking about death,— partly from taste, and partly as a duty. And now that I am waiting it at any hour, the whole thing seems so easy, simple and natural that I cannot but wonder how I could keep my thoughts fixed upon it when it was far off. I cannot do it now. Night after night since I have known that I am mortally ill, I have tried to conceive, with the help of the sensations of my sinking-fits, the act of dying, and its attendant feelings; and thus far I have always gone to sleep in the middle of it. And this is after really knowing something about it; for I have been frequently in extreme danger of immediate death within the last five months, and have felt as if I were dying, and should never draw another breath. Under this close experience, I find death in prospect the simplest thing in the world,—a thing not to be feared or regretted, or to get excited about in any way.—I attribute this very much, however, to the

nature of my views of death. The case must be
much otherwise with Christians,—even independently
of the selfish and perturbing emotions connected with
an expectation of rewards and punishments in the
next world. They can never be quite secure from the
danger that their air-built castle shall dissolve at the
last moment, and that they may vividly perceive on
what imperfect evidence and delusive grounds their
expectation of immortality or resurrection reposes.
The mere perception of the incompatibility of immortality and resurrection may be, and often is deferred
till that time ; and that is no time for such questions.
But, if the intellect be ever so accommodating, there
is the heart,—steady to its domestic affections. I,
for one, should be heavy-hearted if I were now about
to go to the antipodes,—to leave all whom I love,
and who are bound up with my daily life,—however
certain might be the prospect of meeting them again
twenty or thirty years hence ; and it is no credit to
any Christian to be 'joyful,' 'triumphant' and so
forth, in going to 'glory,' while leaving any loved
ones behind,—whether or not there may be loved
ones ' gone before.' An unselfish and magnanimous
person cannot be solaced, in parting with mortal
companions and human sufferers, by personal rewards,
glory, bliss, or anything of the sort. I used to think
and feel all this before I became emancipated from the
superstition ; and I could only submit, and suppose
it all right because it was ordained. But now, the
release is an inexpressible comfort ; and the simplify-
ing of the whole matter has a most tranquillising
effect. I see that the dying (others than the aged)
naturally and regularly, unless disturbed, desire and

sink into death as into sleep. Where no artificial
state is induced, they feel no care about dying, or
about living again. The state of their organisation
disposes them to rest; and rest is all they think
about. We know, by all testimony, that persons who
are brought face to face with death by an accident
which seems to leave no chance of escape, have no
religious ideas or emotions whatever. Where the
issue is doubtful, the feeble and helpless cry out to
God for mercy, and are in perturbation or calmness
according to organisation, training, and other circumstances : but, where escape appears wholly impossible, the most religious men think and feel nothing
religious at all,—as those of them who have escaped
tell their intimate friends. And again, soldiers
rush upon death in battle with utter carelessness—
engrossed in other emotions, in the presence of which
death appears as easy and simple a matter as it does
to me now.—Conscious as I am of what my anxiety
would be if I were exiled to the antipodes,—or to
the garden of Eden, if you will,—for twenty or
thirty years, I feel no sort of solicitude about a
parting which will bring no pain. Sympathy with
those who will miss me, I do feel of course : yet not
very painfully, because their sorrow cannot, in the
nature of things, long interfere with their daily peace;
but to me there is no sacrifice, no sense of loss,
nothing to fear, nothing to regret. Under the eternal
laws of the universe, I came into being, and, under
them, I have lived a life so full that its fulness is
equivalent to length. The age in which I have lived
is an infant one in the history of our globe and of
Man ; and the consequence is, a great waste in the

years and the powers of the wisest of us; and, in
the case of one so limited in powers, and so circumscribed by early unfavourable influences as myself, the
waste is something deplorable. But we have only to
accept the conditions in which we find ourselves, and
to make the best of them; and my last days are
cheered by the sense of how much better my later
years have been than the earlier; or than, in the
earlier, I ever could have anticipated. Some of the
terrible faults of my character which religion failed to
ameliorate, and others which superstition bred in me,
have given way, more or less, since I attained a truer
point of view: and the relief from old burdens, the
uprising of new satisfactions, and the opening of
new clearness,—the fresh air of Nature, in short,
after imprisonment in the ghost-peopled cavern of
superstition,—has been as favourable to my moral
nature as to intellectual progress and general enjoyment. Thus, there has been much in life that I am
glad to have enjoyed; and much that generates a
mood of contentment at the close. Besides that I
never dream of wishing that any thing were otherwise
than as it is, I am frankly satisfied to have done with
life. I have had a noble share of it, and I desire no
more. I neither wish to live longer here, nor to find
life again elsewhere. It seems to me simply absurd
to expect it, and a mere act of restricted human
imagination and morality to conceive of it. It seems
to me that there is, not only a total absence of
evidence of a renewed life for human beings, but so
clear a way of accounting for the conception, in the
immaturity of the human mind, that I myself utterly
disbelieve in a future life. If I should find myself

mistaken, it will certainly not be in discovering any existing faith in that doctrine to be true. If I am mistaken in supposing that I· am now vacating my place in the universe, which is to be filled by another, —if I find myself conscious after the lapse of life,— it will be all right, of course; but, as I said, the supposition appears to me absurd. Nor can I understand why any body should expect me to desire any thing else than this yielding up my place. If we may venture to speak, limited as we are, of any thing whatever being important, we may say that the important thing is that the universe should be full of life, as we suppose it to be, under the eternal laws of the universe: and, if the universe be full of life, I cannot see how it can signify whether the one human faculty of consciousness of identity be preserved and ·carried forward, when all the rest of the organisation is gone to dust, or so changed as to be in no respect properly the same. In brief, I cannot see how it matters whether my successor be called H. M. or A. B. or Y. Z. I am satisfied that there will always be as much conscious life in the universe as its laws provide for; and that certainty is enough, even for my narrow human conception, which, however, can discern that caring about it at all is a mere human view and emotion. The real and justifiable and honourable subject of interest to human beings, living and dying, is the welfare of their fellows, surrounding them, or surviving them. About this, I do care, and supremely; in what way I will tell presently.

Meantime, as to my own position at this moment, I have a word or two more to say.—I had no previous

conception of the singular interest of watching human
affairs, and one's own among the rest, and acting in
them, when on the verge of leaving them. It is an
interest which is full even of amusement. It has been
my chief amusement, this spring, to set my house and
field in complete order for my beloved successor;—
to put up a handsome new garden fence, and paint the
farming man's cottage, and restore the ceilings of the
house, and plan the crops which I do not expect to see
gathered. The mournful perplexity of my good farm-
servant has something in it amusing as well as touching;—the necessity he is under of consulting me
about his sowings, and his plans for the cows,—
relating to distant autumn months, and even to
another spring,—the embarrassing necessity that this
is to him, while his mind is full of the expectation
that I shall then be in my grave. In the midst of
every consultation about this or that crop, he inter-
poses a hope that I may live to see his hay, and to eat
his celery and artichokes and vegetable marrow, and
to admire the autumn calf; and his zeal for my
service, checked by the thought that his services are
in fact for others, has something in it as curious as
touching.—And so it is, more or less, with all my
intercourses—that a curious new interest is involved
in them. Mere acquaintances are shocked that the
newspapers should tell that I am 'in a hopeless
state,' that 'recovery is impossible,' &c., while my
own family and household have no sort of scruple
in talking about it as freely as I do. A good many
people start at hearing what a cheerful,—even merry
—little party we are at home here, and that we sometimes play a rubber in the evenings, and sometimes

laugh till I, for one, can laugh no more. To such
wonder, we answer—why not? If we feel as usual,
why not do as usual? Others, again, cannot conceive
how, with my 'opinions,' I am not miserable about
dying; and declare that they should be so; and this
makes me wonder, in my turn, that it does not strike
them that perhaps they do not comprehend my views
and feelings, and that there may be something in the
matters more than they see or understand. There is
something very interesting to me in the evidences of
different states of mind among friends and strangers
in regard to my 'good' or 'bad spirits,'—a matter
which appears to me hardly worth a thought. As it
happens, my spirits are good; and I find good spirits
a great blessing; but the solicitude about them, and
the evident readiness to make much of bad spirits, if
I had them, are curious features in my intercourse
with acquaintance or strangers who are kind enough
to interest themselves in my affairs. One sends me a
New Testament (as if I had never seen one before)
with the usual hopes of grace &c., though aware that
the bible is no authority with me; and, having been
assured that I am 'happy,' this correspondent has
the modesty to intimate that I ought not to be
happy, and that people sometimes are so 'without
grounds.' It is useless to reply that, as I have
not pursued happiness as an aim, all this kind of
speculation is nothing to me. There is the fact; and
that is enough.—Others, again, who ought, by their
professions, to know better, are very glad about this
'happiness,' and settle it in their own minds that
Christian consolations are administered to me by God
without my knowing it. If so, I can only say it is

a bounty not only gratuitous, but undesired. Christian consolations would certainly make me any thing but happy, after my experience of them in contrast with the higher state of freedom, and the wider sympathies opened by my later views.

The lesson taught us by these kindly commentators on my present experience is that dogmatic faith compels the best minds and hearts to narrowness and insolence. Even such as these cannot conceive of my being happy in any way but theirs, or that there may be views whose operation they do not understand. In a letter just received, a dear friend says ' I have seen no one since I left you who is "sorry" about you (about my "opinions"). Still I see that the next row, and the next, still more so, are "very sorry" and "very, very sorry."' The unconscious insolence revealed in this ' sorrow ' is rebuked by the more rational view of others who are no nearer agreeing with me than the second and third ' row.' ' Not agreeing,' says my friend, ' they still see no more reason for lamentation over you than for you to lament over them. " *Il y a aussi loin de chez toi chez moi que de chez moi chez toi,*" is the perfectly applicable French proverb.' Another, who professes to venerate martyrs and reformers (if only they are dead) is ' sorry ' again because this, that, or the other Cause suffers by my loss of influence. The mingled weakness and unconscious insolence of this affords a curious insight. First, there is the dereliction of principle shown in supposing that any ' Cause ' can be of so much importance as fidelity to truth, or can be important at all otherwise than in its relation to truth which wants vindicating. It reminds me of an incident which happened when I was in America, at the time of the severest trials of the Abolitionists. A pastor from the Southern States lamented to a brother clergyman in the North the introduction of the Anti-slavery question, because the views of their sect were 'getting on so well before!' 'Getting on!' cried the Northern minister. 'What is the use of getting your vessel on when you have thrown both captain and cargo overboard?' Thus, what signifies the pursuit of any one reform, like those specified,— Anti-slavery and the Woman question,—when the freedom which is the very soul of the controversy, the very principle of the movement,—is mourned over in any other of its many manifestations? The only effectual advocates of such reforms as those are people who follow truth wherever it leads. The assumption that I have lost influence on the whole exposes itself. Nobody can know that I have lost influence on the whole, either in regard to ordinary social intercourse or to subjects of social controversy; and I have reason to believe that I have (without at all intending it) gained influence in proportion to the majority that the free-thinkers of our country constitute to the minority existing in the form of the sect in which I was reared, or any other.

As to the curious assortment of religious books and tracts sent me by post, they are much what I have been accustomed to receive on the publication of each of my books which involved religious or philosophical subjects. They are too bad in matter and spirit to be safe reading for my servants; so, instead of the waste-basket, they go into the fire. I have not so many anonymous letters now as on occasions of publication; but some which are not anonymous are scarcely wiser or purer. After

the publication of ' Eastern Life,' I˙ had one which
was too curious to be forgotten with the rest. It was
dated ' Cheltenham,' and signed ' Charlotte'; and
it was so inviting to a reply that, if it had borne any
address, I should have been tempted to break through
my custom of silence in such cases. ' Charlotte'
wrote to make the modest demand that I would call
in and destroy all my writings, ' because they give
pain to the pious.' It would have been amusing
to see what she would think of a proposal that ' the
pious' should withdraw all their writings, because
they give pain to the philosophical. It might have
been of service to suggest the simple expedient, in
relief of the pious, that they should not read books
which offend them. After the publication of the
'Atkinson Letters,' anonymous notes came in elegant
clerical hand-writing, informing me that prayers would
be offered up throughout the kingdom, for my rescue
from my awful condition, ' denying the Lord that
bought me,' &c. Now, the concern seems to be of a
gentler sort, and to relate more to my state of spirits
at present than to my destiny hereafter.—But enough
of this. I have referred to these things, not because
they relate to myself, but because the condition of
opinion in English society at present affords material
for profitable study; and my own position at this
moment supplies a favourable opportunity. In the
midst of the meddlesomeness, I do not overlook the
humanity thus evidenced. My only feeling of concern
arises from seeing how much moral injury and suffering is created by the superstitions of the Christian
mythology; and again from the chaotic state of
opinion among Christians themselves, and among

those who would fain retain the name, while giving up all the essentials, and unfurnished with a basis of conviction, while striving to make the fabrics of the imagination serve the purpose.—As for me, who unexpectedly find myself on the side of the majority of thoughtful persons on these questions, I am of course abundantly solaced with sympathy which I can accept ; and I am more and more sensible, as I recede from the active scenes of life, of the surpassing value of a philosophy which is the natural growth of the experience and study,—perhaps I may be allowed to say,—the progression of a life.   While conscious, as I have ever been, of being encompassed by ignorance on every side, I cannot but acknowledge that philosophy has opened my way before me, and given a staff into my hand, and thrown a light upon my path, so as to have long delivered me from doubt and fear.   It has, moreover, been the joy of my life, harmonising and animating all its details, and making existence itself a festival.   Day by day do I feel that it is indeed

> Not harsh and crabbed as dull fools suppose ;
> But musical as is Apollo's lute.

A state like mine of late has its peculiar privileges,—the first felt of which is its freedom from cares and responsibilities.   I have hitherto loved solitude perhaps unduly ; partly, no doubt, on account of my deafness, which, from its attendant fatigues, has rendered solitude necessary, to husband my strength, ---(always, I now suspect, below the average) for my work ; but partly also from the unusual amount of intellectual labour which it has been my duty to undertake. Now, when my work is done, I am enjoying genuine holiday, for the first time for a quarter of a century. I relish, very keenly, the tending of affection, and the lawful transference of my responsibilities to the young and strong, and those who have a tract of life before them, and who are pausing on their way to give me the help I need. I am now free for intellectual luxury,—to read what charms me most, without the feeling that I am playing truant from the school of technical knowledge, for which I shall have no further occasion. Again, I enjoy the free expenditure of my resources. It is something pleasant not to have to consider money— the money which I have earned, and laid up to meet such an occasion. But it is more and better not to grudge my time. My hours are now best spent in affectionate intercourses, and in giving a free flow to every passing day. I need not spare my eyes, nor husband my remaining hearing. I may, in short, make a free and lavish holiday before I go.

Such is the selfish aspect of the case; and I am bound, having begun, to tell the whole case.—Far greater are the privileges I enjoy in regard to the world outside my home. I need not say that one's interests in regard to one's race, and to human life in the abstract, deepen in proportion to the withdrawal of one's own personal implication with them. Judging by my own experience, one's hopes rise, and one's fears decline as one recedes from the action and personal solicitude which are necessary in the midst of life, but which have a more or less blinding and perturbing influence on one's perception and judgment. When at the zenith, clouds are apt to come between one's particular

star and the wide world; whereas, on the clear
horizon, at the moment of the star's sinking, nothing
intervenes to shroud or distort the glorious scene. I
was always hopeful for the world; but never so much
so as now, when I am at full leisure to see things as
they are, and placed apart where the relation of the
past and the future become clear, and the meeting-
point of the present is seen in something like its due
proportion. It appears to me now that, while I see
much more of human difficulty from ignorance, and
from the slow working (as we weak and transitory
beings consider it) of the law of Progress, I discern
the working of that great law with far more clearness,
and therefore with a far stronger confidence, than I
ever did before.

When I look at my own country, and observe the
nature of the changes which have taken place even
within my own time, I have far more hope than I once
had that the inevitable political reconstitution of our
state may take place in a peaceable and prosperous
manner. There have been times in my life when,
having a far obscurer view than I now entertain of the
necessity of a total change in the form of government,
I yet apprehended a revolution in the fearful sense in
which the word was understood in my childhood, when
the great French Revolution was the only pattern of
that sort of enterprise. I now strongly hope that,
whenever our far-famed British Constitution gives
place to a new form of government, it may be through
the ripened will of the people, and therefore in all good
will and prudence. That the change must be made,
sooner or later, was certain from the time when the
preponderance of the aristocratic over the regal ele-

ment in our state became a fact. From the natural alliance between king and people, and the natural antagonism of aristocracy and people, the occurrence of a revolution is always, in such a case, a question merely of time. In our case, the question of time is less obscure than it was in my childhood. The opponents of the Reform Bill were right enough, as every body now sees, in saying that the Constitution was destroyed by that act; though wrong, of course, in supposing that they could have preserved the balance by preventing the act of reform. A constitution of checks and balances, made out of old materials, can never be more than a provisional expedient; and, when the balance is destroyed,—when the power of the Crown is a mere lingering sentiment, and the Commons hold the Lords in the hollow of their hand, while no recent House of Commons has been in any degree worthy of such a trust, the alternative is simply between a speedy revolution with an unworthy House of Commons, or a remoter one, with a better legislature in the mean time. The circumstances of the hour in which I write seem to show that so much social change is near as may be caused by the exposure of administrative incompetence under the stress of the war. It may be this, or it may be something else which will rouse the people to improve the House of Commons: and under an improved House of Commons, the establishment of a new method of government may be long delayed. From the general state of prosperity and contentment at home, the retrieval of Ireland, the rapid advance of many good popular objects, and the raising of the general tone of the popular mind, we may hope that what has to be

done will be done well.—Meantime, the thing that
causes me most anxiety, in regard to our political
condition, is the universal ignorance or carelessness
about the true sphere of legislation.   Before the
people can be in any degree fit for the improved institutions, it is highly necessary that they should understand, and be agreed upon, the true function of legislation and government; and this is precisely what
even our best men, in and out of parliament, seem to
know nothing about.   I regard this as a most painful
and perilous symptom of our condition,—though it
has been brought to light by beneficent action which
is, in another view, altogether encouraging.   Our
benevolence towards the helpless, and our interest in
personal morality, have grown into a sort of public
pursuit; and they have taken such a hold on us that
we may fairly hope that the wretched and the
wronged will never more be thrust out of sight.   But,
in the pursuit of our new objects, we have fallen back,
—far further than 1688,—in the principle of our
legislative proposals,—undertaking to provide by law
against personal vices, and certain special social con-
tracts, while refusing that legitimate legislative boon,
—a system of national education,—which would
supersede the vices and abuses complained of by
intelligence more effectually than acts of parliament
can ever obviate them by penalty.   If I were to form
one hope rather than another in relation to the
political condition of England, it would be that my
countrymen should rise to the level of their time, and
of their intelligence in other respects, in regard to
the true aims of government and legitimate function
of legislation.

As to the wider political prospects outside our own empire, I am of much the same opinion now as when I wrote a certain letter to an anti-slavery friend in America in 1849, which I will subjoin.   That letter was published in the newspapers at the time by my correspondent, and it has been republished in England since the outbreak of the war with Russia :—

'October 1st, 1849.

'MY DEAR ——; We can think of little else at present than of that which should draw you and us into closer sympathy than even that which has so long existed between us.   We, on our side the water, have watched with keen interest the progress of your War of Opinion,—the spread of the great controversy which cannot but revolutionize your social principles and renovate your social morals.   For fifteen years past, we have seen that you are " in for it," and that you must stand firm amidst the subversion of Ideas, Customs and Institutions, till you find yourselves encompassed by " the new heavens and the new earth " of which you have the sure promise and foresight.

'We,—the whole population of Europe,—are now evidently entering upon a stage of conflict no less important in its issues, and probably more painful in its course.   You remember how soon after the conclusion of the Napoleonic wars our great Peace Minister, Canning, intimated the advent, sooner or later, of a War of Opinion in Europe; a war of deeper significance than Napoleon could conceive of, and of a wider spread than the most mischievous of his quarrels. The war of Opinion which Canning foresaw was in fact a war between the further and nearer centuries,—between Asia and Europe,—between despotism and self-government. The preparations were begun long ago. The Barons at Runnymede beat up for recruits when they hailed the signature of Magna Charta; and the princes of York and Lancaster did their best to clear the field for us and those who are to come after us. The Italian Republics wrought well for us, and so did the French Revolutions, one after the other, as hints and warnings; and so did the voyage of your Mayflower,—and the Swiss League, and German Zollverein, and in short, everything that has happened for several hundreds of years. Everything has tended to bring our continent and its resident nations to the knowledge that the first principles of social liberty have now to be asserted and contended for, and to prepare the assertors for the greatest conflict that the human race has yet witnessed. It is my belief that the war has actually begun, and that, though there may be occasional lulls, no man now living will see the end of it.

'Russia is more Asiatic than European. It is obscure to us who live nearest to her where her power resides. We know only that it is not with the Emperor nor yet with the people. The Emperor is evidently a mere show,—being nothing except while he fulfils the policy or pleasure of the unnamed power which we cannot discern. But, though the ruling power is obscure, the policy is clear enough. The aim is to maintain and extend despotism; and the means chosen are the repression of mind, the corruption of conscience, and the reduction of the whole composite population of Russia to a brute machine. For a great lapse of time, no quarter of a century has passed without some country and nation having fallen in, and become a compartment of the great machine; and, the fact being so, the most peace-loving of us can hardly be sorry that the time has come for deciding whether this is to go on,— whether the Asiatic principle and method of social life are to dominate or succumb. The struggle will be no contemptible one. The great tarantula has its spider-claws out and fixed at inconceivable distances. The people of Russia, wretched at home, are better quali-fied for foreign aggression than for anything else. And if, within her own empire, Russia knows all to be loose and precarious, poor and unsound, and with none but a military organisation, she knows that she has for allies, avowed or concealed, all the despotic tempers that exist among men. Not only such Governments as those of Spain, Portugal, Rome and Austria are in reality the allies of Eastern barbarism; but all aristocracies,—all self-seekers,—be they who and where they may. It is a significant sign of the times that territorial alliances are giving way before political affinities,—the mechanical before the essential union : and, if Russia has not for allies the nations that live near her frontier, she has those men of every nation who prefer self-will to freedom.

This corrupted 'patriarchal' system of society, (but little superior to that which exists in your slave States) occupies one-half of the great battle-field where the hosts are gathering for the fight. On the other, the forces are ill-assorted, ill-organised, too little prepared; but still, as having the better cause, sure, I trust, of final victory. The conflict must be long, because our constitutions are, like yours, compromises, our governments as yet a mere patch-work, our popular liberties scanty and adulterated, and great masses of our brethren hungry and discontented. We have not a little to struggle for among ourselves, when our whole force is needed against the enemy. In no country of Europe is the representative system of government more than a mere beginning. In no country of Europe is human brotherhood practically asserted. Nowhere are the principles of civilisation of Western Europe determined and declared, and made the ground-work of organised action, as happily your principles are as against those of your slave-holding opponents. But, raw and ill-organised as are our forces, they will be strong, sooner or later, against the serried armies of the Asiatic policy. If, on the one side, the soul comes up to battle with an imperfect and ill-defended body, on the other, the body is wholly without a soul, and must, in the end, fall to pieces. The best part of the mind of Western Europe will make itself a body by dint of action, and the pressure which must bring out its forces; and it may be doubted whether it could become duly embodied in any other way. What forms of society may arise as features of this new growth, neither you nor I can say. We can only ask each other whether, witnessing as we do the spread of Communist ideas in every free nation of Europe, and the admission by some of the most cautious and old-fashioned observers of social movements that we in England cannot now stop short of 'a modified communism,' the result is not likely to be a wholly new social state, if not a yet undreamed-of social idea.

'However this may be,—while your slave question is dominant in Congress, and the Dissolution of your Union is becoming a familiar idea, and an avowed aspiration, our crisis is no less evidently approaching. Russia has Austria under her foot, and she is casting a corner of her wide pall over Turkey. England and France are awake and watchful; and so many men of every country are astir, that we may rely upon it that not only are territorial alliances giving way before political affinities, but national ties will give way almost as readily, if the principles of social liberty should demand the disintegration of nations. Let us not say, even to ourselves, whether we regard such an issue with hope or fear. It is a possibility too vast to be regarded but with simple faith and patience. In this spirit let us contemplate what is proceeding, and what is coming, doing the little we can by a constant assertion of the principles of social liberty, and a perpetual watch for opportunities to stimulate human progress.

'Whether your conflict will be merely a moral one, you can form a better idea than I. Ours will consist in a long and bloody warfare—possibly the last, but inevitable now. The empire of brute force can conduct its final struggle only by brute force; and there are but few yet on the other side who have any other notion or desire. While I sympathise wholly with you as to your means as well as your end, you will not withhold your sympathy from us because our heroes still assert their views and wills by exposing themselves to wounds and death in the field, and assenting

once more to the old *non sequitur* about Might and
Right. Let them this time obtain the lower sort of
Might by the inspiration of their Right, and in
another age they will aim higher. But I need not
thus petition you; for I well know that where there
is most of Right, there will your sympathies surely
rest.

‘Believe me your friend,

‘ HARRIET MARTINEAU.’

I have no doubt whatever of the power of France
and England to chastise Russia, without the aid of
any other power. I should have no doubt of the
power of England alone (if that power were well
administered) to humble Russia, provided the case
remained a simple one. But that is precisely what
appears impossible, under the existing European
dynasties. I now expect, as I have anticipated for
many years, a war in Europe which may even outlast
the century,—with occasional lulls; and I suppose
the result must be, after a dreary chaotic interval, a
discarding of the existing worn-out methods of government, and probably the establishment of society under
a wholly new idea. Of course, none but a prophet
could be expected to declare what that new idea will
be. It would be rational, but it is not necessary here,
to foretell what it would *not* be or include. But all
that I feel called on to say now, when I am not
writing a political essay, is that the leading feature of
any such radical change must be a deep modification
of the institution of Property ;—certainly in regard
to land, and probably in regard to much else. Before
any effectual social renovation can take place, men

must efface the abuse which has grown up out of the transition from the feudal to the more modern state; the abuse of land being held as absolute property; whereas in feudal times land was in a manner held in trust, inasmuch as every land-holder was charged with the subsistence of all who lived within his bounds. The old practice of Man holding Man as property is nearly exploded among civilised nations; and the analogous barbarism of Man holding the surface of the globe as property cannot long survive. The idea of this being a barbarism is now fairly formed, admitted, and established among some of the best minds of the time; and the result is, as in all such cases, ultimately secure.

These considerations lead my thoughts to America; and I must say that I regard the prospects of the republic of the United States which more pain and apprehension than those of any other people in the civilised world. It is the only instance, I believe, of a nation being inferior to its institutions; and the result will be, I fear, a mournful spectacle to the world. I am not thinking chiefly, at this moment, of American slavery. I have shown elsewhere what I think and expect about that. Negro slavery in the United States, as regards the existing Union, is near its end, I have no doubt. I regard with a deeper concern the manifest retrogression of the American people, in their political and social character. They seem to be lapsing from national manliness into childhood,—retrograding from the aims and interests of the nineteenth century into those of the fifteenth and sixteenth. Their passion for territorial aggrandisement, for gold, for buccaneering adventure, and for vulgar praise, are seen

miserably united with the pious pretensions and fraud-
ulent ingenuity which were, in Europe, old-fashioned
three centuries ago, and which are now kept alive only
in a few petty or despised States, where dynasty is on
its last legs.   I know that there are better men, and
plenty of them, in America than those who represent
the nation in the view of Europe; but those better
men are silent and inactive ; and the national retrogression is not visibly retarded by them.   I fear it
cannot be.   I fear that when the bulk of a nation is
below its institutions,—whether by merely wanting
the requisite knowledge, or by being in an immature
moral condition,—it is not the intelligence and virtue
of a small, despairing, inactive minority that can save
it from lapse into barbarism.   I fear that the American nation is composed almost entirely of the vast
majority who coarsely boast, and the small minority
who timidly despair, of the Republic.   It appears but
too probable that the law of progression may hold
good with regard to the world at large without preventing the retrogression of particular portions of the
race.   But the American case is not exactly of this
kind.   I rather take it to be that a few wise men,
under solemn and inspiring influences, laid down a
loftier political programme than their successors were
able to fulfil.   If so, there is, whatever disappointment, no retrogression, properly speaking.   We
supposed the American character and policy to be
represented by the chiefs of the revolution, and their
Declaration of Independence and republican constitution; and now we find ourselves mistaken in our
supposition.   It is a disappointment; but we had
rather admit a disappointment than have to witness
an actual retrogression.

Effacing these national distinctions, in regarding the peoples as the human race, the condition of humanity appears to one who is taking leave of it very hopeful, though as yet exceedingly infantine.   It is my deliberate opinion that the one essential requisite of human welfare in all ways is scientific knowledge of human nature.   It is my belief that we can in no way but by sound knowledge of Man learn, fully and truly, any thing else; and that it is only when glimpses of that knowledge were opened,—however scantily and obscurely,—that men *have* effectually learned any thing else.   I believe that this science is fairly initiated; and it follows of course that I anticipate for the race amelioration and progression at a perpetually accelerated rate.   Attention is fully fixed now on the nature and mode of development of the human being; and the key to his mental and moral organisation is found. The old scoff of divines against philosophers must now soon be dropped,—the reproach that they have made no advance for a thousand years;—that there were philosophers preaching two thousand years ago, who have hardly a disciple at this day.   In a little while this can never more be said; nor could it be said now by any one who understood the minds of the people among whom he lives.   The glorious aims and spirit of philosophy have wrought for good in every age since those ancient sages lived; and the name and image of each is the morning star of the day in which each lived.   In this way were the old philosophers truly our masters; and they may yet claim, in a future age, the discipleship of the whole human race.   But to them scientific fact was wanting: by them it was unattainable.   Their aim and their spirit have led

recent generations to the discovery of the element
wanting,—the scientific fact; and, now that is done,
the progression of philosophy is secure. The philosophy of human nature is placed on a scientific basis;
and it, and all other departments of philosophy, (for
all depend mainly on this one) are already springing
forward so as to be wholly incomparable with those of
a thousand years ago. There is no need to retort the
scoff of divines, as facts are against them. There is
no need to inquire of them what is the state of Christianity at the end of 1800 years, nor what it has done
in regenerating human nature, and establishing peace
on earth and goodwill among men, according to its
promise. Leaving divines on one side, as professionally disqualified for judging of the function and
prospects of philosophy, and looking at the matter in
a speculative, and not an antagonistic way, I should
say that the time cannot be far off when, throughout
the civilised world, theology must go out before the
light of philosophy. As to the fact, the civilised
world is now nearly divided between gross Latin or
Greek Catholicism and disbelief of Christianity in any
form. Protestantism seems to be going out as fast as
possible. In Germany the Christian faith is confes-
sedly extinct; and in France it is not far otherwise.
The Lutheranism of Sweden is, in its effects, precisely
like the Catholicism of Spain or Italy, and will issue in
'infidelity' in the one country as surely as in the
others. In England the lamentations of the religious
world, and the disclosures of the recent Census, show
how even outward adhesion to Christianity is on the
decline: and if they did not, the chaotic state of
religious opinion would indicate the fact no less

reliably.   In America we see Protestantism run wild, —each man being his own creed-maker; and the result,—a seeking ere long for something true and stable,—is secure.—Not only is such the state of the civilised world, but it must be so.   Precisely in proportion to Man's ignorance of his own nature, as well as of other things, is the tendency of his imagination to inform the outward world with his own consciousness.   The fetish worshipper attributes a consciousness like his own to everything about him; the imputation becomes more select and rare through every rising grade of theology, till the Christian makes his reflex of himself invisible and intangible, or, as he says, 'spiritual.'   His God is an invisible idol, fading away into a faint abstraction, exactly according to the enlightenment of the worshipper, till he who does justice to his own faculties gives up the human attributes, and the personality of that First Cause which the form of his intellect requires him to suppose, and is called an Atheist by the idolaters he has left behind him.   By the verification and spread of the science of human nature, the conflict which has hitherto attended such attainment as this will be spared to our successors. When scientific facts are established, and self-evident truths are brought out of them, there is an end of conflict;—or it passes on to administer discipline to adventurers in fresh fields of knowledge.   About this matter, of the extinction of theology by a true science of human nature, I cannot but say that my expectation amounts to absolute assurance; and that I believe that the worst of the conflict is over.   I am confident that a bright day is coming for future generations. Our race has been as Adam created at nightfall.   The solid earth has been but dark, or dimly visible, while the eye was inevitably drawn to the mysterious heavens above.   There, the successive mythologies have arisen in the east, each a constellation of truths, each glorious and fervently worshipped in its course ; but the last and noblest, the Christian, is now not only sinking to the horizon, but paling in the dawn of a brighter time.   The dawn is unmistakeable; and the sun will not be long in coming up.   The last of the mythologies is about to vanish before the flood of a brighter light.

With the last of the mythologies will pass away, after some lingering, the immoralities which have attended all mythologies.   Now, while the state of our race is such as to need all our mutual devotedness, all our aspiration, all our resources of courage, hope, faith and good cheer, the disciples of the Christian creed and morality are called upon, day by day, to 'work out *their own* salvation with fear and trembling,' and so forth.   Such exhortations are too low for even the wavering mood and quacked morality of a time of theological suspense and uncertainty.   In the extinction of that suspense, and the discrediting of that selfish quackery, I see the prospect, for future generations, of a purer and loftier virtue, and a truer and sweeter heroism than divines who preach such self-seeking can conceive of.   When our race is trained in the morality which belongs to ascertained truth, all ' fear and trembling ' will be left to children ; and men will have risen to a capacity for higher work than saving themselves,—to that of ' working out ' the welfare of their race, not in ' fear and trembling,' but with serene hope and joyful assurance.

The world as it is is growing somewhat dim before my eyes; but the world as it is to be looks brighter every day.

END OF THE AUTOBIOGRAPHY.

APPENDIX A.

MEMORIAL

AGAINST PROSECUTION FOR OPINION, SIGNED BY DR. CHANNING AND 166 OTHERS.

Page 42.

To his Excellency the Governor of the Commonwealth of Massachusetts :—

The undersigned respectfully represent that they are informed that Abner Kneeland, of the city of Boston, has been found guilty of the crime of Blasphemy, for having published, in a certain newspaper called the ' Boston Investigator,' his disbelief in the existence of God, in the following words :

' Universalists believe in a God, which I do not ; but believe that their God, with all his moral attributes (aside from nature itself), is nothing more than a chimera of their own imagination.'

Your petitioners have learned, by an examination of the record and documents in the case, made by one of their number, that the conviction of said Kneeland proceeded on the ground above stated. For though the indictment originally included two other publications, one of a highly irreverent and the other of a grossly indecent character ; yet it appears by the Report, that, at the trial, the prosecuting officer mainly relied on the sentence above quoted, and that the Judge who tried the case confined his charge wholly to stating the legal construction of its terms, and the law applicable to it.

In these circumstances, the undersigned respectfully pray, that your Excellency will grant to the said Kneeland an unconditional pardon, for the offence of which he has been adjudged guilty. And they ask this, not from any sympathy with the convicted individual, who is personally unknown to most or all of them; nor from any approbation of the doctrines professed by him, which are believed by your petitioners to be as pernicious and degrading as they are false; but

Because the punishment proposed to be inflicted is believed to be at variance with the spirit of our institutions and our age, and with the soundest expositions of those civil and religious rights which are at once founded in our nature, and guaranteed by the constitutions of the United States and this Commonwealth;

Because the freedom of speech and the press is the chief instrument of the progress of truth and of social improvements, and is never to be restrained by legislation, except when it invades the rights of others, or instigates to specific crimes;

Because, if opinion is to be subjected to penalties, it is impossible to determine where punishment shall stop; there being few or no opinions, in which an adverse party may not see threatenings of ruin to the state;

Because truths essential to the existence of society must be so palpable as to need no protection from the magistrate;

Because the assumption by government of a right to prescribe or repress opinions has been the ground of the grossest depravations of religion, and of the most grinding despotisms;

Because religion needs no support from penal law, and is grossly dishonoured by interpositions for its defence, which imply that it cannot be trusted to its own strength and to the weapons of reason and persuasion in the hands of its friends;

Because, by punishing infidel opinions, we shake one of the

strongest foundations of faith, namely, the evidence which arises to religion from the fact, that it stands firm and gathers strength amidst the severest and most unfettered investigations of its claims ;

Because error of opinion is never so dangerous as when goaded into fanaticism by persecution, or driven by threatenings to the use of secret arts ;

Because it is well known that the most licentious opinions have, by a natural reaction, sprung up in countries where the laws have imposed severest restraint on thought and discussion ;

Because the influence of hurtful doctrines is often propagated by the sympathy which legal severities awaken towards their supporters ;

Because we are unwilling that a man, whose unhappy course has drawn on him general disapprobation, should, by a sentence of the law, be exalted into a martyr, or become identified with the sacred cause of freedom ; and lastly,

Because we regard with filial jealousy the honour of this Commonwealth, and are unwilling that it should be exposed to reproach, as clinging obstinately to illiberal principles, which the most enlightened minds have exploded.

Boston, Massachusetts, 1839.

APPENDIX B.

Page 92.

A MONTH AT SEA.

The following is an account of a real voyage, perfectly true, except in one respect. For obvious reasons the names are all changed. As to every other particular, the scene is presented exactly as it appeared to the eye and the imagination of a lands-woman.

Some weeks before the sailing of the packet, I went on board, as she lay alongside the wharf on the East River, New York, to select my state-room. I engaged one for myself and Miss Saunders, who was one of the party with whom I had arranged to cross the ocean. I bore in mind the exhortation I had received from an experienced sailor, to secure a berth on the starboard side of the ladies' cabin; for the sake, among other reasons, of being out of the way of the scents and sounds of the steward's pantry. The state-room I secured was on the starboard side. The captain wrote my name and Miss Saunders's on slips of paper, which he pinned to the curtains of the berths. He then introduced me to the stewardess, Margaret, a bonny, obliging Scotch girl, whose countenance and manner pleased me exceedingly.

The ship, which I shall call the 'Eurydice,' was not so new, so clean, or so convenient, as most on the line; but there were considerations in favour of our going by her which overbalanced these objections. The high character of the captain, and his being a personal friend of some of our party, were the chief inducements to us to go by the 'Eurydice.' She sailed too on the first of August, which was the season at which we wished to cross.

The day before we were to sail, I was informed that Miss Lamine, a passenger, had been to the ship, and had removed Miss Saunders's ticket from the curtain of the berth, and substituted her own, on the ground of Miss Saunders's passage having been only conditionally engaged. This was true ; but it was no excuse for the lady's ill-manners. As anything is better than squabbling anywhere, and particularly on board ship, where people cannot get out of each other's way, I gave up the point, surrendering my berth to Miss Saunders, who was an invalid, and taking up with a state-room on the larboard side, which I had to share with a young orphan girl, Kate, who, being left destitute by the recent death of both her parents, was allowed by the captain's kindness to work her way over to her friends in Wales, by assisting the stewardess.

My things were packed so as to occasion the least possible trouble to myself and the people on board. Some passengers are not so considerate as they should be about this. The ladies' cabin is small enough at best ; and it should never be crowded with trunks and bandboxes, for people to tumble over in rough weather. Such encumbrances are unsightly, too ; and in a situation like that of being on board ship, every care should be taken to avoid offence to eye or mind. The ladies' cabin should be as neat as any parlour in a private house. A carpet-bag and bandbox, such as the state-room will easily hold, may be made to contain all that is necessary for a month's voyage ; with the addition of a few good books, in which the owner's name should be written, and which should not be too fine to be willingly lent.

I carried no stores. Everything requisite for good eating and drinking is so abundantly provided on board these packets, that it is useless to burden oneself with anything more   Some of the ladies found comfort in ginger lozenges, and each should have a vinaigrette. I do not remember that anything else was in request. Warm clothing is essential to comfort. While basking in a July sun on shore, it is difficult to believe how bitter the cold will be a few miles out at sea : but no amount of cloaks furs, and woollen over-shoes can be too great for comfort during, the first and last days of a voyage, usually the coldest of the term. There is much comfort in having two cloaks ; one to wear, and another to wrap round the feet on cold days, and in a high wind.

The first of August was an intensely hot day : I looked with amazement at my boa, fur tippet, warm cloak and gown, and wondered whether it was possible that I should in a few hours be shivering, in spite of them all. About eleven o'clock, the passengers assembled on board a steamboat which was to convey them to their ship. Some, of whom I was one, were attended by friends who meant to accompany them as far as Sandy Hook, the southern point of New York bay. It was a dismal morning, sad with the sorrows of parting. We tried to amuse ourselves after we had stepped on board by showing the ship to the children who were to return. I was rather dismayed to see the range of water-casks on deck, looking like a very ugly encumbrance. In the more modern packets they are out of sight.

We were towed out of the harbour by a steamer ; and the motion was so smooth, the shores so bright, and the luncheon in the cabin so good, that the children evidently thought a voyage must be an extremely pleasant affair. They little knew how heavy were the hearts of their parents and friends round the table, with the parting glass at their lips, and parting emotions struggling in their hearts.

A certain square box of mine contained some papers of value ; and this circumstance was mentioned to the captain by a mutual friend, without my knowledge. The captain said the box should not go down into the hold with the rest, but should stand under the table in the gentlemen's cabin, where it would be in nobody's way, and would be kept dry.   It will be seen what grew out of this small circumstance.

The character of the passengers will appear in the course of the narrative.   At present they may be thus indicated.   My own party consisted of Professor Ely and his lady ; Miss Saunders ; Mr. Tracy, a youth just from college, and going to travel in Europe with the Professor and his lady; and Lieutenant Browning, of the American navy.   With Miss Lamine was an old Dutch lady, Mrs. Happen.   A very stout widow lady, with her two daughters, Irish, and strangers to us all, and Miss Taylor, the captain's invalid sister, made up the number of ladies.   An elderly Scotch gentleman, Mr. Bruce, appeared after two days, having been laid up in his berth with a bruised leg.   Some young men from New Orleans and Mobile; Dr. Sharp, Mr. Simpson, Mr. Larkin, and Mr. Mann, were the only others that I now remember.

By four o'clock we were off Sandy Hook, and it was necessary for our New York friends to return.   I promised to send them a minute journal of the events of our voyage.   With a few suppressions and amplifications, the following is what I sent them :—

August 3.   Already I feel or believe myself able to write ; if you can but manage to read an unsteady scrawl on damp paper.   Fortified by chicken broth, red with cayenne paper, I begin my journal : –

Before we had quite lost sight of your steamer the pilot began to be in a hurry off.   'Haul away, boys, and no humbugging ! ' cried he.   Soon after, he told the captain to 'sail due east, and keep the white buoy on his weather bow,' and departed—too soon—before we were over the bar ; and the captain was too anxious to go down to dinner.   Mrs. Ely was too much of something else, and so sat still in the round-house (the sort of summer-house on deck, built round the head of the stairs leading down into the cabin).   Miss Saunders went down with

APPENDIX.

me, still declaring that no Saunders was ever yet sea-sick since the world began. Presently, however, she said at table, 'Shall I pass you?' and glad enough she was to get into the air. The motion of the ship now became unpleasant, and I was not sorry when the ladies left their dessert to repair to the deck.

I found that Mrs. Ely did not present a model of colouring for a portrait-painter; her eyes and lips being yellow, and her cheeks ash-colour. I tried to read the Boston newspapers I had received in the morning, but was too heavy at heart, and found them strangely uninteresting. Just before I went down for the night, at seven o'clock, I was cheered by a single charm in Miss Saunders—a precious look and gesture of fun in the midst of distress. O the worth of good humour at sea! What a contrast was here to Miss Lamine, who made a noise all evening and night, such as was never heard in these upper regions before, I should think. She was evidently anxious that everyone on board should know the extent of her sufferings. The captain told me in the morning that he had been explaining to his sister that 'noise does no good, and is not fair.'

When in the morning with much toil I got myself on deck (the only lady), the captain congratulated me on our rough sea and rapid progress: 'very good for the sea-sick.' These favourable circumstances, however, sent me down before noon, to reappear no more till evening. The captain is as kind as a brother, and as handy as a lady's maid. In the midst of our distresses, Margaret's innocent face and kind voice are a comfort to see and hear. To set against these solaces, the flies are almost intolerable, notwithstanding my state-room (which it was thought would not be wanted) being luxuriously hung with cobwebs. These flies must be of American extraction, to judge by the pertinacity of their disposition. Only two or three showed the breeding of English flies in keeping away after a certain number of rebuffs. What can be the reason of the difference between your flies and ours in pertinacity? If Margaret was driven at last to throw her apron over her face, what must have been the annoyance to us invalids ? I lay on the sofa. I wish you had seen the august captain approach, pepper-box in hand, and followed by a cup of hot chicken-broth. I felt seasoned for half a century, and took to the 'Life of Mackintosh,' of which I read half a volume before laying the book down. Then I thought of three particularly pleasant things, which you said to me on Sunday and Monday. Can you remember or imagine what they were ? I will only say that they were nothing personal. Then I toiled up on deck to see the sun set ; admired him the minute before ; and then forgot all about him till he had disappeared. Lieutenant Browning offered me the astronomical comfort of assuring me that I had really seen the last of the sun, and that it was only the refraction that I had missed. This was about as effectual as consolation usually is.

Thinking that the captain looked grave about his poor flock of ladies, and knowing that nothing is more dispiriting to the captain than the absence of passengers from the table, I plunged down into the cabin to tea, and stayed an hour, beguiled by some pleasant conversation.

Some remarkable events have happened to-day. Mrs. Happen's cat has caught a mouse. This opens a prospect of some unlooked-for provisions, in case of our voyage being three months' long, and our stock failing. Professor Ely has donned his sea-dress, popping his head up the stairs in a cap, which must have been a grenadier's. We dubbed him Captain Ely. Dr. Sharp is disconsolate for want of ' two small buttons ' for the straps of his pantaloons. He implored the steward to furnish him with some —in vain. The under-steward—in vain also. The captain. The captain was brought down into the cabin, to hear this petition ; and offered that ' two small buttons ' should be cut off his own pantaloons for Dr. Sharp's use ;—which Dr. Sharp accepted ! Miss Saunders saw a Portuguese man-of-war before I did, which makes me jealous. Do you know why this little fish is thus called ? I have endealoured in vain to learn. Some wag says that it is because, as soon as a gale rises, it fills and goes down ;

but this must be said out of some special grudge against the Portuguese navy. I have seen these beautiful little mariners of the deep of various hues and sizes, some as large as my fist, some as small as my grandmother's teacups. I have seen them of a rich violet, of a pale lilac, and of a dingy pink; their hue evidently not depending wholly on the sunshine or shade in which they may be gliding. Before I became acquainted with them, I fancied that they floated only in sunshine, and on a calm sea; but I have seen them in almost all weathers. They are most beautiful when shining on the surface of a deep blue sea; but they allow themselves to be tossed about on the crests of troubled waves, and turned over and over in rough weather, before 'they fill and go down.' I never handled one. The sailors are unwilling to catch them; and when they do, are careful to fetch them up in bowls or nets, and to avoid touching the fish; as, on being touched, it discharges a fluid which raises a large blister on the skin, and is very painful. The part of the fish which answers to the shell of the nautilus is soft—a mere membrane; but its form is that of a nautilus shell, and it floats like a tiny but substantial boat, the fibrous parts of the little fish depending and moving as it changes its direction. Except the dolphin, I think the Portuguese man-of-war the prettiest of the inhabitants of the deep which come to the surface to delight the eye of the passenger.

I saw to-day two Mother Carey's chickens. We shall have them now sporting about our ship all the way. I wish we could change our swarms of flies into these pretty creatures.

Mrs. Happen's quick eye saw my box under the table in the gentlemen's cabin. She says, 'If some people's boxes are taken care of, so shall other people's be;' and she has actually ordered the steward to bring up her trunks from between decks, and put them in the same place. Her jealousy being once roused, there will be no more peace in her mind all the voyage. She quarrelled with the captain at the dinner-table, for letting the lamp in the ladies' cabin blow out at two in the morning. He answered by sending us the binnacle lamp, which cannot blow out. He is much too good to her. She is on bad terms with several of the passengers already.

The captain has been making war against the flies, sweeping thousands of them out of the skylight to the birds ; so that they will be changed into Mother Carey's chickens in a different way from what I meant. He brought me down a chick of Mother Carey's brood. Pretty creature ! with its long legs and yellow web-feet, and curious hooked beak ! It stumbled and fluttered about the deck, and then we let it get away. I never could conceive before how these birds walked on the water, which I saw they certainly did. They never leave us, flitting about, apparently without rest, from the time we are out of sight of land, till we come near it again. They are in flocks of from two or three to thirty or forty. They feed on the refuse food thrown from the ship.

The captain lashed up a stool on the rail, to serve for the back of a chair. Here I sat in the breeze, enjoying some feelings of health again, and proceeding rapidly with 'Mackintosh's Life,' which is very interesting.

Mrs. Ely is on deck to-day, dizzy but better. The other ladies are still disconsolate, and show no disposition to be sociable.

4th. A heavenly day : the perfection of sailing. It is unreasonable to expect more than one such a day in a month's voyage. The wind was fair, mild, and balmy ; the sea radiant in all directions. The captain gave orders to 'square the yards ' (a delightful sound always), and we cut steadily through the waves all day,—perceiving only in the cabin that we were on the sighing bosom of the deep. Our sails being all set, the captain and crew seemed quite at leisure. I saw no less than six Portuguese men-of-war, wetting their lilac sails in the purple sea. I could not leave such a sight, even for the amusement of hauling over the letter-bags. Mr. Ely put on his spectacles ; Mrs. Ely drew a chair ; others lay along on deck to examine the superscriptions of the letters from Irish emigrants to their friends. It is wonderful how some of these epistles reach their destination; the following, for instance, begun at the top left-hand corner, and elaborately prolonged to the bottom right one :—' Mrs. A. B. ile of man douglas wits sped England.' The letter-bags are opened for the purpose of sorting out those which are for delivery in port from the rest. A fine day is always chosen, generally towards the end of the voyage, when amusements become scarce, and the passengers are growing weary. It is pleasant to sit on the rail, and see the passengers gathered round the heap of letters, and to hear the shouts of merriment when any exceedingly original superscription comes under notice. Though the ladies seem by this time all well, some of them show no disposition to render themselves agreeable; and the captain was thus tempted to an early development of all his resources of amusement.

Mrs. Happen presently came up, and indulged in a passion of tears. Her cat is missing, and she is sure some cruel person has thrown it overboard, because somebody wrung her Poll-parrot's neck on her first voyage. We suggested that it was more probable that pussy, feeling frightened, had hidden herself, and would re-appear. But the weeping lady was sure that all was over with pussy. At dinner, her eyes were much swollen, but she was disposed for some turkey, and sent her plate to Mr. Ely for some, begging that it might be without bone. He sent her a plump wing, which she returned with an order to him to take the bones out. In the evening there was a bustle on deck : all the stewards were running with hot water and cold, and the ladies with 'eau-de-Cologne.' Mrs. Happen was hysterical,—fainting, from the news having been too suddenly imparted to her that her cat had re-appeared in the cabin. Mrs. Happen's negro-maid, Sally, has orders to keep her mistress's state-room so shut up (in August) as that pussy may not hide herself again.

The two Miss O'Briens appeared to-day on deck, speaking to

nobody, sitting on the same seats, with their feet on the same letter-bag, reading two volumes of the same book, and dressed alike, even to the yellow spectacles, which are so far unbecoming as that they make good grey eyes look grass-green. Their mother has not yet appeared at table, and keeps her pillows about her; but I twice saw her during dinner steal to the steward's pantry, and come forth with a replenished plate, in addition to the lobster-salad we sent her. There is fear that she will not shrink materially, though she assures Mrs. Ely that 'a spare diet is the only thing at sea.' In this opinion I do not agree with her. I have reason to think a full and generous diet necessary to health at sea,—and particularly during the season of sickness. The reason, I believe, why some do not think so, is that they feel ill and miserable after eating : but they should remember how ill and miserable they felt before eating; and how much more so they might have been without eating. Disagreeable as is the effort to eat during sea-sickness, I am persuaded that, where it can be made, it obviates much suffering.

We began to be uneasy about knowing nothing of the steerage passengers. To be in the same bottom, on the wide ocean, and to be strangers, cannot be right. If some of the ladies prefer alienation, so be it : but we mean to give the rest of the people the means of acquaintanceship with us, if we can do it without intrusion. What can these worthy folks, amidst their real privations, think of the story of Mrs. Happen's troubles, if the tale should reach their end of the ship ?

The stars came out softly in our wide sky; and the sun set amidst indications of continued fair winds. Mr. Browning shows me our place on the chart every noon. We are about 400 miles from New York ;—going further from you, the more we exult in our fair breeze. We meant to have had a rubber to-night, but found the cabin too warm. Every body is on deck, except some gentlemen who are at cards. I am going to see how the dim ocean looks under the stars.

I found less dimness than light upon deck. The captain

never knew so sultry a night in this latitude. The sea was luminous; the exquisite light spreading in a flood from every breaking wave. There were explosions of lightning from the cloudy west. We dashed through the sea, and made great progress during the night, having accomplished one-fifth of our voyage by morning.

What a loss has there been of this glorious day to such as were stormy within while all was bright around!

August 5th. A day as disagreeable as yesterday was the contrary. Damp, stifling, with much rain, and rolling, which threw us back upon our patience. Miss Saunders is gentle and merry. Every body begins to praise her. The ship is very inferior to the one I came out in;—in stewards, and in all manner of arrangements; but I can scarcely regret this, as it is the means of displaying the captain's virtues. We are in constant admiration of his patience, ingenuity, and consideration of everybody. Mrs. Happen's insults only make him more generous.

Before breakfast, for two dreary hours, Mrs. Ely beguiled us with capital sketches of character;—oddities. She does this very well: a little coarsely, perhaps, and not absolutely simply; but with much power. I read the first half of her book in the proofs.

...   .

Mr. Simpson began talking to me to-day about some mutual acquaintance. He can tell me every thing about Mexico, where he has been living. He has a true understanding of the Texan cause. He says the Mexicans hate all foreigners, and call them all English. It is too bad to mix us up with the Texans; though, as I am sorry to say, there have been English in the Texan ranks.

An hour before dinner, the clouds parted, and the wind became fresher and drier. I fell asleep on the rail, while looking for sea-sights, and woke refreshed.

In the afternoon, Miss Saunders and I had a long talk on the rail on the difference between religion, spontaneous and artificial; natural.and arbitrary; professionally and unconsciously administered; with examples : all this arising out of some lines she brought me about gradual and sudden death. I amazed her by telling her of the incessant conflict in ——'s mind, between her free and joyous nature, and the separate, arbitrary religion which she has had imposed upon her; but which will not for ever prevent her discovering that religion has a natural affinity with whatever is free, pure, lofty, and exhilarating. She is one who would certainly break loose, or grow hypocritical in time, if she could not get liberty for her devotional spirit.'

Then followed, our own party having assembled, not a few tales of travel, I furnishing an account of my Michigan trip. In the evening, the Elys, Mr. Tracy and I played a rubber. They are slow and young players, but pleasant partners and adversaries. Tracy will play well.—On deck, to see that there was nothing to be seen this moonless night. So uncomfortable with the damp heat of the day as to be unwilling to go down but it is against my conscience to keep the girls up; and they will not go to rest till we do. I slept pretty well after all.

6th. I really cannot write down all Mrs. Happen's freaks. The captain is now busy with hammer and nails, trying to please her. She is jealous of a bandbox of Kate's, standing in the entire state-room which her negro maid is allowed to have. She cannot possibly spare the curtains from the berth in her stateroom, that she does *not* sleep in; and so forth.

I like Mr. Browning. He has been telling me some anecdotes of greatness, all full of the richest moral beauty. When he was at Marseilles, he went about hunting for the house where Guyon died. Nobody knew anything about Guyon!

At breakfast, five or six of us had a long talk about dressing-boxes, of all things. This led to the display of our respective ones, which was very amusing. Mrs. Ely's was the most nice and complete; and Lieutenant Browning's perhaps the most commodious,—being nothing else than a stocking! He thinks us worthy to hear the whole truth about our voyage; and so tells us that to-day we are going slowly, four points out of our course; that we got too far south at the outset; that we shall not cross 'the Banks,' and shall therefore see neither icebergs nor cod-boats; that we have got into a region of calms and light winds, and shall probably have a long voyage. My heart sank for a moment,—I had so long counted the days which had home at the end of them: but I esteem it a sin to let one's countenance fall on board ship; and we all joked upon the matter.

Found on deck Mr. Bruce, who has been in his berth nursing a wounded leg ever since we came on board. He is Scotch, acquainted with divers literary folk in London; droll, and pretty sensible:—an acquisition, particularly to the captain, as he has promised to turn his novelty to good account with Mrs. Happen, who has quarrelled with everybody else. He is going to lay himself out to amuse her. He has written some things for 'Hood's Comic Annual.' He will get some fine new material here.

Dr. Sharp asks the captain to-day if rain is quite fresh at sea.

Mrs. Happen owns she had a prejudice against Mr. Tracy from the moment she saw him.—She supposes Mrs. Ely and I enjoy the voyage from knowing that we shall never be in such society again.—She begs Mr. Browning to inform her rightly about our course; for she never saw such mates in *her* life. Miss Lamine is very nearly as bad. She complains of everything, and has nicknamed everybody. The captain told her not to feel uneasy at being of the same party with Mrs. Happen, as no one supposed Miss Lamine to have anything to do with the old lady's behaviour. Miss Lamine went directly and told Mrs. Happen every word that the captain had said.

Scene. Ladies' Cabin.

Miss Lamine writing on the sofa; Margaret and Sally.

Marg.—'Where's the cat now?

Sally.—'In Missus's state-room.'

Marg.—' She'll get away, as sure as she's alive.'

(*A groan from Sally.*)

Marg.—' Why don't you tie her up ? '

Sally.—' I vow I will, if I can get a bit o' cord.'

Marg.—' Only, perhaps, your mistress will tie *you* up, if the cat happens not to like it.'

Sally.—' Perhaps she will: only then she must get a pretty strong cord ; that I can tell her.'

Scene. Deck.

Mr. Mann and the Mate.

Mate.—' I'll tell you what, sir—we've got this head-wind, all because you will keep catching Mother Carey's chickens. If you go on catching them, we shall have a gale ahead.'

Mr. Mann.—' In that case, I should advise your throwing the cat overboard.'

Mate.—' Then we shall have a gale within ship that will last us all the way to Liverpool.'

11th. Found it calm : chickens ' tripping a ballet,' as Mrs. Ely says ; and Lieutenant Browning predicting a fair wind,—which has this moment arrived. The weather has been deplorable, and we have been rolled about, in the midst of one of those pelting rains which make everybody busy in keeping dry without being stifled. Mr. Ely was wholly and happily absorbed in Southey's ' Cowper.' The rest of us talked and laughed in the round-house till poor Mrs. O'Brien (who begins to show herself a second Mrs. Happen) abruptly left the company, and burst into the cabin, exclaiming that we were all the lowest and most ignorant society she ever was in. For my part, I thought some of the conversation, particularly the captain's, Mr. Browning's, and Miss Saunders's, very clever and entertaining. After a while, the weather conquered most of us. In vain the captain sent round his champagne, and his jokes, and kind sayings. Poor man! when the stars showed themselves, and the long tempest seemed over, and he was going to bed, after two days and a night of toil, the weather changed, and he could not leave the deck for hours. What a life it is!

Mr. Browning put on his sea-coat and went out into the storm, and came back, the rain streaming from his hat and chin, to praise the ship. He knew few that would stand such a wind under so much sail. I was glad to hear this, for certainly her inside is not to be praised. How strange it is to see music and lyres stuck up all over her, old and dirty as she is! and to see black coal buckets, with 'Eurydice' painted on them! Miss Lamine lays down the law that 'each passenger ought to have a whole state-room, twice the size of ours; but the people try to make money instead of accommodating the passengers.' The question is, whether she would like to pay accordingly. She never uses her berth, after all, but sleeps on the sofa.

Mrs. Happen could not perceive that there was any particular motion to-day. On the instant over went her rocking chair on one side, throwing her into Miss O'Brien's lap.

12th. We do long for a little cheery weather. The captain is somewhat serious about it. He never knew so much damp, changeable weather at this season. We are past the Banks without having seen anything. Only one porpoise has shown himself. Only one ship has been hailed, and she did not answer; all which sounds very dull. I have been reading Southey's 'Cowper,' which has not mended the matter much. It is as interesting as possible, but most dismal.

I feel very small in the presence of the sailors. How they must look down upon us, fleeing in from every drop of rain; getting under the awning as soon as the sun shines, and going to bed comfortably every night, whatever the weather may be! I feel myself truly contemptible.

The captain and I had a full hour's talk in the evening, when he was tired, after forty-eight hours of toil. He told me a great deal about his wife and children, and all about the loss of his brother last winter. The death of this brother has made a deep impression upon him. He asked me much about the degree of faith which it is possible to have in a future life, and gave me his own conceptions of it. I was heartily sorry when the tea-bell rang. The simplicity of this man, with all his other qualities, is beautiful. So serious, so funny (he has now been peeping down upon us through the skylight, with his round face in a lady's long deck bonnet); so brave and cheerful, so amiable with his cross passengers, and his inefficient crew ! Mrs. Ely says he is just as gentle with his crew in the midst of a stormy night, as with Mrs. Happen at table. Her room is where she can hear all that passes on deck. One miserable day, he looked himself to the making of the pea-soup, ordering the ham-bone in ; then he mended the lock on Mrs. Ely's room-door; then he came and talked of this life and other with me.

Mr. Browning is not in very good spirits. He says he has had more experience of bad company than ever before ; and he now associates only with us. Poor Mrs. Happen sits all alone on deck. People speak kindly to her, but she makes no sort of answer. I am glad to see she reads a good deal.

The box of books, sent on board for the steerage by a benevolent gentleman, was brought up a few days ago, and immediately emptied. It is a fine resource for the idle men, and I like to see them perched on casks and chests absorbed in their books. We cannot succeed in making acquaintance with these people. Perhaps they have found out that our end of the ship is squally.

Yesterday the captain shouted, for the first time, ' Splice the main brace ' (give out grog). Mrs. Ely and I had previously done it in a small private way, without having so earned the comfort. The captain is now heard giving orders to kill the finest pig to-night. I think I shall ask him to shave and soap its tail first, and set the passengers to catch it. It might unite them in a common object, and restore good-humour. The cow was not milked on our two roughest days, at which the complainers profess to be very angry, and threaten to report the captain for it.

If I were he, I would set them to try what milking cows in a rolling sea is like. Miss Saunders's geranium pines, and will be as yellow as the mast before we land.

The captain told me this evening, what he does not wish the other ladies to know till we are within sight of port, lest they should be alarmed, that the mate behaved so ill as to be necessarily sent back with the pilot. The second mate was made first, and the carpenter second mate; and neither of them knows much of his business; so the captain has hard work to do. He says, 'There is Lieutenant Browning to command, if anything should happen to me.'

Mr. Bruce gave me a dreadful account to-day of his sufferings from tic-doloureux, and of his cure, which he ascribes to his having taken nightly a pill consisting of three grains of mercury and one of stramonium. He is well now, and very kind and agreeable.

15th. Better news. For some hours we had a fair wind and delicious weather. We have been becalmed for days, between two winds, catching all the bad consequences of each, and none of the good. But these are the times for feeling that one stands between two worlds; looking forward and back upon the divisions of human society, and able to survey them without prejudice, and to philosophize upon them without interruption. These are the times for feeling as if one could do something for one's race by toiling for it, and by keeping aloof from the storms of its passions and its selfish interests; humbly, not proudly, aloof. Such thoughts arise in the isolation of a voyage, as if they came up from the caverns of the deep. On the centre of the ocean one is as in another state of existence, with all one's humanity about one.

Everybody's ailments are gone, and all but the two unhappy old ladies look cheery this morning. I saw a whale yesterday. Mr. Bruce pronounced it 'no orator, because it did not spout well;' but I was quite satisfied with its performances—heaving its black carcass, and wallowing and plunging in the dirty-looking boiling sea. How different was everything the next morning! The sapphire sea, with its fleet of Portuguese men-of-war; a single land-bird flitting and fluttering, from New-foundland no doubt. Pity it had not faith to come on board, for I fear it will never get back.

I saw three flying fish—very pretty—leaping from the crest of one wave into another: but nothing was to me so beautiful as the transparent ripple, seen above the surface when the sun got low. After reading ——'s capital sermon, I read no more, but sat with Miss Saunders on the rail all day, having much talk with long intervals of silence. Mrs. Ely wrote all the morning; but I could not bear to lose a breath of balmy air, or a hue of the sweet sea. In the afternoon we repeated poetry and sang, and promised each other scientific lectures on deck daily this next week. Do not laugh at us. You would have promised anything whatever on such an afternoon.

In the evening, five of us had a long conversation on European politics and American democracy, till the captain came to take me, first to the bows, to see the full sails swelling against the star-lit sky, and then to the stern, to see how bright a train of light we left behind us, as we dashed through at the rate of ten knots an hour. Professor Ely gave us a little history of the improvements in astronomy and navigation, the elements of these sciences being furnished by observation in the bright regions of the East to the foggy and scientific West. When these improvements are carried back to the star-lit east, what may not the science become!

The captain brought me to-day a book, about the size of the palm of my hand, that I might look at a short poem,—rather pretty. He was very mysterious: the book was not published; was written by some one on board. We all guessed Mr. Bruce. But no; everybody had been told in a whisper, before two hours were over, that it was by Mr. Kitton, the artist and poet. Mr. Kitton was a poor sick gentleman, who had been in his berth ever since we sailed, and who now began to creep out into the sunshine. Dr. Sharp attended him professionally, and he had a friend to nurse him. We saw nothing of him except when he sat on deck in the middle of the day. He looked wretchedly, but I believe his complaints were not alarming.

Mrs. Happen treated the captain cruelly to-day. He looks grave, though he owns he ought not to mind her. The ship we saw on Thursday kept dallying about us for three days, and would not speak when hailed. I wish Mrs. Happen could have been put on board of her; they would suit exactly.

There is one thing interesting about the Miss O'Briens. They are very attentive and affectionate to their mother; which, considering how she sometimes treats them, speaks well for their tempers. She may well pronounce them 'very steady girls.' But their conversation is of that kind which, however often one may hear it, one can scarcely credit on recollection. I set down one specimen, as a fair example. Dr. Sharp was called yesterday to one of the crew who was ill. As he returned, looking rather thoughtful, Mr. Mann observed to the O'Brien family that the doctor was quite a man of consequence to-day. Thereupon ensued,—

First Miss O.—'La! Doctor, how consequential you look!'

Second Miss O.—'Well! Doctor, how consequential you look!'

Mrs. O.—'Why, the Doctor does look consequential indeed!'

First Miss O. (*to Mr. Mann.*)—'La! Sir, how consequential the Doctor does look!'

Second Miss O.—'Now doesn't the Doctor look quite consequential?'—And so on, for above ten minutes.

The captain has just been unpacking a hundred towels; a goodly sight for those who rehearse drowning every morning (in salt water), as I do. I am certain that no practice is so beneficial to health at sea as plenty of bathing, with friction afterwards. A large foot-bath, or small tub, may easily be procured; and the steward will draw up a bucket or two of sea-water every morning.

A sea-faring friend told me this before I sailed; and I have often been thankful for the advice.

Our cargo is partly turpentine. The vessel leaks and so do the turpentine casks; and what comes up by the pumps is so nauseous as to cause much complaint among the passengers. There was no time at New York to get the copper bottom mended; and the crew are hard worked with the pumping. The captain says if the leak increases, he shall employ the steerage passengers at the pumps. Mr. Browning shows me the chart. We are rather more than half way. He considers it two-thirds, as the best is all to come. 'All down hill now,' he says.

August 17th. Going on most prosperously. We have never slackened on our course since I made my last entry. Kind-hearted Margaret came to my bed-side early this morning, to tell me that at four o'clock we were going twelve knots, right on our course. If we hold on till noon, we are pretty sure of being carried straight in by this blessed wind. All are well, and in better temper, unless it be Mrs. Happen. Yesterday, while all was bright and gleesome, she was 'low.' She did not know that we should ever arrive! Betting is the order of the day with the idle young men. As the weather is not wet, and they cannot therefore bet upon the raindrops running down the cabin windows, they are obliged to find or make other subjects for bets. Yesterday at dinner they betted about whether they could roll up bits of bread so tight as not to break when thrown down on deck! Also whether they could swallow a pill of bread so rolled up, the size of the end of the thumb. They were so impatient they could not wait till the cloth was removed, but missed their dessert for the sake of this thumbed bread. They bet at cards, and one of them declared he had lost sixteen dollars,—4*l*. After having talked very loud over their cards, till just midnight, last night Dr. Sharp got his flute, and played execrably, till requested to be quiet till morning. It did not occur to him that he was disturbing anybody.

The captain is very grave, while all looks so prosperous.

His sister says, with tears, that 'it is a hard voyage to him;' but we tell her it will not matter a month hence, when his unamiable passengers will have dispersed to the four winds. He discovered yesterday that the stewards have been leaving the ice-house door open, so that the ice is nearly all gone; and he fears he shall lose some of his best joints of beef. Upon this he good-humouredly said, 'Sea-captains are not intended to be good-tempered. It should not be looked for. At the top of a heap of little vexations, comes a gale; and then they should not be expected not to shout pretty sharply to their crews.' We do not believe he ever does. He showed good manners yesterday to a ship that we hailed. In the early morning, when the fog drew up, there was an etherial vision of a ship on our horizon. We overtook her just at noon. (We overtake every thing.) She looked so beautiful all the morning, that we did nothing but watch her. As we approached we went to leeward, the captain explaining, in answer to our questions, that it is worth losing a little time to be civil. She was the St. Vincent of Bristol, thirty-three days from Jamaica. I pitied the poor ladies on board, of whom we saw many on deck. The captains each asked the other to report him, in case of arriving first. Our young men laughed at the idea of our being reported by a ship thirty-three days from Jamaica; but our captain looked grave, and said it looked presumptuous to make sure of our having no accident; and uncivil to assure the St. Vincent that she could not, by possibility, be of any service to us. She could have spared us some limes; but it would have used up too much time to send a boat for them; so we dashed on, and she was out of sight westward before the afternoon. I never saw a greater press of sail than she carried; but her bows were like a breakwater, so square and clumsy.

In the afternoon I read 'Much Ado about Nothing,' and watched a shoal of porpoises. They are welcome visitors in any weather; but they seem extremely lively in a rough sea, chasing one another, and shooting through the midst of a rising billow.

They are sometimes caught and killed, to be eaten more as a curiosity than a delicacy. I am told that the meat resembles coarse and tough beef. The mate wounded one to-day; and its companions crowded on it to eat it up. Some Jaques on board asked me if this was not the way of the world; to which I indignantly answered, No !

18th. Still dashing on. Mr. Browning expects that we shall get in on Tuesday of next week : the captain says Thursday or Friday. I listen to neither, knowing how little such calculations are to be depended upon.

21st, Sunday. We have been rolling about so that it has been impossible to write. We have had a fine run for eight days now. Yesterday's observation gave 220 miles for the twenty-four hours. The captain says we are pretty sure of running straight up to Liverpool. By to-morrow morning we may see land. I dreamed last night that I saw it first ;—a lovely Irish hill. It is almost too cold now to be on deck, with any amount of cloakage : a sign of being near land. The joke since we passed half-way, has been to annoy me by ascribing all evils whatever to the foggy English climate. Mr. Browning began ; the captain carries it on ; and the ingenuity with which they keep it up is surprising. Something of the sort drops from the captain's lips, like a grave passing observation, many times a day. I shall have no respite now; for every one will be too cold till we land.

We had a prodigious run last night. While we were at our rubber, the news spread (as news does on board ship) that the captain was on deck, taking in sail, ordering in the dead-lights (the shutters which block up the cabin-windows in the stern), and 'expecting a blow.' Under the idea that it was raining, I was, for once, about to retire to my room without running up on deck ; but the captain came for me, thinking I should like to see what was doing : and indeed he was right. Though he had taken in the studding-sails, mainsail, and royals, we were flying through at the rate of twelve knots. The clouds were blown down the eastern sky,—and the stars so bright, they looked as if they were coming down. But below us, what a sight! The dazzling spray was dashed half a mile off, in a level surface which looked like a white marble floor, gemmed with stars. The captain says, people talk of the monotony of the sea; but the land is to him monotonous in comparison with the variety in which he revels in his night-watches. It is evidently a perpetual excitement and delight to him. But, truly, the contrast between the deck and the cabin is wonderful. When I came down at midnight, I thought it possible that some of the ladies might be alarmed; and I therefore told Margaret, in a voice loud enough to be heard by any who might be trembling in their berths, that the captain said it would be a fine night, and that the stars were already bright. Half-an-hour after, when I was asleep, Miss Saunders came down, and the following took place :—

A trembling voice from somewhere cried, ' Miss Saunders! Miss Saunders ! '

Miss Saunders peers into all the ladies' rooms, and finds it is Miss O'Brien who calls.

Miss O.—' Miss Saunders, is the storm *very* bad?—is there much danger ? '

Miss S.—' There is no storm, ma'am : only a brisk, fair wind. I heard nothing of any danger.'

When Miss Saunders is falling asleep, she is roused by another call. She puts on a cloak, and goes to Miss O'Brien's room.

Miss O.—' O, Miss Saunders ! haven't we shipped a sea ? '

Miss S. looks round the cabin. ' No, ma'am : I do not see any sea.'

Before she is quite asleep, she hears Miss Lamine's voice from the sofa, to which the captain has kindly lashed chairs, to prevent her falling off ; as she persists in sleeping there, though retaining her berth.

Miss Lamine.—' O Mrs. Happen ! Mrs. Happen ! '

Mrs. H.—'Well! what *do* you want?'

Miss L.—'We are sinking, ma'am. I feel the ship sinking!'

Miss Saunders wakes up to assure the ladies that the ship is on the surface. Mrs. Happen grumbles at her first sleep being broken. She slept no more; and of course is out of humour with the whole universe to-day. Nothing is on her lips but that Miss Lamine broke her first and only sleep.

I have had a talk, prodigious for its breadth, length, depth, and earnestness, with Mr. Browning, about the duty of republicans exercising the suffrage; brought on by his saying that he had never voted but once in his life. I believe we said an octavo volume between us,—I hope to some purpose. He is a good man, with a warm simple heart, a full sense of what he owes to his excellent wife, and a head which only wants to be put a little in order. He is full of knowledge, and fond of thinking.

Mrs. O'Brien has, we suppose, kept her temper in check as long as she can; for now it is coming out worse than Mrs. Happen's, if that be possible. At dinner, the other day, she began to scold her daughters, in the presence of passengers and servants: but the captain warded it off by saying that he would not have the young ladies found fault with, for that I had been telling him that I thought them very attentive and affectionate daughters. She look gratified and complacent: but not for long. In the evening, she complained to Mrs. Ely, who was on the sofa, very unwell, of her own sensibilities; and confessed she felt very hysterical. The confession from her lips is always a signal for the cabin being cleared; every one dreading a scene. It was so now; and there were no hysterics. This morning, however, the sensibilities thus repressed have broken out; and a most unsanctified scene has disgraced our Sunday. The lady was cold in the night. Margaret was sorry: would have been happy to supply her with as many blankets as she pleased, if she had but asked for them. The lady would perish rather than ask Margaret for anything. She would have no breakfast. Margaret entreated : the daughters implored, with many tears. The lady compelled them to go to the breakfast-table with their swollen eyes ; but no breakfast would she have. Margaret, in the kindness of her heart, prepared a delicate breakfast,—strong tea, hot buttered roll and sliced tongue. The woman actually threw the breakfast at the girl's head ! Margaret was fluttered, and said she did not know whether to laugh or cry. I advised her to do neither, if she could help it. At breakfast, the captain, knowing nothing of this scene, called— ' Margaret, why don't you carry Miss O'Brien some breakfast ? ' ' I did, sir,' replied the girl in a whisper ; 'and she hove the bread at me.' ' O ho ! ' said the captain. Presently, he strode down the room, and into the ladies' cabin, both doors of which he shut. He soon came forth, looking his gravest. The lady was very 'hysterical' all day. Every heart ached for her weeping daughters.

We have been asking Mr. Browning to propose the captain's health, with an expression of thanks and friendship on the part of the passengers, the day before we land. This is the usual practice, we believe, when the captain has done his duty. Mr. Browning heartily consents, saying that it is only the captain's temper which has kept any order at all. We hope that Mrs. Happen may be so overawed as not to dare to move an amendment.

Afternoon. Mr. Browning says he fears we must give the matter up. The young men have been abusing the captain so grossly over their wine,—particularly for not having the cow milked these two days, and for letting Mr. Tracy have a room to himself, that something disagreeable would certainly arise out of any attempt to gratify our good friend. Our acknowledgments must be made individually. Mr. Bruce drew up a very good letter of thanks ; but any formal proceeding from which one-third of the passengers would probably choose to exclude themselves, would give the captain as much pain in one way as pleasure in another.

We took our seats at the bottom of the table at the outset, to avoid any contention about precedence. It is well we did ; for the captain's immediate presence is required to keep the conversation from being really offensive : it's being very silly, even the captain cannot prevent. Here is a specimen or two.

Mr. Mann.—' Mr. A. has so many bales of cotton for sale this year.'

· *Mr. Larkin.*—' I am sure I have not got that number of bales of cotton.'

Dr. Sharp.—' No ; because you are a bale of cotton yourself.' (*Roars of laughter.*)

Dr. Sharp.—' Somebody always says to me at tea-time, " Sir, will you have black tea or green tea ? "—I expect somebody will say to me some day, " Sir, will you have red tea or yellow tea ? "' (*Roars of laughter.*)

Since I came on board, I seem to have gained a new sense of the value of knowledge, of an active, reasonable mind, as well as of a disciplined and benevolent temper. Notwithstanding the occasional mirth of these people, and their ostentatious party merriment, I think I never saw persons so unhappy. No suffering from poverty or sickness ever struck me so mournfully as the misery of these ship-mates, from vacuity of mind ; from selfishness, with all its little affectations ; from jealousy, with its intolerable torments. How they get on in their homes I have no means of knowing ; but the contrast at sea between them and such of their fellow-passengers as are peaceable, active, employed, and mutually accommodating is one of the most striking and instructive spectacles I ever witnessed. The mischief has not stopped with their immediate suffering from *ennui* and ill-humour : some have been led to plot crime, which it is no merit of their own that they do not execute. I cannot enter here upon this part of their disgusting history : suffice it that the captain's vigilance and authority are too strong for them.

The wind blew us on gloriously all day ; and there was every expectation at bed-time that we might see land at daybreak. In the evening, we sketched out European tours, by the map, for such of our party as were going to travel; and we were all in fine spirits. The young men at the upper end of the table had an argument as to whether Sunday was over, so that they might go to cards. They appealed to Miss Lamine whether Sunday was not over when the sun set. She decided in the negative; so Dr. Sharp began doling forth a Report of a Charity, in the most melancholy voice imaginable; and the whole coterie moved off very early to bed.

22nd. The young men are making up for last evening's abstinence. They are busy at cards, almost before breakfast is cleared away. What can they suppose religion is?

I have seen some Irish earth. On sounding, we find sixty fathoms; and some sand came up on the lead. Mr. Browning thinks it not so clean and neat as American sand. A calm fell at five o'clock; and we are moving very slowly. There is fog at a distance; but we *have* seen a faint, brief line of coast. I do hope the sun will come out, and the wind freshen at noon. Meantime, the sea has lost its deep blue beauty, and we have not arrived at the beauty of the land; so I think it an excellent time for writing.

You should see how faded and even rotten our dresses look, from head to foot. To-morrow or Wednesday we hope to have the pleasure of dressing so as not to be ashamed of ourselves and one another. But it is a piece of extravagance, which none but silly people are guilty of, to dress well at sea, where the incessant damp and salt ruin all fabrics and all colours. Silks fade; and cottons cannot be washed; stuffs shrink and curl. Dark prints perhaps look neat the longest. Mrs. Ely's drawn bonnet, of gingham, looks the handsomest article of dress now on board; unless it be Miss Taylor's neat black-print gown.

23rd. The rest of yesterday was very interesting. On going up, before noon, I found Ringan Head visible at forty-five miles off; and three other points of high land. At one, a favourable breeze sprang up, and lasted till evening, when it died away.

We drew nearer and nearer to land, till we were within twelve miles. This was off the Point of Kinsale, where we were when the calm fell. The captain called me up after dinner, to show me where the 'Albion' was lost; the packet commanded by Captain Williams, which was lost, with all the crew and passengers but two or three, I think some ten or twelve years ago. I could see the spot distinctly; a bay between two high points of land. The captain ran into this bay in thick weather, and was unable to get out again. If the 'Albion' had struck a few rods further on, she would have gone on a sloping sand-beach, and the passengers might have got out, almost without wetting their feet. As it was, she struck against a perpendicular wall of rock.

The captain stayed talking with me all the afternoon, and we watched for the kindling of the light on the high Point of Kinsale, 400 feet above the sea. It looked so beautiful and so friendly that we could attend to nothing else. The last light I saw was the Fort Gratiot light, on the wild evening when I left lake Huron in a thunder-storm. How familiar did the Kinsale light look in comparison! The captain's heart was quite opened by it. 'I shall stand here,' he had declared, 'till I see that light. It is of no consequence to me; I know where I am, and how to steer, but it is pleasant to me to see those lights. They ought to have kindled it by this time. I wonder we don't see it. There! there it is! You can't see it well yet. It will be deep red presently. So many pleasant thoughts belong to such a light—so many lives saved—so many feelings made comfortable!' *I* felt it like the first welcome home. The dim outline of land in the morning was pleasant but mute: here were human hands at work for us. It was, to all intents and purposes, a signal; and I could not turn my eyes from it.

We saw, this afternoon, a fishing-boat with its dark brown sails. Through the glass, I discerned two men in her, and cried out that I had seen two Irishmen. Every body laughed at me. To be sure, we have more than that on board; and you may

meet 100 per hour in New York; but that is not like seeing
them in their own boat, fishing in their own sea. Sail hovered
about us all day. Mrs. O'Brien is busy in the cabin among her
handboxes, quilling and trimming. I shall not take out any of
my land-clothes yet, to get mildewed, when we may still be
some time in reaching port. I am afraid of growing restless if
I prepare for shore too soon. One would shun the heart-sickness
of hope deferred when one can. Pouring rain to-night; so we
sit down to our rubber as if we had not seen the land. This
is chiefly (as it has been throughout) for Mr. Ely's sake. He
is very poorly, and reads quite enough by daylight. He seems
to enjoy his rubber in the evening.

This morning the weather is not favourable. The wind has
been round to every point of the compass during the night, and
is now blowing from the north-east, 'right a-head.' I do not
feel very impatient at present. Miss Saunders is rather glad of
the delay. She dreads landing among strangers, though she
knows they are already friends.

Mrs. Ely has been very bold this morning with Mrs. O'Brien
(as the lady had no buttered roll by her) about the fees to the
stewardess. The stewardess depends solely upon the fees paid
by the lady passengers; and the service is so important, and so
extremely fatiguing, that it ought to be well paid. The
stewardess has to attend upon the ladies, night and day, in their
sea-sickness; to keep their state-rooms; to wait at meals in the
large cabin; to be up before all the ladies, and go to rest after
them. Among such a company of ladies there are usually some
who rise early, and always some who go to rest very late; and
commonly a few who cannot be easily pleased, and who keep
their attendant on the foot at all hours, without any consideration. When all this is considered, and it is remembered how
helpless and uncomfortable the ladies would be without such a
servant, it is clear that the stewardess should be handsomely
paid. The captain interested us particularly for Margaret, by
telling us that she was extremely poor, as she sent every shilling

she could spare from her absolute wants to her old father and mother in Scotland. Judging by what we knew to have been done in similar cases, we agreed that Margaret should have a sovereign from each of us. Miss Lamine, and Miss Taylor, and the ladies of our party paid this; but Mrs. O'Brien declared she would pay nothing, as Margaret had shown her no attention at all! It will be too bad if, in addition to the many crying fits this woman has occasioned to the poor girl, and all the toil she and her daughters have imposed upon her, night and day, she defrauds her of the money she has fairly earned. Mrs. O'Brien became so 'hysterical' that Mrs. Ely had to desist for this time; but she does not mean to let the matter stop here. As for Mrs. Happen, she not only refused to give anything, but, in her passion at being asked, sent the plate down the whole length of the table. There is something really terrifying in such tempers. Mrs. Ely changed colour as if she had been in the wrong, instead of the right. Mr. Browning says there are occasions on which people show their real selves,—in the treatment of their servants. I own that I was as much surprised as I was indignant, to find that people of good property, as these ladies both are, could stoop to accept the hard service of a very poor girl, with the knowledge all the time that they meant to defraud her of her wages. They might at least have given her warning, that she might know that she was conferring charity upon them in serving them. I trust they will think better of the matter, and repair their injustice to her at last.

We are now between Cork and Milford Haven, out of sight of land.

25th. Now, did you not expect that the next entry would be of our arrival? Far from it. There is much to be said first. I was obliged to quit my writing, last time, by the rolling of the ship; and for the rest of the day, we were treated with a gale, far more stormy than any we had during the voyage. It blew tremendously from the north-east. With the tide in our favour, and every sail snug, we were driven in the direction of the Devonshire coast ; and thankful we were that we had plenty of sea-room. Mrs. Ely and others were as sick as ever ; and at dinner there was the well-remembered scene of every thing solid slipping about the dishes, and every thing liquid being spilled: though the frames were on,—the wooden frames, made to fit the tables, with holes for the bottles and glasses. It was a truly uncomfortable day, though there was nothing to occasion fear in any but the most timid persons.

Yesterday morning we had the alternative of being sick below, or half-sick and half-frozen on deck. We preferred the latter, and were ere long repaid. We were going over the ground lost the day before, standing in for the Irish coast. There were large flocks of Neptune's sheep (waves breaking into foam); and the sky was so clear that Mr. Browning, with his malicious eye-glass, could not discern a streak of English fog all day.

About noon, the outline of the Dungarvon Mountains appeared, and the bay of Tramore, with three white towers at one extremity, and one at the other, and the town of Tramore, at the bottom of the bay. We saw, too, the high lighthouse at the extremity of Waterford Bay, and a steamboat in the entrance. Seven other sail were about us, and we felt in the midst of society once more. Before we tacked we came near enough to see the recesses in the sharp-cut rocks or cliffs on the shore, and the green downs sloping up from their summits. With the glass I could distinguish the windows of three large houses in Tramore. The outline of the mountains behind was very fine, and the lights and shadows on them delicious to behold. We tacked all day, and amused ourselves with watching the points of the shore, advancing and receding; with speaking the ship 'Georgia of Boston,' bound to New York, which we hope will report us to you ; and with admiring the clear setting sun, and the rising moon, almost at the full. She never looked finer since she was first set spinning.

There was some sad nonsense among us, even on this important and pleasurable day. Mrs. O'Brien looked cold, as she sat on the rail, in the breeze, and Mr. Simpson caused his warm broad-cloth cloak to be brought for her. Mrs. Happen, who was sitting on deck, sheltered and in the sun, growled out, 'You never offered me your cloak.' Immediately after dinner, when the gentlemen were at their wine, she sent Sally down for Mr. Simpson's cloak, and wore it all the afternoon.

The captain promised us the quietest night we had had since we left New York; and I accordingly went to sleep, nothing doubting, though the last thing I was aware of was that there was a prodigious tramping upon deck, which I concluded was from the crew shifting the sails. I slept till daylight, and thus missed a scene, partly dreadful, partly ridiculous. This tramping excited the attention of the ladies; and Mrs. Ely next heard a cry of distress from the deck, and then another, a sort of scream. The gentlemen rushed from their rooms, and up on deck; the ladies screamed, and said it was fire, the ship sinking, running foul of another ship, and much besides. Miss Taylor (still very delicate) heard every voice calling ' Captain! Captain!' and naturally supposing that something had happened to her brother, fainted away in her berth, where she was found some time after still insensible. One gentleman brought out his pistol, and Mrs. Happen entreated that she might not be shot. Mrs. Ely and Miss Saunders remained in their rooms, and were presently told that there was no danger, that it was all over. The captain put forth his authority, and ordered every body to bed. How much the passengers really knew of the cause of this bustle I cannot say; but the affair was this. The captain had a bad crew. Yesterday, at the instigation of a mischievous fellow among them, there was a sort of mutiny about their beef; a silly complaint, particularly foolish when preferred almost within sight of port. Mr. Browning knew that the captain meant to shut up the ringleader in the ice-house (now as warm as any part of the ship) at midnight, when the passengers should be asleep. The man resisted, making so much noise over the passengers' heads, that the captain sent him into confinement in the forepart of the ship : but it was too late for secrecy. The captain is much annoyed at the confusion created ; and I do not think he is aware that any of us know the cause.

All is quiet enough this morning. It is bright and cold. We are off Tusca lighthouse, the extreme south-east point of Ireland ; and the little wind there is is fair. This mutiny is a good hint. If we grow dull, I shall propose a mutiny about the handles of the milk pitchers, which were broken off in the gale ; the pitchers being thus rendered inconvenient to hold.

At this moment, Mr. Tracy brings news that the captain expects to be off Holyhead this evening ; so I jump up, and run to unpack and arrange for landing, that I may have the last few hours free. O, with what pleasure I took out gown, shawl, bonnet and gloves for to-morrow ! packing up books ; putting away everything sea-spoiled, and being completely at liberty by dinner-time !

In the afternoon, the captain found a dry seat on the binnacle for Miss Saunders and me ; and then went and stood by himself, too much excited for conversation. Mr. Browning told us we could not understand the emotions of the captain of a ship on concluding his voyage. We talked of our homes on either side of the water ; and looked out through the fog and rain, dimly discerning a ship which we supposed to be the packet of the 24th.—After tea we played, for Mr. Ely's sake, our final rubber : but we could not attend to our cards, and were glad to throw them away. At half-past ten o'clock, we ran up to see the Holyhead light. As we passed in the dark, there could be no telegraphic communication to Liverpool of our approach, and we must give up the hope of seeing our friends on the pier.

26th. At six, Miss Saunders came to my room, dressed, and talked for an hour, the cabin being in great confusion with the preparations of the ladies. We sent Margaret to learn where we were. About thirty miles from Liverpool ; but the tide would not allow us to get to port before eleven. Every body was assembled early on deck, dressed for landing ; and each, as he appeared, more spruce than the last. The cook could not be prevailed upon to let us have a slovenly breakfast early, that we might be wholly at leisure at the last. By a little after nine, however the steams of breakfast ascended; and before that time I saw, through the glass, the church steeples of Liverpool. The Welsh mountains looked lovely through the thin haze, which Mr. Browning chose to call a fog.

Mr. Bruce gratified me by a piece of truly kind consideration. He said that, from the absence of notice of our approach from Holyhead, my friends would not probably be awaiting me. He was alone, with time to spare. If I would give him a line to my friends, he would be the first to step ashore, and would bring them to me. I promised to accept his good offices, if, after reasonable waiting, no familiar faces appeared on the pier.

Soon after breakfast we saw the floating lights and the castle at the mouth of the Mersey; then New Brighton, with its white houses, trim gardens and plantations; and then some golden harvest-fields. The post-office boat was soon seen coming towards us—a sign we were expected. Then came the custom-house boat, to deposit an officer on board. We pointed out to Miss Saunders the gable of a house covered with ivy;—a plant which she had read of, since she could read at all, but never seen, as it does not grow in America. She was surprised at the narrowness of the Mersey; Mr. Bruce apologized for it; —a bad habit which he had learned in America, we told him.

As we hove alongside the pier groups began to assemble; chiefly work-people from about the docks. All had their hands in their pockets; and Miss Saunders asked me, laughing, whether she was to conclude that all Englishmen carried their hands there. In a few minutes breathless gentlemen came running down the Parade. Among them I found the face I was looking for. A watchman had given notice, from the top of the Exchange, that the ' Eurydice ' was coming up the river, and in an incredibly short time the news spread over the town.

With eager kindness the captain fixed the plank, and handed me on shore.

I am sure this gentleman must by this time have more of your esteem and regard than ever. We, his passengers, feel that we are more deeply indebted to him than he knows of; not only for his professional qualities and hospitality, but for a lesson on the value of good temper, and the dignity of greatness of mind.

As for the rest, they kept up their characters to the end. Miss Lamine's last act on board was ordering the steward to throw overboard Miss Saunders's geranium, brought from Dr. Channing's garden in Rhode Island, and kept alive through the voyage by great care. Wherever these ladies may have gone (and we have heard nothing of them since), they carry with them our sincerest pity. Others of the company of shipmates nave since repeatedly met, and enjoyed, as shipmates do, the retrospect of the brighter days of their Month at Sea.

APPENDIX C.

Page 178.

CORRESPONDENCE ABOUT A PENSION.

Putney Park,
Sunday, 27th December, 1840.

Dear Miss Martineau,

I have often regretted that Lord Grey's intention had been so strenuously resisted by you, and that he had not remained in power long enough to afford time for you to reconsider your first impulse.

I write now to say that although I have only spoken to *one* person on the subject, we were both strongly of opinion that it *ought* to be a gratification to Lord Melbourne to do what Lord Grey would have done ; and I only wish to know that, if such a step were taken, it would not be resisted by you.

I do not wish to give you the trouble of writing to me on this subject. Your silence will be quite sufficient ; and I trust you know me well enough to confide in the discretion of,

Dear Miss Martineau,

Your's very faithfully,

R. HUTTON.

Tynemouth, December 29, 1840.

My dear Mr. Hutton,

      Our friend has given me your letter. She would not keep back for a day what she knew would be so sure a gratification to me. You would not easily believe the delight your note has afforded me, as a fresh instance of your faithful and generous friendship.

      It is a pleasure to me to answer your note : but, if it were not, I should write, on account of the interpretation which my silence would bear. My objections to Literary Pensions, conferred otherwise than immediately by Parliament, remain in full force. I owe it to your kindness to state the grounds of my objections to this mode of provision : but I own to you, that (apart from all scruples of pride) my feelings against receiving a pension are full as strong as my reason, and would, I believe, induce me to give my present answer, if I had no reasons to offer.

      The first of these reasons is that I think money conferred as a reward for public service should be given by the public served, —such service having been altogether irrespective of Government. If such pensions were conferred by the representatives of the people, instead of by the ministers, (whom I cannot look upon as true exponents of the popular desire in this instance) I might perhaps thankfully accept what, under present arrangements, I must decline.—Again, I am certain that I should lose more or less of my freedom of speech, if not of thought. I am aware how generously it is desired that the recipients of pensions should divest themselves of this feeling. But with me this would be impossible. I could never again deny to myself that I was under a personal obligation to the Premier and others ; and I need not specify to you what restrictions would follow of course.

      Again, I am sure that my personal influence, and that which I exercise through the press would suffer much—not with all, but with many. If I were fully satisfied as to the act being unexceptionable, I should probably disregard any misinterpretation that might be put upon it.   But, feeling as I do, I should suffer from any consequent decline of my influence, without having a right to complain ; accompanied as such decline would be by a loss on my own part of self-respect.   I have a strong suspicion that if I accepted a pension, I should never again address the public with freedom and satisfaction.

You will not, I am sure, suspect me of blaming any who take the sort of pension which I feel myself compelled to decline.   If they think and feel differently, they are right in acting differ-ently.   I speak only for myself.

Let me assure you that I do not feel the need of this assist-ance.   My wants are small, and thus far I have supplied them. I am still able to work.   If I lose this power. I have a little in store to meet what will then probably be but a short exigency. If I continue able to work, I hope to remain as free from anxiety about the means of subsistence as I am at present.

I do not say that I, in common with other authors, have not a claim for aid ; just cause to complain of my poverty ; but the claim is one which cannot be met by royal or ministerial bounty. If literary property had been protected by law as all other pro-perty is, I should now have been enjoying more than a competence, together with advantages of another kind, which I value far more. In this direction, my dear friend, you may be able to benefit, not me, perhaps,—it may be too late for that, but many authors in a future time, who may be happier in the protection of the laws than literary labourers of this generation.   To ministers who will see to the carrying out of laws already passed for our protec-tion, and to Members of Parliament who will urge the passing of others, I promise gratitude as strong as if I owed them a situation of pecuniary ease for life.

I shall feel henceforth that fresh strength has been added to the respect and regard with which I have ever been

Your's most truly,

H. MARTINEAU.

India Board,

Wednesday, August 18th, 1841.

Dear Miss Martineau,

Lord Melbourne having heard of your present illness, as well as of the inconvenience to which you are subjected by the mode in which your money is settled, has desired me as a friend of yours to inquire whether you would accept a pension of 150*l*. per annum on the Civil List. It is out of his power to offer you more in the present state of things : but I hope you will not refuse him the opportunity of giving this proof of his respect for your writings and character, inadequate as the amount proposed may be.

If you will accept this offer, have the goodness to write *me* word to that effect ; and let me have the answer by return of post, as Lord Melbourne is desirous of completing the arrangement before he goes out of office.

I cannot tell you how grieved I have been by recent accounts of your sufferings : and how rejoiced I shall be if the offer which I have now the pleasure of communicating to you shall have the effect of contributing in any degree to your comfort.

Believe me,

Dear Miss Martineau,

Your's very truly,

CHARLES BULLER, Junr.

12, Front Street, Tynemouth,

August 19th, 1841.

Sir,

I am requested by my sister, Miss Harriet Martineau, to acknowledge the receipt of your kind communication of yesterday's date. She is too unwell, I regret to have to state, to write to-night. She commissions me therefore to give *from her* her answer to the most considerate proposal with which she has

been honoured by Lord Melbourne. Her answer is that she
cannot accept it. She hopes in a few posts to send explanations
which will show that her decision arises neither from disrespect
nor insensibility to the kindness: least of all from any regard
to the amount.

I have the honour to remain,

Sir,

Your's with much respect,

ROBERT MARTINEAU.

CHARLES BULLER, Esq., M.P., &c., &c.

———

Tynemouth, August 21st, 1841.

Dear Mr Buller,

I am far from wishing to trouble Lord Melbourne or
you with my views on Literary Pensions; but the great consideration and kindness shown in Lord Melbourne's remembrance
of me at this untoward time require from me something more
than the very abrupt reply I was compelled to send by Friday
morning's post.

I should like Lord Melbourne to understand that my decision
is no hasty one ;—that it rests on no passing feeling or prejudice, but on a real opinion that I should be doing wrong in
accepting a pension. My opinion has been held through some
changes of persons as the proposed givers, and through some
vicissitudes in the circumstances of myself as the proposed receiver, of such a pension. The first mention of a provision of
this kind was made to me in November 1832, when I was informed that I was to have a pension of the amount now specified
on the conclusion of my work on the Poor Laws. I should
doubtless then have taken it, if it had been actually offered.
On reflection I changed my mind: and when I found that Lord
Grey had still a wish that the thing should be done, I wrote to

Lord Durham, (then in Russia) to request that nothing more should be said about it, as I could not conscientiously accept a provision from this source. I have since had occasion to make the same reply to two inquiries from different quarters whether I would agree to such an arrangement for my benefit.

Lord Melbourne will not, I think, wonder at my feeling of repugnance to touch the proceeds (except as salary for public service) of a system of taxation so unjust as I have in print, for long and at large, declared it my opinion that ours is. It matters not how generously the gift may be intended, how considerately it may be bestowed,—how specifically it is designed to benefit such a case as mine. These considerations affect, most agreeably, my personal feelings towards those who would aid me; but they cannot reconcile me to live upon money (not salary) levied afflictively upon those, among others, whom I have made it my business to befriend, (however humbly)—the working classes. Such services as I may have rendered to them are unconsciously received by them; and I cannot accept reward at any expense to them. If this provision be not designed as recompense, but as aid,—as a pure gift,—I cannot take it, as they who provide the means have no voice in the appropriation of it to me personally. About the principles of taxation, a surprising agreement has grown up on our side of late. Whenever we obtain a just system of taxation, the time may perhaps follow when, among other minor considerations, some plan may be discovered by which the people's representatives may exercise the power of encouraging and rewarding merit and services working through the press; and then even the most scrupulous, with no better view of their own claims than I have, may be happy to receive, in their time of need, aid from the public purse. Meanwhile I seriously and truly feel that I had rather, if need were, (to put an extreme case) receive aid from the parish, and in the work-house, where I could clearly read my claim, than in the very agreeable manner proposed, where I can see no excuse for my indulgence.—If it be true that in the case of gifts, we do not nicely measure the grounds of *claim*,—surely there is an exception in the one case of gifts from the public purse.

Some of my friends would persuade me that my great losses from the defective protection afforded to literary property in this country entitle me to compensation in whatever form I can obtain it. But I see the matter differently. Taking compensation from those who have not injured me, leaving inequitable profits in the hands of those who have, seems to me only making a bad matter worse.

But this pension is offered with another view than this. It is offered in remedy of a case such as the fund is expressly provided to meet. Be it so : but while I know that the members of a government are (as they ought to be) otherwise employed than in looking into the retreats of suffering, to discover for themselves what poverty and sickness it is most just to aid from the public purse,—while I know that such gifts from the hand of the most discriminating and the most kind of ministers must be but a set of chances as to their gradations of justice,—I should be forever mistrusting my own happy chance. On the one hand, I should see public benefactors before whom I am nothing, pining in privation from which my pension would relieve them : and, on the other, I should be haunted by images of thousands and hundreds of thousands of poor tax-payers,— toiling men who cannot, with all their toil, keep their children in health of body,—to say nothing of their minds. 'Mighty visions about a small matter,' you may perhaps think : but, small or great, the moment I had acted on it, this matter would become no less than all-important to my peace of mind. Indeed, I would rather in the present circumstances of the country, put my hand into the fire than into the public purse.

Let me assure you that I do not need this pension as my friends suppose. They know my means well enough, but they over-rate my wants. This very sum which you speak of apologetically would quite meet my wants in the way I live here. I have no permanent uneasiness about income. If I should ever be well enough to work again (from which I am now, at last, driven) I trust I shall find, as hitherto, that my head and hands will keep my life. If my enforced illness should continue very long, I hope to keep my expenditure within my actual means.

I beg you to assure Lord Melbourne that my feelings of respectful gratitude to him are exactly the same as if I could have accepted the proposed gift. My refusal arises from causes which are out of any one's control. Of the comfort I should have derived from this annual income no one can be so sensible as myself; and I consider myself his debtor for what it would have been.

One of my pleasures, this summer, has been the Liskeard election.* How hearty it was!

My friends are too anxious about my 'state of suffering.' There is little enough of good prospect about the case; but by excellent medical management, the suffering is reduced to something very inconsiderable. The repose of such retreat is delightful.

Believe me very truly yours,

H. MARTINEAU.

India Board, August 26th.

My dear Miss Martineau,

I am very sorry that you have not thought it right to accept the pension which has been offered to you: but I cannot but respect most highly the conscientious feelings which induced you to decline it. And I am most glad to find that you so justly and kindly appreciate Lord Melbourne's conduct in making the offer. He regrets that it has been unavailing: but let me assure you that he is very sensible of the kind terms in which you expressed yourself about him, and of the high motives by which you have been actuated in your refusal.

* Mr. Charles Buller's election.

I would fain hope from the language of your letter, and from seeing that you have of late been publishing new works, that you do not suffer much, or rather, so much as I had been led to believe. I trust that you are not doomed to the long inaction which you yourself apprehend: and that you may, if not soon, at any rate at some time, be restored to your former vigour and enjoyment of life.

•••   •••   •••   ••   •••   •••   •••

Yours very truly,

CHARLES BULLER, Junr.

Howick Monday, October 31st, 1842.

My dear Miss Martineau,

I am very sorry that the publication of our correspondence should have caused you a moment's uneasiness. I did not first see it in the ' Chronicle :' and the paper in which I did see it (I think it was the ' Times ') did give a letter from ———— showing that the publication took place without your sanction. This was all that was requisite to satisfy me, for the correspondence itself is most honourable to you, very much so to Lord Melbourne, and even a little so to me. I cannot regret that the world should know it : nor can he.

I should have written to him to give the little explanation necessary to set every thing right with him, had I not been prevented by hearing of his illness. It is, I am sorry to hear from too good authority, far more serious than the papers like to represent it : for it was a paralytic stroke, which deprived him for a while of the use of one side : and though he has already partly recovered this, they say he will probably never again be able to take an active part in public life. When I return to town, which will be before the end of the week, I will explain the matter to him, if I hear that he is well enough to entertain the subject.

I am much nearer you than you imagined; and did hope to be able to go to see you in my way to London.   But I fear that I shall be obliged to hurry back in great haste.

...   .

I wish you had given me better tidings of your health.   I did hear a better account of it: but I fear from what you say that you have no immediate prospect of returning strength.

Believe me, dear Miss Martineau,

Very truly your's,

CHARLES BULLER, Junr.

If you would like to know more about Virago books, write to us at Ely House, 37 Dover Street, London W1X 4HS for a full catalogue.

Please send a stamped addressed envelope

VIRAGO
Advisory Group

Book Tokens

Give them
the pleasure of choosing
Book Tokens can be bought
and exchanged at most
bookshops